Middle-Class Democracy
and the Revolution in
Massachusetts, 1691–1780

Middle-Class Democracy and the Revolution in Massachusetts, 1691–1780

By ROBERT E. BROWN

Michigan State University

NEW YORK / RUSSELL & RUSSELL

Preface

FOR the past fifty years or more a thesis has been current in the teaching and writing of American history, political science, and literature that the society which produced the American Revolution and the federal Constitution was not a democratic society. There are differences of opinion as to just how undemocratic this society was, but in general the point is usually made that even though eighteenth-century America was more democratic than Europe, democracy as we know it did not arrive in this country until the time of Andrew Jackson.

This concept of an undemocratic society is based on two major assumptions: one, that property qualifications for voting eliminated a large portion of the free adult male population from participation in political affairs; the other, that inequitable representation heavily favored the older aristocratic commercial areas along the seacoast at the expense of the more recently settled inland agricultural areas. Hence it followed naturally that colonial political and economic life was dominated by the upper economic classes.

Writers who accept the thesis that colonial society was undemocratic have also generally followed the interpretation that the American Revolution was a "dual" revolution. On one hand, there was the conflict between Great Britain and her American colonies—what might be called the "War for Independence." But accompanying this, and of equal or perhaps greater significance, was a struggle within the colonies over which class would dominate economic and political life. According to this theory, the second phase of the conflict, which might well be designated the "American Revolution" to distinguish it from the "War of Independence," was primarily an effort by the unenfranchised and dissatisfied lower classes to gain economic, political, and social equality with their betters.

Both the "War of Independence" and the "American Revolution" succeeded to a greater or lesser extent in their objectives, according to most writers. The first won political independence for the colonies from Great Britain, although economic independence was not achieved until the War of 1812. The second succeeded by the elimination of colonial ruling classes, or a reduction in their power, and by the elevation of the "common man" to a position of importance in society which he had not hitherto enjoyed. This was reflected in the elimination or diminution of such manifestations of aristocratic domination as property qualifications for voting, inequitable representation, established churches, and entail and primogeniture in the distribution of inheritances. Later, aristocratic upper classes staged a "counterrevolution" by putting over a conservative Constitution on the people, and it was not really until the time of Andrew Jackson that democracy came fully into its own.

In the following pages I have raised some questions about this accepted interpretation as it applies to one colony and state, Massachusetts from 1691 to 1780. Did an upper economic class control economic life in the colony? Were property qualifications for voting sufficiently high to exclude an important number of adult men from participation in politics? Is the "American Revolution" interpretation a valid one, and if not, what part did democracy play in the "War for Independence?" And did the Revolution result in social changes in the state of Massachusetts significant enough to justify the concept of an "internal revolt"?

In the process of gathering material for this work, I have also seen sufficient evidence to suggest the need for reconsideration of assumptions with regard to other colonies as well as to Massachusetts.

Some of the basic ideas in the following pages first made their appearance as a doctoral dissertation at the University of Wisconsin in 1946. Since then, additional research has added much new material, and much rewriting has changed the original organization materially. But most of the general thesis presented in the original dissertation withstood the test of additional research; in fact, much of it was greatly strengthened by new material. Naturally for a work of this scope there are sources which I did not consult, but I reached a point where additional sources were merely adding more weight to points already well documented.

In the process of gathering material and writing the book, I incurred obligations almost too numerous to mention. At Wisconsin, Professor Curtis P. Nettels was most helpful in the early stages of the book, and he has continued to be a great encouragement. Professor Fred Harvey Harrington saved the writer many serious mistakes through his critical suggestions. Librarians at Wisconsin, Harvard, Worcester, Massachusetts Archives, Forbes Library in Northampton, Massachusetts Historical Society, New York Public Library, Boston Public Library, and the Library of Congress have undoubtedly forgotten the trouble I caused, but their help was indispensable. Of particular significance was the confidence with which the many town clerks throughout the state allowed the use of valuable town and tax records. These unpublished records proved to be gold mines of information and need to be worked to a much greater extent than they have been. I wish to acknowledge here my gratitude to the Alumni Board of Trustees at the University of Virginia for allowing me time from a Thomas Jefferson Fellowship to do the necessary revisions on the manuscript. Historians, or for that matter writers of any kind, probably owe much more to the efforts of their wives than they are willing to acknowledge. My own wife, B. Katherine Brown, did much more than the usual typing and proofreading. Her assistance in the research and writing of the book would entitle her to a place on the title page if she were willing to accept it. And finally, my appreciation goes to the members of the Albert J. Beveridge Committee, who spent many long hours on the manuscript and whose suggestions have been especially valuable in shaping the finished product.

Michigan State University   ROBERT E. BROWN
September 1955

Contents

Middle-Class Democracy
and the Revolution in
Massachusetts, 1691–1780

[CHAPTER I]

Economic Democracy

THE term "democracy" has come to mean many things to many people. In common usage, Lincoln's definition—government of the people, by the people, and for the people—expresses the accepted idea of political democracy. But "democracy" can also mean the right to choose one's religion freely, a chance for all to be educated, and an opportunity to participate in the material benefits of the community.

In colonial days, as is so well known, there was a close connection between political democracy and what, for want of a better term, we might call "economic democracy," that is, the opportunity which the average man had to acquire property and to get ahead in society. This connection was close because there were property qualifications for voting, which meant that if a man could not acquire property he would never be entitled to political rights.

Therefore, any understanding of colonial democracy must of necessity be prefaced by a discussion of some of the economic aspects of Massachusetts society. Since the right to vote depended on the possession of worldly goods, we would want to know how much property was required, what part of the population possessed property, how much property men had, and what opportunity existed for the acquisition of property by those who did not have it. Was there a political aristocracy which rested on the existence of an economic aristocracy, or was

1

there much economic opportunity, that is, economic democracy, so that the average man could acquire property? Was the "common man" excluded from political life because he lacked the opportunity to acquire sufficient property, or could he easily become a property holder and therefore a voter?

Some of the available information on economic conditions in colonial America deals with the colonies in general. The inference is that there was not much difference in the colonies and that what applied to one applied to all. Until the evidence proves otherwise, we can assume that references to the colonies included Massachusetts.

Contrary to the accepted interpretation,[1] one thing on which both foreign observers and contemporary Americans concurred was the vast difference between European and American societies. There was little doubt in their minds that the people who came here from Europe had not simply transplanted their old-country class structure to the New World. In fact, observers

[1] Although some specialized works are not in accord with the accepted interpretation as presented in the preface, most textbooks follow it, reflecting what is generally accepted by some of our leading writers. Students generally read the textbooks rather than the specialized monographs and articles. Instances of this view appear in: John D. Hicks, *A Short History of American Democracy* (Boston, 1949), pp. 48–49, 53–54, 85, 100, 103–06, 119, 124–26, 128–30, 148, 154–55, 187–88, 224–26; Samuel Eliot Morison and Henry Steele Commager, *The Growth of the American Republic*, 2 vols. (New York, 1950), I, 116, 163–67, 171–75, 179–82, 198–99, 234, 237, 239–40, 274–81, 296–98, 300, 303, 309, 311, 316, 335, 381, 382, 393, 468–71; Arthur Cecil Bining, *A History of the United States*, 2 vols. (New York, 1950), I, 185, 187, 194, 198, 219–20, 230–31, 250–52, 276–77, 287, 394–97; Oscar Theodore Barck, Jr., Walter L. Wakefield, and Hugh Talmage Lefler, *The United States: A Survey of National Development* (New York, 1950), pp. 91–92, 152, 167, 186–87, 192–93, 209–10, 215–16, 227, 229, 243, 285, 306–07; Merle Curti, Richard H. Shryock, Thomas C. Cochran, and Fred Harvey Harrington, *An American History*, 2 vols. (New York, 1950), I, 115–17, 144–45, 158–62, 192–96, 202–03, 209, 212, 251, 253, 446–49; Leland D. Baldwin, *The Stream of American History*, 2 vols. (New York, 1952), I, 151–52, 157–58, 184–87, 202, 205, 223–24, 239, 269–73, 276, 289–90, 295–99, 304, 306, 315–45, 440–42; William Anderson, *American Government*, 3d ed. (New York, 1946), pp. 24, 31, 36, 51, 54, 57–58; Claudius O. Johnson, *Government in the United States*, 3d ed. (New York, 1944), pp. 3–4, 123–24; Frederic A. Ogg and P. Orman Ray, *Introduction to American Government*, 9th ed. (New York, 1948), pp. 12–13, 15, 25–26, 78; John H. Ferguson and Dean E. McHenry, *Elements of American Government* (New York, 1950), pp. 24, 33, 41, 44; Vernon Louis Parrington, *Main Currents in American Thought*, 3 vols. in 1 (New York, 1930), I, 140–47, 179–82, 187, 200–01, 232, 283, 355.

agreed that a unique social order had developed in the American colonies.

One of the best known of the European observers, and one who was particularly struck by the contrast between Europe and America, was the French immigrant, Michel-Guillaume Jean de Crèvecoeur. Unlike Europe, said Crèvecoeur, America did not have a few great lords who possessed everything and a herd of people who had nothing. There were no aristocratical families, no courts, no kings, no bishops, no great manufacturers employing thousands of workers, and no great refinements of luxury. There was not the wide gulf between the rich and the poor that existed in Europe. In the rural districts the traveler did not see, as he did in Europe, the hostile castle and haughty mansion in contrast with the clay hut or miserable cabin, where men and animals lived together in meanness and indigence, keeping each other warm. America had no princes for whom to toil, starve, and bleed. The poor of Europe had come to America because Europe offered them neither bread nor land—nothing but penury, starvation, and the abuse of the rich. Europe, in short, contained few distinctions but lords and tenants, rich and poor.

What, then, were the characteristics of this American society which differed so markedly from that of Europe? Crèvecoeur called it a country of fair cities, substantial villages, and extensive fields, filled with decent houses, good roads, orchards, meadows, and bridges. The immigrant found a society differing from what he had seen. Except for the inhabitants of a few towns, the people from Nova Scotia to West Florida were farmers. They were motivated by a spirit of industry which was unfettered and unrestrained because each person worked for himself, not for others. There was a pleasing uniformity of decent competence throughout the country, with the poorest log cabin a dry and comfortable habitation. Lawyer, merchant, or farmer were the only titles in a country where the dictionary was short on words of dignity or honor. Among the Sunday congregation of respectable farmers and their wives there was not an esquire except the unlettered magistrate, and even the minister himself was a simple farmer who did not live in luxury on the labor of others. America, said Crèvecoeur, was the most perfect society then in existence, where men were as free as they ought to be —a predominantly middle-class, equalitarian society.[2]

The reason for this, continued Crèvecoeur, was the abundance of economic opportunity. Immigrants received ample compensation for their labor, and this in turn enabled them to procure land. Their labor was founded on self-interest, the fruits of which were not claimed by despotic princes, rich abbots, or mighty lords. Their land gave them the rank of independent freeholders, which in turn conferred all the political honors in the society. Europe had no such class as this. It was in America that the idle were employed, the useless became useful, and the poor became rich—rich not in terms of gold and silver, but in cleared lands, cattle, good houses, and good clothes. The immigrant did not find a crowded society as in Europe, but one in which there was room for everyone. If he were a laborer, he would soon be hired, well fed at the table of his employer, and paid four or five times as much as he could get in Europe. If he wanted uncultivated lands, there were thousands of acres from which to make a cheap purchase. Not everyone would become rich in a short time, but industry would procure an easy, decent maintenance. The rich stayed in Europe; only the middle class and poor migrated. For laborers or men of middle stations, Crèvecoeur concluded, Europe with all its pomp was not to be compared with America.[3]

Another observer who had firsthand knowledge of the differences between European and American societies was Benjamin Franklin. Franklin pointed out that the population rate in any country was directly proportional to the prevailing economic

---

[2] Hector St. John de Crèvecoeur, *Letters from an American Farmer* (London and New York, 1940), pp. 39–42, 55. Throughout this work I have used exact quotations except for contractions and capitalization.

[3] *Ibid.*, pp. 42, 44, 45, 56–58. Among the earlier historians, George Bancroft stressed the existence of economic as well as political democracy in colonial America, much as Crèvecoeur did, but Bancroft has long been out of favor with modern historians (*History of the United States of America*, 10 vols. [Boston, 1834–1875], IV, *passim*). For a current estimate of Bancroft, see Russell B. Nye, *George Bancroft, Brahmin Rebel* (New York, 1944), *passim*.

opportunity. In Europe, all the land was occupied, forcing some men to work for others; labor was plentiful, which meant low wages; and the result was a slow increase in population. But conditions in America were just the opposite. Land was plentiful and so cheap that a laboring man could soon save enough money to buy a farm, raise a family, and be assured that cheap land would provide economic opportunity for his children. Economic opportunity meant that in America there were twice as many marriages and twice as many children per marriage in proportion to the population as there were in Europe, so that the population in America doubled about every twenty years. Even so, land was so easy to obtain and so plentiful that conditions in Europe would not be duplicated in this country for many ages. Labor would never be cheap in America, for no man continued to work for others very long; either he acquired a farm or, if he were an artisan, went out to a new settlement to set up for himself.[4]

Later Franklin, like Crèvecoeur, advised Europeans that this country particularly offered opportunities for people of the middle and lower income groups who had to work for a living. America, he said, was predominantly middle class—few were as miserable as the poor of Europe, but also very few were rich. A general happy mediocrity prevailed. There were few great proprietors of land and few tenants; most people cultivated their own lands or were merchants or artisans. Not many men were rich enough to live on their rents or incomes, and there were no offices of profit for the rich or well born. A title was valuable in Europe, but it was a commodity that could not be carried to a worse market than America. People there did not ask a man what he was but what he could do. The test was a man's usefulness. Farmers and mechanics were respected because of this

---

[4] Benjamin Franklin, *The Writings of Benjamin Franklin*, ed. by Albert Henry Smyth, 10 vols. (New York, 1907), III, 63–65. Frederick Jackson Turner, *The Frontier in American History* (New York, 1920), has Turner's famous thesis of the influence of the frontier on democracy. See also Percy W. Bidwell and John I. Falconer, *History of Agriculture in the Northern United States, 1620–1860* (Washington, 1925), pp. 33–49, who emphasized cheap land, scarcity of labor, and democratic land tenure.

quality. In short, America was what Franklin called "the land of labour," a land in which an "almost general mediocrity of fortune" prevailed among the people.[5]

Given this middle-class society, who should migrate to America? Franklin declared that a young man who understood farming could easily establish himself there, for land was cheap and he could obtain a hundred acres of fertile soil near the frontier for eight or ten guineas. If he did not have money, a little saved from the good wages he received while working for others would enable him to buy land and start his own farm. Many people, who would have remained poor in Europe, had thus become wealthy farmers in a few years. The rapid increase in population also created a continual demand for artisans, who would easily find employment and be well paid. If they were poor, they started as servants or journeymen, but if they were frugal and industrious, they could soon establish their own business. America was no place for large-scale manufacturing: labor was too expensive and too difficult to keep, for either the worker wanted to be a master, or cheap land lured him away from a trade and into agriculture. Factories required poor laborers who would work for small wages, such as Europe had, but these poor workers would not be found in America until all the land had been occupied. Persons of moderate fortune could also secure estates for themselves and their posterity in America. Franklin said he had known several instances of land purchased on the frontier for ten pounds a hundred acres which increased in value in twenty years to three hundred pounds, without any improvement and simply because of the expanding settlement.[6]

<hr/>

[5] Franklin, *Writings*, VIII, 603–07, 613. Joseph Dorfman has interpreted the period in terms of an aristocratic society in which commerce, rather than agriculture, was the determining factor (*The Economic Mind in American Civilization*, 3 vols. [New York, 1946–1949], I, preface, p. 111 *et passim*).

[6] Franklin, *Writings*, VIII, 607–09. Most historians of the period are familiar with the writings of Crèvecoeur and Franklin and, in fact, some even quote passages from their writings, yet these historians have interpreted early American history in terms of sharp class conflict. James Truslow Adams, *The American: The Making of a New Man* (New York, 1944), pp. 3, 100, 172; *Provincial Society, 1690–1763* (New York, 1927), p. 256; *Revolutionary New England, 1691–1776* (Boston, 1923), preface, pp. 252–54; "The Unexplored Region in New England History,"

Franklin then compared the apprentice systems in Europe and America as further evidence of the economic opportunity which the latter offered. In Europe the arts, trades, professions, and farms were all so crowded that a poor man experienced difficulty in placing his children where they could earn a living. Artisans there, fearing future competition, refused to take apprentices unless they were well paid, which poor parents could not afford to do, so children were forced to become soldiers, servants, or thieves. The rapid increase of population in America, on the other hand, removed the fear of competition. Artisans not only accepted apprentices willingly, but would even pay for the opportunity. Many poor parents had thus raised enough money to buy land and establish themselves in agriculture. Then having served his apprenticeship, the artisan could establish himself in business in some new settlement.[7]

Still another observer who stressed the economic opportunity in America compared with that of Europe was a customs official, Comptroller Weare. Like Franklin, Weare pointed out that the tremendous growth of population was due to the fact that the means of gaining a livelihood were so easily obtained in America that no one avoided marriage because of the expense of a family. Moderate labor gained a plentiful subsistence, he said, while industry and economy often resulted in opulence. Under

American Historical Review, XXVIII (July 1923), 673–81; Merle Curti, The Growth of American Thought (New York and London, 1943), pp. 2, 11, 123, 491; Willard Thorp, Merle Curti, Carlos Baker, American Issues, 2 vols. (Chicago, 1941), I, 103–10; Vernon Louis Parrington, Main Currents in American Thought, 3 vols. in 1 (New York, 1930), I, 140–47, 179–206, 233–47; Marcus W. Jernegan, The American Colonies, 1492–1750: A Study of Their Political, Economic and Social Development (New York, 1941), pp. 271–72, 357–58; John C. Miller, Origins of the American Revolution (Boston, 1943), ch. iii.

7 Franklin, Writings, VIII, 610, 612–13. For contrasting views of early American labor, see John R. Commons and associates, History of Labor in the United States, 2 vols. (New York, 1918), who picture the worker as an artisan-entrepreneur interested in price and quality of products, and Philip S. Foner, History of the Labor Movement in the United States from Colonial Times to the Founding of the American Federation of Labor (New York, 1947), who views the colonial laborer as one of the exploited masses. Marcus W. Jernegan, Laboring and Dependent Classes in Colonial America, 1608–1783 (Chicago, 1931), also stresses internal conflict as a factor in the worker's environment, but not to the extent that Foner does. Dorfman did not consider the town laborer as of any significance until well into the nineteenth century (The Economic Mind, Vol. I, preface).

democratic colonial governments, all mortifying distinctions of rank were lost in common equality, and the way to wealth and preferment was alike open to all men. When they discovered these things, Weare said, the poor of Europe would leave their necessitous and servile condition for independence in America, where the lowest orders lived better than journeymen artificers did in London, and corresponding classes all lived better than did their prototypes in England.[8]

In England government officials sometimes stressed the differences between England and the colonies as bases for certain colonial policies. For instance, when Parliament considered a proposal for using the British Mutiny Act on colonial soldiers, the objection was made that British and American soldiers represented different economic and social classes, and would therefore have to be treated differently. Members of Parliament maintained that British soldiers came from the lowest classes and needed strict discipline, but American soldiers were gentlemen, freeholders, farmers, and master tradesmen—men who were economically independent, who could not be forced to serve in the army and who would not volunteer if they thought they were subjecting themselves to the same kind of treatment given to British regulars.[9]   In a letter to Lord Shelburne during the Revolution, one James Anderson said that migration from Scotland and Ireland to America had reached such alarming proportions that the government would be forced to take action to prevent it and would have to consider the problem after the war was over. Declared Anderson: "The disease evidently originated from an idea prevailing of the comparative advantages that British subjects in America enjoyed above those in Europe."[10]

These three discussions described all the colonies in general. Of particular concern here, however, is whether they applied equally well to Massachusetts.

[8] Comptroller Weare, "Observations on the British Colonies on the Continent of America," in Massachusetts Historical Society *Collections*, 1st ser., I, 67–82.

[9] *The Parliamentary History of England from the Earliest Period to the Year 1803*, ed. by W. Cobbett, 36 vols. (London, 1813), XV, 378–82, 390–94.

[10] James Anderson to Lord Shelburne, May 28, 1782, Library of Congress Transcripts, Shelburne Papers, LXVII.

Among Crèvecoeur's many observations was his remark that New Englanders held a special place in the American scene. They, too, came in for a great share in the pleasing perspective displayed in the thirteen colonies, he said, for there never was a people situated as they were who had done so much with such ungrateful soil.[11] A presumption might be that if there was economic democracy in New England, and in Massachusetts in particular, there was probably as much or more in the other colonies.

In spite of its ungrateful soil, however, even New England seems to have been something of a promised land compared with Europe. Franklin noted the contrast on a tour he made through Ireland and Scotland:

In those countries a small part of society are landlords, great noblemen, and gentlemen, extreamly [sic] opulent, living in the highest affluence and magnificence: The bulk of the people tenants, extreamly poor, living in the most sordid wretchedness, in dirty hovels of mud and straw, and cloathed only in rags.

I thought often of the happiness of New England, where every man is a freeholder, has a vote in public affairs, lives in a tidy, warm house, has plenty of good food and fewel [sic], with whole cloaths from head to foot, the manufacture perhaps of his own family. . . .

. . . Had I never been in the American colonies, but was to form my judgment of civil society by what I have lately seen, I should never advise a nation of savages to submit to civilization: For I assure you, that, in the possession and enjoyment of the various comforts of life, compar'd to those people every Indian is a gentleman. And the effect of this kind of civil society seems only to be, the depressing multitudes below the savage state that a few may be rais'd above it.[12]

As for Massachusetts, there is ample evidence that the social order there was also relatively equalitarian rather than sharply divided into classes. The Massachusetts agent in England, William Bollan, argued against extension of the Mutiny Act

[11] Crèvecoeur, Letters, p. 41.

[12] Franklin, Writings, V, 362–63. 1772. In view of these many statements, it is difficult to understand how historians have arrived at the conclusion that American class structure was simply more or less the transplanted class structure of Europe.

to the colonies on the ground that the people of Massachusetts were freeholders and persons of some property or business, not the class of men who became professional soldiers.[13] John Adams spoke of the "equality of knowledge, wealth, and power" which prevailed,[14] maintaining that this equality was fostered by a colonial law for the distribution of intestate estates which resulted in frequent divisions of landed property and prevented monopolies of land.[15] On another occasion he declared that the land was divided among the common people in every state so that nineteen-twentieths of the property was in their hands.[16] The Boston merchant-politician Andrew Oliver also explained to an English friend that land did not descend to the eldest son or heir as in England, but that the law provided for an equal distribution of all property, real and personal, among all the children except for a double portion for the eldest son.[17] And Thomas Hutchinson, merchant, legislator, judge, historian, and colonial governor, wrote as follows: "Property is more equally distributed in the colonies, especially those to the northward of Maryland than in any nation in Europe. In some towns you see scarce a man destitute of a competency to make him easy." [18]

Travelers in particular were impressed by the middle-class, equalitarian society of colonial Massachusetts. A British officer said the country around Boston was rough and stony, yet it produced all kinds of English grains and roots "in plenty and perfection." He said he never saw such quantities of apple and pear trees—all the roads were lined with them, and "the poorest farmer, or rather proprietor" had one or more orchards and drank cider as a common beverage. He expressed surprise at finding such respectable names as Howard, Wentworth,

[13] Massachusetts Archives, CCCIII, 275.

[14] John Adams, *The Works of John Adams,* ed. by Charles Francis Adams, 10 vols. (Boston, 1856), II, 167.

[15] *The Familiar Letters of John Adams and His Wife Abigail Adams during the Revolution,* ed. by C. F. Adams (New York, 1876), pp. 120–21.

[16] Adams, *Works,* IV, 359.

[17] Andrew Oliver Letter Book, II, 19–20, Massachusetts Historical Society.

[18] Mass., Arch., XXV, 207. Entail and primogeniture were of little importance in Massachusetts. For legal aspects see Richard B. Morris, "Primogeniture and Entailed Estates in America," *Columbia Law Review,* XXVII (1927), 24–51.

Pelham, Dudley, and others among the common people. The reason, he said, was that the "levelling principle here, everywhere operates strongly, and takes the lead, everybody has property, & everybody knows it." He also remarked that at dances, "every girl who has a pretty face and good clothes, is free to come, and is well received at public places there, where there is no sort of distinction of persons." [19] Another traveler noted that in spite of the hilly land and great abundance of rocks and stones, the countryside looked prosperous. The land was well cultivated, the neat and substantial farmhouses with their leaded windows were thickly settled on the land, there was an abundance of fine large cattle, and the people looked hale and hearty. Near Marblehead, the land looked "as bare, rocky & uncomfortable" as could be imagined, yet the houses were "as thick seated" and looked as well as any he ever saw in the most fertile country. He said he mentioned this because it did "so much honour to the incomparable industry of the inhabitants." [20]

As both Crèvecoeur and Franklin emphasized, one reason for the prevailing economic democracy was the favorable conditions for workers and for ordinary people in America. John Woolman recorded in his *Journal* in 1772 that workingmen near London received 10*d.* a day and had to provide their own food. During harvest, they received 1*s.* a day and food.[21]

---

[19] "Journal of an Officer . . . 1765," Library of Congress Transcripts, British Museum, King's MSS., CCXIII, 126.

[20] Robert Honyman, *Colonial Panorama, 1775: Dr. Robert Honyman's Journal for March and April*, ed. by Philip Padelford (San Marino, Cal., 1939), pp. 39–40, 49. Historians differ over the extent of economic prosperity in the colonies. In order to explain the Land Bank of 1740, John C. Miller had Massachusetts in the depth of a depression, but offered no evidence to prove his contention. "Religion, Finance and Democracy in Massachusetts," *New England Quarterly*, VI (March 1933). Others have contended that there was a good deal of prosperity in the colonies after 1730. Adams, *Revolutionary New England*, pp. 5, 9, 11; Carl L. Becker, *The Beginnings of the American People* (Boston, 1915), pp. 162, 165–66; Jernegan, *The American Colonies, 1492–1750*, pp. 271–72; Charles McLean Andrews, *Colonial Folkways: A Chronicle of American Life in the Reign of the Georges* (New Haven, 1918), pp. 24–26, 65. Available evidence appears to support the latter point of view.

[21] John Woolman, *The Journal and Essays of John Woolman*, ed. by Amelia Mott Gummere (New York, 1922), pp. 305–06.

In Massachusetts, towns paid about 1s.8d. to 2s. a day for work on the highways during the winter months and about 3s. in the summer.[22] One writer claimed that manufacturing failed in Massachusetts because workers there would not take less than 2s. a day and that they could not hope to compete with English workers who received 6d. or 8d. a day.[23] This, of course, was also what Franklin had said. At the same time that wages were higher in the colony than in England, provisions were much lower. Woolman reported that wheat was 8s. and rye 5s. sterling a bushel in England.[24] Colonial prices were 4s. for wheat and 3s. for rye, Massachusetts money, which would make the price of grain in England about double the colonial price.[25] Ann Hulton, English sister of a customs official, complained of the lack of servants in Boston. No one would call anyone else master, she said, and the reason was that there were "no distinctions, scarsly" in the society there.[26]

Two examples illustrate Franklin's contention that artisans could easily set up for themselves in new settlements and that economic opportunity resulted in rapid population growth. The Massachusetts town of Stockbridge, for instance, not only offered Stephen Nash the opportunity of establishing his blacksmith business there, but actually granted him fifty acres of land as an inducement to do so.[27] David Chapman, a North-

[22] Malden Town Records, II, 215; Stockbridge Town Records, 1760–1805, p. 15; Pittsfield Town Records, I, 90. Manuscript town records are located in the respective towns unless otherwise indicated.

[23] Peter Oliver, "Origins and Progress of the *American* Rebellion . . . ," Library of Congress Transcripts, British Museum, Egerton MSS. 2671, p. 116.

[24] Woolman, *Journal*, pp. 305–06.

[25] Hadley Town Records, June 24, 1779; Hatfield Town Records, IV, 284. Prices were 1774 prices.

[26] Ann Hulton, *Letters of a Loyalist Lady* . . . *1767–1776* (Cambridge, Mass., 1927), pp. 49–50. 1772. Richard B. Morris is a good example of the historian who is caught between his evidence and the accepted interpretation. Morris cites copious quantities of evidence to show that workers enjoyed great economic as well as political democracy, yet he says he writes from the standpoint of Madison's *Federalist* No. 10, that labor did not enjoy full civil and political rights, that there was social stratification, and that even the Revolution did not achieve democracy. See Morris, *Government and Labor in Early America* (New York, 1946), preface, pp. 32–53.

[27] Town of Stockbridge, "Indian Proprietors 1749–1790," p. 36, Stockbridge Library.

ampton blacksmith, paid neither poll nor estate tax in 1771, paid a poll tax only in 1772, was rated one poll and £9.8.o estate in 1773, and eleven years later, 1784, had a house, seven acres of improved land, twenty-two acres unimproved, and a family of thirteen.[28] If, as Franklin said, the increase of population was directly proportional to economic opportunity, Chapman's family of eleven children within twelve years after he started paying poll taxes ought to be indicative.

Another contributing factor, and perhaps even more important to colonial economic democracy than opportunity for workers, was the availability of free or cheap land. Franklin, Crèvecoeur, Weare, and others emphasized this for the colonies as a whole, but they could have done the same for Massachusetts in particular. In 1755, the general court declared that the colony was a new country with so much land to be given away or sold for a trifling consideration that the means of subsistence were easily obtained. As a result, said the court, every young man who was so inclined could start a family without venturing a farthing—something that could not be done in the old countries of Europe.[29] Nash and Chapman were examples of this. During the French and Indian War, proprietors of land in Maine offered 200 acres to any settler who would begin to build a house within a year after the end of the war, clear five acres within three years, and live on the land seven years.[30] In 1765, this same area had only 1,500 families scattered over 6,000 square miles of land (one family for each four square miles) and though it was a poor frontier community then, the minister who described it said the soil was rich and that future prospects looked good.[31]

Even in Massachusetts proper, there was still much uncultivated land for expansion. Often only a small part of a man's land would actually be improved. For example, in Northamp-

[28] Judd MSS., Northampton, II, 71, 75, Forbes Library, Northampton, Mass.

[29] William Shirley, *Correspondence of William Shirley* . . . , ed. by C. H. Lincoln, 2 vols. (New York, 1912), II, 287.

[30] *Boston Gazette Supplement,* May 21, 1759.

[31] Library of Congress Transcripts, Archives of the Society for the Propagation of the Gospel in Foreign Parts, ser. B, XXII, 98–101. Hereafter cited S.P.G. Archives.

ton, one man had but five of his eighty acres improved, and in Westhampton, the ratio for another man was twenty-seven out of 187 acres.[32] David Chapman had improved only seven of his twenty-nine acres. In 1763, Stockbridge voters whose right to vote had been challenged and who were called "young men," "labourers," and "way fareing men," turned out to have up to £100 sterling in wild lands recently granted by the General Court or purchased from others.[33] As the General Court said, a young man could easily acquire land and start a family if he so desired.

It cannot be overemphasized that with land cheap and plentiful, the great majority of the people were independent, property-owning farmers, in Massachusetts as in the other colonies. As already noted, Crèvecoeur said that, a few towns excepted, the people from Nova Scotia to West Florida were tillers of the soil.[34] Franklin confirmed this view. He said that the great business of America was agriculture, and that for every merchant or artisan he supposed there were at least a hundred farmers, by far the greatest part cultivators of their own fertile lands.[35] On another occasion he characterized Americans as cultivators of land, with few engaged in fishing and commerce compared with the body of the people.[36] In his examination before Commons on repeal of the Stamp Act, he said that the merchants of Boston were a small number compared with the body of the people, and when asked what the body of the people were, he said they were farmers, husbandmen, or planters.[37]

Except for those in the few seaport towns in Massachusetts, even the artisans and laborers generally combined farming with a trade, so that it was difficult to say exactly what they were. Blacksmiths David Chapman and Stephen Nash, as well as the "labourers" in Stockbridge were examples. Josiah Burrage

[32] Judd MSS., Northampton, II, 74.   [33] Mass. Arch., XXXIII, 277–88.
[34] Crèvecoeur, *Letters,* p. 40.   [35] Franklin, *Writings,* X, 117–18.
[36] *Ibid.,* VII, 6.
[37] *Ibid.,* IV, 432. One of the major contradictions in the writings on this period is the fact that many authors will point out that property was easily acquired, yet they revert to the idea that colonial society was sharply divided into classes. Adams, *Revolutionary New England,* pp. 5, 9, 11, 88–96; Miller, *Origins of the American Revolution,* ch. iii; Jernegan, *The American Colonies,* pp. 271–72.

of Lynn, heelmaker, glazier, and joiner, also had a house and thirty-nine acres of land, and a half interest in another house and barn.[38] One Consider Leeds, Dorchester cordwainer, had a house and barn and 102 acres of land.[39] Nathan Bailey, Andover cordwainer, possessed a farm of fifty-six acres with some livestock and husbandry tools; [40] and Skipper Lunt, Newbury joiner, had thirteen acres of land with buildings.[41] Henry Pain, Marblehead shipwright, owned a house, barn, and land worth £240 and a separate piece of land worth £76.[42] Edward Webber, Wenham "yeoman" with a house, barn, and nine acres, was obviously also a jack-of-all-trades, for his estate included "joynery ware," cooper's ware, spinning wheels, and farm tools.[43] Most artisans in the seaport towns owned only their homes and perhaps a shop, or the shop was in the home, but Caleb Parker, Boston blacksmith, owned twelve or fifteen acres of land in Braintree in addition to his house and land in Boston.[44]

Thomas Hutchinson gave a rather graphic description of colonial society in an essay written in 1764, characterizing colonial economic democracy as follows:

I must observe to you that but few farms in the colonies are in the hands of tenants. . . .

In all the colonies upon the continent but the northermost more especially the inhabitants are generally freeholders where there is one farm in the hands of a tenant I suppose there are fifty occupied by him who has the fee of it. This is the ruling passion to be a freeholder. Most men as soon as their sons grow up endeavour to procure tracts in some new township where all except the eldest go out one after another with a wife a yoke of oxen a horse a cow or two & maybe a few goats and husbandry tools a small hut is built and the man and his family fare hard for a few.[45]

---

[38] Essex County Probate Records, CCCXLVII, 19 (1771).
[39] Suffolk County Probate Records, LXXII, 12–13 (1772).
[40] Essex County Probate Records, CCCLI, 148–51 (1775).
[41] *Ibid.*, CCCXLVII, 289 (1771).   [42] *Ibid.*, p. 303.
[43] *Ibid.*, CCCXLVIII, 71 (1773).
[44] Suffolk County Probate Records, LXXI, 77–78 (1771). Convict labor and indentured servants, except apprentices, were not important in Massachusetts. Abbot Emerson Smith, *Colonists in Bondage: White Servitude and Convict Labor in America, 1607–1776* (Chapel Hill, 1947); James D. Butler, "British Convicts Shipped to the American Colonies," *American Historical Review*, II (Oct. 1896), 12–33.
[45] Mass. Arch., XXVI, 95–96.

Here the essay ended, but the implication was that after a few years the young farmer eventually found himself in better circumstances. Hutchinson later wrote to Governor Wentworth of New Hampshire that he had written the essay at Wentworth's request, but he was sure that Wentworth was acquainted with all the information in it.[46]

Almost any Massachusetts town would demonstrate the generalizations made thus far, but the available records make Northampton a particularly good example. The tax lists show that almost all the people were property owners, that the spread in the amount of property owned was not wide, and that the vast majority of men were farmers. Furthermore, a comparison of tax lists for different years shows that practically all men increased their holdings over a period of years.[47] A list of shops in Northampton in 1773 reveals that workers other than farmers were not day laborers who worked for wages, but skilled artisans who worked for themselves—blacksmiths, goldsmiths, joiners, tanners, weavers, tailors, clothiers, traders, shoemakers, barbers, sadlers, coopers, and hatters. Furthermore, the fact that most of them owned substantial amounts of real estate indicates that they were both farmers and artisans. In fact, the wealthiest man in town, Seth Pomeroy, was listed as a blacksmith. Most of these artisans were town proprietors, that is, men who owned a share in the common lands, and many were town officials, including some who were not proprietors.[48]

Although not as new as many Massachusetts towns, Northampton was still an area with plenty of room for expansion. There were unincorporated sections such as Westhampton, Southampton, Easthampton, Pascommack, Bartlett's Mill, and Nashawamuck where land was still available. A tax list for Pascommack, Bartlett's Mill, and Nashawamuck in 1769 lists twenty-nine persons who were not proprietors of Northampton yet most of whom owned substantial farms.[49] A Westhampton

---

[46] *Ibid.*, p. 99.

[47] Northampton Town Records, I, 296–99 (1748); II, 123–24 (1765); Andover Tax Lists (1754 and 1774); Hatfield Town Records, I, 182–85 (1743), and Hatfield Assessors' List (1772).

[48] Judd MSS., Northampton, II, 71; Northampton Town Records, II, 121, 123–24 (1773).

[49] Judd MSS., Northampton and Westhampton, II, 80.

list of nonresidents of Westhampton, taken in 1778 before the town was incorporated, shows that many men had done what Hutchinson said they did—acquired land in some unsettled township. Some were substantial property owners in Northampton, but fifteen of the thirty-nine were not town proprietors of Northampton. Their holdings were 50, 80, 40, 160, 187, 80, 90, 150, 105, 120, 30, 12, 40, 260, and 140 acres respectively, an indication that land was available in sizable amounts for others besides town proprietors even in relatively settled areas.[50]

Strange as it might seem, even the poorhouses confirm the generalization that American society was an equalitarian, middle-class society. Jefferson made the statement that from Portsmouth to Savannah one seldom met a beggar, and then only in the larger towns, but these were usually foreigners who had never obtained a settlement in any parish. Jefferson said he never saw a native American begging in the streets or highways, for a subsistence was easily gained here.[51] The Boston poorhouse, by far the largest in Massachusetts, contained twenty-nine people in 1768. There were eight children, twelve women, and nine men, most of them immigrants from England, Ireland, Scotland, and France. Most of the adults were listed as distracted, blind, weakly, lame, infirm, subject to fits, or aged. None was capable of working to earn a living. So the poorhouse served the multiple purpose of a children's home, hospital, mental hospital, old folks' home, and poorhouse, not a place for people who were on charity because they could not find employment.[52]

I am not contending that the people of Massachusetts were all equal economically, but only that there was relative equality

[50] *Ibid.*, Northampton, II, 74; Northampton Town Records, II, 123–24. These figures would indicate that town proprietors did not monopolize the land as has sometimes been suggested. Adams, *Revolutionary New England*, p. 88. Roy H. Akagi, *The Town Proprietors of the New England Colonies* (Philadelphia, 1924), maintains that the proprietors often conceded land rights to others, even though by law they could have held the land for themselves.

[51] Thomas Jefferson, *The Writings of Thomas Jefferson,* ed. by P. L. Ford, 10 vols. (New York, 1892–1899), III, 239.

[52] Mass. Arch. CXVIII, 329. Robert W. Kelso, *The History of Poor Relief in Massachusetts, 1620–1920* (Boston and New York, 1922), gives a legal and institutional approach. The author does not attempt to determine the extent of poverty, but he does contend that widows constituted the largest group of the poor.

compared, for example, with Europe at that time or America today. The probate records show that a few men had little property when they died, particularly sailors and fishermen in towns such as Boston, Salem, and Marblehead, but these were few compared with those who were property owners.[53] At the other extreme there were a few well-to-do. Thomas Hutchinson estimated the Apthorp estate between £20,000 and £30,000 sterling, which he called "a large property." [54] Andrew Oliver's estate was valued at £9,121,[55] and Thomas Gerry, father of Elbridge Gerry, had property worth £7,919.[56] But between these extremes was the vast majority of the population, men of middling property, farmers whose farms were not only their homes but also their capital stock. These farms generally averaged from 75 to 150 acres, with a value of from £300 to £1,200. For example, a farm of 86 acres was worth £702, one of 98 acres was worth £854, one of 123 acres was worth £920, and one of 170 acres was worth £1,395 for the land alone.[57] The Adams' homestead in Braintree (Quincy), consisting of buildings and 53 acres of land, would have been considered a small farm in colonial times, yet the land and buildings alone were worth £440.[58] So while there was a spread of ten or fifteen to one between the estates of Andrew Oliver or Thomas Gerry and that of an average farmer, this difference is small indeed compared with the difference in the estates of men in similar circumstances today.

It is difficult to tell what such titles as esquire or gentlemen meant, but in Massachusetts they were certainly not marks of economic class distinction. In Boston, William Tailer, John Neal, William Sheaffe, and Francis Bernard, Jr., son of Governor Francis Bernard, were all distinguished by the title "Es-

[53] Suffolk County Probate Records, LXXI, 53 (1771); LXXII, 47, 136 (1772); Essex County Probate Records, CCCXLVII, 15, 23 (1771).

[54] Mass. Arch. XXVII, 384 (1772).

[55] Hutchinson-Oliver Papers, Massachusetts Historical Society. Estimate of the estate of Andrew Oliver, 1775.

[56] Essex County Probate Records, CCCLI, 132–43 (1775).

[57] *Ibid.*, CCCXLIII, 413–15; CCCXLVIII, 53–55; CCCLI, 101–03; CCCXLVIII, 194–96.

[58] Adams, *Works*, II, 326.

quire," yet they were worth respectively £68, £91, £233, and £27.[59] Three of them had less than the "labourers" out in Stockbridge. Richard Reith, "Gentleman" of Marblehead, was insolvent, and Charles Pierce, "Gentleman" of Newbury, had only £281.[60] Stephen Bartlett of Almsbury, "Capt. and Gentleman," possessed £709, an amount that hundreds of farmers in the colony could have matched.[61]

Even slavery, which might be considered a barometer of class society, did not serve that function in Massachusetts. Joseph Coolidge, Boston gunsmith, had no real estate, a total estate of only £122, yet owned a Negro boy worth £33. Caleb Parker, Boston blacksmith, counted a Negro man in his total estate of £256. Captain Robert Erskine, probably of Boston, had no real estate in his total estate of but £244, yet he owned three Negro men worth £120. John Mellony, Boston mariner, had two tenements (£160), a Negro woman (£40), and total property of £234. And Cord Cordis, Boston liquor merchant who was bankrupt in 1758, possessed £489 including two Negroes when he died.[62] Needless to say, economic democracy did not exist for slaves, but ownership of slaves was not a mark of wealth.

When we interpret the society of Massachusetts which produced the American Revolution and the Constitution, we need to remember that, economically speaking, it was a relatively equalitarian, middle-class society in which there was a great deal of economic opportunity. Land was cheap and easy to acquire, and most men acquired some; wages were high, so that a worker could save money to buy land; apprentices could easily become masters and owners of their own small business

---

[59] Suffolk County Probate Records, LXXII, 5, 7–8, 18, 135 (1772).

[60] Essex County Probate Records, CCCXLVII, 369; CCCXLVIII, 3–4.

[61] *Ibid.*, pp. 33–34.

[62] Suffolk County Probate Records, LXXI, 57–59, 77–78, 91–95; LXXII, 110, 137. The only comprehensive work on Negro slavery in New England is Lorenzo Johnston Greene, *The Negro in Colonial New England, 1620–1776* (New York, 1942). The author believed that slaves were sufficiently numerous to influence the social institutions of their masters, but his figures on page 76, giving a percentage of 1.4 for Massachusetts in 1790, hardly justify this interpretation. The author also says, p. 103, that "a large proportion of the slaves worked on farms," but immediately below he weakens this statement as follows: "How many slaves were employed at farm labor is not known."

in some new community; few men could be called day laborers, or if they were, few remained day laborers for long; most "workers" were self-employed artisans, not day laborers. Even men who were designated "laborers" were nevertheless owners of considerable land. More than 90 per cent of the people were farmers, most of whom owned their own farms. In fact, a vastly greater part of the population owned property then than now, and there was a much smaller gap between the wealthy and the ordinary people. These are some of the factors we need to keep in mind when we consider the problem of political democracy.

[CHAPTER II]

The Province
Voting Franchise

EVEN if there was economic opportunity in colonial Massachusetts and most men owned property, there would still not have been political democracy if the colony had voting requirements which most men could not meet. We need to know what the voting franchise was and what it amounted to in terms of understandable property values. In this chapter, therefore, I have attempted to ascertain the voting qualifications for province elections and to compare these qualifications with values expressed in real estate, rentals, commodities, and wages. Voting qualifications for town elections differed from the province franchise and will be considered in a later chapter.

Voting in province elections depended on the possession of two kinds of property, but there is some confusion in the records as to just how much property was required. This confusion was due to a mix-up in the charters granted to Massachusetts by the English government in 1691. The original charter, kept in London, required that voters in the colony have a 40s. freehold (real estate that would rent for 40s. a year) or any property, real or personal, worth £50 sterling. In the copy sent to the colony, however, the requirement was a 40s. freehold or any property worth £40 sterling.[1] Just why the two charters differed has never been satisfactorily explained.

For a while there was some difficulty in Massachusetts because the two charters were not the same. The colony followed its copy of the charter in passing election laws, and these laws had the 40s. and £40 qualification.[2] When the election laws were sent to England for approval, as was required, the Lords of Trade consulted the original charter and disallowed the laws because they did not contain the £50 requirement.[3] The Massachusetts General Court then made the change to £50 in the election law as the Lords of Trade demanded, and this was made a perpetual law.[4] This evidence would indicate that the requirement for voting in province elections was a 40s. freehold or £50 of property.

At the same time, however, there is evidence that £40 of property was the legal qualification. While one election law stipulated £50, another election law, passed in 1693 and overlooked by the Lords of Trade, required only £40. This law said that if any man were challenged in his right to vote, he could qualify himself simply by swearing that he had a freehold worth 40s. a year or any property worth £40 sterling.[5] So the election law which fixed the form of writs for holding elections called for £50, but the second law said that a challenged voter could qualify simply by swearing that he had £40.

---

[1] Francis Newton Thorpe, ed., *The Federal and State Constitutions, Colonial Charters, and Other Organic Laws* . . . , 7 vols. (Washington, 1909), III, 1878–79. Hereafter cited Thorpe, *Constitutions and Charters;* Albert Edward McKinley, *The Suffrage Franchise in the Thirteen English Colonies in America* (Philadelphia, 1905), p. 354; *The Acts and Resolves, Public and Private, of the Province of Massachusetts Bay* . . . , 21 vols. (Boston, 1869–1922), I, 363n. Cortlandt F. Bishop's *History of Elections in the American Colonies* (New York, 1893) is based mainly on laws, describes the qualifications for voting and the machinery of government, but does not attempt to determine how restrictive the franchise was. Kirk Harold Porter, *A History of Suffrage in the United States* (Chicago, 1918), accepts the work of Bishop and McKinley on the colonial period as definitive but does not indicate what their figures really mean.

[2] *Acts and Resolves,* I, 80, 202.

[3] *Calendar of State Papers, Colonial Series, America and West Indies, 1693–96* (London, 1880), pp. 497–98; J. Franklin Jameson, "Did the Fathers Vote?" *New England Magazine,* n.s., I (Jan. 1890), 486.

[4] *Acts and Resolves,* I, 249, 315.   [5] *Ibid.,* pp. 147–48.

To make the confusion complete, editions of the colonial laws were printed in 1714, 1726, 1742, and 1759, and these contained both qualifications. The election law fixing the form of election writs and the election law by which a challenged voter could qualify for voting were both retained, and they had different qualifications.[6] Moreover, each of these editions of the laws has a copy of the charter, but while the charter in the editions of 1714 and 1726 has the £50 qualification, the charter in the editions of 1742 and 1759 requires only £40.[7]

Legally speaking, both qualifications were presumably in effect in the election laws as well as in the printed copy of the charter. The problem is to find out, if possible, which one the province actually used. Some of the evidence for this is equally confusing. Braintree, for example, usually used such vague terms as "freeholders," "legal freeholders," or "inhabitants" in references to voters. Only twice, once in 1705 and again in 1728, were the exact qualifications given, and both times the amount was £50.[8] Marblehead used £50 in 1732 but reverted to £40 in 1749 and 1773.[9] This might well have reflected the change in the charter as printed in the edition of the Laws of 1742. An election notice for Salem in 1769 also specified £40.[10] But two other towns, Andover and Fitchburg, required £40 before 1776, then changed to £50 in the election of 1776.[11] One might suspect that when the colony claimed its charter rights perhaps these towns took a look at the charter and discovered that

[6] *Acts and Laws of Her Majesties Province of the Massachusetts-Bay in New-England* (Boston, 1714), pp. 54, 95; *Acts and Laws of His Majesty's Province of the Massachusetts-Bay in New-England* (Boston, 1726), pp. 55, 95; *Acts and Laws of His Majesty's Province of the Massachusetts-Bay in New-England* (Boston, 1742), pp. 55, 88; *Acts and Laws of His Majesty's Province of the Massachusetts-Bay in New England* (Boston, 1759), pp. 48, 79.

[7] *Laws* (1714), p. 7; *Laws* (1726), p. 7; *Laws* (1742), p. 7; *Laws* (1759), p. 7. See also the paper on the franchise by Ellis Ames, in Massachusetts Historical Society, *Proceedings, 1867–69*, X (Boston, 1869), 370–75.

[8] *Records of the Town of Braintree, 1640–1793*, ed. by Samuel Austin Bates (Randolph, Mass., 1886), pp. 61–62, 127.

[9] Marblehead Town Records, III, 147, 387; IV, 141.

[10] *Boston Gazette,* June 5, 1769.

[11] Andover Town Records, May 17, 1774, and May 21, 1776; *The Old Records of the Town of Fitchburgh Massachusetts* . . . , compiled by Walter A. Davis, 8 vols. (Fitchburg, 1898–1913), I, 115, 124.

the qualification was £50, but of course this is speculation.

The reader will begin to understand at this point why the seemingly simple problem of ascertaining the voting qualifications is not so simple after all.

In spite of the confusion and apparent contradictions, there is a great deal of evidence that the general practice in elections was to require £40 rather than £50. Thomas Hutchinson, the Boston merchant-politician-historian, was apparently unaware that the £50 qualification existed, and he should have known what the current practice was.[12] Governor Francis Bernard told the Lords of Trade that the qualification of a voter was his oath that he had a 40s. freehold or £40 of property.[13] In a disputed Watertown election in 1757, the General Court gave the 40s. freehold or £40 qualification in calling for a new election, and challenged voters took the oath that they were worth £40 sterling.[14] In another disputed election in Stockbridge in 1763, voters took the oath that they were worth £40, and a committee of the General Court used the £40 qualification in settling the dispute.[15]

For all practical purposes, therefore, we can safely assume that the accepted voting qualification in province elections, especially after 1740, was the possession of a freehold that would rent for 40s. a year or any property, real, personal, or both, that was worth £40 sterling. In determining colonial values and their relation to voting qualifications, I have converted sterling money to lawful Massachusetts money. As lawful money was rated at four to three for sterling, 40s. sterling would be 53s. 4d. lawful money and £40 would be £53.4.0 lawful money.[16]

The next step is to determine how much property a 53s.4d. freehold (40s. sterling) or £53.4.0 in property (£40 sterling) represented. Was it sufficiently high to be restrictive, as most writers think, or was it something that the "common man" could meet without too much difficulty? There are numerous comparisons that can be made, so we can get a fairly accurate

[12] Thomas Hutchinson, *History of the Colony and Province of Massachusetts-Bay*, ed. by Lawrence S. Mayo, 3 vols. (Cambridge, Mass., 1936), II, 7–8; Mass. Arch., XXVII, 339.

[13] *Acts and Resolves*, IV, 628.   [14] Mass. Arch., CXVII, 298–301, 306–07.

[15] *Ibid.*, XXXIII, 277–88.   [16] *Acts and Resolves*, III, 494–95.

picture of just what the voting qualifications meant to the people of that day.

Since many writers, even those who consider colonial society undemocratic, agree that most farmers and artisans owned their own farms or homes, a natural approach to the value of the voting qualification would be through a comparison with real estate values and rentals. This is easily done, for the probate records give us countless examples of farm and town property values, and since all real estate was assessed for tax purposes according to its rental value, we can ascertain without much difficulty what a 53s.4d. freehold amounted to.

Before we investigate the values of farms we need to rid ourselves of a popular misconception about the size of farms in colonial days. For example, farms of 31 and 75 acres were advertised in the newspapers as "small" farms,[17] and a widow in a petition to the General Court said that her husband had left her a "small estate" which included 47 acres of land.[18] A farm of 200 acres was called a "fine large farm" and one of 300 acres "large and comodious [sic]." [19] Fifty farms advertised in the *Gazette, Evening Post, News-Letter,* and *New England Weekly Journal* from 1725 to 1760 ranged from 30 acres (a minister's farm) to 1,000 acres. Thirteen were under 100 acres, thirty-seven were over 100 acres, and fifteen of these were over 200 acres. The average was 181 acres, but this was doubtless high for the typical farm, which, as the probate records will show, usually contained from 80 to 150 acres.

In Table 1, I have listed some typical holdings of average to small farmers, the men whose right to vote might be questioned. Obviously most of them had several times the £53.4.0 needed for voting. Even Richard Cobb of Hingham, with only a house and twelve acres of land, had more than twice the voting qualification. Almost any farm with a house, barn, and five acres of land would qualify its owner, which meant that any man who made a living for himself and family by farming could qualify. If some 90-odd per cent of the people were

---

[17] *Boston Gazette,* Jan. 30, 1758; May 26, 1760.
[18] Mass. Arch., XVII, 787.
[19] *Boston Gazette,* April 26, 1748; Nov. 15, 1756.

farmers, and if, as Hutchinson said, forty-nine out of fifty owned their own farms, a large percentage of Massachusetts farmers were qualified voters.

Table 1. Average and Small Farms

Name and place	Total real estate		Personal estate	Total estate
Ebenezer Frie [20] of Andover	72 acres	£278.0.0	£52.3.1	£330.3.1
Zebadiah Johnson [21] of Andover	90+ "	407.0.0	40.1.4	417.1.4
Timothy Abbot [22] of Andover	86 "	500.0.0	202.4.3	702.4.3
Samuel Barker [23] of Andover	100 "	583.6.8	110.15.2	672.11.6
Stephen Runnels [24] of Boxford	c.46 "	256.8.0	123.7.7	379.15.7
Nehemiah Carlton [25] of Bradford	174 "	1,036.0.0	134.16.11	1,170.16.11
Paul Dodge [26] of Ipswich	94 "	348.11.8	223.13.6	572.5.2
Joseph Moody [27] of Almsbury	98 "	704.0.0	150.6.3	854.6.3
Ebenezer Knowlton [28] of Ipswich	59 "	241.0.0	96.3.2	337.3.2
John Wilson [29] of Andover	c.125 "	745.2.8	200.6.1	945.8.9
Joseph Harrington [30] of Weston	72 "	443.15.0	99.6.2	543.1.2
Nehemiah Barker [31] of Methuen	39 "	134.0.0	51.5.8	185.5.8

[20] Essex County Probate Records, CCCXXXIII, 370–71 (Dec. 23, 1755).
[21] *Ibid.,* CCCXLVI, 209 (April 6, 1770).
[22] *Ibid.,* CCCXLIII, 413–15 (March 3, 1767).
[23] *Ibid.,* CCCXLVII, 28 (June 13, 1771).   [24] *Ibid.,* pp. 230–31.
[25] *Ibid.,* p. 309.   [26] *Ibid.,* CCCXLVIII, 41–45 (March 23, 1773).
[27] *Ibid.,* pp. 53–55.   [28] *Ibid.,* pp. 62–64.
[29] *Ibid.,* CCCLI, 52–54 (Sept. 23, 1774).
[30] Middlesex County Probate Records, LVI, 472–73 (March 13, 1776).
[31] Essex County Probate Records, CCCXLVII, 1a (March 25, 1771).

Name and place	Total real estate		Personal estate	Total estate
Nathaniel Fairfield [32] of Beverly	36	" 261.6.8	1.2.10	262.9.6
John Tenny [33] of Rowley	43	" 124.0.0	36.4.10	160.4.10
Robert Rogers [34] of Newbury	30	" 236.0.0	51.2.10	287.2.10
Richard Cobb [35] of Hingham	12	" 100.0.0	9.3.0	109.3.0

Probably most of the 2 per cent who were tenants could also qualify on the strength of their livestock, household goods, and clothing. The probate records give examples of men who had no real estate, but whose personal estate was more than sufficient as a voting qualification. Benjamin Hager of Weston was listed as a "husbandman," but his personal estate was £133.[36] Benjamin Harrington of Weston possessed the usual personal effects of a small farmer—household goods, farm utensils, two oxen, three steers, three cows, two calves, four heifers, two yearlings, and three swine—yet his estate was valued at £96.[37] Even if a few farmers did not own real estate, they could still vote on the strength of their personal estates; and, of course, most farmers owned land.

When we turn to what has sometimes been mistakenly termed the "city proletariat" or the "propertyless workers" of the towns, we find the largest disfranchised group, but even that was not very large. In the first place, Boston of some sixteen thousand inhabitants and Salem and Marblehead of some five thousand were the only towns that could be remotely considered as "cities." In the second place, most of the "workers" in colonial times were not day laborers who worked for daily wages, but skilled artisans who owned their own businesses.

[32] *Ibid.*, p. 107.　　　　[33] *Ibid.*, p. 385.
[34] *Ibid.*, CCCXLVIII, 49–51 (March 30, 1773).
[35] Suffolk County Probate Records, LXXII, 41–42 (April 10, 1772).
[36] Middlesex County Probate Records, XXXIII, 137 (March 1758).
[37] *Ibid.*, LI, 212–13 (March 1768).

Probably most "laborers" were apprentices who were not old enough to vote. And in the third place, the probate records show that most, but not all, of these artisans had sufficient property to be voters even when they owned no real estate. Table 2 gives a few typical samplings of the estates of town dwellers.

Table 2. Estates of Town Workers or Artisans

Name and occupation	Real estate	Personal estate	Total estate
Caleb Parker [38] Boston blacksmith	House ....£133.6.8 12 acres 57.17.4	Negro man Other	£256.13.10
Joseph Coolidge [39] Boston gunsmith	None	Negro boy Other	122.9.11
John Mellony [40] Boston mariner	Two tenements £160.0.0	Negro woman Other	234.16.10
Thomas Templeton [41] Boston mariner	None	Only clothing and travel books	26.19.0
John Hewett [42] Boston mariner	None	Sloop Household goods	248.18.10
Edward Stone [43] Boston mariner	House and garden £100.0.0	Personal items	116.12.8
John McCleveland [44] Boston—no trade given	House and land £80.0.0	Nine items of personal estate	85.0.9
David Wheeler [45] Boston blacksmith	None	Household goods Blacksmith tools	78.4.8
Samuel Boden [46] Marblehead fisherman	House & land £130.0.0 Half a pew £7.0.0	Household goods	151.12.8
Caleb Woodbury [47] Gloucester fisherman	10 acres ....£83.9.4 Fishhouse ...... 6.0.0 Half a pew 4.0.0	Household goods Some livestock	144.9.6

[38] Nov. 20, 1771, Suffolk County Probate Records, LXXI, 77–78. The best work on colonial population is Evarts B. Greene and Virginia D. Harrington, *American Population before the Federal Census of 1790* (New York, 1932). Figures for Boston, Salem, and Marblehead, pp. 22–23.

[39] Suffolk County Probate Records, LXXI, pp. 57–59.   [40] *Ibid.*, LXXII, 110.

[41] *Ibid.*, p. 141.   [42] *Ibid.*, pp. 172–73.   [43] *Ibid.*, p. 17.

[44] *Ibid.*, LXXI, 40.   [45] *Ibid.*, LXXII, 90–91.

[46] Essex County Probate Records, CCCXLVI, 187–88 (April 20, 1770).

[47] *Ibid.*, CCCXLVII, 386.

Name and occupation	Real estate	Personal estate	Total estate
Thomas Foot [48] Marblehead fisherman	House, barn, and land £220.0.0	Household goods	240.1.2
Stephen Pettingall [49] Newbury mariner	None	Household goods 6 sheep, 1 swine	71.14.5
Henry Brookins [50] Newbury mariner	House and 1/10 acre £66.13.4	Household goods	103.9.11
Thomas Cross [51] Newburyport ship-wright	House and land £100.0.0	Notes Household goods	386.14.1
Willson Hickman [52] Marblehead fisherman	2/3 house £60.0.0	Household goods	84.10.2

Just to show that these qualified town voters and artisans were not living in affluent circumstances, I have included the entire inventory of the property of Willson Hickman, whose estate was fourth lowest in Table 2.

A case of draws 48/ . a looking glass 48/ a table 30/ a ditto 12/	£6.18.0
6 chairs 18/ . a ditto 12/8. broken table 1/4 a warming pan 6/ trammel 4/	2.2.0
handirons 2/8. shovel & tongs 1/6. a pot 2/. a kettle 2/. a tea kettle 4/	0.12.0
an old pr bellows 4d old iron ware 3/4. bed, bolster & pillows 60#@ 1/4	4.3.8
a quilt 20/. 1 pr blankets 6/. a bedstead 6/. an under bed 4/	1.16.0
Old curtains 12/. Vallens 4/. 7 sheets 18/4. 3 pr. pillow cases 2/	1.16.4
A table cloth 1/6. 15# pewter 15/. glass ware 6/. china ware 3/	1.5.6
Delph ware 2/. Tea pot 1/4d. Old pictures 6d. old toaster & gridiron 1/	0.4.10
A beaver hat 12/. a surtout 12/. a broad cloth coat 20/. an old do. 4/	2.8.0
5 jackets 24/. 2 pr. breeches 6/. 4 p. house 5/4. a cradle 1/4	1.16.8
9 old shirts 24/	1.4.0
2/3 dwelling house with land under & adjoining	60.0.0
	£84.7.2
A spinning wheel 3/	.3.0
	£84.10.2

[48] *Ibid.*, p. 19.   [49] *Ibid.*, p. 303.   [50] *Ibid.*, p. 106–07.
[51] *Ibid.*, CCCXLVIII, 158 (May 13, 1773).
[52] *Ibid.*, CCCLI, 57 (Dec. 4, 1774).

The circumstances of Benjamin Franklin's father, Josiah Franklin of Boston, furnish a good example of the relationship between the property of a town worker and the voting qualification. The elder Franklin was trained in England to be a dyer, but on coming to Boston he changed his trade to that of tallow-chandler and soap-boiler since there was no demand for dyers. That he was not affluent is attested by Franklin's statement that his father was too poor to send him to college, and also that his father, though a man of good judgment, was never able to engage in public affairs because his family of thirteen children and "the straitness of his circumstances" kept him "close to his trade." [53] Yet, in 1752, Josiah Franklin's household goods sold for a little more than $400 (which would be £120 lawful or £90 sterling) and his house and land were appraised at $2,000 (which would be £600 lawful or £450 sterling).[54] Here was a town artisan, working at a trade for which he was not trained and unable because of his economic condition to engage in politics or to send his son to college, yet possessing property worth more than thirteen times the voting qualification.

The examples in Table 2 show that town artisans even in the seaport towns did not need much property to qualify as voters. Almost any town house, or even a part of a house, was enough, while of the five who did not own real estate, only one had insufficient personal estate. The records indicate that this one was obviously an itinerant sailor. There were doubtless a few town dwellers who were not voters, probably more in proportion to the population than could be found in the rural areas, but they were not many. We need to be extremely careful, therefore, in talking about a "city proletariat" or "propertyless mechanics" who were disfranchised.

Sometimes the probate records are misleading. There are examples of men who did not have enough property to be voters at the time of their death, but the tax records show that they had ample property when they were alive. Henry Leadbetter of Weston had a total estate of only £8.5.6 at the time of his death in 1762.[55] Yet the tax records reveal that he was rated at £10 real estate and from £5 to £14 personal estate

[53] Franklin, *Writings*, I, 228–35.   [54] *Ibid.*, III, 105.
[55] Middlesex County Probate Records, Original No. 13828.

between 1758 and 1760, indicating total property of some
£200 or more.[56] James Boyd, Salem mariner, had only £26
when he died,[57] but the tax list shows that he owned part of a
house worth £3 annual rent, property which did not appear on
the inventory of his estate.[58] The inventory of the estate of
John Lamson, Weston farmer, listed only £36 in household
furniture.[59] But his will shows that he gave his widow and son
his house, lands, and livestock, and that his three daughters
received bequests of £40, £70, and £40 respectively.[60] Then
there was the following comment by the appraisers of the
estate of Ebenezer Hammond of Weston: "There is a dwelling
house and barn with 50 or 60 acres of land which we know said
Hammond died possess'd of but the adm r declined showing it
to us & we look'd upon it we are not to apprize any thing but
what they show us." [61]

In any consideration of democracy and the voting franchise,
we need to be extremely careful in grouping the creditors, gentlemen, and professional men among the voting aristocracy
and the common men and debtors among the disfranchised.
Sometimes we find that the wealthier people were also the
largest debtors, while some of the "aristocracy" had less property
than the poorest fishermen and farmers. And of course anyone
who talks about "debtor farmers" or "debtor backcountry" and
"creditor seaboard" is indulging in pure armchair speculation,
for no one has ever established who the debtors were and what
areas were debtor or creditor. A few examples will show the
danger of such interpretations.

As indicated in the previous chapter, if the probate records
are correct, there were "gentlemen," "esquires," "captains," and
"doctors" who had much less property than the small farmers.
William Tailer, Esquire, of Boston owned no real estate but
had a Negro boy and a total estate worth £68.13.6.[62] John Neal,
Boston Esquire, owned a silver-hilted sword, a gold watch, and

---

[56] *Town of Weston, The Tax Lists, 1757–1827*, ed. by Mary Frances Peirce
(Boston, 1897), lists for 1757–1761.
[57] Essex County Probate Records, CCCXLVII, 308.
[58] Mass. Arch., CXXXIV, 69.
[59] Middlesex County Probate Records, XXXII, 323 (Nov. 1757).
[60] *Ibid.*, XXVII, 261.   [61] *Ibid.*, XXIV, 285–87.
[62] Suffolk County Probate Records, LXXII, 5 (July 1772).

sixteen ruffled shirts, but he had no real estate, and his total estate was only £91.15.0.[63] Francis Bernard, Jr., son of Governor Francis Bernard, died with total assets of £27.12.2.[64] Richard Reith, Marblehead gentleman, had a "mansion house" worth £45, but he was insolvent with debts of £132.19.4.[65] Daniel Cahill, Marblehead doctor, had no real estate and died insolvent,[66] while Dr. John Hill had a personal estate of only £45.2.4.[67] Of several men who were called "Captain," none had real estate, and one, Barnabas White of Boston, was worth £43.14.8,[68] Richard Watts of Chelsea had £31.18.6,[69] Simeon Freeman of Boston had £129.2.1,[70] and Jonathan Lord, Boston, had £81.14.4.[71] Almost any small farmer and many artisans had more property than these captains, esquires, and gentlemen.

Debtors and creditors included all groups ranging from the poor to the wealthy, making any division of voters on debtor-creditor lines extremely tenuous. As we have seen, James Boyd, Salem mariner, was a poor man worth only £26, but £16 of this was out at interest.[72] Thomas Cross, Newburyport shipwright, had £170 at interest,[73] while Benjamin Hagar of Weston had £109 of his £133 estate at interest.[74] On the other hand, Samuel Pike, Newbury mariner, had assets of £800 but debts of £1,013.[75] The owner of a farm worth £5,000 and rented to a tenant for £150 sterling a year had to sell his farm to pay his son's debts.[76] Even the "aristocratic" Oliver family was not above the debtor status. Andrew Oliver, who lived in a £2,000 home in Boston, owed James Boutineau £1,000 from 1761 to 1774.[77] Another Oliver, Peter, claimed he was in "much distress" because of a debt, and appealed to Thomas Hutchinson for a loan of £800 sterling.[78] Francis Bernard, Jr., son of the governor,

[63] *Ibid.*, pp. 7–8.   [64] *Ibid.*, p. 135.
[65] Essex County Probate Records, CCCXLVII, 369 (March 1772).
[66] *Ibid.*, CCCXLVI, 158–59, 431–34.
[67] May 1772, Suffolk County Probate Records, LXXII, 31–32.
[68] *Ibid.*, LXXI, 97–98.   [69] *Ibid.*, pp. 32–34.   [70] *Ibid.*, LXXII, 97.
[71] *Ibid.*, LXXI, 98–99.   [72] Essex County Probate Records, CCCXLVII, 308.
[73] *Ibid.*, CCCXLVIII, 1–2.
[74] Middlesex County Probate Records, XXXIII, 137.
[75] Essex County Probate Records, CCCXLVIII, 33.
[76] Andrew Oliver Letter Book, I, 138–39.
[77] Hutchinson-Oliver Papers, II, May 10, 1761.
[78] Samuel Adams Papers (New York Public Library), I, April 27, 1768.

owned a stillhouse worth £1,000 sterling but this was not enough to pay his obligations.[79]

Neither can we segregate sections into debtor and creditor areas in any discussion of the franchise, at least until we have more evidence than we now have. If Oliver and Bernard were debtors in Boston, their creditors were also in Boston. Usually debtors and creditors lived in the same area, and often included members of the same family. Mrs. Rebekah Dresser of Rowley loaned most of her money to Stephen and John Dresser.[80] Reverend Timothy Woodbridge of Hatfield held notes from Haynes and Dudley Woodbridge, at least one of which was considered a "bad debt."[81] Thomas Bridgman of Northampton owed money to other Northampton men—Quartus Pomeroy, James Shepherd, Timothy Dwight, and Simeon Strong.[82] The tax list for Northampton in 1772 lists twenty-eight men in the town who had money out at interest in amounts from £6 to £500.[83] In short, we need much more evidence than we now have before we can speak accurately of the debtors and creditors.

In addition to an evaluation of the voting franchise in terms of those who did or did not own property, a second approach is through the rental of property. Most people owned property, but there were enough renters to give us some conception of what a 53s.4d. (40s. sterling) freehold entailed. Andrew Oliver handled the rental of a 200-acre farm which rented for £40 a year, or thirteen times the voting requirement.[84] Another farm of 533 acres, rented "by the halves," brought its owner £150 sterling a year or seventy-five times the voting qualification.[85] Oliver rented a garden spot in Boston for £5.6.8 a year, or twice the qualification, and said that rooms in Boston rented at £6 to £8 a year, about two or three times the voting requirement.[86] Henry Hulton, one of the commissioners of customs in Boston, claimed that he could not rent a house for less than £50 sterling, and also said that board and lodging for a single person in Boston was £35 sterling a year.[87] This would mean

[79] Mass. Arch., XXVII, 386, 394.
[80] Essex County Probate Records, CCCXLVIII, 129–30.
[81] Hampshire County Probate Records, XII, 1.
[82] Ibid., pp. 34–35.
[83] Judd MSS., Northampton, II, 69.
[84] Andrew Oliver Letter Book, I, 159.
[85] Ibid., pp. 138–39.
[86] Ibid., II, 93.
[87] Hulton, Letters, p. 42.

that a 53s.4d. freehold would be real estate that would yield a yearly rent sufficient to pay board and room for a single person for twenty-one days.

Other available figures on rentals show just how little was needed to meet the 53s.4d. freehold requirement. The Reverend Mather Byles received £100 a year in salary and paid £25 sterling a year for rent.[88] At Newburyport, the minister was allowed £10 sterling a year for rent.[89] Andrew Oliver's seven tenements on Oliver's Dock were valued at £500 and rented for a total of £54.8.0 a year.[90] At this rate, Boston property worth £25 rented for enough to qualify its owner. John Hancock claimed the loss of £100 sterling for a year's rent on his house as a result of the Boston siege, just fifty times the voting qualification.[91] And finally, the Boston tax lists for 1771 show that there was not a single house in Boston with a yearly rental of less than 60s. and only a few that approached this low figure.[92] So anyone who owned a house in Boston was a qualified voter.

Still another way to get a proper perspective of the voting qualifications is through a comparison of colonial and present-day wages in terms of purchasing power. As I have already said, wages were much higher in the colonies than in England, averaging about two shillings a day for common labor in the winter and three shillings in the summer.[93] At this rate, a 53s.4d. freehold would be real estate with a yearly rent equal to twenty-seven days' wages for common labor in the winter or eighteen days' wages in the summer. Allowing $12.00 a day for similar work at the present time, this would mean property which would rent for $216.00 to $324.00 a year in 1955, or $18.00 to $27.00 a month. Such figures do not make the voting qualification look very formidable, as this amount would scarcely pay for room rent now.

[88] S.P.G. Archives, ser. B, XXII, 146–47. [89] *Ibid.*, p. 80.
[90] Estimate of the real estate of Andrew Oliver, Hutchinson-Oliver Papers, II.
[91] Chamberlain Collection, John Hancock (Boston Public Library), p. 147.
[92] Mass. Arch., CXXXII, 92–147.
[93] Woolman, *Journal*, pp. 305–06; Peter Oliver, "Origins and Progress . . . ," Egerton MSS., 2671, p. 116; Malden Town Records, I, 162; Stockbridge Town Records, 1760–1805, p. 15; Pittsfield Town Records, I, 90.

Similar comparisons can be made with soldiers' wages, and soldiers have certainly never been rated in the upper income brackets. In 1775, Marblehead voted to pay 2s. a day for a private, 3s. for a sergeant or drummer, 4s. for a second lieutenant and 6s. for a captain.[94] During the war, Hadley paid 40s. a month to soldiers, later raising this to 60s., the money to be equivalent to the purchasing power of prewar money, so there was no problem of inflated money.[95] On this basis a 53s.4d. freehold would be real estate that would yield a yearly rent equivalent to about one month's pay for a private or eighteen days for a sergeant. In terms of present wages for privates and sergeants, this would mean real estate renting from $72.00 to $100.00 a year or $6.00 to $9.00 a month.

Ministers' salaries also give a fair indication of what the voting qualifications meant in practical terms. In 1764, Pittsfield paid its minister £60 with £5 a year increase until the salary reached £80, and also provided forty cords of firewood a year.[96] Northampton did better for the man who succeeded Jonathan Edwards. He was given £266.13.4 to settle, a starting salary of £80 with a £5 yearly increase until his pay reached £100, and £6.13.4 to purchase firewood.[97] Timothy Woodbridge of Hatfield received £90 in salary and £15 for firewood at 6 shillings a cord.[98] Dover paid Jeremiah Belknap £100 a year as colleague of the Reverend Jonathan Cushing, and also agreed to give him £150 to provide his own house, or, if he preferred, the town would furnish a convenient house, barn, and garden.[99]

What do these figures mean? A minister's salary, including fuel and housing, was about twice as much as the amount of property required for voting. At the present time, real estate worth half the salary of a small-town minister would not be much. A minister's yearly fuel bill would be from two to five times the yearly income of real estate that would yield enough to qualify its owner. Jeremiah Belknap's allowance for a house would be almost treble the amount of property needed. By way

[94] Marblehead Town Records, IV, 207–08.
[95] Hadley Town Records, June 24 and 28, 1779.
[96] Pittsfield Town Records, I, 69, 74.
[97] Northampton Town Records, II, 1.   [98] Hatfield Town Records, IV, 165.
[99] *Belknap Papers*, Mass. Hist. Soc., *Collections*, 6 ser., IV, 11.

of contrast the governor of Massachusetts received £1,000 sterling or £1,333 lawful money a year. Ministers were obviously not considered in the upper economic groups, for it should be remembered that Franklin's father decided not to educate Benjamin for the ministry in part because of "the mean living many so educated were afterwards able to obtain." [100]

A final comparison to indicate the value of the voting qualifications is between various colonial prices and the 53s.4d. freehold requirement for voting. Livestock was valued as follows: horses £5–£20, cows £2–£5, hogs £1–£2.8, calves 13s.–20s.[101] A man could be a voter if he had property which, if rented for a year; would yield enough to purchase half a cheap horse, one average cow, two hogs or three calves. Northampton offered to pay 40s. a year to anyone who would keep one of the town bulls, another indication of what 40s. represented.[102] Grain, a basic commodity, was valued by the bushel as follows: wheat 4 or 5s., rye 3 or 4s., corn 2 or 3s., and oats 2s.[103] Figured in wheat, a 53s.4d. freehold represented something between eleven to sixteen bushels of wheat. The records show that land in Massachusetts produced twelve to twenty-five bushels of grain to the acre, and that farmers produced from fifteen to 120 bushels of grain a year.[104] So the yield from one acre of wheat would usually be more than the rental of a 53s.4d. freehold. In terms of other commodities, a 53s.4d. freehold represented seventy-five pounds of butter, forty ducks, seventy-five chickens or nine cords of firewood.[105] The town of Hadley paid a shilling bounty for each crow killed,[106] a set of coach harness came at £6 or £7,[107] and a lock on a door cost 16s.[108]

[100] Franklin, *Writings*, I, 233.

[101] Hampshire County Probate Records, XII, 62–64; Suffolk County Probate Records, LXXI, 12–13, 46–47; LXXII, 12–13; Middlesex County Probate Records, XXXIV, 275–76; LVII, 319; Essex County Probate Records, CCCXLVII, 28, 272, 304; CCCXLVIII, 9–12.

[102] Northampton Town Records, II, 40.

[103] Hatfield Town Records, IV, 284; Hadley Town Records, July 24, 1779. Prices were listed as of 1774.

[104] Mass. Arch., CXXXII, 5; CXXXIII, 68, 69, 74, 76.

[105] Hutchinson-Oliver Papers, II, Dec. 13, 1766; Hulton, *Letters*, p. 36.

[106] Hadley Town Records, March 5, 1770.   [107] Oliver Letter Book, I, 52.

[108] Judd MSS., Diary of Jonathan Judd, Jr., June 18, 1773. Hereafter cited Judd, Diary.

The almost inevitable conclusion from this evidence would be that not many adult men in colonial Massachusetts were excluded from voting because of property requirements. Cheap land, high wages, and economic opportunity promoted almost universal property ownership, while the amount of property needed for voting was extremely modest. We need to place the property qualifications in their proper perspective, for it makes a tremendous difference in our interpretation of the colonial, revolutionary, and constitutional periods whether more than 90 per cent or only 10 per cent of the adult men could vote. And unless £50 of property meant more in other colonies than it did in Massachusetts, we ought to take a closer look at democracy in those colonies as well.

CHAPTER III

Political Democracy
in Province Elections

IF THE tentative conclusions in Chapters I and II are correct
—that property ownership was widespread in colonial Massachusetts and that the voting qualification did not represent
much property—the sources ought to show that most men actually could vote in province elections. It is essential to have
this information before one can decide whether the Revolution
was a dual movement—a war for independence and a conflict
to democratize American society. We would need to know
whether most men could vote, whether they actually did vote,
or whether property qualifications for voting created an upper-
class aristocracy which controlled colonial politics.[1]

[1] Much of the material presented in this chapter appeared in an article, "Democracy in Colonial Massachusetts," *New England Quarterly*, XXV (Sept. 1952).
It is published here with the permission of the *New England Quarterly*. Writers
who hold that Massachusetts society was undemocratic usually make such statements without any supporting evidence or cite McKinley, *The Suffrage Franchise*.
James Truslow Adams maintained that practically not a single workman, laborer,
fisherman, sailor, mechanic, or small tradesman had the vote in province affairs,
that voting in all the colonies "was rigidly restricted to but a fraction of the
population," and that there were fewer voters proportionately in New England
than in the other colonies. See *Revolutionary New England*, pp. 161, 315–16. The
late Charles McLean Andrews also contended that the colonies were not democratic. The colonies had self-government, he said, but this did not imply democracy, if by democracy we mean political equality, universal suffrage, majority
rule, and government by consent of the governed. See *Colonial Background of the*

The task of discovering the number of qualified voters in colonial times is not easy, because the colonists did not consider voting records important. The historian must resort to all sorts of indirect approaches to arrive at his conclusions.

One bit of circumstantial evidence on the existence of democracy was the indiscriminate way in which the terms "qualified voters," "families," and "freeholders" were used interchangeably in the election laws and in references to elections. The first law on representation under the Charter of 1691 specified that a town with forty freeholders or other inhabitants, qualified to vote according to the charter, must send a representative to the General Court.[2] This law was changed in 1726, with the term "families" used instead of qualified voters, as though most adult men were heads of families and legal voters.[3] In 1731, the law was altered again, and this time the terms "qualified voters" and "families" were used interchangeably.[4] Towns which were fined for failure to send representatives often used the word "families" instead of qualified voters in justifying their failure.[5] Individuals frequently used the same terminology. One writer, in advocating a curtailment of representation in the colony, said that towns were entitled to two representatives when the number of their "families" increased to 120.[6] Similarly, Governor Francis Bernard used the word "freeholders" to mean legal voters as though all freeholders qualified as voters.[7] Even the Lords of Trade, in referring to representation in Massachusetts, used "families" to mean qualified voters.[8] Such widespread use of these terms could not have been accidental, and certainly

---

American Revolution (New Haven, 1924), p. 201; *The Colonial Period of American History*, 4 vols. (New Haven, 1934–1938), IV, 423n. Adams, as have many other writers, cited J. Franklin Jameson and Albert Edward McKinley, whose work I shall discuss at length in footnote 55.

2 Acts and Resolves, I, 88–90 (Nov. 1692).

3 *Ibid.*, II, 406 (Nov. 1726); *Journal of the House of Representatives*, 25 vols. (Boston and Watertown, 1715–1777), VII, 114.

4 *Acts and Resolves*, II, 592–93 (April 1731).

5 Mass. Arch. CXVI, 767–68; CXVII, 628–30; CXVIII, 44.

6 Andrew McFarland Davis, ed., *Colonial Currency Reprints*, in Prince Society, *Publications*, 4 vols. (Boston, 1910–1911), IV, 35, 343–44.

7 *Acts and Resolves*, IV, 628–29 (April 1763).

8 Mass. Hist. Soc., Miscellaneous MSS., VIII (July 16, 1764).

would not have been had the question of voting been a very pressing one.

Excellent material on colonial democracy is to be found in the records of disputed elections. Since some of these elections were extremely close and often bitterly contested, it can be presumed that a larger number of qualified voters took part than in ordinary elections. Hence it is possible through the use of various figures on population to estimate with some degree of accuracy the percentage of voters among the adult males.

For one thing, there is evidence that sometimes boys under twenty-one years of age voted. In one dispute, Hezekiah Noble of Sheffield testified that Zonas Higgins, about nineteen years, put his vote for representative "into the hat" with the other votes—a statement which also reveals something about voting methods.[9] Joseph Noble, selectman of the same town of Sheffield, testified that Peter Ingersole, aged eighteen, tried to vote but was refused. Then one of the candidates, David Ingersole, argued "with the utmost earnestness" that Peter was a voter because he possessed his deceased father's estate, was a "town born child," and so was an inhabitant. After this argument, Nathaniel Austin, another selectman, accepted the vote of Peter Ingersole; and strange to say, when the votes were counted, candidate David Ingersole had one more vote than his opponent.[10]

A disputed province election in Stockbridge, in 1763, furnishes some excellent evidence on the number and kind of voters in a Massachusetts town. The election was close, some figures are available for statistical estimates, and an investigation by the General Court gives some conclusions that can hardly be doubted. The big issue seems to have been that the town was fairly evenly divided between Indians and whites, with the whites determined to capture control of political affairs.

The Indians, who lost the election by a vote of twenty-nine to thirty-two, accused the victors of unethical voting practices.

[9] Mass. Arch., VIII, 277. On methods of voting, see Charles S. Sydnor and Noble E. Cunningham, Jr., "Voting in Early America," *American Heritage*, IV (Fall 1952), 6–8.
[10] Mass. Arch., VIII, 278.

They said that the opposition, knowing that many of the Indians could not write, used written ballots for the first time, which was contrary to established custom. The Indians also claimed that their opponents imported unqualified voters to swing the election. Some of these, said the Indians, "were poor fellows that we never heard had any business in this town only as they were hired to work and we have reason to believe to vote likewise." The Indians also declared that the voting population had suddenly jumped from about forty to more than sixty, some of whom were not people of the town, but were there "only as day labourers." They had no interest in the town or its government, the Indians concluded, and they possessed only "some wild lands," were "but way fareing men," and set their own value on their estates, swearing they were qualified to vote. In all, they accused nine men of voting illegally.[11]

After a thorough investigation, however, a committee of the General Court, which had been sent to Stockbridge to settle the dispute, came to the conclusion that all the men who were challenged were qualified as far as property was concerned and that most of them were qualified as town residents. The facts as set forth by the committee, and agreed to by both contending parties, were as follows:

The alleged illegal voters were "three young men, sons of Mr. Jones, Mr. Brown, and Mr. Pixley, one Ball a hired man of Major Williams, one Curtis, Whitney, Patterson, Roe and Halluck."

Of the three young men, Abraham Brown, aged twenty-two, had a freehold of wild or unimproved land worth £100 "at least," Elijah Jones had a similar freehold of the same value, and David Pixley had "a freehold of like value with a saw mill upon it of the yearly rent of 40/ sterling [40s.] had also a yoke of oxen and a horse."

The "hired man," Nathan Ball,

was sworn at the town meeting that he was worth £40 Sterl. and offered to swear the same before the committee; but the petitioners declared themselves satisfied on that point, and allowed also that he was qualified as an inhabitant. True, he was hired by Majr. Williams

11 *Ibid.*, XXXIII, 249–52, 265–68.

as a labourer; but he declared that Majr. Williams never asked him, or sent him to attend the meeting, nor was there any evidence, but hearsay that Majr. Williams made use of any undue influence with any other person to obtain a vote—

Titus Curtis had lived occasionally in Stockbridge for the past two years, and was then living with his father who was an inhabitant. He was sworn at the meeting that he was worth £40 sterling, and said he was ready to swear it before the committee. The petitioners declared their objection to him was not based on lack of property but on the fact that he was not a legal inhabitant.

Phineas Whitney had lived in Stockbridge the greater part of two years, was twenty-three years old, and "was sworn at the meeting that he was worth £40 sterling."

Joseph Patterson, a laborer, claimed he was worth £40 sterling in lands at Mt. Ephriam granted by the government, was sworn at the meeting, and said he was also worth £20 sterling in money.

Abel Roe, a laborer, conceded at the town meeting to be worth £40 sterling in lands, was not sworn.

Stephen Halluck was conceded to have land which the Indians had sold to a "Dutchman." Halluck declared that he gave £70 lawful money for it, had a warranty deed, had built on the land, and had laid out £40 or £50 on it since he purchased it. It did not appear that he was concerned in a fraudulent purchase as the petitioners had suggested.[12]

When the committee finished its investigation, then, all these "labourers," "poor fellows," "way fareing men" proved to be property owners and qualified voters. The committee declared the election legal, but recommended separation of the Indians and whites in their political capacities.[13]

An investigation of the deeds for Berkshire County merely confirms the committee's findings that these laborers were property owners. In 1765, two years after the election, Joseph Patterson, designated a "labourer" in the dispute, sold two lots of land at Mt. Ephriam for £60 and £10 respectively.[14] At the

[12] *Ibid.*, pp. 277–88.
[13] *Ibid.*, pp. 256–57 (Feb. 3, 1764); *Acts and Resolves*, XVII, 500.
[14] Berkshire County Register of Deeds, III, 322; IV, 85.

same time, he bought 100 acres from Abraham Brown, one of the three young sons, for £90.[15] Brown also sold two other lots for £60 and £10.[16] In 1766, Nathan Ball, the "hired man," was able to borrow £85 on fifteen acres of his land, which was designated as part of the lot on which he lived.[17] And in 1764 and 1765, Titus Curtis sold two lots for £15 and £50 respectively.[18]

In addition to showing that young men and laborers were voters, this disputed Stockbridge election also produced evidence that practically all adult men in the town could vote. The committee of the General Court said there were thirty-seven adult Indian men, twenty of whom were qualified on the basis of their improved lands, and the assertion was made that all of them could vote if their interest in the common Indian proprietary lands was counted as a qualification. The committee also said that the town contained about thirty-two white families, but that forty-five white men were admitted as qualified voters in the disputed election for representative, and that one of the candidates was not present, making at least forty-six white voters.[19] If there were forty-six qualified voters in a town with

Table 3. Estimated Adult Males and Qualified Voters,
Stockbridge, 1763–1765 [20]

Committee figures, 1763	Census figures, 1763–1765
32 white families	34 houses of whites
45 white men voted in election	39 white families
1 candidate not at election	50 white males under 16 years
206 total Indians:	64 white males over 16 years
37 males over 21 years	[48 adult white men, using 25%
20 qualified voters on basis of improved lands	as number of men 16–21]
37 qualified voters on basis of proprietary lands	217 total whites
18% of Indian population were adult men.	221 total Indians

[15] *Ibid.*, III, 342.   [16] *Ibid.*, pp. 45, 340 (1764–65).   [17] *Ibid.*, IV, 537–39.
[18] *Ibid.*, II, 460; IV, 15.   [19] Mass. Arch., XXXIII, 277–88.
[20] *Ibid.*; Joseph B. Felt, "Statistics of Population in Massachusetts," in American Statistical Association, *Collections* (Boston, 1847), I, 156, 196. Hereafter cited Felt, "Statistics."

only thirty-two families, there could not have been many men in town who were not legal voters.

Other figures given in Table 3 verify the view that most adult men in Stockbridge were qualified voters. The census was probably taken in 1765, since the Indian population had increased from 206 to 221; by 1765 there should also have been a few more adult white men in the town than in 1763. As will appear later, the colonial population was a young population so that about 25 per cent of the polls (males over sixteen) were under twenty-one and therefore not qualified to vote. There should have been about forty-eight adult white men in the town at the time the census was taken, and we know there were forty-six qualified white voters in 1763. So the number of adult men and qualified voters must have been about the same.

Another disputed election for representative, this one in Watertown in 1757, demonstrated not only the extent but also the machinations of colonial democracy. In the first ballot the vote was sixty-five for John Hunt and sixty-six for Daniel Whitney, a total of 131 votes. The selectman, who favored Hunt, had objected to four votes cast for Whitney while the Whitney people challenged two votes cast for Hunt. Under the circumstances, the selectmen had declared Hunt the winner. The selectmen defended the two Hunt voters by saying that one was not "non compos mentis," as accused, but merely had a guardian because he drank too much, and that the other was a carpenter who was not an inhabitant of Lincoln, as claimed, but only went there occasionally to work. The selectmen then said they threw out the four Whitney votes because two of the men were not freeholders of Watertown, had not been born there, had not served an apprenticeship there, and had not obtained the consent of the town to live there. One of them had been hired as a laborer from Lexington, where he was an inhabitant. A third man had been born in Watertown, but had moved to Cambridge where he had rented a farm. The fourth man was an inhabitant of Boston who had married a Watertown widow but had not established a residence in Watertown.[21]

The chief objection to these men as voters seems to have been that they were not residents, not that they did not have sufficient

21 Mass. Arch., CXVII, 291–301.

property to be voters. At one point in the dispute, a petition read as follows: "So it seems that the only test that the select men made of the qualifications of voters was their swearing they were worth forty pounds sterling & the law which forbids persons voting that were not inhabitants were [sic] not regarded." [22]

Accusations of corruption and attempts to swing the election regardless of the vote flew thick and fast. One man swore that Hunt men had offered to lend him as much money as he wanted if he would vote for Hunt, an indication that the voter and not the candidate had the whip hand.[23] A Whitney man claimed that one of the selectmen had "declared he wou'd die, before he would return a precept in favor of Whitney." [24] On one balloting, the selectmen, assuming that all the votes were in, had turned over the hat, counted the votes, and declared the election a tie. Just then a voice from the rear—a voice well-known to the selectmen, according to Whitney men—called out that not all the votes were in, and the selectmen answered, "Let them come forward." But unfortunately for the Hunt men, these four Hunt voters were followed by six others who voted for Whitney.[25]

The dispute, as finally settled by the House of Representatives, was presumably based on the assumption that all the challenged voters were qualified. The selectmen had thrown out three Whitney votes as illegal, which would have given Hunt a majority of one.[26] But the House nevertheless declared Whitney the winner, which obviously meant that the House considered these three votes legal.[27] Later the General Court had to appoint the Honorable Benjamin Lincoln as impartial moderator for the town so that the town could carry on its affairs.[28]

In addition to revealing the workings of democracy in Massachusetts, this disputed Watertown election furnished some figures on voting which, with other statistics on the town, show that practically all the adult men could vote. There were 131

[22] *Ibid.*, pp. 306–07.   [23] *Ibid.*, p. 308.   [24] *Ibid.*, pp. 311–14.
[25] *Ibid.*, L, 85–90.   [26] *Ibid.*
[27] *House Journals, 1758–59,* pp. 31–32, 35.
[28] *Acts and Resolves,* XVI, 318; *Watertown Records,* 6 vols. (Watertown, 1894–1906), V, 208–10.

votes cast in 1757; in the census of 1763–1765, Watertown had 117 families and 179 polls (men over sixteen years of age).[29] In other words, there were fourteen more voters in 1757 than there were heads of families in the town six or eight years later. If we subtract the estimated forty-four men (25 per cent) sixteen to twenty-one years of age from the 179 polls, the result is 135 adult men in 1763–1765 compared with 131 voters in 1757. It is interesting to note also that the population and qualified voters of Watertown, an eastern town, compare very closely with the population and voters of Stockbridge, a western town. Stockbridge, a newer town, seems to have had a slightly higher percentage of adult men in its population than did Watertown, which would be natural for a frontier town.

Still a third disputed election, this one in Weston, a few miles from Boston, showed a high percentage of voters in the adult male population. There were 133 votes cast in this election, which was held in 1773.[30] The Weston tax lists for 1772 show 216 polls,[31] which would probably mean some 162 adult men in the town. If every qualified voter in town voted, the result would be that over 80 per cent of the adult men were qualified voters. However, a valuation list for 1774 lists 154 eligible voters,[32] which would boost the percentage to about 95. At any rate, any minimum estimation would give a high percentage of qualified voters among the adult men, and there is little reason to suppose that Weston differed much from Watertown and Stockbridge, or that these towns differed from most of the agricultural towns in Massachusetts.

Another way to determine how many adult men were probably qualified voters is by comparing the tax and probate records. The problem was to find someone who died the same year in which he was taxed, and Andover furnished the records. David Stevens was worth £152 when he died, which would be 2.8 times the voting qualification of £53.4.0 lawful money.[33] Stevens also paid 10s.8d. in taxes the same year, which, deducting the poll tax of 3s.4d., would leave 7s.4d. in property

29 Felt, "Statistics," p. 150.   30 Mass. Arch., L, 452–55.
31 *Weston Tax Lists*, pp. 72–77.   32 *Ibid.*, pp. 83–84.
33 Essex County Probate Records, CCCXXXIII, 287.

tax.[34] If Stevens had 2.8 times as much property as he needed to vote and paid 7s.4d. in property taxes, anyone who paid 2s.7d. in property taxes should have been worth at least £54. Of the 400 men on the tax list, about 300 (deducting the 25 per cent between 16 and 21) should have been adults. Some 290 of these paid estate taxes of 2s.7d. or more, or about ninety-five per cent. Such figures are about the same as those for Watertown and Stockbridge.

An objection might well be made that the poor would not appear on the tax lists and that therefore these lists are not indicative. This would certainly be true, for there were doubtless a few men too poor to be taxed. But on the other hand, the error would be more apt to be the other way—that is, there might be many men who could vote but whose names would not appear on the lists, since property such as unimproved land, money not at interest, furniture, farm tools, mechanic's tools, and young livestock was not taxed but could be counted to qualify for voting.[35] The nine men whose votes were challenged in Stockbridge all had sufficient property to be voters, yet none of this property except the sawmill and livestock was taxable.[36]

A tax list for a portion of Northampton in 1769 shows what a typical agricultural community must have been like in colonial times. There were forty-eight men listed and sixteen extra polls, indicating that the polls sixteen to twenty-one years of age comprised twenty-five per cent of the total number of polls. Of the forty-eight men, only five—John Black, Nathaniel Kentfield, Daniel Kentfield, Rufus Brown, and John Smith—could possibly have had insufficient property to vote. Two men, John Black and Nathaniel Kentfield had houses and were probably qualified, and all five might well have owned unimproved lands as did the challenged voters in Stockbridge. Assuming that all five were disqualified, the percentage of those who were undoubtedly qualified would still be nearly ninety.[37]

One additional statistical method remains for ascertaining the minimum percentage of qualified voters in Massachusetts

[34] Andover Tax Lists, 1754, pp. 433–38.   [35] *Acts and Resolves*, IV, 422–23.
[36] Mass. Arch., XXXIII, 277–88.
[37] Judd MSS., Northampton and Westhampton, II, 80.

before the Revolution. This method is based on a change in the basis of representation which the colony made in 1776. Under the charter, a town with forty voters had to send one representative, a town with 120 voters could send two, but only Boston could send more than two, and Boston was entitled to four.[38] Such a proportioning of representation might have been equitable in 1692, but by 1776 there was a marked spread in the size of towns, and inequitable representation had resulted. In 1776, the General Court provided that a town could send an additional representative for each hundred voters it had above 120; that is, if a town had 220 voters, it could send three delegates.[39] Boston, for instance, assumed that it could send twelve or more under the new law—an indication that the town probably did not know how many voters it had. But Boston had to have at least 1,120 voters, although only 272 voters actually participated in the election of these twelve representatives.[40]

The debates over this new law provide some interesting information on the number of voters in the province. In August 1775, the General Court had first acted to increase the number of small towns which could send representatives.[41] Some of the larger towns protested, and in April 1776, there was a call for a convention in Essex County to discuss the problem. The complaint was that while the General Court had increased the representation of the smaller towns, it had done nothing about towns containing from 300 to 3,000 freeholders.[42] This is significant in the first place because the word "freeholder" was used to mean qualified voter. In the second place, the inference is that at least one town had 3,000 freeholders, which could mean only Boston, and 3,000 freeholders would include about all the adult men in Boston.

This law equalizing representation for the larger towns also provides some figures for estimating legal voters. The method

[38] Acts and Resolves, I, 88–90 (Nov. 1692).   [39] Ibid., V, 502–03 (May 1774).

[40] Boston Town Records in Reports of the Record Commissioners . . . , 39 vols. (Boston, 1876–1909), XVIII, 234.

[41] Acts and Resolves, IV, 419.

[42] "Broadside," in Essex Institute, Historical Collections (Salem, 1859–), XXXVI, 104.

is rather simple. If a town sent three representatives, it must have had at least 220 qualified voters; if it sent six, it must have had at least 520 voters. Hence by checking on representation after 1776 it is possible to find the minimum number of qualified voters in any town. The result would be only a minimum, for towns seldom sent as many representatives as they were entitled to send, and the town which sent three representatives might well have had 300 qualified voters instead of the minimum of 220. These minimum figures, in turn, can be compared with census figures on the estimated adult male population in any town. The result is an estimated minimum percentage of the adult male population which could qualify as voters.

One other explanation is essential to an understanding of Table 4. Taxation was determined by polls (men sixteen years and over) rather than by adult men, so the records give only the number of polls in a town. This means that the polls sixteen to twenty-one must be eliminated to get figures on the adult male population. As stated above, the population in colonial times was a young population, so that about 25 per cent of the polls were under twenty-one. In his "Notes on Virginia," Jefferson gave figures of 53,289 free men over twenty-one and 17,763 free men sixteen to twenty-one, which would be 24.9 per cent.[43] Northampton had 234 men listed on the tax records in 1748 and 100 extra polls, which would be 29.9 per cent.[44] By 1769, one section of the town had forty-eight men and sixteen extra polls, or 25 per cent.[45] Hatfield also had 29.4 per cent in 1743 and 25.2 per cent in 1772.[46] So in Table 4, I have deducted 25 per cent of the polls to get the estimated adult male population of any town.

I stress again that these percentages in Table 4 are minimum figures, and a quick check will show that most of them were far below the true figures. In all probability, only the estimates for Northampton, Worcester, and Charleston came close to actuality. There is no reason to suppose, for instance, that any of the agricultural towns in Massachusetts differed very much from

[43] Jefferson, *Writings,* III, 490.   [44] Northampton Town Records, I, 296–99.
[45] Judd MSS., Northampton and Westhampton, II, 80.
[46] Hatfield Town Records, I, 182–85; Hatfield Assessors' List, 1772.

these three towns. If more than 90 per cent of their adult men could vote, chances are that the same percentage would hold for most of the country towns. We know that the estimate for Watertown based on 120 voters is low because Watertown had 131 actual voters in the disputed election of 1757. There is no valid reason why Salem should have a larger percentage than

Table 4. Estimated Percentage of Voters in the Adult
Male Population [47]

Town	County	No. of reps.	Least no. of voters	No. of polls	Est. polls 16 to 21	Est. No. adult males	Est. % of adult male voters
Roxbury	Suff.	3	220	356	89	267	82.4
Watertown	Mid.	2	120	185	46	139	86.3
Northampton	Hamp.	4	320	451	113	338	94.6 (1777)
Worcester	Worc.	4	320	438	109	329	97.2
Charlton	Worc.	3	220	308	77	231	95.2
Boston	Suff.	12	1120	2664	666	1998	56.0
Salem	Essex	7	620	1193	298	895	69.2
Ipswich	Essex	5	420	1016	254	762	55.1
Marblehead	Essex	5	420	1047	262	785	53.5
Gloucester	Essex	5	420	939	235	704	59.6
Newbury	Essex	5	420	704	176	528	79.5
Medford	Mid.	2	120	190	47	143	83.9
Monson	Hamp.	2	120	197	49	148	81.0 (1777)
Bridgewater	Ply.	6	520	1130	282	848	61.3
Leicester	Worc.	2	120	212	53	159	75.4 (1777)
New Braintree	Worc.	2	120	185	46	139	86.3 (1777)
Sheffield	Berk.	3	220	338	84	254	86.6 (1777)

Ipswich and Marblehead, and it is obvious, as later evidence will show, that the figure for Boston is far out of line. In the first place, the town did not know how many voters it had or how many representatives it was entitled to send. Hutchinson estimated the number of legal voters in town affairs at 1,500 in 1770,[48] which would make the Boston figure 75 per cent rather than 56 per cent. And, as I will show in a later chapter, this

[47] *Acts and Resolves,* XIX, 418–20; XX, 4–6; Felt, "Statistics," pp. 158–70.
[48] Mass. Arch., XXVI, 464.

would doubtless mean many more were qualified to vote for representatives. Sudbury sent only one representative from 1776 on, yet in 1753 the town claimed "two hundred or more voters." [49]

A work of this nature must naturally include some reference to the fact that even though most men probably could vote, a large percentage of them often failed to exercise their rights at the polls. That, of course, is nothing new, for it is still a problem. But it is one thing whether only 10 per cent of the adult men *could* vote and the other 90 per cent could not and wanted to, or whether more than 90 per cent had the franchise and only ten per cent used it. As Thomas Paine said, if a man fails to vote, he has no one to blame for the consequence but himself.[50]

Actually, as the records of Boston show so graphically, the people turned out in sizable numbers when there was an important issue at stake and presumably failed to vote when they were satisfied with existing conditions. In 1729, for instance, there were 192 voters, but when paper money became an issue in 1732, the vote jumped to 655.[51] The beginning of trouble with Great Britain attracted the greatest number of voters, for the number increased from 334 in 1761 to 1,089 in 1763.[52] There was also some interest exhibited in the election of 1772, testing Samuel Adams' control of the town meeting, when 723 voters turned out.[53] But the next year, with Adams securely in command, the vote dropped to 419, and it fell to the lowest point in thirty-seven years when only 272 participated in the 1776 election just before the Declaration of Independence.[54]

In dealing with the problem of voting, it is highly misleading to confuse those who *did* vote with those who *could* vote or to give the percentage of voters in terms of the whole population. Those who did and those who could were two entirely different problems, then as now. Anyone who assumes that the number of people who participate in present-day elections is representative of the number who can vote would be just as far from the

[49] *Ibid.*, CXVI, 373–74.

[50] Thomas Paine, *The Complete Writings of Thomas Paine*, ed. by Philip S. Foner, 2 vols. (New York, 1945), II, 302.

[51] *Boston Town Records*, XII, 7, 31.   [52] *Ibid.*, XIV, 57, 88.

[53] *Ibid.*, XVIII, 78.   [54] *Ibid.*, pp. 129, 235.

mark as he would be in making the same assumption for colonial times. Furthermore, percentages of voters in terms of the entire population give a distorted picture. In colonial days, more than 60 per cent of the people were minors, and even in these enlightened times we still consider such people unqualified to vote. Half of the remainder were women, so that only about one person in five or six was an adult man. Jefferson gave the figure as 18.7 per cent of the population in Virginia, and the population of Massachusetts could not have been much different.[55] The only valid approach, therefore, is to find out how many adult men could vote out of the total adult male population.

[55] Jefferson, *Writings*, III, 490. The question of percentages of those who could and did vote presents an interesting study in the use of historical evidence. J. Franklin Jameson maintained, without use of evidence, that in an agricultural society in which most men owned property, not many would be excluded from voting by the property qualifications. He estimated that 20 per cent of the people would be adult men (which was probably a little high) and that adult sons still at home and the propertyless would cut this figure down to 16 or 17 per cent *of the whole population*. In terms of adult men, Jameson meant 16 or 17 out of 20 could vote, or 80–85 per cent. Jameson apparently assumed that everyone would understand this. See "Did the Fathers Vote?" *New England Magazine*, n.s., I (Jan. 1890), 484–90. Albert Edward McKinley simply accepted Jameson's figures, but took the lower one of 16 per cent *of the entire population*. See *The Suffrage Franchise*, pp. 356–57. McKinley neglected to point out that 16 per cent of the population, of which 20 per cent were adult men, meant that 80 per cent of the adult men could vote. Whereas a reader could not be misled by Jameson's article, the use of 16 per cent by McKinley could easily be mistaken to mean that only one *man* out of about six could vote. Actually, both Jameson and McKinley were saying that at least four men out of five, or more, were voters, figures not too different from my own, though somewhat lower.

From that day to this, however, writers have cited Jameson and McKinley to prove that the franchise requirements greatly restricted the number of voters. In *Seedtime of the Republic: The Origin of the American Tradition of Liberty* (New York, 1953), p. 20, Clinton L. Rossiter says that accurate figures on qualified voters are difficult to establish. He estimates that the figures varied from one out of two to one out of eight, or from 12 to 50 per cent. Rossiter accepts Jameson and McKinley as authorities (p. 461, footnote 33) in spite of the fact that they present no evidence. In the same footnote, he rejects my work regardless of the evidence, even though I am in substantial agreement with Jameson and McKinley. One might suspect that the Jameson article was more often cited than read. Rossiter and also Max Savelle, in *Seeds of Liberty: The Genesis of the American Mind* (New York, 1948), develop the thesis that the seeds of democracy were present in colonial times but had not yet developed. Obviously such a thesis is incompatible with the evidence presented in this chapter.

In addition to using statistics for determining colonial democracy, we can also find out what the people themselves thought at the time. Men are often motivated by what they believe to be true, not necessarily what is true. So we need to know two things: (1) did colonials believe that most of the people could vote, and (2) did the political machine operate in their interests once they had voted, or was political control in the hands of a colonial aristocracy?

Because it aroused intense interest and antagonism, the Massachusetts Land Bank or Manufactory Scheme of 1740 shows how democracy worked in that colony when there was a popular issue at stake. Thomas Hutchinson, Boston merchant-politician and bitterly opposed to the Bank, was one witness. He said the partners were seven or eight hundred persons, "some few of rank and good estate, but generally of low condition among the plebians [sic] and of small estate and many of them perhaps insolvent." In addition to the partners, Hutchinson continued, "the needy part of the province in general favored the scheme." Then having said that the Land Bank was backed by the lower economic orders, Hutchinson made this significant statement: "One of their votes will go as far in popular elections as one of the most opulent." [56]

Hutchinson's statement that the vote of a "needy" person counted as much in a democracy as the vote of the "most opulent" was amply substantiated by later developments in the Land Bank controversy. Another rabid opponent of the Bank, Dr. William Douglass of Boston, blamed the popular or democratic part of the government, which he said was usually in debt but had too much weight in elections.[57] Douglass also declared that the Land Bankers openly threatened to defeat any representative or councilor who opposed the Bank,[58] a threat which they carried out with a vengeance in the election of 1741. Hutchinson said the House of Representatives was so overwhelmingly pro-Land Bank that it was later "distinguished by the name of the Land Bank House." [59]

56 Hutchinson, *History*, II, 299–300.
57 *Colonial Currency Reprints*, III, 326.   58 *Ibid.*, IV, 74–78.
59 Hutchinson, *History*, II, 300.

The completeness of democratic control appeared in Salem, second largest town in the province and a place where there should have been a large voteless "proletariat" if such had existed. Benjamin Lynde, chief justice in the colony, and his son Benjamin, Jr., Salem merchant, politician, and opponent of the Bank, told what happened. Previous to the Land Bank controversy, the younger Lynde had been moderator and town treasurer and had been elected to the Council of the General Court by the largest vote of any councilor.[60] The revolution began at the March elections for town officers when the Land Bankers swept the election,[61] and it continued in the May election for representatives. The old representatives, Browne and Lee, who actually favored public paper money but not the Land Bank, did not receive twenty votes in a town which usually had from 136 to 265 voters.[62] When the General Court met soon after the election, said Lynde, Jr., "most of the members were Land Bankers." These men then proceeded to clear the Council of all who had opposed the Bank, just as they threatened to do. Sixteen of the eighteen councilors allotted to Massachusetts lost their seats, among them Benjamin Lynde, Jr. The governor rejected thirteen of these, then seeing how hopelessly he was outnumbered, threw up his hands and dissolved the General Court.[63] The only obstacle to colonial democracy was the British government, not a local "aristocracy," and the British soon stepped in to kill the Land Bank.

Two other instances of colonial democracy cropped up shortly after the Land Bank controversy. As one solution for the problem of paper money, the General Court had passed a law for adjusting depreciated paper money in the payment of debts. The House, the Council, or the justices of the superior court were given the responsibility of determining the value of paper currency every six months. But according to Hutchinson and

[60] *Diaries of Benjamin Lynde and of Benjamin Lynde, Jr.,* ed. by F. E. Oliver (Boston, 1880), pp. 143–60. Hereafter cited *Lynde Diaries.*

[61] *Ibid.,* pp. 102, 162.

[62] *Ibid.,* pp. 143, 154, 162; *House Journals,* XVII, 208.

[63] Jonathan Belcher, *Belcher Papers* (Mass. Hist. Soc., *Collections* 6th ser., VII [1894]), II, 396; *Boston Weekly News Letter,* May 28, 1741; *Lynde Diaries,* pp. 163–64.

another contemporary writer, the law became a dead letter because the popular cry was against it, and those entrusted with fixing the depreciation never had the firmness to go against this popular cry.[64] A second item was the problem of a fixed salary for the governor instead of annual grants by the legislature. Governor William Shirley, who took over during the Land Bank controversy, reported to the Lords of Trade that the people generally had a strong aversion to a fixed salary, an aversion which made the issue so unpopular among the representatives that even those who favored it dared not support it because they were elected annually and were extremely dependent on their constituents.[65] So democracy operated in economic as well as political spheres.

Later in his career as governor, Shirley had an unpleasant experience for which he blamed colonial democracy. The incident was a riot in Boston brought about by an attempt on the part of a British officer to impress colonial sailors. Shirley called out the militia to restore order, but the militia, sympathizing with the rioters, refused to act, and the governor sought the protection of Castle William, a fort in Boston harbor. In reporting this incident to the Lords of Trade, Shirley placed the blame on the democratic government in Boston. Any ten persons could petition a town meeting, he declared, and at these meetings the poorest inhabitants, by their constant attendance, were generally the majority and outvoted the gentlemen, merchants, traders, and better part of the inhabitants.[66] There is little hint here of a controlling "merchant aristocracy" in Boston.

Undoubtedly Shirley's unpleasant experience with Boston democracy influenced the advice he gave the British on ways to check democracy in a new government to be set up in Nova Scotia. He recommended triennial instead of annual elections because he thought that the representatives curried the favor of the voters by opposing the governor, especially just before an election. He also advocated limitations on the number of representatives and councilors, and preservation of the balance

[64] Hutchinson, *History*, II, 306–07; *Colonial Currency Reprints*, IV, 174–84.
[65] Shirley, *Correspondence*, I, 88–89.   [66] *Ibid.*, p. 418.

between them—a balance which he said had already been destroyed in Massachusetts. But above all, the king should control the incorporation of towns. Experience had demonstrated the pernicious influence of Boston on other towns and their representatives, he concluded, for in Boston, all points were carried "by the mobbish factious spirit of the populace" in their town meetings.[67]

Thomas Hutchinson could also vouch for the effectiveness of Boston democracy. Hutchinson made himself unpopular with his constituents by advocating that a parliamentary grant of £183,000, to compensate for overexpenditures in the late war with France, be used to retire outstanding paper money. After the next election in 1749, Hutchinson wrote plaintively to his friend Israel Williams of Hatfield: "You have heard my fate. I could make but about 200 votes in near 700. They were the principal inhabitants but you know we are governed not by weight but by numbers."[68]

Like Hutchinson, John Adams expressed the opinion that the colony was governed by numbers rather than by weight. Adams made the statement in 1761 that all an artful man had to do to win the vote of the "rabble" that frequented the taverns was to win the favor of the tavern keeper. The rabble, he continued, comprised "a very large, perhaps the largest number of voters" in many towns.[69]

Trouble between the colonies and Great Britain furnishes so much evidence of colonial democracy that a problem in illustrating the topic becomes one of deciding what examples to exclude. It is difficult to understand how anyone who has examined the sources can hold the view that colonial Massachusetts was undemocratic, that the government was in any way controlled by a merchant aristocracy in the seacoast towns, or that one of the chief motivations of the Revolution was the prospect of gaining more internal democracy.

The Stamp Act controversy of 1765–1766, for example, brought many statements of the extent of democracy and the

[67] *Ibid.,* pp. 473 ff.
[68] Israel Williams Papers, II, 140 (May 19, 1749). Mass. Hist. Soc.
[69] Adams, *Works,* II, 112.

effectiveness of its control in the colony. A British officer traveling through the colonies emphasized the equality which prevailed because of "the levelling principle" or "that ancient rugged spirit of levelling, early imported from home, and too successfully nursed, and cherished. . . ." The "better sort," he continued, lamented their plan of government because the popular branch had too much power.[70] The Loyalist, Peter Oliver, said it was imprudent for men of sense to interfere in events of the time, for the government of Massachusetts "was in the hands of the mob, both in form and substance." [71] He also accused Samuel Adams of duping John Hancock into building unprofitable houses and wharves so that many artisans would be given employment. These artisans would then support Adams politically, said Oliver, "and such men chiefly composed the voters of a *Boston* Town Meeting." [72] And Governor Bernard stated that the colony was democratic in all respects except the appointment of a governor.[73]

That the Stamp Act had no connection with a dual or internal revolution is best attested by Hutchinson in a statement made during the Stamp Act upheaval:

Had our confusions, in this province, proceeded from any interior cause we have good men enough in the country towns to have united in restoring peace and order and would have put an end to the influence [of] the plebeian party in the town of Boston over the rest of the province. In the town of Boston a plebeian party always had and I fear always will have the command and for some months past they have governed the province.[74]

Hutchinson should have known, for the plebeian party had defeated him for elective office, and his aristocratic connections were of no avail in getting him restored to popular favor.

Among the Hutchinson papers is the following draft of a letter which does not leave much doubt about Hutchinson's views as to whether or not Massachusetts was democratic:

[70] "Journal of an Officer . . . 1765," Library of Congress Transcripts, King's MSS., CCXIII, 126.
[71] "Origins and Progress," Egerton MSS., 2671, p. 118.   [72] *Ibid.*, p. 74.
[73] Francis Bernard, *Select Letters on the Trade and Government of America* (London, 1774), pp. 42–43.
[74] Mass. Arch., XXVI, 227.

Altho I have lived all my days here, yet you know as much of our Constit. as I do particularly that every town is a body corporate but without any form of government an absolute democracy which exists hardly anywhere else all being upon a level. . . . The town of Boston is an absolute democracy and I am mistaken if some of the inhabitants don't wish for an independence upon province authority as much as they wish to see the province independent of the authority of Parliament. Every man in the government being a legislator in his town thinks it hard to be obliged to submit to laws which he does not like & which were made by a house of representatives consisting of 100 men for one or two only of which he could give his vote and it is harder that a council who are still in a more distant relation to him should have a share in these laws and harder still that a governor in whose appointment he had no voice should control or restrain both council and house. . . .[75]

As later events demonstrated, the people of Massachusetts were hardly the anarchists Hutchinson depicted, but there is certainly little evidence here of a restricted electorate or a ruling merchant aristocracy, especially in Boston.

The Townshend Acts and efforts to enforce them merely strengthened, rather than decreased, the power of the democratic elements in Massachusetts. Bernard wrote that the faction in Boston which ruled there was composed of "the lowest kind of gentry," and the reason for their absolute control was that Boston was "governed by the lowest of the people." [76] He also explained how the selectmen, using the displeasure of the town as a threat, had ordered the return of thirty hogsheads of smuggled molasses which had been removed from a schooner. The customs officials, judge of admiralty, chief justice, or governor could not have prevailed on anyone to tell where the molasses had been hid or to aid in its recovery. But, said Bernard, "to serve a purpose of the people the selectmen in a summary way can do the business in a trice. So we are not without a government: only it is in the hands of the people of the town, and not of those deputed by the king or under his authority." [77]

---

[75] *Ibid.*, XXV, 226–27 (Nov. 19, 1767).

[76] To Hillsborough, May 19, 1768, Francis Bernard, Letters 1768–1769, Force Transcripts, No. 2, Library of Congress.

[77] July 11, 1768, *ibid.*

Bernard had dissolved the General Court and had not called a new one because, as he said, the only change would be the exclusion of the few representatives who had upheld the British government.[78]

Repeal of the Townshend Acts in 1770 brought a temporary relief in the tension between Britain and her colonies, but it seems not to have changed in any way the control which the democratic forces had in the colony. The lower orders continued to rule Boston, for, as Hutchinson said, "in most of the public proceedings of the town of Boston persons of the best character and estates have little or no concern. They decline attending town meetings where they are sure to be outvoted by men of the lowest order, all being admitted and it being very rare that any scrutiny is made into the qualifications of voters." [79] Later Hutchinson wrote that Boston was the source of trouble and that considering the town constitution it could not be otherwise. If met anywhere else, he said, the majority which conducted town affairs would be called a mob, "there being no sort of regulation of voters in practice." [80]

A few more examples will suffice to show that whatever present-day historians might think about early Massachusetts, men at the time at least considered it democratic. There is the statement by Benjamin Franklin that in New England every man was a freeholder and had a vote in public affairs.[81] There is also the quoted interview of a veteran of the Revolution: "Young man, what we meant in going for those red-coats, was this: we always had governed ourselves and we always meant to. They didn't aim we should." [82] And Carter Braxton, in reporting the prospects for independence in the Second Continental Congress, wrote the following:

Two of the New England colonies enjoy a government purely democratical the nature and principle of which both civil and religious are so totally incompatible with monarchy that they have ever lived

[78] Bernard to Hillsborough, Aug. 6, 1768, Mass. Hist. Soc., Miscellaneous MSS., XIII.

[79] To Hillsborough, April 19, 1771, Mass. Arch., XXVII, 151.

[80] May 24, 1771, ibid., pp. 171–73.   [81] Franklin, Writings, V, 362.

[82] Quoted in Mellen Chamberlain, John Adams, the Statesman of the American Revolution (Boston, 1898), p. 248.

in a restless state under it. The other two tho' not so popular in their frame bordered so near upon it that monarchical influence hung very heavy on them. The best opportunity in the world being now offered them to throw off all subjection and embrace their darling democracy they are determined to accept it.[83]

If there be those who still think colonial Massachusetts was undemocratic and governed by a merchant aristocracy, let them read the following letter which Hutchinson sent to Lord Hillsborough. He said he was sending a copy of the *Boston Gazette* containing the proceedings at the election and Boston's instructions to its representatives. These were criminal, he declared, but were looked upon as a matter of course,

the meetings of that town being constituted of the lowest class of the people under the influence of a few of a higher class but of intemperate and furious dispositions and desperate fortunes. Men of property and of the best character have deserted these meetings where they are sure of being affronted. By the constitution forty pounds sterl.—which they say may be in cloaths household furniture or any sort of property is a qualification and even into that there is scarce ever any inquiry and anything with the appearance of a man is admitted without scrutiny.[84]

If anything with the appearance of a man could vote, there was little problem of a restricted electorate.

As far as Massachusetts is concerned, colonial society and the American Revolution must be interpreted in terms of something very close to a complete democracy with the exception of British restraints. There were doubtless a few men who could not vote, but they must have been few indeed. Obviously the common man had come into his own in Massachusetts long before the time of Andrew Jackson.

[83] Edmund C. Burnett, ed., *Letters of Members of the Continental Congress,* 8 vols. (Washington, 1921–1936), I, 420–21.
[84] May 29, 1772, Mass. Arch. XXVII, 339.

[C H A P T E R   I V]

Representation and
Its Restriction

CLOSELY associated with the right to vote, in the accepted
interpretation of colonial society and the American Revolution,
is the problem of equitable representation.[1] Students of this
period of American history are familiar with the idea that a
dominant seaboard aristocracy of wealthy merchants in the
North and wealthy planters in the South controlled colonial
legislatures by refusing to grant equal representation to western
sections. Equally familiar is the idea that equitable representation became an issue in the Revolution—the view, made famous
by the late Carl Becker, that the question was not merely home
rule but who should rule at home.[2]

---

[1] Some of the material in this chapter appeared as an article, "Restriction of
Representation in Colonial Massachusetts," in *Mississippi Valley Historical Review*, XL (Dec. 1953), and is published here by permission of the *Review*.

[2] Typical statements of the accepted interpretation may be found in Jernegan,
The American Colonies, pp. 272, 289–91; Hicks, *A Short History of American De-
mocracy*, pp. 49, 85; Morison and Commager, *Growth of the American Republic*,
I, 163, 167; Rossiter *Seedtime of the Republic*, pp. 114–15; Adams, *Revolutionary
New England*, pp. 162–63. Most of these accounts are merely statements unsupported by evidence. Adams, however, cited Harry Alonzo Cushing, *History of the
Transition from Province to Commonwealth Government in Massachusetts* (New
York, 1896), p. 20 and note. Adams injected the internal struggle into his own
account by saying that conservative merchants were behind the move to restrict
representation. But Cushing did not give this view. Cushing was correct in interpreting the problem of representation as imperial rather than internal. See Cush-

In our estimate of democracy in colonial Massachusetts, therefore, we would need to know just how representation was apportioned in the legislature, what groups if any were over- or under-represented, what restrictions were placed on representation, and who placed these restrictions. Even if we conceded that most men could vote, we would still want to see how the colony was represented and whether a merchant aristocracy along the coast controlled the legislature. The problem of representation has remained one of the most vexing of all problems in democratic government, for even though we have universal suffrage now, we still have unequal representation in the Senate and in many of the states. Unequal representation in colonial times could have given control of the legislature to the coastal area regardless of the fact that nearly all men could vote. In short, was the desire for equitable representation of sufficient importance to be a factor in an internal or dual Revolution?

Under the Charter of 1691, the General Court was to consist of a governor, a Council, and a House of Representatives, each with different powers and selected by different methods. The governor, chosen by the king, had various executive powers, including the right to veto legislation. The Council, consisting of twenty-eight members, acted both as an upper house of the legislature and also as an advisory board for the governor. The governor could reject men selected for the Council, but the Council was also a check on the governor since some of his duties could be performed only with its consent. The first Council under the charter was appointed, but succeeding councils were to be chosen "by the General Court or Assembly." This ambiguous wording was finally interpreted to mean that the newly elected House of Representatives would join with the old outgoing Council to elect a new Council. Then there was a House of Representatives which was elected by qualified voters.[3] Since the Council and House were chosen by the colo-

---

ing, *Transition*, pp. 20–26. Becker's famous statement has found its way into many books. See his *The History of Political Parties in the Province of New York* (Madison, Wis., 1909), p. 22. See Hicks, p. 85, and Morison and Commager, p. 163, above.

[3] Thorpe, *Constitutions and Charters*, III, 1878–83; Hutchinson, *History*, II, 6–7.

nists, we will be particularly interested in their composition and actions, especially those of the House of Representatives.

Representation in the colony was established by provisions in the Charter of 1691 and by an apportionment law passed in 1692. The charter said only that representatives had to be free-holders, but did not specify what the value of the freehold had to be. The charter also gave the General Court the power to determine how representation should be apportioned, which the General Court soon did. Under the law of 1692, towns with less than forty qualified voters could send representatives if they desired, but representation was not mandatory. Towns with more than forty qualified voters had to send representatives. If a town had 120 or more legal voters, it could send two dele-gates, though it was required to send only one. Regardless of how large it became, no town could send more than two except Boston, which could send four.[4] Except for a short interval, ap-portionment of representation in Massachusetts was based on this law of 1692 until hostilities with Britain started in 1775.

Far from establishing a "seaboard merchant aristocracy," however, the law of 1692 meant that the Massachusetts House of Representatives could be dominated by the small agricultural towns. The smallest country town could be represented if it wished to be, while towns with forty voters, also small towns, had to send delegates. As the colony expanded westward and as new towns were added, the agricultural towns could increase their total representation in proportion to the growth of the colony. On the other hand, there were only five or six coastal towns large enough to merit the name "seaports," yet their combined representation could never exceed a total of fourteen,

[4] Thorpe, *Constitutions and Charters,* III, 1878; *Acts and Resolves,* I, 88–90. To the author's knowledge, no satisfactory work has been done on representation in Massachusetts from 1691 to 1780. George Henry Haynes covered the period before 1691, "Representation and Suffrage in Massachusetts 1620–1691," *Johns Hopkins University Studies,* 12th ser., VIII–IX (Baltimore, 1894), and the period after the Civil War, "Representation in New England Legislatures," *Annals of the Ameri-can Academy of Political and Social Science,* VI, no. 2 (Philadelphia, 1895). W. Neil Franklin covered the problem in Massachusetts only up to the charter of 1691 and then gave an erroneous account of the charter provisions in "Some Aspects of Representation in the American Colonies," *North Carolina Historical Review,* VI (Jan. 1929), 43.

regardless of how big they became. In other words, as long as this apportionment law was in effect, which was most of the time between 1692 and 1775, there could never be any question of political control by a merchant aristocracy through restriction of backcountry representation.

In 1694, the General Court placed restrictions on representation which further insured that the small towns would be well represented. Apparently to save travel expenses, some of the distant towns elected men who lived in Boston as their representatives. Probably these Bostonians owned land in the town they represented but were not residents. So the law of 1694 decreed that a representative must be both a freeholder in and resident of the town that elected him.[5] Several representatives protested that a man might be the largest freeholder in the town yet be ineligible to represent the town if he lived elsewhere—a protest which in itself is doubtless good evidence for the purpose of the new law.[6] There were also fines imposed on officials who failed to call elections and on representatives who failed to attend the General Court.[7]

As a result of the apportionment law of 1692, the backcountry or agricultural areas, far from demanding more representation, were soon complaining that they had too much representation. Compulsory representation for towns of only forty voters was more than they wanted, so they petitioned to have the figure of forty voters raised. The House attempted to comply with the request in 1726 by increasing the number of voters from forty to a hundred for mandatory representation. This, of course, would not prevent a town with less than a hundred voters from being represented if it so desired. Strangely enough, the opposition to an increase came from the Council, or upper house of the legislature, a fact which should not have been true if the Council represented a seacoast merchant aristocracy. Theoretically, the Council and merchants should have welcomed any decrease in representation from the small agricultural towns. In any event, a compromise of sixty voters for compulsory representation was finally accepted by both houses.[8]

[5] *Acts and Resolves*, I, 80, 202, 315; Mass. Arch., XLVIII, 239, 246.
[6] Mass. Arch., XLVIII, 224.   [7] *Acts and Resolves*, I, 146–48.
[8] *House Journals*, VII, 114; *Acts and Resolves*, II, 406.

Some towns felt that even sixty voters for compulsory representation were too few, and in 1731 the legislature tried unsuccessfully to increase the number. A new law said that any towns with eighty qualified voters had to send a representative. A town with fewer than eighty voters could still send a delegate if it desired, but it was not forced to do so.[9] This time, however, the General Court ran into opposition from Britain. The Lords of Trade recommended disallowance on the ground that the act of 1726 was temporary and that at its expiration the earlier law of 1692 again became effective.[10] So while the Massachusetts legislature was willing to change the basis of representation, the British government would not permit it. As a result, the colony reverted to the old apportionment of 1692 by which towns with less than forty voters could send representatives, towns with forty or more voters had to send representatives, and towns with 120 voters or more could send two representatives.

In spite of the British veto and the fact that towns of forty voters were theoretically required to be represented, there is evidence that the House of Representatives actually used the eighty-voter figure in practice. Towns were fined for failure to send representatives, and town petitions for abatement of the fine show what the practice was. In Chelsea, just across the bay from Boston, there was the argument that the town should not send a representative in 1757 because it was not obliged by law to send one, yet there were forty-five voters in the town.[11] Raynham claimed in 1760 that it should not be fined for failure to send a representative because the town was not obliged to do so on the basis of its seventy-four qualified voters, and the General Court remitted the fine.[12] Southborough in the same year claimed exemption from the fine on the excuse that it had only sixty voters.[13] Apparently the General Court paid little attention to Britain's disallowance of the apportionment law.

That Massachusetts towns considered themselves overrepresented rather than underrepresented is attested by the fact that

[9] *Acts and Resolves*, II, 592–93.
[10] *Calendar of State Papers, Colonial Series, America and West Indies, 1731*, p. 368.
[11] Mass. Arch., L, 20–22, 25.   [12] *Ibid.*, CXVII, 609.
[13] *Ibid.*, p. 630.

towns sometimes avoided sending delegates altogether or sent a minimum rather than a maximum number. Seventeen towns in 1739 were fined a total of £390 for failure to send delegates, while other towns were excused from representation.[14] Marblehead, which could not claim either remoteness or inability, voted not to elect any representatives in 1752, even though the town was entitled to two.[15] Brookline, just outside Boston, voted not to elect a representative in 1762 "by reason not obliged to send by law." [16] In 1742, Governor William Shirley said there were 160 towns, most of which could send two members if they desired, but that few except Boston, Salem, Ipswich, and Newbury ever sent more than one.[17] And in 1763, Governor Francis Bernard told the Lords of Trade that of 168 towns in 1762, most of which could send two representatives, 104 sent delegates, sixty-four defaulted, and only four sent more than one member.[18]

These figures demonstrate not only that lack of representation was no problem, but also that the agricultural towns had complete control. Of the potential 350 or more representatives, the less than twenty seaport delegates could not have done much in a showdown between merchants and farmers. The policies of both the Council and the British government contributed to this agricultural predominance, a fact which the British government, at least, later regretted.

There can also be little doubt that once elected, representatives had to follow the mandates of their constituents or suffer the consequences. Malden voted that its representatives could keep only 2s.8d. of his allotted pay (about the pay of ordinary labor), and if any man refused to serve under these conditions, the town would elect someone else.[19] In the Land Bank controversy, the Land Bankers promised to carry the legislature, with the result that more than half of the representatives lost their seats between 1740 and 1741.[20] As noted previously, the "aristo-

[14] *House Journals,* XVII, 37.   [15] *Marblehead Town Records,* III, 441.

[16] *Muddy River and Brookline Records, 1634–1838* (Brookline, Mass., 1875), p. 203.

[17] To Lords of Trade, Oct. 18, 1742, *Acts and Resolves,* III, 70.

[18] Jan. 10, 1763, *ibid.,* IV, 627.   [19] Malden Town Records, I, 169.

[20] *Acts and Resolves,* XII, 668–69; XIII, 4–5.

crat" Thomas Hutchinson displeased his Boston constituents in 1749 and could muster only 200 out of 700 votes.[21] Hutchinson was never again able to win a popular election in Boston. And Governor Shirley said that the granting of a fixed salary to the governor was so unpopular among the people that even those representatives who favored it, being annually elected and extremely dependent on their constituents, dared not support the measure.[22]

The tax lists give us a method for ascertaining just who the representatives were and how they rated on the economic scale compared with their fellow townsmen. Major Joseph Fry, representative from Andover in 1754, was taxed 8s.10d. On this list, four men paid the same tax, while 242 men paid more, the highest being £2.9.3, or about six times as much as Fry paid.[23] By 1766, Fry had become a colonel, was moderator of the town meeting, and had risen to 145th place on the tax list.[24] In 1755, Joshua Fry was elected instead of Joseph, and Joshua ranked thirty-seventh on the tax list.[25] Hatfield sent Oliver Partridge in 1743, and Partridge rated sixteenth.[26] In a society in which most men were property owners, one would expect the towns to elect substantial citizens as representatives, but this did not necessarily mean the largest property owners.

From the town records we gather the impression that being a representative in colonial times was not always as attractive a position as it is now considered. Ebenezer Davis refused to serve as Brookline representative in 1768, and though he went to the legislature in 1769, he again turned down an election to the post in 1770.[27] Hatfield elected John Dickinson as its delegate in 1741, and then after Dickinson declined, the town decided not to send a representative but instead to petition the General Court to be excused.[28] Of course, as I pointed out in

[21] Israel Williams Papers, II, 140.
[22] To Lords of Trade, June 23, 1742, Shirley, *Correspondence,* I, 88–89.
[23] *Acts and Resolves,* XV, 166; Andover Tax Lists, 1754, pp. 433–38.
[24] Andover Town Records, March 3, 1766; Andover Tax Lists, 1766.
[25] *Acts and Resolves,* XV, 324; Andover Tax Lists, 1755, pp. 444–51.
[26] *Acts and Resolves,* XIII, 326; Hatfield Town Records, I, 182–85.
[27] *Muddy River and Brookline Records,* pp. 221, 223, 226.
[28] Hatfield Town Records, IV, 3.

Chapter III, there were some hotly contested elections for representative, but there were also many examples to show that some men did not relish the honor.

To this point there appears to have been no problem of inequitable representation, especially of the backcountry, or of control of representation by a merchant aristocracy. If any towns were underrepresented, they would be the seacoast towns, but there is nothing in the records that I have seen which would indicate that these coastal towns were dissatisfied.

Eventually there was an effort to restrict representation in Massachusetts, but this originated with the British government, not with a merchant aristocracy bent on controlling the legislature. This restrictive effort came because of British fears that a growing House of Representatives would gradually overpower the governor and Council, especially since the membership of the Council was fixed by the charter at twenty-eight members. British restrictions failed to accomplish their purpose, but they do throw a great deal of light on the problem of representation in Massachusetts.

The first evidence of British concern over a dominant House of Representatives appeared in a report to the king in 1735, when paper money was the big issue. The report shows not only what the British thought of the lower house but also of the kind of men who composed the assembly. Stated the report:

Thus altho' the government of this province is nominally in the crown, and the governor appointed by Your Majesty, yet the unequal balance of their constitution having lodged too great a power in the assembly: this province is, and is always likely to continue in great disorder. They do not pay a due respect to Your Majesty's instructions, they do not make a suitable provision for the maintenance of their governor, and on all occasions they effect too great an independence on their mother kingdom.

The report then went on to blame the law of 1693 which

provided that no person shall be capable of representing any town or borough, where such person is not a freeholder, and settled inhabitant, from whence it happens, that the assembly is generally filled with people of small fortunes, and mean capacities, who are easily led into any measures that seem to enlarge their liberties, &

privileges, how detrimental soever the same may be to Great Britain, or to Your Majesty's royal prerogative.[29]

This hardly looks like a legislature dominated by aristocratic commercial interests, but it does reflect British fears that a strong House of Representatives was definitely a threat to colonial dependence on Great Britain.

Not until the Land Bank or Manufactory Scheme episode of 1740–1741, however, did the British attempt any checks on the Massachusetts assembly. As noted in Chapter III, that incident demonstrated how completely the lower house could dominate the governor and Council whenever the occasion demanded, and it was this dominance which prompted the British to take action.

The initiative was taken by William Shirley, an ardent British imperialist who had succeeded Governor Jonathan Belcher at the height of the Land Bank controversy. Shirley had vetoed three bills which divided some old towns and made two towns where only one had existed before. In justifying his actions to the Lords of Trade, Shirley said the division of towns doubled the representation, and that he had found by the activities of the General Court for several years past that the number of representatives was already sufficiently large to embarrass the king's government in the colony. So he proposed that in the future governors should prevent an increase in the House, particularly through stopping the practice of splitting old towns. Instead of towns, there should be districts or precincts with all the powers of towns except that of sending a representative. There were some 160 towns, he said, most of which could send two representatives if they desired. Few except Boston, Salem, Ipswich, and Newbury ever sent more than one, he concluded, but in an emergency they had it in their power to double or treble the number of representatives if they should desire to dispute with the governor.[30]

A contemporary writer, defending Shirley's actions in the Land Bank controversy and after, spelled out the problem in

[29] Library of Congress Transcripts, British Museum, Additional MSS. 35907, Hardwicke Papers, DLIX, 18–19.
[30] *Acts and Resolves,* III, 70.

even greater detail. He said it was a governor's duty to see that His Majesty's Council was not over-balanced by the House of Representatives. The recent governor, Belcher, had not done his duty; in fact, he had indulged the House in the practice of splitting old towns and had thus contributed more to the destruction of the balance between the House and the Council than any other governor. Shirley, he said, had stopped this "pernicious practice" by declaring his determination not to allow additions to the House. There were already between 110 and 120 sitting delegates, and there could be sixty more if the present towns wanted to send them. When all the towns grew to 120 "families," there would be about 300 representatives, and within another century, there would be more than there were members of the British Parliament. Meanwhile, the Council consisted of twenty-eight members, its size was fixed by the charter, and even these twenty-eight members were annually chosen by the representatives in the House and by the old Council.[31]

Actually, the assembly's practice of dividing old towns was one method of restoring equitable representation, but it was not done especially to aid a seaboard aristocracy. Dividing a town compensated for population growth, since the law did not provide for increased representation for towns larger than 120 voters. But the practice followed no pattern—towns all over the colony were divided, regardless of whether the division increased representatives from commercial or agricultural areas. Newburyport was separated from Newbury because Newburyport was a commercial town and could not agree with agricultural Newbury.[32] On the other hand, Danvers was set off from Salem because Danvers was an agricultural town and could not agree with commercial Salem.[33] About the only pattern discernible in the assembly's actions was its desire to increase the potential membership and power of the assembly.

If the House of Representatives had as many potential members as contemporaries said, any attempted restrictions were obviously too late, but the British government adopted Shirley's

---

[31] *Colonial Currency Reprints*, IV, 35, 343–44; Hutchinson, *History*, III, 119.
[32] *Acts and Resolves*, IV, 699.   [33] *Ibid.*, III, 598.

recommendations anyway. The Lords of Trade instructed the governor not to consent to bills for dividing old towns, unless such bills contained suspending clauses preventing the bill from becoming effective until it had been reviewed in England. He could permit the incorporation of districts as towns were divided, but these districts were not to enjoy the right of separate representation.[34] Such a policy would presumably check the growth of the House of Representatives, even if it did not reduce the number.

The new policy of restricting representation turned out to be a proposition of buying insurance after the house burned down, but it did serve as a bone of contention between the House and the executive. In 1749, the lieutenant governor refused his consent to a bill incorporating part of Leicester into a new town unless the bill expressly excluded representation and also contained a suspending clause. The House sent back a sharp reply. They were at a loss to understand why he could not sign, they said, for there were only two excuses for his actions: (1) reason and the nature of the act, and (2) some restraint in the charter. These were the only rules of government in this, His Majesty's province, and the House could find nothing in either to prevent his signing the bill. The end of government was the king's honor and the happiness of his subjects, the House concluded, and a full representation of the people would contribute to both.[35] Since Leicester was an agricultural town, and since the Council had also passed the incorporation bill, there is nothing in this incident to indicate that the Council was acting to strengthen a seaboard merchant aristocracy.

It was Shirley himself who allowed the first breach in his new policy, a breach which resulted in a sharp reprimand from the British government. In 1754 he signed a bill incorporating Lincoln with full power of representation and without the attached suspending clause. This brought a pointed rebuke from the Lords of Trade, but they said they would allow the act

[34] *Journal of the Commissioners for Trade and Plantations from April, 1704, to May, 1782*, 14 vols. (London, 1920–1938), VIII, 71, 76, 109.
[35] *Acts and Resolves*, III, 653, 665–66.

because repeal might result in inconvenience. At the same time they warned the governor to be more careful in the future.[36] Once again the Council had concurred in violating British instructions and had done so to set up an agricultural town.

Another clash came in 1757, in which the House lost the battle and won the war, and again the incident involved an agricultural rather than a commercial town. The town was Danvers, which had been set off from Salem in 1752 as a district. The reasons given were that the inhabitants were too far from the town house and school, that Salem was composed of merchants while Danvers was composed of farmers, and that they quarreled over taxes.[37] In short, there was a conflict between two property-interest groups, not between those with and those without property. The House brought in a bill to give Danvers full powers as a town in 1757, when Shirley had left for England, his successor Pownall had not arrived, and Lieutenant Governor Phips had died. The act, which had passed the House and Council, the latter acting as the executive also, was dissented to by Thomas Hutchinson, a member of the council, on the ground that it increased representation in violation of instructions and did not contain a suspending clause. In England the act was vetoed, but Danvers continued to elect a representative regardless, and the House took no steps to stop it.[38]

Toward the close of the French and Indian War, new conditions forced the British to modify their restrictive policy on representation. Defeat of the French had resulted in rapid expansion into Maine, and the new towns being established were demanding representation. At first the Lords of Trade refused to modify their position, but eventually they changed their minds. They decided that new towns did not fall in the same category as those divided off from old towns and that both reason and justice required that Maine towns should be represented,[39] so that even though representation could not be

[36] *Ibid.*, p. 728.　　　　　[37] *Ibid.*, p. 598.
[38] *Ibid.*, IV, 5, 93n.; XVI, 204, 364, 564; XVII, 4, 218; Hutchinson, *History*, III, 39.
[39] *Acts and Resolves*, IV, 349–51.

increased by the division of old towns in Maine, it could be increased whenever a new town was established.

Shortly after the decision on new Maine towns, the question of representation for new towns in Massachusetts arose. The House divided Hampshire County into two counties, Hampshire and Berkshire, and then incorporated five new towns in these counties. Governor Bernard objected to the bills because they did not prohibit representation. He said that "the towns themselves were willing to waive their right of sending representatives, but some gentlemen in the house opposed the allowing them to waive their privilege." Bernard vetoed four of the bills, but consented to the incorporation of Pittsfield because it was to be the county seat for Hampshire County. In his letter to the Lords of Trade, Bernard took the position that his instructions not to incorporate towns were not designed to prevent representation from newly settled counties, but only to stop the multiplication of representatives from the old towns. It was obvious to him that the new counties had a right to be represented. He said he feared the increase in the house, and wished that it could be stopped, "without denying new settlers the natural and constitutional right of being represented." [40]

Again this is not evidence of a governing merchant aristocracy. The towns involved were agricultural western towns, not eastern seaports, and while the people of the towns were willing to waive representation, the House of Representatives was not. Had a merchant aristocracy been in control, it certainly should have welcomed any opportunity to restrict representation from these western towns.

Resigning themselves to the inevitable, the Lords of Trade in 1762 arrived at the same solution for representation of the new towns in Massachusetts proper as they had for Maine. Old towns were not to be divided to increase representation, but new towns, they declared, had an indisputable right to a share in the formation of the laws by which they were to be bound and governed. The evil they were trying to remedy, the domination of the growing House over the Council, was the result of the

[40] *Ibid.*, pp. 432, 450–52.

charter and laws confirmed by the king, they declared, and nothing could be done to stop an increase in the number of representatives who came from new towns.[41]

This new policy after 1762—giving representation to new towns but denying it to towns divided off from old ones— should have settled the problem of restricted representation once and for all, but such was not true. Either the Lords of Trade forgot their final decision or there were new members among them, for in 1763 they wrote to Bernard asking about incorporating acts and also requesting information about the whole system of representation in the colony. Obviously they were still troubled about the problem of a dominant House of Representatives.[42]

In his letter of explanation to the Lords of Trade, Bernard both summed up the whole system of representation in Massachusetts and gave figures showing how hopeless attempts to restrict the House had become:

But as the sending of a member is a burthen upon a town instead of being exerted, it is avoided as much as possible, so that it scarce ever happens that a town which has a right to be excused sends a representative; and of those which are obliged by law to send one, a great many make default; that it is frequent for the house of representatives to fine towns for not sending members. . . . In the list of 1762 . . . there appear to be 168 towns (reckoning joint towns as one) which are supposed to be obliged to send members of which 64 have made default and 104 have returned: Of these last only 4 have sent more than one member, so that there appears to be 110 . . . representatives returned. I will suppose that much the greater part of these towns have the right, if they please, to send two representatives, and that there are many other towns not named in this list which have a right to send one representative. . . .[43]

Bernard also proposed a remedy, but in spite of the fact that the people failed to take advantage of the right of representation, Bernard was not certain that they would willingly relinquish the right. Said he:

In short, My Lords, it were to be wished that some proper method could be devised to limit the general number of representatives, but

41 *Ibid.*, pp. 452–53.   42 *Ibid.*, p. 627.   43 *Ibid.*, pp. 628–29.

it seems to me that it should be done rather by contracting those of the old counties than by preventing a new county from being completely represented.

I don't apprehend that the difficulty of this reform will be so great in the planning the work as in the reconciling the people to an alteration which tends to the contracting their representation. It might be done effectively by enlarging the number of freeholders that shall give a town a right to send one member and as for towns that have not such a number to join them together in chusing [sic] a representative as many already are.[44]

Perhaps, if they had known, the Lords of Trade might have regretted the fact that their predecessors had disallowed an act of 1731 which would have cut down on the House of Representatives in the very way that Bernard proposed.

Bernard's figures show not only the potential representation but also that the House could dominate the Council and that the agricultural towns could dominate the seaports if circumstances required. The House could undoubtedly have numbered more than 350 had the people wished, compared with twenty-eight for the Council and fourteen representatives for the six major seaports. That explains why the towns sent only 110 representatives in 1763—more were not necessary. A House of 350 would have meant one representative for less than 1,000 people, figures to be compared with the 240 representatives, or one for each 19,543 persons, at the present time in Massachusetts. In other words, colonial Massachusetts had a potential representation 2,000 per cent greater and, when 110 representatives attended, an actual representation more than 600 per cent greater than the people of Massachusetts enjoy today. In this respect, one might easily say that there was more democracy in colonial times than now.

Under the policy of restriction as finally adopted by the British, many towns were incorporated with full representation and many others were simply divided off from old ones. After 1761, forty-six new towns with representation and thirty-three districts without representation give ample evidence of the tremendous expansion following the French and Indian War.[45]

[44] *Ibid.*   [45] *Ibid.*, IV and V, *passim.*

Usually governors followed instructions on representation very carefully, but not always. Once Bernard was tricked into violating his instructions. Newbury and Newburyport desired to be separated because one was agricultural and the other commercial, so Bernard agreed on condition that the two representatives would be divided and each town would send only one. This, of course, would not increase representation, since the combined towns had previously sent two members. But agricultural Newbury continued to send two representatives after the separation regardless of the bargain, and the House refused to rule them out. Bernard went to great lengths to justify his actions to the Lords of Trade.[46] Thomas Hutchinson also permitted the incorporation of four towns that had been districts as well as the setting off of West Springfield with full powers of representation.[47]

On one occasion in 1764 the desire to restrict representation was the deciding factor in denying a land grant. The land was near Nova Scotia, and the grant would have involved the extension of Massachusetts' jurisdiction. The Lords of Trade advised against the grant on the ground that the Massachusetts constitution either allowed or compelled every town to send representatives. They said the size of the lower house was already so large that it not only caused great disorder and embarrassment to the administration of government, but also destroyed the balance between the House and the Council when they voted together.[48]

In 1767 the Lords of Trade finally admitted defeat in their efforts to restore some balance between the assembly and the other branches of government in Massachusetts. With relations between colony and mother country strained almost to the breaking point, the Privy Council asked the Lords of Trade about a number of incorporating acts which had come to the king for approval. The Lords had to confess that any new town was naturally entitled to representation, even though this contributed to a further disproportion between the House and

[46] *Ibid.*, IV, 699.   [47] *Ibid.*, V, 50, 124, 327, 335, 389.

[48] Report of Lords of Trade to Lords of the Committee of the Council for Plantation Affairs, July 16, 1764, Mass. Hist. Soc., Miscellaneous MSS., XIII.

the other branches of the government. They still wished that some method could be devised for limiting and restraining the assembly, but were not sure what method should be adopted and said they were leaving the final decision to the king.[49]

Actually the battle of restricted representation had been lost before it got started in 1743, and the intervening years to 1767 had merely added to the hopelessness of the situation. Domination by the lower house at the time of the Land Bank episode should have warned the British that their restrictive policy would prove fruitless. Bernard's figures of 168 towns required to send delegates and many more able to do so merely accentuated the inevitable. The fact that the British did nothing further about representation after 1767 is probably sufficient evidence that they had finally recognized their failure. But again it should be noticed that restriction was a British policy, not that of a dominant ruling merchant aristocracy along the coast, and that the agricultural towns, not the seaports, could dominate the assembly at any time.

[49] *Acts and Resolves,* IV, 870.

CHAPTER V

Town-Meeting Democracy

IN ADDITION to province elections and province representation, Massachusetts had another political institution in which democracy might or might not find expression. This was the town meeting, where a myriad of local issues were raised and decided, and where the people, or at least those qualified to participate in town elections and town affairs, decided many problems now handled by state and national governments. To understand democracy in Massachusetts, therefore, we need to know what restrictions, if any, were imposed on town electors and whether or not democratic processes prevailed in town affairs.

Massachusetts towns were separate corporations established under the implied powers of the Charter of 1691 and acts of 1692 and 1715. The Crown implied recognition of the practice of incorporating towns by saying that certain groups, including "corporate towns," were to retain all their lands and estates. The charter also granted the General Court full power to make all laws necessary for the welfare of the province and its inhabitants.[1] So in 1692 the General Court passed an act which provided for the incorporation of towns. This act gave the inhabitants wide latitude in the annual election of town officers and in the conduct of town affairs.[2] A later act provided more

[1] Thorpe, *Constitutions and Charters*, III, 1877, 1882.

[2] *Acts and Resolves*, I, 64–68. Robert Francis Seybolt, *The Town Officials of Colonial Boston, 1634–1775* (Cambridge, Mass., 1939), and William H. Whitmore, *Massachusetts Civil List for the Colonial and Provincial Periods, 1630–1774* (Albany, 1870), provide convenient sources for data on town officials.

specifically for the regulation of town meetings. There was to be a moderator, elected by a majority of the voters present, who would have power over the orderly conduct of affairs. No one could speak without permission of the moderator, no one could speak when someone else was speaking, and there was a fine for violations. Also the town was to act only on the specific items contained in the warrant for the meeting, but a petition signed by any ten inhabitants could force the leading town officers, the selectmen, to place any item in the warrant.[3]

As established by these laws, the town meeting, with the exception of one factor, was a democratic institution. Annual elections insured that no undesirable official could remain in office very long. The provision that any ten persons could have an item inserted in the warrant meant that majority opinion could not be thwarted by a small group. The wide range of affairs governed by the town meeting gave the people ample opportunity to participate in the regulation of important problems relating to their daily lives. The one exception to these democratic institutions was a voting qualification attached to participation in town affairs. The extent of democracy in the town meeting, then, depends on how restrictive this voting qualification was.

One of the most persistent misconceptions about early Massachusetts history has been the accepted notion that there was more democracy in the town meeting than in elections for

[3] Dec. 22, 1715, *Acts and Resolves,* II, 30. John Fairfield Sly, *Town Government in Massachusetts, 1620–1930* (Cambridge, Mass., 1930), Kirk Harold Porter, *County and Township Government in the United States* (New York, 1922), and Ernest S. Griffith, *History of American City Government: The Colonial Period* (New York, 1938), all deal with town government from an institutional rather than a historical point of view. They consider the machinery of town government but make no effort to determine how democratic or undemocratic the town meeting was. Herbert Baxter Adams, *The Germanic Origin of New England Towns* (Baltimore, 1882), Edward Channing, *Town and County Government in the English Colonies of North America* (Baltimore, 1884), and Charles Francis Adams et al., *The Genesis of the Massachusetts Town and the Development of Town-meeting Government* (Cambridge, Mass., 1892), engaged in a warm verbal controversy over whether the town originated in the German forest, as H. B. Adams contended, in the English common law parish of 1600, as Channing believed, or whether the towns were indigenous and their development depended on new conditions, as C. F. Adams contended.

province representatives. Unless the student is wary, the mistake is easily made. Province elections called for £40 of property, while town elections required the voter to be "ratable at twenty pounds estate, to a single rate besides the poll." [4] At first glance, the inclination might well be to say that the town qualification was £20, which was only half the requirement for voters in province elections, and that therefore town elections were more democratic than province elections. The joker, however, is the term "ratable," and the problem is to see how a £20 "ratable estate" compared with a 40s. freehold or £40 sterling in property.

To eliminate as much difficulty as possible in dealing with a complex problem, I shall start with a town election law of 1735 rather than the first law of 1692. This law said there had been many "doubts and controversies" about town voting because the election law of 1692 required a voter to have a £20 ratable estate but had not defined what rule of valuation was to be used in determining the £20 ratable estate. The 1735 law then defined precisely who could vote and how the qualification was to be determined. [5]

1. The voter must be an inhabitant of the town where he voted and have a £20 ratable estate *in the town.* In province elections, a man's estate could be anywhere in the province.

2. A ratable estate meant the *assessed* value of a man's *taxable* property, not its full value, and was to be determined as follows. Real estate was to be assessed at the rent it would bring if rented at a reasonable rate for six years. Taxable personal estate and faculty (income from labor or profession)

----

[4] *Acts and Resolves,* I, 64–68. For example, Rossiter says that in province elections one out of two to eight could vote, but in town elections the ratio was one out of two to five (*Seedtime of the Republic,* p. 20). Carl Bridenbaugh, "The New England Town: A Way of Life," in American Antiquarian Society, *Proceedings,* LVI (1947), 301, says the local franchise was much broader than that of the colony. See also Jernegan, *The American Colonies,* pp. 166–68, and J. T. Adams, *Revolutionary New England,* p. 195. Adams says that the town franchise became so widened as to include practically all male inhabitants of legal age, of whom perhaps only one-fifth to one-fourth possessed the provincial franchise. Elisha P. Douglass, *Rebels and Democrats* . . . (Chapel Hill, 1955), pp. 141–42, has all free adult males as voters.

[5] *Acts and Resolves,* II, 761–62.

were to be estimated as they were in province taxes. The tax laws, in turn, provided for an assessment on livestock old enough to return an income (oxen four years and older at 40s., horses three years and older at 40s., cows three years and older at 30s., swine one year and older at 8s., and sheep or goats one year and older at 3s.), and income or faculty according to the best judgment of the assessors.[6] Later tax laws included real and personal estates, rents, slaves, vessels of ten tons and up, stock in trade, money at interest, productive livestock, tilled land, and pasturage.[7] Income from trade, faculty, interest, or commissions was to be assessed at 1s. on the pound, that is, at 5 per cent.[8] In short, taxes were levied on the assessed valuation of anything that yielded an income. A £20 ratable estate, therefore, represented *assessed* value, which value could be, and generally was, only a fraction of a man's total property.

3. Disputes in town elections were to be settled by the simple process of checking the tax lists which were to be lodged with the town clerk.

4. A special method was to be used to determine town voters in those towns where the people did not declare their assessable property but were "doomed" by the assessors for what they thought each person could pay. In such towns, a man was a voter if he paid a property tax equal to two-thirds of a poll tax. The lawmakers must have considered such a tax equivalent to a £20 ratable estate.

5. This act was not to disqualify anyone from voting in province elections if he qualified for those elections according to the charter.[9]

---

[6] *Ibid.*, I, 165–69, 213, 413; II, 734–35.   [7] *Ibid.*, IV, 422–23.
[8] *Ibid.*, V, 104–06.

[9] *Ibid.*, II, 761–62. Much confusion exists about the role of town proprietors in town government. Whatever their position at an earlier time, in the later period, town proprietors were concerned solely with their grant of land and did not have exclusive voting privileges in the town. Much of the confusion appears to stem from a misinterpretation of Akagi, *The Town Proprietors of the New England Colonies.* But as Akagi says, pp. 4–5, men could become "legal inhabitants and freemen of the town and obtain a voice in town meetings, or even be freemen of the colony. . . . The freemanship implied the exercise of the franchise, while the proprietorship was exclusively a property right." Akagi leaves the impression that the proprietors exercised a great deal of economic

When we work backward from this 1735 law, we can readily understand why there were many "doubts and controversies" about town voting. For one thing, many different methods were used to assess real estate, all of which would effect the town voting qualification. At different times the assessed value of real estate was fixed at rentals for seven years, fourteen years, twenty years, seven years again, one year, and after 1700, six years.[10] Unless there was some easy solution used at the time to obviate these difficulties, and one that does not appear in the records, it is little wonder that the problem of town voting was perplexing. It would certainly make a tremendous difference in voting qualifications whether the £20 ratable estate was estimated on one year's rent or twenty years' rent.

With the law of 1735 as a guide, we are now in a position to compare the voting qualifications for province and town elections. The best measure of the difference is the freehold qualification, for this requirement entered into both types of elections. The 40s. freehold for province elections needs no elaboration, but the £20 ratable estate does. Figured in real estate, a £20 ratable estate meant real estate which would bring £20 for a total of six years at a reasonable rent. This would be £3.6.8 or 66s.8d. a year, which would mean that the town qualification was 26s.8d. or 66⅔ per cent more than the 40s. province qualification—provided both the province and town qualifications were expressed in the same kind of money.

Thus far the going is not too rough, but at this point we

---

and political power, but the evidence he presents, pp. 129–44, shows that the nonproprietors and the town meetings really had much the best of whatever conflict existed. The author also implies that the proprietors were few compared to the nonproprietors, thus leading to minority rule, but he does not cite concrete evidence to prove this. Two examples from the sources raise the question about making the proprietors the minority as Akagi does. A Hatfield list, undoubtedly based on proprietors and nonproprietors, had 146 who were entitled to a share in the division of the town's money and 41 who were not, including five apprentices. See Hatfield Town Records, IV, 326–29. In Northampton, 255 names of proprietors were listed in 1765 for division of the common lands. See Northampton Town Records, II, 123–24. We need much more exact information about town proprietors than Akagi gives us before we can generalize about them.

[10] *Acts and Resolves,* I, 91–95, 165–69, 213, 386, 413.

encounter the nightmare of colonial paper money, for the province qualification was expressed in terms of sterling, while the town qualification was Massachusetts money, and the two were by no means the same. This in itself would not be too discouraging, except for the fact that Massachusetts money was almost never the same at any two points of time. Before 1750, the colony used "lawful money" geared to the Spanish dollar, at other times it used old, middle, and new tenor paper money which started as lawful money and depreciated; and finally, after 1750, the colony went back to a lawful money expressed in both Spanish and English silver, and this lawful money did not depreciate.

As money values fluctuated, the £20 ratable estate for town voting also fluctuated. A few generalizations will show what the situation was and help the reader grope his way through the difficult maze of colonial money values as I explain them later. From 1692 until about 1711, when Massachusetts money began to depreciate, the town qualification was probably higher than the province qualification. As Massachusetts paper money depreciated, however, the two qualifications doubtless came first to approximate each other and then the province requirement became the higher. It is difficult to tell how much the difference was, but the town qualification could have gone to a point as low as one-third the province qualification. The issue of new tenor money at lawful money values, and the basing of town qualifications on new tenor, probably in 1735 and certainly in 1738, again raised the town qualification above that of the province. New tenor depreciated in turn, so that by 1750 the town qualification was some 36s., or much lower than that of the province. Then, in 1750, the colony returned to a permanent lawful money basis, making the town qualification once again higher than that of the province.

As I said, the town qualification was doubtless higher than that of the province between 1692 and 1711, but as Massachusetts money was not valued the same as sterling, the difference was not as much as 40s. to 66s.8d. Massachusetts paper money was based on Spanish dollars which were valued a third higher than sterling.[11] The province qualification of 40s. sterling would therefore have meant 53s.4d. in Massachusetts money, and since the town qualification was 66s.8d., the real difference between province and town voting was only 13s.4d. Before 1711, the date when Massachusetts money started to depreciate, the town qualification was approximately 25 per cent higher than the province qualification when both were expressed in freehold values.

From 1711 to 1738, the difficulties involved in determining the value of money, and with it the town voting qualification, become well-nigh insuperable. The 1738 law on town voting contained this phrase about the £20 ratable estate: *"the Value of both Real and Personal Estates being considered as heretofore has been usual, in Bills of the Old Tenor."* [12] This section of the law was deleted by an amendment, and as later evidence will show, the province used the more valuable new tenor in estimating the £20 ratable estate. But it seems obvious from this statement that old tenor had been the value used before 1738. There is also an item in the *Boston Gazette* showing that old tenor depreciated in value in relation to silver from 8s.6d. an ounce in 1713 to 27s.6d. an ounce in 1735.[13] As money depreciated in value, prices of rents and goods naturally increased, making it easier for men to meet the £20 qualification. One modification of this statement would be that evaluations on which tax assessments were made did not occur every year, so that the increase in assessed values would lag considerably behind the depreciation of money. But in general it would probably be safe to say that depreciation of money caused the town

[11] On the complicated problem of colonial money, see Curtis P. Nettels, *The Money Supply of the American Colonies before 1720* (Madison, Wis., 1934), pp. 256–57; Charles M. Andrews, "Current Lawful Money of New England," *American Historical Review,* XXIV (Oct. 1918); William Graham Sumner, "The Spanish Dollar and the Colonial Shilling," *ibid.,* III (July 1898); Andrew McFarland Davis, *Currency and Banking in the Province of Massachusetts Bay* in *Publications of the American Economic Association,* 3d ser., I, no. 4 (New York, 1900), ch. ii.

[12] Mass. Arch., CXIV, 325–28a.

[13] *Boston Gazette,* June 7, 1779. Davis discussed the question of depreciation but was unable to throw much additional light on the problem, which he recognized as "full of difficulty" (p. 88). His chart on page 91, giving prices of silver in terms of paper, shows a depreciation from 8s. in 1711 to 16s. in 1727. See *Currency and Banking,* I, ch. iii.

qualification to fall considerably below that of the province between 1713 and 1735. The attempted amendment of the voting law in 1738 was definite evidence that some legislators wanted to keep the qualification low while others wanted to restore it to its original value.

If the legislature acknowledged in the law of 1738 that there were "many doubts and controversies" about town voting, we will doubtless have to be content with this unsatisfactory account of town elections from 1713 to 1738.

With town qualifications expressed in new tenor, our problem becomes a little less complex after 1738. A selection from an account of a Boston election of 1740 shows not only what the qualification was but also how the election was conducted to check on illegal voters:

Then the Inhabitants were desired to prepare their Votes in writing, either Yea or Nay; and to bring and offer them at One of the Doors of the House—And the Assessors were directed to attend there with their Lists of Valuation of Estates and Facultys, that so no one might be allow'd to Vote in the Affair, Excepting such as were Qualified according to Law—And it is also Declared, That it is determined by the present Meeting, to be the Sense of the Law, that No Person is Qualified to vote in Town Affairs, but such as are Rated in the last Tax Two Shillings and One penny New Tenor, Or Six Shillings and three pence Old Tenor, to the Province Tax, for his Personal Estate and Faculty, including Rents if they be his Own.[14]

This quotation about the Boston election shows that the colony had shifted from old to new tenor as a basis for taxation, and since the voting qualification was stated in money, this shift tripled the town voting qualification. The province tax called for a poll tax of 3s.3d., and the town said that no one could qualify unless he paid 2s.1d. tax in new tenor.[15] Obviously the town was using that part of the election law which said that anyone was a voter if he paid two-thirds as much estate tax as he paid for one poll. The requirement of paying 6s.3d. tax in old tenor meant that old tenor had depreciated to three for one

14 July 14, 1740, *Boston Town Records*, XII, 260.
15 *Acts and Resolves*, II, 962.

in relation to new tenor, so that the shift to new tenor had raised the voting qualification three times.

A Bellingham tax list also reveals that the colony was using new tenor in its tax laws and in determining qualified voters. The tax law of 1738 called for evaluations in bills of new tenor and levied a poll tax of 3s.3d.[16] In the tax return for Bellingham, polls were taxed 3s.3d. Then a note at the end explained how the town determined its qualified voters. It said that each person was taxed 1d. a pound on his assessed valuation, so that anyone who paid 20d. in estate taxes had an estate assessed at £20 and was therefore qualified to vote in town affairs.[17] The 20d. estate tax would be 1s.8d., which would mean that a voter could actually qualify with less property when his property was rated than when the assessors "doomed" the taxpayers. Under the alternate system of determining voters, that is, that a man must pay a property tax equal to two-thirds of a poll tax, a man in Bellingham would have been required to pay an estate tax of 2s.2d. to be a qualified town voter.

Again the town qualification declined in value as new tenor money depreciated between 1735 and 1750. When new tenor first came out, its value, as usual, was that of lawful money, which was valued in the ratio of four for three in sterling, so the town qualification would again be in the ratio of 66s.8d. to 53s.4d. for province voting when both were expressed in lawful money. By 1750, however, new tenor had depreciated to 1.875 to 1 in terms of lawful money, which meant that the £20 ratable estate in new tenor was only £10.13.4 in lawful money.[18] To the extent that evaluations for tax assessments kept pace with depreciation, therefore, the town qualification for voting became less and less between 1735 and 1750. By 1750, the town qualification would have been a 36s. freehold compared with a 53s.4d. freehold for province voting.

After 1750 the going becomes relatively simple compared with the previous period, for stable money prices from that

---

[16] *Ibid.*   [17] Mass. Arch., CXIV, 401–05.

[18] *Acts and Resolves,* III, 430–31, 494–95; Davis, *Currency and Banking,* I, ch. vii. Davis was unable to give any exact scale of depreciation for the years 1735–1750.

time to the Revolution make the voting qualification much easier to determine.

When Massachusetts went back to "lawful money" on a permanent basis in 1750, evaluations for assessing taxes were figured in lawful money and the £20 ratable estate for town voting again became more than the 40s. freehold for province voting. The law gave the value of old tenor, new tenor, and lawful money in relation to sterling, so we have no difficulty in telling just what the town voting qualification was after 1750 and how it compared with the province qualification. One shilling sterling was equal to 10s. old tenor, 2s.6d. new tenor, or 1s.4d. lawful Massachusetts money.[19] This again raised the freehold qualification for town voting to 66s.8d. compared with 53s.4d. for province voting.

Although the province eventually used lawful money in determining the town qualification, the change from new tenor to lawful money did not occur immediately, and an incident which arose over the adoption of lawful money throws additional light on town voting. The General Court said there was a great deal of confusion in town voting when the assessors changed their valuations from new tenor to lawful money. To obviate the difficulty, the legislature in 1751 decided that until it took a new tax valuation, which was done in June, 1752, any person who was rated at £10.13.4 lawful money would be considered a town voter.[20] In lawful money £10.13.4 was the same as £20 new tenor, so the General Court kept the new tenor basis for town voting for a while. A ratable estate of £10.13.4 lawful money would be the same as a 36s. freehold in yearly rent. Under depreciated new tenor, therefore, the province qualification of a 53s.4d. freehold would be considerably higher than the town qualification.

When the province reverted to lawful money for taxes and town voting after 1752, there is ample evidence to prove conclusively that the town qualification was higher and more difficult to meet than the province qualification. The probate

---

[19] *Acts and Resolves*, III, 430–31; *Independent Advertiser*, Sept. 25, 1749; Shirley, *Correspondence*, I, 462.

[20] *Acts and Resolves*, III, 625–36; XIV, 499–500; Mass. Arch., CXV, 826.

records show that Samuel McIntier of Needham, for example, had livestock valued as follows: a horse £10, two oxen £10.12.0, eight cows £26.6.8, fifteen sheep £6, three swine £3.19.0, and a bull £2.6.0.[21] The total value of this livestock, which any average farmer might possess, was £60.7.8, or £7.3.8 more than the £53.4.0 lawful money in property necessary for province voting. We do not have McIntier's tax rating, but even if all these animals were old enough to be rated according to the tax laws, the rating would be £23.9.0, or only £3.9.0 more than the rating needed for town voting.

A comparison of taxes paid by individuals and their probated estates yields additional information showing how much easier it was to qualify for province than for town voting. The real estate of Ebenezer Knowlton of Ipswich was listed at £9.7.6 annual worth which, multiplied by six years, would give a rating of £56.5.0 or a little less than three times the £20 ratable estate required for town voting.[22] An inventory of Knowlton's estate, taken a year later, shows that he had £241 in real estate alone, or more than four and a half times the province qualification of £53.4.0.[23] Nathaniel Goddard of Weston had a total estate of £741, some 13.7 times the province qualification.[24] Goddard's tax rating, however, was only £55, or 2.75 times the £20 ratable estate for town voting.[25] John Potter's £97 estate in Ipswich was more than ample for providence voting,[26] but on the tax list he was rated for two cows, a swine, and real estate worth £2.6.0 annually.[27] His total tax rating would be only £18.8.0, not enough to qualify him for town voting.

The disputed election in Stockbridge, 1763–1764, already discussed at length in Chapter III, provides excellent evidence that some men could qualify for province but not for town voting. There were nine challenged voters, all of whom were qualified to vote in province elections according to the com-

---

21 Suffolk County Probate Records, LXXI, 12–13.
22 1771, Mass. Arch., CXXXIII, 68.
23 Essex County Probate Records, CCCXLVIII, 62–64.
24 Middlesex County Probate Records, LII, 45.
25 Mass. Arch., CXXXIV, 291.
26 Essex County Probate Records, CCCXLVIII, 77–78.
27 Mass. Arch., CXXXIII, 77.

mittee of the General Court sent out to settle the dispute. Most of the property of these challenged voters was in wild, uncultivated land, and while its value ranged from £40 to £100 sterling, the land was not improved and was therefore not ratable for taxes.[28]

When it came to town voting, however, not all of these nine Stockbridge men could qualify. Three of them—Brown, Jones, and Roe—had only wild lands and were certainly disqualified. Five others—Whitney, Curtis, Halluck, Patterson, and Ball— might have qualified, for the records do not say whether or not their property was taxable. Of the nine only Pixley could definitely meet the £20 ratable estate qualification. He had a sawmill worth 40s. sterling a year and also had a horse and a yoke of oxen, which would give him a ratable estate of £22. Pixley had obviously not considered the right to vote in town affairs worth the price of declaring his taxable property and paying taxes until this dispute arose, but from this point on he was rated by the town.[29]

According to the committee, it was also true that many Indians in Stockbridge could qualify for province elections but could not qualify for voting in town affairs. There were thirty-seven adult Indian men, of which about twenty could meet the 40s. freehold requirement on the valuation of their improved lands. The assertion was made, however, that all could qualify if their wild lands were counted. But of the twenty Indians who could qualify for province voting on the valuation of their improved lands, only nine were qualified to vote in town affairs.[30]

A disputed election in Bellingham, another agricultural town, gives a lower percentage of town voters in relation to province voters than should have been true in an agricultural town. Thirty-three men signed a petition accusing the selectmen of illegal procedures. In their own defense, the selectmen sent an attested copy of the town tax list with the explanation that men were taxed a penny for each pound they were rated, so anyone who paid 20d. in real and personal taxes was rated £20 and was therefore a legal voter. On this list those who were

[28] Mass. Arch., XXXIII, 249–52, 277–88.   [29] *Ibid.*, pp. 277–88.
[30] *Ibid.*

qualified had "vt" after their names. When nonresidents were eliminated, some of whom had enough property holdings to vote, about forty-nine or fifty out of some seventy-five resident adult men were qualified. This would be about two-thirds, or 67 per cent. Of the nonvoters, four were fathers whose sons could vote, a probable indication that the sons had taken over the family estate, and several were the younger sons of voters.[31]

With town voting dependent on taxable property, the tax records naturally furnish a clue to the number of qualified town voters. These tax records merely verify the generalization that more men could vote in province than in town elections. As my figures in Chapter III indicate, agricultural towns should have had well over 90 per cent of their men qualified to vote in province elections. On a Hatfield assessors' list for 1743, however, only eighty-four of the 111 men on the list, or 75.6 per cent, were rated at £20 or more.[32] My percentage of province voters in Northampton is 94.6, but for town voting the tax list for 1748 gives only 80.5 per cent,[33] while another list for 1765 gives only 88.1 per cent.[34] In Boston, almost everyone who owned a house could vote in both province and town elections, as there were few houses that rented for less than £4 a year in 1771.[35] But a renter who could count his clothing and furniture to qualify in province elections would not be able to count either personal effects or rented real estate as a qualification for town elections.

Tax and voting lists for Weston show that a large percentage but not all of the adult men could vote. A valuation list of 1757, used for making up the voting list for 1758, contains the names of 155 men. This voting list cannot be found today, but a voting list for 1759, compiled from the tax list for 1758, has 124 men marked as voters. This would mean that 80 per cent of the adult men were qualified town voters, and though this figure would not be completely accurate because of the year's difference in time, it would be close enough to give a fair indication.[36]

[31] *Ibid.,* CXIV, 401–06, 408.   [32] Hatfield Town Records, I, 182–85.
[33] Northampton Town Records, I, 296–99.   [34] *Ibid.,* II, 123–24.
[35] Mass. Arch., CXXXII, 91–147.   [36] *Weston Tax Lists,* pp. 1–7.

As young men acquired wild land in new towns and began to cultivate their lands, there were doubtless many who could not qualify for town voting for a while but who eventually became qualified voters. A petition from Upton in 1746 shows this change. Thirty-six men petitioned the General Court that their town was young, that there were only ten qualified town voters, and that affairs would run more harmoniously if all men could vote in town affairs. The General Court obliged by waiving the town qualifications, but two years later the town petitioned for a restoration of the qualifications on the ground that the number of voters had reached thirty.[37] The men in Stockbridge who had only wild lands were probably town voters within a few years.

Another method of arriving at percentages of legal town voters is to assume that a man was a legal voter if he paid two-thirds as much estate tax as he paid for a single poll tax. This was the method provided by law as an alternative to the £20 ratable estate. On this basis the percentage of qualified town voters in Andover was 75.5 in 1766. The poll tax was 5s.4d.; hence a man who paid 3s.7d. estate and faculty tax, or a total of 8s.11d., should have been qualified. On this tax list were 256 men who paid more than 8s.11d. in taxes, and eighty-two who paid less. Many of these eighty-two nonvoters were obviously younger sons of men who were voters.[38] My estimate for province voters in Andover (Ch. III) was about 95 per cent.

While in theory the town qualification was undoubtedly higher and more difficult to meet during most of the period after 1692, it was not sufficiently high to keep many men from voting or from voting for very long if they really valued the right. For example, Ebenezer Knowlton of Ipswich had fifty-nine acres, which was a small farm by colonial standards, but only twenty-three acres were cultivated and taxable. Yet these alone had an annual worth of £9.7.6, which would be a ratable estate of £56.5.0, nearly three times the £20 qualification.[39] In

[37] Mass. Arch., CXV, 316–20.
[38] *Acts and Resolves*, IV, 897; Andover Tax List, 1766.
[39] Essex County Probate Records, CCCXLVIII, 62–64; Mass. Arch., CXXXIII, 68.

short, a man did not need a very large farm nor many cleared acres to qualify as a town voter.

Rental figures on reality, one of the ways for computing ratable estates, demonstrate that the amount of taxable property required for the vote did not add up to very much. As noted in Chapter II, a farm of 533 acres near Boston, rented "by the halves," returned its owner £150 sterling a year, which would be just sixty times the voting qualification.[40] At this rate, a farm of nine acres would suffice. Another farm of 200 acres rented for £40 a year or twelve times the required amount.[41] At this rate, a farm of about sixteen acres would be ample. In 1772, Andrew Oliver received £5.6.8 a year for one garden spot in Boston, 13s.8d. for another 68 feet by 36 feet, and he said rooms rented in Boston for £6 to £8 a year.[42] Houses in Boston rented for various prices. Merchant John Rowe had one rental unit worth only £8 a year,[43] and Oliver's seven tenements on Oliver's Dock brought a total of £54.8.0 or less than £8 each. These tenements were valued at £500, and at this rate property in Boston worth £30 would have qualified its owner.[44] That these rentals were low is attested by the fact that minister Mather Byles received £100 a year in salary and had to pay £25 sterling a year for rent [45] and that a British customs official Henry Hulton complained that he could not rent a house for less than £50 a year.[46] John Hancock had several houses which he rented and for which he claimed compensation as a result of the Boston siege. These he valued variously at £20, £25, £30, £80 and £133 a year, the latter his own mansion house.[47] For voting purposes, these figures are to be compared with the qualification of £3.6.8 yearly rental.

Wages and commodity prices can also serve as a standard for estimating the practical value of the town qualification just as

[40] Andrew Oliver Letter Book, I, 138–39. [41] *Ibid.*, p. 159.
[42] *Ibid.*, II, 93.
[43] *Letters and Diary of John Rowe, Boston Merchant, 1759–62, 1764–69*, ed. by Anne R. Cunningham (Boston, 1903), p. 111. Hereafter cited Rowe, *Diary.*
[44] Estimate of the estate of Andrew Oliver, 1775, Hutchinson-Oliver Papers, II.
[45] SPG Archives, Series B, XXII, 146–47. [46] Hulton, *Letters*, p. 42.
[47] Chamberlain Collection, John Hancock, p. 147.

they did in Chapter III with the province franchise. Based on wages of 2s. to 3s. a day for common labor, the £3.6.8 yearly rental required would mean some thirty-three days' wages in the winter or twenty-two days' wages in the summer. At 4s. a bushel for wheat, the rental would be some seventeen bushels or perhaps the yield of one acre of land. These figures are somewhat higher than comparable ones for province voting, but they are still not formidable.

If in theory the town franchise was based on taxes and some 75 or 80 per cent of the adult men could qualify, in practice there were deviations from the legal requirement to permit some unqualified voters to vote and to exclude some who were qualified.

If we can believe the charges and countercharges in disputed elections, the right to vote occasionally seems to have depended much more on who controlled the election machinery than it did on the payment of sufficient taxes. A petition from Boxford in 1739 accused the moderator of allowing six unqualified persons to vote and refusing to use the tax list to determine their qualifications. An attested copy of the tax list was inclosed to prove that the six men were not qualified.[48] At Rehoboth, the right of several persons to vote was challenged, but the selectmen refused to test them by the tax lists. One selectman said the men in question claimed the right to vote and he knew of no law to the contrary, "for the law was oute." [49] After hearing the selectmen, the General Court granted the petition, evidence that the selectmen were allowing disqualified men to vote.[50] In 1742 at Brunswick the accusation was made that the election notice had been posted, according to the law, but was placed on the inside of the meetinghouse door so the opposition could not see it. The opposition also claimed that the moderator purged the meeting of some men who were actually legal voters, yet allowed others to vote who were not. There was also the claim that the assessors had not rated some men as much as they had done in previous years, but after the election, raised

48 Mass. Arch., CXIV, 343, 345, 348–49.   49 Ibid., p. 533.
50 Ibid., p. 535.

the assessment again. At the same time, the assessors increased the rating of other men to qualify them, one of whom had only a cow as taxable property.[51]

Other towns sent similar complaints of illegal or questionable voting practices designed to win an election for one or the other faction in the town. There was the claim from Haverhill in 1748 that the selectmen disfranchised many of the opposition who were not only qualified by their real estate but were tradesmen with incomes alone sufficient to give them the vote. There was also the farmer who had considerable stock and many hundreds of pounds out at interest but was disqualified because he was a tenant, while the vote of another tenant, rated much lower on the tax list, was accepted. The clerk accepted three other illegal votes and refused to produce the valuation lists as a check.[52] The General Court set aside an election in Westborough on the ground that qualified voters had not been permitted to vote.[53] At Needham an attempt was made to disqualify four voters by counting only two years' instead of six years' income from real estate. There was the added accusation that the moderator was allowing all freeholders to vote regardless of taxes, a charge which seems to be born out by the minutes of the meeting.[54] At Middleton in 1751 all freeholders were also allowed to vote, a practice sanctioned by some of the "principle men," although some of these voters had never paid taxes in the town.[55]

Some evidence already presented and other available evidence raises an interesting question in relation to the tax rates and town voting. That question is this: how many men valued the right to vote sufficiently to declare the full value of their taxable property and thus pay all the taxes they should have paid? Swearing that they were worth enough to vote in province elections cost nothing, for their property was not taxable, but voting in town elections carried a price. We know that there was much indifference among the voting population then as now, and one could suspect that some men would rather pay low

[51] *Ibid.*, CXV, 36, 56.
[53] *Ibid.*, CXV, 628–32.
[55] *Ibid.*, VIII, 279.

[52] *Ibid.*, p. 300; CCCIII, 51.
[54] *Ibid.*, pp. 614–27a.

taxes and not vote than pay high taxes and vote. This was true for David Pixley in the disputed Stockbridge election. Up to the time of this election he had not declared his taxable property, and while he did not have the privilege of voting in town affairs, he also had avoided the privilege of paying taxes.[56] One man was rated for nine acres of salt marsh on a tax list, but the inventory of his estate has fifteen acres.[57] John Hancock's property was "doomed" in the tax lists of 1771, with his house valued at £60 annual rent.[58] But when he valued the house for compensation as a result of the Boston siege, he placed the annual worth at £133.[59] Just how widespread the underestimation of taxable property was would be difficult to ascertain, but it would certainly be a factor that would have to be considered.

On different occasions two governors testified that the tax returns were not a true indication of either the estates or the numbers of inhabitants in the towns. Governor Bernard maintained that the people of Massachusetts did not always give a true accounting of their taxable property. He said that estimates of population in the colony were based on tax returns, but that such estimates were not too reliable for these tax returns were "certainly short of the truth." [60] Thomas Hutchinson went even further in 1773. The British government had asked for the number of ratable estates and polls in the province. Hutchinson said that he would send the 1761 list and estimates made since then but that these estimates were not to be depended upon. Every town was desirous of keeping both the inhabitants and estates as low as possible, he said, for their part of the province tax was set in proportion to the number of inhabitants and estates.[61]

While statistical evidence would seem to indicate that perhaps a fourth of the adult men could not qualify as town voters, some contemporary observers give the impression that in prac-

---

56 *Ibid.*, XXXIII, 277–88.
57 *Ibid.*, CXXXIII, 74; Essex County Probate Records, CCCXLVIII, 130–31.
58 *Ibid.*, CXXXII, 92–147.
59 Chamberlain Collection, John Hancock, p. 147.
60 King's MSS., CCV, pt. 1, pp. 398–400.
61 To Dartmouth, Oct. 1, 1773, Mass. Arch., XXVII, 546.

tice almost any adult man was a voter. John Adams, for instance, did not seem to think that voting was particularly restricted by the tax qualification. Writing in 1775, he said:

The division of our territory, that is, our counties, into townships; empowering towns to assemble, choose officers, make laws, mend roads, and twenty other things, gives every man an opportunity of showing and improving that education which he received at college or at school, and makes knowledge and dexterity at public business common.[62]

On another occasion, Adams told how certain men took advantage of a storm to get themselves elected town selectmen. They did not have the influence to win in a full meeting, but were "mean enough to seize the opportunity, when three-fourths of the town were detained at home by the storm, to assemble their crew of debtors and laborers, and accomplish their projects as they pleased." [63] If "debtors and laborers" could vote, voting qualifications must not have been very restrictive, and these same "debtors and laborers" had to be tax payers. As in province elections, it should be remembered, as Hutchinson said, that there were few tenants who might be disqualified and scarcely a man destitute of a competency to make him easy.[64]

Boston, in theory, should have had more unqualified voters than any other town, but if so, Governor William Shirley was not aware of it. In an altercation with the town over impressment of colonial seamen by the British navy, with a riot the result, Shirley blamed the democratic constitution of Boston. He declared that any ten persons could petition for a town meeting, and that the "meanest inhabitants," by their constant attendance at these meetings, were generally the majority and outvoted the gentlemen, merchants, traders, and better part of the inhabitants.[65]

If we can believe Thomas Hutchinson, in practice there was not much difference in Boston between province voters and town voters. In Chapter III, Hutchinson was quoted to the ef-

[62] Adams, *Familiar Letters*, pp. 120–21.   [63] Adams, *Works*, II, 66.
[64] Mass. Arch., XXV, 207; XXVI, 95–96.
[65] Dec. 1, 1747, Shirley, *Correspondence*, I, 418.

fect that anyone with the appearance of a man was a voter in province affairs. As for town voting in general and Boston in particular, he wrote:

Although I have lived all my days here, yet you know as much of our Constit. as I do particularly that every town is a body corporate but without any form of government an absolute democracy which exists hardly anywhere else all being upon a level saving that at every meeting of the inhabitants one pro hac vice is raised above the rest to put their questions or motions to a vote.

In the draft of this letter, the following was crossed out:

Every town is of course a distinct corporation with powers of making by laws, raising money etc. & hold their meetings when and as often as they please. All matters are determined by the majority of voices and altho the province law provides that a man who does not pay a small tax shall not be deemed a qualified voter yet it is not one time in 20 that any scrutiny is made. 5 or 6 hundred are upon the floor together upon a level to all intents and purposes only one excepted who pro hac vice only is raised above the rest to put to vote such questions as are called for. The town of Boston is an absolute democracy. . . .[66]

Before we close this discussion of town-meeting democracy, a word needs to be said about town officials. This is particularly true if one thinks in terms of a dominant colonial ruling aristocracy. Who were these town officials and what did they represent in the way of wealth?

---

[66] Nov. 19, 1767, Mass. Arch., XXV, 226–27. Carl Bridenbaugh in *The Colonial Craftsman* (New York, 1950), chs. i–vi, gives a contradictory account of town voting, sometimes refuting Hutchinson's views and sometimes concurring with them. Basing his account almost entirely on sources, Bridenbaugh gives an excellent account of the middle-class status of colonial craftsmen or artisans and of the many opportunities they had for bettering themselves economically and socially. In fact, his material confirms the evidence presented in Chapter I of this work. Yet in Chapter VI he reverts to the old interpretation of a controlling merchant aristocracy in the cities. On page 170, he first says that artisans in the cities did not have sufficient property or pay enough taxes to vote in either local or provincial affairs, but on the same page he maintains that in the larger New England towns, including Boston and Salem, it could be said in general that every householder who was the head of a family could vote. Unfortunately, Bridenbaugh relied heavily on a misinterpretation of McKinley, *The Suffrage Franchise*. (For my discussion of McKinley see Ch. III, footnote 55.)

In the first place, an official could be anyone, as far as qualifications were concerned. The law simply said that the leading
officials, the selectmen, must be "able and discreet, of good conversation." Of the other town officials the law said nothing.[67]

In practice, men of all sorts seem to have been chosen to
town offices. Northampton furnishes good examples both because the records are available and because the town seems to
have had about an average number of qualified voters. Of the
fifty-eight offices in the town, twenty-seven were occupied by
men who were not town proprietors and did not have a share
in the common lands. On the tax rating for 1765 to divide the
common lands, men were rated from £10 to £625. Officials
who can be checked on this list rated as follows: three actually
were rated under £20 or the amount required for voting in
town meeting, nineteen of the twenty-nine were rated under
£70, and the wealthiest was rated under £200. Of the total
population, 129 men rated under £70 and 98 rated over £70, so
the bottom 57 per cent of the population had 65 per cent of the
town officials. Three of the five selectmen were also rated under
£70. The wealthiest selectman, Deacon Ebenezer Hunt, a hatter,
was rated at £166, which was twelfth on the list. Six men were
rated higher than the highest town official. In other words, the
town offices were not controlled by an upper-class aristocracy
but by men who represented an average cross-section of the
population.[68]

[67] *Acts and Resolves,* I, 64–68.

[68] Northampton Town Records, II, 121, 123–24; Judd MSS., Northampton, II,
69. Again Bridenbaugh has a contradictory account of town democracy or lack
of democracy in his article "The New England Town: A Way of Life." Sometimes
the farmers lived in substantially built and well-proportioned houses (pp. 20,
41), and sometimes they lived in severely simple farmhouses (pp. 21, 24–25). At
times the society exhibited a definite hierarchy of social classes, the pure crystal
of democracy was not to be found anywhere in eighteenth century New England,
class distinctions sprang full blown into being when the lands were first divided,
and members of the gentry ran town affairs because of wealth, ability, or education, either by getting themselves elected or securing the election of those who
saw things their way (pp. 22–24). But at other times, the society was composed
of happy yeomen, the middling sort, who were self-respecting, not subservient to
superiors, socially as well as politically sure of themselves. These farmers were
jealous of their rights and insisted on their rights as freeholders, independent
farmers, and voters. In fact, nearly every man had a voice in the town meeting, as

Although the Andover records are not as complete as in Northampton and there is some difference between the two towns, a comparison of Andover's town and tax records for 1766 shows that a town official might be anyone. Here the man rated highest, Samuel Phillips, did hold office, but the important post of moderator was held by Joseph Frye, who ranked 146th on the tax list. The selectmen ranked 27th, 5th, 52nd, 24th, and 42nd respectively, and the wardens 5th, 80th, 1st, and 134th.[69]

From all this evidence on town-meeting democracy, several conclusions seem warranted. In theory, and sometimes in practice, the town voting qualification was higher and more restrictive than the province qualification. Neither was very high nor difficult to meet. Still, a man might well have property that would qualify him for province elections, but if his property was not taxable, he would not be qualified to participate in town affairs. At the same time there is other evidence that actual voting sometimes depended on the election officials, and that in practice the qualification excluded few from the franchise. At all events, it seems perfectly clear that anyone who was a town voter could also qualify for province elections. Anyone who concedes that the town meeting was democratic must perforce admit that province elections were even more democratic.

---

the local franchise was much broader than that of the colony. The farmers were conservative, suspicious of innovation, and *saw eye to eye with the larger property owners* (pp. 24, 26–27, 30. Italics mine).

[69] Andover Town Records, March 3, 1766; Andover Tax Lists, 1766.

CHAPTER VI

Religion, Education, and Democracy

IN ANY evaluation of democracy or of internal revolution in colonial society, consideration of the religion and education of the community is naturally important. Both can be judged as factors determining democratic or undemocratic society. Did the people have a large share in determining their religion and enjoy religious toleration, or did they live under an authoritarian state church? Did the provisions for education emphasize the few or the many, the rich or the poor? Religion and education were closely associated in Massachusetts, and both contributed to the development of a democratic society.

As Thomas Hutchinson explained it, the church in Massachusetts before the Charter of 1691 was a mixture of Brownism, Congregationalism, and Presbyterianism. He said that the Puritans would have remained in the Church of England had they stayed in England, but in America they followed the Separatists of Plymouth. The churches became Congregational churches, something midway between Brownism and Presbyterianism, with each church ordaining its own minister. By the Cambridge Platform of 1648 the churches were linked together loosely, but there was no binding tie. And while church and state were also connected through religious qualifications for voting, he said, both church and state were as "popular as could be conceived," for there were few people in the colony of any denomination except Congregational.[1]

According to Hutchinson, then, Massachusetts had developed a completely different religious organization from that used in England. Instead of a church anchored to the prerogatives of an hereditary monarchy and possessing a hierarchy of archbishops, bishops, and lesser clergy, the Massachusetts churches laid their foundations on the popular basis of individual congregations. Each congregation ordained its own minister, and both congregation and minister were on the same level with other congregations and ministers. It was a religious organization in which authority came from the people, not from an authoritarian church.

The Charter of 1691 was important to religion both for what it said and for what it left unsaid. On the positive side, religion and politics in the colony were separated more than they previously had been by the provision that voting was to be based on property rather than religion. In addition, the charter provided for the same kind of religious toleration in Massachusetts that prevailed in England as a result of the Toleration Act of 1689. This was liberty of conscience for all Christians except Catholics, and though it excluded both Catholics and non-Christians, it was still a long step toward religious toleration compared with previous practices. On the negative side, the charter neither established the Church of England as the official

---

[1] Hutchinson, *History*, I, 352. For anti-Puritan accounts, see Brooks Adams, *The Emancipation of Massachusetts* (Boston, 1887), and Charles Francis Adams, *Massachusetts, Its Historians and Its History; An Object Lesson* (Boston, 1894). Brooks Adams attributes the emancipation from Puritan domination to liberal control of the Brattle Street Church and Harvard College and to the rise of lawyers in the colony. Charles Francis Adams contended that Massachusetts had its ice age, and he condemned Puritan historians for glossing over or even praising what was undesirable in the colony's history. To C. F. Adams, this period, which he called the theological or glacial age, extended from 1637–1760. An opposing point of view is presented by Bertrand Max Wainger, "Liberal Currents in Provincial Massachusetts, 1692–1766," unpublished thesis, Cornell University, 1934. Perry Miller maintains that business men, wanting an increase in the population, were willing to sacrifice religious standards for economic gain. See "Declension of a Bible Commonwealth," in American Antiquarian Society, *Proceedings* LI (1942), 37–94. On the percentage of Congregationalists in Massachusetts, 1691–1780, see footnote 28.

church nor prohibited the establishment of a different church.[2]

Given this choice by the charter, the General Court soon attempted to re-establish the Congregational Church as the official church. A law of 1692 required that each town should be constantly provided with an able, learned, orthodox minister or ministers "of good conversation." These ministers were to be suitably encouraged and maintained by all the inhabitants of each town. The Court of Quarter Sessions had power to force towns to provide support for their ministers, and if a town was without a minister for six months, the court could order the town to get one. If the town then failed to comply, the court could procure and settle a minister, ordering the expense to be paid by the town.[3] Even though other Christian denominations except Catholics were tolerated and could conduct their own services, they had to contribute to the support of the orthodox Congregational minister. This, of course, was the system used in England except that the established church there was the Church of England. Massachusetts, then, started out under the Charter of 1691 with an established religion, an institution that we do not consider democratic today.

[2] Thorpe, *Constitutions and Charters*, III, 1881. Perry Miller has emphasized the intellectual and literary aspects from 1660 to about 1730 in Massachusetts during its transition from a Bible commonwealth to a secular province. Doctrinal conflicts were replaced by social conflicts as religion tended to align itself with property in the predominantly secular state. See *The New England Mind: From Colony to Province* (Cambridge, Mass., 1953). While Deism was making progress in the colonies and did influence the thinking of men such as Joseph Hawley, John Adams, Charles Chauncy, and Jonathan Mayhew, it never gained a strong foothold in Congregational Massachusetts. See Herbert Monfort Morais, *Deism in Eighteenth Century America* (New York, 1934).

[3] *Acts and Resolves*, I, 62–63. On the question of church and state, see Susan M. Reed, *Church and State in Massachusetts, 1691–1740* (Urbana, Ill., 1914). Jacob Conrad Meyer, who extended Reed's study from 1740 to 1833, also has an excellent detailed account of the attempt and failure in Massachusetts to maintain a state church. Efforts by Baptists, Quakers, and Episcopalians for equal status with Congregationalists, breaks within the Congregational church such as the Brattle Street Church, control of Harvard, and the Great Awakening, and pressure from the British government as well as fear of what the British government would do all worked for religious toleration in Massachusetts. Meyer maintained that a large majority in the province favored a tax-supported church, but he did not give any figures on percentages of Congregationalists and others. See *Church and State in Massachusetts from 1740 to 1833: A Chapter in the History of the Development of Individual Freedom* (Cleveland, 1930), ch. i.

There were some elements of democracy, however, in this religious law of 1692. For one thing, individual churches were to exercise and enjoy all their privileges and freedoms respecting divine worship, church order, and discipline. This meant a good deal of autonomy for each church, which certainly was more freedom than many churches enjoy at the present time. A second democratic provision was that the minister should be elected by a majority of the qualified inhabitants at a town meeting legally called for that purpose. So instead of a minister appointed from above, he was to be elected by the voters of each town, including those who were not orthodox Congregationalists.[4]

The workings of democracy in town dealings with ministers is clearly apparent from the sources. On occasion, a town might haggle with various ministers over a period of several years before terms satisfactory to both town and minister could be reached.[5] Sometimes a town used diplomacy in dealing with its minister in spite of the fact that it had the power to choose and dismiss. Sheffield selected a committee and gave it instructions "to treat with the Reverend Mr. Hubbard in a calm Christian like mannor to see if he will not be persuaded to desist from preaching any longer amongst us since there are so many difficulties arise between us." [6] On the other hand, a congregation might exercise its prerogatives of keeping a minister who desired to move elsewhere. When the Reverend Edward Holyoke of Marblehead was chosen president of Harvard in 1737, a committee of the college's overseers had to go to Marblehead to negotiate with both Holyoke and his congregation. At first

---

4 *Acts and Resolves,* I, 62–63. On the influence of the Congregational church in the development of democracy, see a recent work by Ola Elizabeth Winslow, *Meetinghouse Hill, 1630–1783* (New York, 1952). Winslow places the meetinghouse not only in the center of religious life but of political and social life as well. Democracy manifested itself in the varied controversies which raged around the meetinghouse. Her work is something of a balance for those writers who have emphasized economic influences, such as J. T. Adams and V. L. Parrington. If the meetinghouse was perhaps not as predominant in the molding of New England democracy as Winslow says, it was certainly one of the most important influences.

5 Pittsfield Town Records, I, 21–26, 36–39, 69.

6 Sheffield Town Records, Nov. 9, 1763.

the congregation refused to release Holyoke, and it required another committee and much prayer before they could be brought to see the light.[7]

Even the few Church of England congregations adopted the prevailing system of democratic election of ministers, though the election had to be sanctioned by the Society for the Propagation of the Gospel in London. In Boston there was a heated controversy among the congregation of Christ Church over the election of a minister to succeed the one who had died, and the minister of King's Chapel attempted to compromise the issue.[8] Church of England ministers at Cambridge and Newport were also elected, subject to approval by the Society.[9]

With voting dependent on property and taxes rather than church membership, however, the official church establishment quickly began to break down. Eventually the colony, for practical purposes, ceased to have a truly "established church."

The system of electing ministers by town voters—that is, by both church members and nonchurch members—proved unsatisfactory and soon had to be changed. The big complaint seems to have been the election of ministers by towns having more than one church, not the election of Congregational ministers by non-Congregationalists. To eliminate this difficulty, a

---

[7] "Autobiography of the Reverend John Barnard of Marblehead" in Mass. Hist. Soc., *Collections*, 3d ser., V, 177–242. The older work on the Congregational church by Joseph Sylvester Clark, *A Historical Sketch of the Congregational Churches in Massachusetts, from 1620 to 1858* (Boston, 1858) has been outdated by two later works. Williston Walker, *A History of the Congregational Churches in the United States* (New York, 1903), has an exceptionally good account, especially of the intricate differences in theology and conflicts over doctrine within the church. Gaius Glenn Atkins and Frederick L. Fagley, *History of American Congregationalism* (Boston, 1942), relied heavily on Walker, but place their emphasis more on Congregational church organization rather than on church doctrine. These writers believed that congregationalism contributed much to democracy in New England.

[8] SPG Archives, XXII, ser. B, pp. 226–29, 233.

[9] *Ibid.*, pp. 195, 229. The best picture of the difficulties confronting Anglican ministers is to be found in the collection of their letters to England during the period. See William Stevens Perry, ed., *Historical Collections Relating to the American Colonial Church*, 5 vols. (Hartford, Conn., 1870–1878), III, *passim*. Of the secondary accounts, *The Anglican Episcopate and the American Colonies* (New York, 1902) by Arthur Lyon Cross is still the best, especially on British attempts to establish an Anglican bishop in the colonies.

law of 1693 said that "each respective gathered church" in any town could choose its minister. Then this choice was to be ratified by the majority of inhabitants who usually attended that particular church and were duly qualified to vote in town affairs. Once elected, the minister was to be supported by all the ratable inhabitants within each church parish. An exception was made for Boston, where the churches were to choose and maintain their ministers in their accustomed way. A new element was also injected by this law of 1693. If a town did not have a "gathered church," the ratable inhabitants, "with the advice of three neighboring ordained ministers," were to elect an orthodox minister.[10]

In spite of their privileged position, some of the established churches soon ran into difficulties in their efforts to maintain orthodoxy. A petition to the General Court from a group of ministers in 1694 pointed out that opposition to the churches by other inhabitants in the town caused trouble. Obviously some of the inhabitants were blocking the ratification of the minister chosen by the "gathered church." The petition proposed that a council of elders and messengers of three or more churches be called in to examine the charges made against any minister chosen by a church. If the council approved the choice, the minister was to stay regardless of the vote of the town.[11] In all probability, Quakers and Anabaptists were blocking the choice of an orthodox minister to avoid paying ministerial taxes. The General Court complied with the proposals in the petition by the passage of a suitable law in 1695.[12]

Although there were never many Quakers in Massachusetts except those on Nantucket Island, Quakers did cause some difficulties for the Congregational church. Opposition by Quakers and others, probably active in 1694, received official recognition by 1702. The preamble of an additional church law stated that in various towns the Quakers and other irreligious persons opposed the public worship of God and the maintenance of a learned orthodox minister and found ways to elude the law providing for the support of religion. Steps were taken,

10 *Acts and Resolves*, I, 102.   11 *Ibid.*, VII, 537.
12 *Ibid.*, I, 216–17.

therefore, to insure that these Quakers and others should pay their just share for maintaining the established church.[13]

But the Quakers and "other irreligious persons" proved to be more ingenious than the orthodox church members, for the General Court had to continue its efforts to find ways to collect ministerial taxes. In 1706, the law stated that the grand jury was to investigate towns without ministers, and the Court of General Sessions was then to enforce the law. To make sure that the orthodox minister received adequate support, taxes were to be levied and paid into the province treasury and paid out to the minister by warrant of the governor and Council.[14] This presumably was intended to undermine the Quakers and others in towns where they had control of town taxes, but it failed. In 1715, the law directed a grand-jury investigation and vigorous execution of the laws by the courts; and if the orders of the courts were not obeyed, there was to be a report to the General Court. The General Court would then provide an orthodox minister and tax the inhabitants in the province tax to support him.[15]

In their opposition to ministerial taxes, the Quakers of Massachusetts eventually received indirect aid from Great Britain. The colonial agent in England, Jeremiah Dummer, wrote in 1719 that colonial Quakers had sent large sums of money to their friends in England to carry their fight against what they called persecution "for not paying the demands of the priest." The Quaker complaint, he said, was based on the religious toleration granted in the charter and the fact that the church in Massachusetts was established only by Massachusetts law. Dummer said paying ministerial taxes did not violate religious toleration, but he suggested that the General Court might do well to relax the ministerial laws, for the Quakers in England were a powerful body, and Massachusetts was in trouble enough in England as it was.[16] In short, Dummer was suggesting a relaxation of the laws for the established church in order to

---

[13] *Ibid.*, pp. 505–06. See Rufus Matthew Jones, *The Quakers in the American Colonies* (London, 1911), ch. vi.

[14] *Acts and Resolves*, I, 597.   [15] *Ibid.*, II, 26–27.

[16] Mass. Arch., LI, 319–35.

silence colonial Quakers and perhaps prevent any British interference in the Massachusetts government or churches.

Eventually the Quakers and "other irreligious persons" in
Massachusetts won their fight against compulsory taxes to support the orthodox church. Dummer's advice was not followed
immediately, but by 1728 the colony had relaxed its religious
laws somewhat. An act of that year said that Quakers and Anabaptists who alleged scruples of conscience for refusal to pay
ministerial taxes would henceforth not be required to support
the established church. There were certain qualifications, however. The exempt had to be enrolled in some church, they had
to attend this church, and they had to live within five miles
of their meeting. Quakers also had to take an oath of allegiance
to the king and of denunciation of the pope, subscribe a confession of belief in the Christian concept of the Trinity, and acknowledge the divine inspiration of the Old and New Testa-
ments. And finally, persons exempted from ministerial taxes
were not to vote in ministerial affairs.[17]

Within a short time, however, even these qualifications were
removed from the laws regarding Quakers and Anabaptists.
Some of the impetus came from Governor Jonathan Belcher,
who urged that prudence and wisdom dictated a policy which
would quiet Quaker opposition.[18] A law of 1731 exempted

[17] *Acts and Resolves*, II, 494–96. The Baptists, or Anabaptists as they were
called, have had numerous historians. One of the leading Baptist ministers, Isaac
Backus, in his *Church History of New England from 1620 to 1804* (Philadelphia,
1853), pp. 137, 138, 176, shows that Baptists were elected to town offices and as
representatives, that they were graduated from Harvard, and that there were only
nine Baptist congregations in 1741. Robert George Torbert, *A History of the
Baptists* (Philadelphia, 1950), made use of three earlier standard works: Albert
H. Newman, *History of the Baptist Churches in the United States* (New York,
1894); Henry C. Vedder, *Short History of the Baptists* (Philadelphia, 1897); and
Thomas Armitage, *A History of the Baptists* (New York, 1899). Torbert, ch. viii,
and Newman, pp. 172, 195, also show that Baptists were representatives and went
to Harvard. Newman, p. 271, said there were thirty Baptist churches in Massachusetts by 1768, and that by 1790 there were 92 churches and 6,234 members.
This would mean approximately 2,000 Baptist church members in the province
in 1768. After the Great Awakening of 1740–1741, some of the strict laws about
Baptists and Quakers were actually aimed at the Separates who broke off from the
Congregational church and desired to avoid paying the ministers' taxes to Congregational ministers (Newman, p. 246).

[18] *Boston Gazette*, Sept. 14, 1730; *Acts and Resolves*, II, 635.

Quakers from all restrictions, but this was criticized in Britain because it did not apply to all denominations, and the governor was ordered not to consent to future acts unless they conformed to the terms of the charter.[19] A law of 1735 exempted Anabaptists except that it had the qualification that exemption from ministerial taxes was not to apply to the settlement of a new town until the town had built a church and established an orthodox minister there. This was one of the conditions on which land was granted.[20] Eventually Quakers were even exempt from military service on condition that all Quakers in the town be taxed to pay the £13.6.8 required for each exemption.[21]

Evidence from the towns shows that the dissenters from the Congregational church were enjoying both religious toleration and freedom from ministerial taxes. Raynham claimed exemption from a fine for failure to send a representative to the General Court on the ground that about twenty of its voters, some of them men of good estates, went to the Baptist Society and did not help to pay for the minister.[22] The implication is that the town could not afford a representative because it was supporting two ministers. Pittsfield also abated the minister's rates of its Baptists.[23]

Thus did the established church come to an end in colonial Massachusetts, if by the term "established church" we mean a church which was by law supported financially by all the people whether or not they belonged to the church. In theory, the only vestige of the established church to remain was in the settlement of new towns. Legally, a group of Quakers, Anabaptists, or members of the Church of England could not get a grant of land on the frontier and set up their own religion until

[19] *Acts and Resolves,* II, 619, 636.

[20] *Ibid.,* pp. 714–15, 876–77; IV, 67. Apparently this law was not always adhered to. An Anglican church was established in the new town of Pownalborough before a Congregational church was built. See Perry, *Historical Collections,* III, 562.

[21] Dec. 31, 1759, *ibid.,* IV, 49.

[22] Mass. Arch., CXVII, 609.

[23] Pittsfield Town Records, I, 165. Apparently the Baptist ministers collected their salaries by way of taxation, for the historians of the Baptists, who condemn the Congregationalists for other practices, do not include nonpayment of salaries as one of the grievances.

they had first built a Congregational church and established an orthodox Congregational minister. How such a provision as this worked in practice was probably a different story, in view of the persistent opposition of Quakers and Anabaptists to the orthodox Congregational church.

There is a faint hint that the Quakers, once they became a majority in the town, in turn did what they could to freeze out the Congregational church. A law of 1759 said that when half or more of the assessors of collectors of any town were Quakers, the non-Quakers could elect an equal number of non-Quaker assessors who would have full power to act by themselves in making rates for building and repairing a church and settling and supporting a minister.[24] The implication is that Quaker assessors were perhaps not too diligent in levying town taxes for the support of the orthodox church.

In dealing with religion in colonial Massachusetts, we must always bear in mind that the vast majority of the people were Congregationalists. Church of England minister William Clark said that in Stoughton and Dedham only about twenty-five families belonged to his church, and that he met with all the discouragements that could be expected "in a country where the generality of the people have so great an antipathy to our mode of religion." [25] Even in Boston, where the Church of England was strongest, three-fourths or more of the people were Congregationalists.[26] The customs officer, Henry Hulton, said there were three Church of England churches, one Presbyterian, and twelve Congregational.[27] In the rural areas, of course, the

24 *Acts and Resolves,* IV, 180–81.

25 SPG Archives, XXII, ser. B, pp. 274–75, 281.

26 "Extracts from Capt. Francis Goelet's Journal," *New England Historical and Genealogical Register,* 94 vols. (Boston, 1847–1941), XXIV, 63. Hereafter cited "Goelet's Journal."

27 Hulton, *Letters,* 39. Except in Boston and Marblehead, the Church of England was never very strong in Massachusetts. At one time there were fourteen ministers in the colony, but most of them spoke of their congregations as extremely small. They almost always spoke hopefully of the future, since they were supported almost wholly by the Society for the Propagation of the Gospel, but on at least one occasion the archbishop of Canterbury said some of them were sending back too favorable reports which misled the people in England as to the true strength of the church in the colonies (Perry, *Historical Collections,* III, 493–96 and *passim*).

proportion of Congregationalists to Episcopalians was much greater than in Boston. Jonathan Mayhew, the famous Boston minister, estimated the ratio of Congregationalists over other religions in the colony at fifty to one.[28] This predominance of Congregationalists does not justify whatever religious intolerance existed, but it does mean that most people were Congregationalists and that religious life was not dominated by a minority which was able to force compliance by the majority.

Just as Congregationalists over the years failed to impose the Congregational church as the established church, so also they failed in their efforts to impose a strict observance of Sunday by the people at large. A blue law in 1692 prohibited Sunday work, games, travel, or the entertainment of any but

As the Revolution approached, Anglicanism was weakened rather than strengthened. In 1768, Mather Byles said the late disturbances had considerably decreased and impoverished his church, while William Clark in 1774 went to Stoughton twice when not a single person came to church. Several times he read services to one, two, or three people, and seldom were there more than five (*ibid.*, 544, 566).

Of the Anglican clergymen licensed to the American colonies from 1745 to 1781, only five went to Massachusetts, thirty-six went to New England, and 141 went to Virginia alone (George Woodward Lamb, "Clergymen Licensed to the American Colonies by the Bishops of London, 1745–1781," *Historical Magazine of the Protestant Episcopal Church* XIII [June 1944], pp. 131–43).

[28] Mayhew to Jasper Mauduit, in *Jasper Mauduit, Agent in London for . . . Massachusetts-Bay . . .* , in Mass. Hist. Soc., *Collections*, LXXIV, 37. The question of the number of Congregationalists in Massachusetts raises an interesting problem in the use of evidence. Anson Phelps Stokes (*Church and State in the United States*, 3 vols. [New York, 1950], I, 229) cites William Warren Sweet to the effect that New England did not have more than one church member for every eight persons. Sweet ("Church Membership," *Dictionary of American History*, ed. by James Truslow Adams, 5 vols. [New York, 1940], I, 372) said one to eight, but cited another of his own works where the figures were one to five (*Religion in Colonial America* [New York, 1942], pp. 334–35). Sweet rejected an estimate by Ezra Stiles in 1760 of 445,000 Congregationalists and only 62,000 others in New England (*Extracts from the Itineraries and Other Miscellanies of Ezra Stiles . . .* [New Haven, 1916], pp. 92–94), but he did not offer other supporting evidence.

Sweet obviously confused "communicants" with people who went to the Congregational church or sympathized with it. Actually, only one or two persons out of each family were communicants, but this did not mean that the rest of the family opposed the Congregational church (Perry, *Historical Collections*, III, 501–02, 516). Half-way Covenanters belonged to the church but were not communicants (Walker, *History of the Congregational Church*, p. 164). Anglican ministers certainly believed that most of the people in Massachusetts were Congregationalists (Perry, *Historical Collections*, III, 517–18, 524, 539, 545, 550).

guests and strangers at public houses, with a fine of 5s. for labor or games and 20s. for travel.[29] Penalties for anyone who could not pay the fine were the stocks, the cage, whipping up to ten stripes, or twenty-four hours in jail.[30] In 1716 the law stated that many people worked and traveled on Sunday in violation of the statutes, that the fine was to be 10s. for working and 20s. for traveling, and that anyone who was able but failed to attend church for one month must pay a fine of 20s.[31] In 1727 the fine was raised to 15s. for work or games on Sunday and 30s. for traveling, again on the charge that there were many violations of the law.[32] Finally in 1761 the General Court repealed all laws governing conduct on the Lord's Day and passed a new one, saying that the laws had not been enforced and that the Lord's Day had been greatly and frequently profaned. This new act modified the Sunday restrictions somewhat. There was a 10s.– 20s. fine for business or diversions, except for charity and necessity, a 20s. fine for traveling unless the traveler had been delayed, restrictions on entertaining any but strangers and lodgers in public houses or on unnecessary walking or assemblying, and a fine for anyone absent one month from church. The law seemed to be aimed particularly at Boston, as though that town had been the greatest violator.[33]

From the wording of these statutes, one can only conclude that the law specifying what the people could or could not do on Sunday had little relation to what the people actually did on Sunday. If we accepted only the provisions of the law, we would believe that Massachusetts authorities were extremely strict about Sunday observance. By the same token, we could read the laws and believe that no one drank any intoxicating liquor between 1920 and 1933. This is not to say that the blue laws are to be condoned, but we do need to keep in mind their practical application.

Other evidence shows something of a contradiction between the law and practice as far as enforcement of the Sunday observance laws was concerned. On the one hand, there is the statement of one Captain Francis Goelet that there was very

[29] *Acts and Resolves,* I, 58–59.   [30] *Ibid.,* p. 123.   [31] *Ibid.,* II, 58–59.
[32] *Ibid.,* pp. 456–57.   [33] *Ibid.,* IV, 415.

strict observance of the Sabbath in Boston and that anyone but doctors found on the streets was compelled to go to church.[34] John Adams also said that New England institutions for the support of religion, morals, and decency exceeded those of all others and obliged every parish to have a minister and every person to go to meeting.[35] At the same time, however, Goelet also told about being too tired to go to church, so he stayed home, went over his papers, then dined with a large company. The next Sunday he dined with another large company of both men and women, declaring that after dinner the company was "very merry." [36] No wonder the ministers complained that the Sunday laws were often disregarded.

Just how widespread this disregard for the laws extended is difficult to say, but the following account indicates that violation of the Sunday laws was by no means confined to Boston. In a disputed election in Bellingham, 1739, one side said that most of the men on the other side claimed the right by law to be exempt from all ministerial taxes, that scarcely three of them had been to church three times in the past year, yet these men invaded the rights of those who were qualified to vote in ministerial affairs. Furthermore, one of their number, Joseph Scott, a selectman, had obtained the proclamation for the last general fast, kept it concealed from those who usually went to church and from the minister, and "made games & mock d at it." [37] Obviously the Sunday laws had little influence in Bellingham.

In terms of religious toleration and freedom, Massachusetts probably ranked about midway between the religious practices of Pennsylvania and those of England. There was not the complete freedom of religion enjoyed in Pennsylvania, but there was more religious freedom than there was in England. Benjamin Franklin explained the differences when, as agent for Massachusetts, he had to answer charges that the people of New England were intolerant and especially that they taxed and persecuted members of the Church of England. Franklin said that the first settlers had required any town to support a minis-

---

[34] "Goelet's Journal," pp. 62–63.
[35] Adams, *Familiar Letters,* pp. 120–21.
[36] "Goelet's Journal," pp. 53–55.   [37] Mass. Arch., CXIV, 399, 408.

ter and a free school, and that what was called Presbyterianism became the established religion. Later, other religious groups, such as Quakers, Baptists, and Anglicans, had protested against supporting the established church. Unlike England, where dissenters still had to pay tithes to the established church, Massachusetts had provided that church taxes paid by non-Congregationalists should be used for their own churches. On this score, Massachusetts was more liberal than England. Massachusetts had gone much further than England in other religious provisions, continued Franklin. In spite of the fact that the legislature was "almost to a man" composed of dissenters, there was no religious test to prevent Churchmen from holding office, sons of Churchmen could attend the universities, and church taxes paid by Churchmen went to the Episcopal minister. In England, on the other hand, dissenters were excluded from all offices of profit and honor, only sons of Churchmen could attend the universities, and dissenters had to support both their own churches and the Church of England.[38]

Internal religious discontent, then, was of little importance in the background of the Revolution, but this does not mean that religion was a negligible factor in the controversy with England. Most of the people were Congregationalists and somewhat satisfactory concessions had been made to other groups long before 1760. After 1760, however, religion played an important role in the controversy with the mother country, as will appear in a later chapter, and the connection between religion and democracy will become increasingly apparent.

Closely associated with religion and democracy were the provisions for education in the colony. The same law of 1692 which set up the established church also attempted to provide compulsory education, and in the end, the colony was more successful in its educational than in its religious program. A town of fifty householders was required to be constantly provided with a schoolmaster to teach reading and writing. Every town of 100 householders or families had to provide a Latin grammar

---

[38] Franklin, *Writings*, V, 399–404. The Anglican minister at Marblehead said that that town in 1766 sent the only Churchman then sitting in the assembly (Perry, *Historical Collections*, III, 524).

school, with "some discreet person of good conversation, well instructed in the tongues, procured to keep such school." The schoolmaster was to be encouraged and paid by the inhabitants, and a £10 fine was to be assessed on any town that neglected to have a schoolmaster for one year.[39]

Evidently the legislature experienced as much difficulty for a while in forcing education on the people as it did in forcing religion on them. A law of 1701 said that towns had shamefully neglected to observe the "wholesome and necessary" school law, that penalties for violation of the law had not been re-

[39] *Acts and Resolves,* I, 62–63. Much difference of opinion exists over the nature of colonial education. In *Evolution of the Massachusetts School System* (New York, 1894), ch. ii, George H. Martin maintained that education was better in the seventeenth than in the eighteenth century. John Seiler Brubacher thought that frontier conditions hindered education but that improved economic circumstances in the eighteenth century resulted in more interest in education (*A History of the Problems of Education* [New York, 1947], p. 79).

Many writers have interpreted colonial education from the viewpoint of a society controlled by and for the upper classes. Lawrence A. Cremin, *The American Common School: An Historic Conception* (New York, 1951), chs. i and ii, tied the development of the schools to political and social democratization which culminated in the election of Jackson. Merle Curti, *The Social Ideas of American Educators* (New York, 1935), ch. i, also found that schools in colonial times were predominantly instruments of the upper economic and religious groups. The Curti interpretation is based mainly on secondary works. The evidence which he cited on page 9 from the *Hutchinson Papers,* II, 295, however, fails to show that education was the handmaid of a ruling aristocracy. The issue in Randolph's letter was between Anglicanism and Congregationalism and Royalism and independence. Leonard Woods Labaree, *Conservatism in Early American History* (New York, 1948), p. 91, contends that colonial education was essentially conservative, that compulsory education laws in Massachusetts were never adequately carried out, and that the educational system made no effective advances in basic philosophy, method, or content in the hundred years before the Revolution.

In opposition to writers who stress class conflict and conservative control, Carl Bridenbaugh shows that there was a great interest in public education and much respect for learning in New England ("The New England Town: A Way of Life," pp. 32–36). In another work in which he emphasizes the role of the towns rather than the frontier, Bridenbaugh contends that the educational system in Boston was the best there was anywhere (*Cities in the Wilderness: The First Century of Urban Life in America, 1625–1742* [New York, 1938], pp. 441–42). Clifford K. Shipton held that the Puritans were interested in education not merely for the sake of religion. He quoted evidence to show that education was widespread and accused J. T. Adams of using secondary writers and ignoring good evidence to prove the Adams' thesis ("Secondary Education in the Puritan Colonies," *New England Quarterly,* VII [Dec., 1934], 646–61).

quired, and that the result was the fostering of ignorance and irreligion. So the fine was raised to £20 for failure to keep a school one year, and provision was made for enforcement by justices of the peace and the grand jury. Education was linked with religion to some extent by the fact that the grammar schoolmaster, but not the writing schoolmaster, had to be approved by the board of ministers, although no minister could himself be a schoolmaster.[40] By 1712, anyone who set up a school to teach "reading, writing, or any other science" had to receive the approval of the town selectmen.[41]

Schoolteachers were obviously held in higher esteem then than now, for they enjoyed privileges not now bestowed on teachers. Among other things, they were exempt from military training and also from the payment of poll taxes and estate taxes, provided the estate was in their own hands and under their own improvement.[42]

Failure to force schools on the towns continued to plague the efforts of the legislature, at least as far as the establishment of Latin grammar schools went. A law of 1718 said that in spite of good and wholesome laws and a fine, "sad experience" had demonstrated that some towns preferred to pay the fine rather than keep the grammar school, even though such towns were fully capable of supporting a school. So the fine was increased £10 for each additional fifty families in the town, making the fine £40, for example, in a town with 200 families.[43] Then the legislature turned its attention to individuals who neglected to educate their children. The court branded such neglect as a great scandal to the Christian name and of dangerous conse-

---

[40] Acts and Resolves, I, 470.   [41] Ibid., pp. 681–82.
[42] Ibid., pp. 29–36, 130, 167, 747.
[43] Ibid., II, 100. Harry Gehman Good, in A History of Western Education (New York, 1949), pp. 373–76, points out that the common people of the time were apparently satisfied with a moderate degree of education for their children, wanting their children taught reading and religion but little else. He also contends that the legislature was in the hands of the rich, but this raises a contradiction. If the rich controlled the legislature, why did they insist on taxing themselves and their class in the towns for support of schools for all? They would have blocked public education instead of fostering it; the towns would have demanded schools instead of trying to avoid them.

quence to the rising generation. If any persons raised their children in such gross ignorance that they did not know the alphabet at the age of six, the overseers of the poor could bind out such children to good families for a decent Christian education.[44]

Evidence indicates that eventually the legislature had more success in forcing education than in forcing religion. In 1738, Boston had two grammar schools, three writing schools, and 595 students. The selectmen and others who usually visited the schools reported that in justice to the master of the South Writing School, "the writing both of the master and scholars has been of late much improved." [45] In 1768 the selectmen's report showed only four schools, but there were 709 students "all in very good order." [46] Sheffield usually voted to keep school as usual, but in 1774 it took measures to defend itself against a grand-jury indictment for not keeping a grammar school.[47] Hatfield also had to answer a presentment of a grand jury in 1741 for failing to have a schoolmaster, indication that the school law was being enforced.[48] Pittsfield, incorporated in 1761, spent only £16 for schooling in 1763. In 1764, the town built three schoolhouses at the expense of £36 and then voted £30 to operate them. By 1771 the town had five schools operating at an expense of £60, and in 1773 the town voted £100 for school-

---

[44] July 3, 1735, *Acts and Resolves*, II, 758–59. One author contends that apprenticeship was not so much a training for a trade as it was a means of providing a general elementary education—that apprenticeship was "the most fundamental educational institution of the period" (Robert Francis Seybolt, *Apprenticeship and Apprenticeship Education in Colonial New England and New York* [New York, 1917], p. 22). Seybolt also did two well-documented works on education in Boston: *The Private Schools of Colonial Boston* (Cambridge, Mass., 1935) and *The Public Schools of Colonial Boston, 1635–1775* (Cambridge, Mass., 1935). In another work, *The Evening School in Colonial America* (Urbana, Ill., 1925), Seybolt shows that evening schooling was available in the larger towns for apprentices, workers, women, and others. Curti (*Social Ideas of American Educators*, p. 22) and Good (*History of Western Education*, pp. 375–76) look on the apprenticeship system as evidence of upper-class domination, but their contentions are not supported by evidence.

[45] *Boston Town Records*, XII, 213.

[46] Mass. Hist. Soc., Miscellaneous MSS., XIII.

[47] Sheffield Town Records, Nov. 9, 1763, March 28, 1764, Nov. 24, 1764, Nov. 15, 1765, Feb. 25, 1774.

[48] Hatfield Town Records, IV, 3.

ing.[49] As early as 1737, Springfield had five schools in operation.[50]

If schooling was not free, as apparently it was not in some towns, provision was still made for educating those who could not afford to pay. Northampton required each student to furnish a load of wood, but that seems to have been the only tuition demanded.[51] Marblehead found 122 children in the town with parents too poor to send them to school, and so the town voted in 1772 to provide not more than £100 for their schooling.[52] Seaport towns always had the extra problem of widows and children of lost seamen. Braintree voted in 1700 that each student should pay a shilling a quarter for every quarter in the school year which started August 18.[53] The next year, the fee was 5s. a year for resident students and 20s. a year for out-of-town students, but poor people were to receive part or all of their tuition.[54] Later the town cut its reading and writing school to six months a year, October through March, doubtless the months during which the children were least useful on the farms.[55]

The colony even attempted to force its ministers to be educated men, though with just what success is difficult to say. In 1760, the General Court declared that some towns had chosen ignorant and illiterate persons as ministers despite the law to the contrary. Then the legislature enacted that it was unlawful for a town to assess taxes to support a minister unless the minister had been educated at some university, college, or academy for instruction of youth in learned languages, the arts, and sciences, or had obtained testimonials from the major part of the settled ministers in the county that he was qualified by his learning.[56] Just what happened with a group that supported its minister by voluntary contributions rather than taxes the law did not say.

That education was a democratic rather than aristocratic

49 Pittsfield Town Records, I, 62, 74, 90, 135–36, 153.
50 Springfield Town Records, IV, 17.
51 Northampton Town Records, I, 177; II, 83.
52 Marblehead Town Records, IV, 122.
53 Braintree Town Records, p. 47.   54 Ibid., p. 51.
55 Ibid., p. 88.   56 Acts and Resolves, IV, 288.

institution in colonial America was clearly pointed out by Franklin. Speaking of the colonies in general, he declared that all worth-while books and pamphlets published in England were within a few weeks to be found in the colonies, "where there is not a man or woman born in the country but what can read." [57] Perhaps this account is somewhat exaggerated, but it does show what Franklin thought. In 1783, just as the Revolution came to a close, Franklin described the American people as follows:

We are more thoroughly an enlightened people, with respect to our political interest, than perhaps any other under heaven. Every man among us reads, and is so easy in his circumstances as to have leisure for conversations of improvement and for acquiring information.[58]

Thus was political, educational, and economic democracy interlaced in Franklin's views.

Statements similar to those of Franklin were made about New England and Massachusetts in particular. In 1769, the Reverend Andrew Eliot of Boston said that the law requiring grammar schools in every town was a "prime" law and that there were scarcely any among them who could not read and write with some tolerable propriety.[59] On one occasion Edmund Burke reminded his fellow members of Parliament that colonial governments were popular governments, that political ideas were strengthened by religious ideas, and that education also promoted freedom in America.[60] John Adams summed up his views of education: "The public institutions in New England for the education of youth, supporting colleges at public expense, and obliging towns to maintain grammar schools, are not equaled, and never were, in any part of the world." [61]

In evaluating colonial religion and education, we must place both in their proper perspective. The correct comparison is with other religious and educational systems of the day, not with those of today. In this respect the religious institutions, and especially the educational institutions, of colonial Massa-

[57] Franklin, *Writings*, V, 209.   [58] *Ibid.*, IX, 87–88.
[59] Mass. Hist. Soc., *Collections*, 4th ser., IV, 436.
[60] *Parliamentary History*, XVIII, 478ff.
[61] Adams, *Familiar Letters*, pp. 120–21.

chusetts stand up well under examination. How both reflected democracy and contributed to the Revolution will be apparent in later chapters, but it seems safe to say that neither was a positive factor in promoting an "internal" revolution.

From the material presented in these six chapters, it would appear that Massachusetts did not offer a very favorable climate for internal class conflict. Voting qualifications were sufficiently low to permit most men to vote in province and town affairs, for in a society which offered much economic opportunity, most men were middle-class property owners. There was no complaint about inequitable representation even though, contrary to accepted opinion, the seaport towns were greatly under-represented in relation to the agricultural backcountry. Equal division of estates nullified the aristocratic practices of entail and primogeniture. There was not much complaint about the semi-established church, particularly in a society in which most people were Congregationalists, for other religions enjoyed toleration and exemption from tithes to support the Congregational church. And finally there appears to have been little demand for more educational facilities in the colony for the common people. In short, the ingredients for an internal revolution were conspicuously absent in the Bay Colony.

[CHAPTER VII]

"Perpetual Discordance,"

1691–1755

IF AN explanation of the Revolution in Massachusetts is not to be found in internal problems, we must look elsewhere for causes of the conflict. The search is not difficult. Evidence of clashes between Britain and her colonies over British imperial policies is as conspicuous by its abundance as evidence of class conflict is conspicuous by its absence.

Interpreting the conflict as a War of Independence rather than as an American Revolution does not mean, however, that democracy was not an issue. It was very much so, not as a condition to be achieved in a class war between privileged upper classes and underprivileged lower classes, but as a force already present —a force which greatly hampered British imperialism. Democracy was fundamental in the Revolution but not in the way current writers have interpreted it.

Writing long after the American Revolution, John Adams declared:

The principles and feelings which contributed to produce the revolution . . . ought to be traced back for two hundred years, and sought in the history of the country from the first plantations in America. Nor should the principles and feelings of the English and Scotch towards the colonies, through that whole period, ever be forgotten. The perpetual discordance between British principles and feelings and of those of America, the next year after the suppression of the French power in America, came to a crisis, and produced an explosion.[1]

It is not necessary to go back two hundred years, as Adams suggested. A brief survey of events from the Charter of 1691 should suffice to reveal some of the clashes and to show the part which democracy played.

The first clash of principles after 1691 came when the General Court attempted to regain the position the colonists had enjoyed under the previous charter. Shortly after the charter became effective, it passed two acts setting forth claims to certain rights and privileges. For the House of Representatives, these included the same freedom of debate and suffrage that the House of Commons enjoyed, the sole right to raise taxes, and the right to supervise expenditure of money. The General Court was to control appointment of all the civil offices not particularly specified by the charter, as well as to provide for salaries of all officials within the province. This latter proposition was to be one of the main obstacles to British colonial policy and one of the keys to an understanding of the change of British policy after 1760. The colonists were to be guaranteed protection of persons and prop-

---

[1] Adams, *Works*, X, 284. The period from 1691 to 1755 has been covered by a number of studies, but except for George Bancroft, either the authors give no interpretation in terms of a democratic society or they interpret the period as undemocratic. James Truslow Adams, in *Building the British Empire: To the End of the First Empire* (New York, 1938), deals mainly with the British side of the period, but as we have seen in his other works, Adams considered colonial society as undemocratic. Edward Channing, in *A History of the United States*, 6 vols. (New York, 1905–1925), II, covers the century 1660–1760. Channing said there was a moderate property qualification for voting (p. 284), but otherwise he did not emphasize democracy as a British-American issue. An account somewhat favorable to the British is that by Lawrence H. Gipson, *The British Empire before the American Revolution*, 8 vols., vols. I–III (Caldwell, Ida., 1936), vols. IV–VIII (New York, 1939–1954). In vol. III, ch. i, the author gives a brief sketch of Massachusetts in the middle of the century. Gipson considers Boston as aristocratic (pp. 5–6), mistakenly assumes that the people of Massachusetts were largely engaged in fisheries, commerce, and shipbuilding (pp. 14–15), gives a good account of the diminished importance of the church in political affairs (pp. 21–28), has an erroneous account of representation (pp. 29–32 note), and ends the chapter with the well-known quotation from John Adams to the effect that Massachusetts had political democracy, a middle-class society, and the best educational system in the world (pp. 38–39).

erty by provision for due process of law, trial by jury, and bail. When these acts setting forth colonial privilege were sent to England, they were disallowed, indicating a difference of principles, but the colonists never ceased claiming the rights expressed in them.[2]

A second difference emerged when the British discovered the importance of one of the claims set forth by the General Court— the right of a democratic legislature to control salaries of British officials. A judge of admiralty, one Colonel Quary, informed the Lords of Trade that it was impossible for a governor to serve the interests of the Crown under the governments of New England. Governors dependent on the people for salaries could not serve the Crown, he said, but would always be tempted to make a bad bargain for the king. The New England constitutions influenced all the other colonial governments, Quary continued, "in most of which I can assure Your Lordshipps, that commonwealth notions and principle, is too much improved within these few years." Quary advocated a standard type of government and a standard currency as the chief remedies. The king should appoint the governor, who should be paid out of a fund contributed by the people but controlled by the Crown.[3] As later events

[2] *Acts and Resolves,* I, 40, 170. The best account of this phase of colonial history is that by Mary Patterson Clarke, *Parliamentary Privilege in the American Colonies* (New Haven, 1943). Clarke said that the assemblies not only asserted their privileges but also developed ingenius devices for nullifying the prerogative as upheld by royal governors.

[3] "Colonel Quary's Memorial . . . ," June 16, 1703, in Mass. Hist. Soc., *Collections,* 3d ser., VII, 222ff. Evarts B. Greene interpreted the period in terms of the constitutional problem of reconciling imperial control with local self-government. To Greene, the fundamental issue was the antagonism between an appointed governor and an elected assembly. See *Provincial America, 1690–1740* (New York, 1905), *passim.* Greene did not deal with the problem of democracy. A second work which stresses the constitutional issues is that by Leonard W. Labaree, *Royal Government in America: A Study of the British Colonial System before 1783* (New Haven, 1930). Labaree considered the conflict between governors and assemblies over the royal prerogative as the central theme in the constitutional history of the colonies (preface). Citing McKinley, *The Suffrage Franchise,* Labaree also said that the colonies were not democratic as the term is understood today (pp. 188–89, note 35). In a study written before the current interpretation became popular, Henry Russell Spencer, *Constitutional Conflict in Provincial Massachusetts . . .* (Columbus, O., 1905), contended that the House of Representatives embodied radicalism, progress, and democracy as opposed to the aristocratic tendencies of the Council. He apparently did not realize that the popular party also gained control of the Council.

demonstrated, Quary had probed one of the thorniest problems to confront British imperialists.

Beginning in 1719, there was strong talk in England that Massachusetts was deviating from British imperial policies and that measures should be taken to restore British control over the colony. The colonial agent, Jeremiah Dummer, warned the colonists of deep prejudices against the charter and of accusations that the colonists were enemies of royal government and not sufficiently dependent on Great Britain. He said there were proposals that the colony pay a yearly revenue to the mother country and that iron manufacturing be prohibited.[4] A report to the king also pointed out that while the colonies paid a £200,-000 balance of trade to Britain, they still refused to obey the king's orders, broke the laws of trade, made laws contrary to British law, and refused to contribute to the defense of other colonies. In particular, the report stressed the danger of colonial independence, and proposed remedies to prevent this. These included the encouragement of colonial products which Britain needed, restraints on colonial manufacturing that competed with British manufacturing, and checks on quit rents, land grants, and use of colonial timber. The most important reform, however, would be to place all colonial governments under a single governor, who in turn should have a salary provided in such a way that he would not be dependent on the colonists or subject to colonial pressure. In these proposed reforms, the colonists would retain their liberties, properties, and religion. They would also be treated as British subjects and favored "in all reasonable things not prejudicial to the interest of Great Britain."[5]

The threat to Massachusetts was sufficient to induce Jeremiah Dummer to write a long defense of the colony's religious, eco-

---

[4] Mass. Arch., LI, 319–35.

[5] Hardwicke Papers, DLIX, 69–70, 94–95, 109–11. The account by Oliver M. Dickerson, *American Colonial Government, 1696–1765: A Study of the British Board of Trade in Its Relations to the American Colonies, Political, Industrial, Administrative* (Cleveland, 1912) gives a detailed account of the machinery by which the British attempted to regulate the colonies. Unlike some other writers (see note 6 below), Dickerson maintains that the rise in importance of the assemblies shifted the center of gravity from Britain to the colonies. His implication is that the American side of the story is the more important one for American history, though the British side is still significant.

nomic, and political practices. The agent attempted to convince the British that their fears regarding the colonies were groundless. He contended that the Congregational church differed from the Church of England in discipline but not in doctrine, that the appointment of a governor and the enforcement of regulations preserved the dependence of the colony on Great Britain, and that Britain benefited through colonial trade, raw materials, and taxes. In particular, he attempted to refute the charge, generally held in England, that the colonies would eventually become independent. He said all ranks in England believed that the growing wealth and numbers of the colonists, combined with their great distance from England, would lead to independence unless the colonies were "curbed in time, by being made entirely subject to the crown." Dummer assured the British that they had nothing to fear, and everything to gain, by leaving the colonies with their charters and by promoting their prosperity.[6]

---

[6] Jeremiah Dummer, *A Defense of the New-England Charters* (Boston, 1765), *passim*. Perhaps as a reaction against the "patriotic" works of George Bancroft, there has been a group of historians who have insisted that the proper perspective for a true understanding of early American history is England rather than the colonies. The trend was undoubtedly started by Herbert L. Osgood. In an article, "England and the Colonies," *Political Science Quarterly*, II (Sept. 1887), pp. 440–69, Osgood accused some historians of being biased by national prejudice, particularly in dealing with the American Revolution, and called for more balance and greater consideration for the British side in the writing of early American history.

Osgood's suggestion was taken up, perhaps too enthusiastically, by one of his students, George Louis Beer. Beer castigated those "unscientific" historians who started with the notion that Britain was tyrannical and who therefore produced books that were notably unjust to the British. He justified mercantilism on the ground that it was a proper policy for the men of that day—a policy of unconscious ignorance, not of conscious malice—and that the colonial system as administered before 1763 contributed but slightly to the bringing about of the Revolution (*The Commercial Policy of England toward the American Colonies* [New York, 1893], pp. 1–9, 157).

With the appearance of *British Colonial Policy, 1754–1765* (New York, 1907), Beer's point of view became even more clearly defined. In the preface he stated that his subject distinctly belonged in the domain of British rather than American history. Although Beer claimed that his writing was strictly objective, the germ of a new point of view appears at the end of the book. Here he stated that the trend in history, especially as exemplified by the British Empire, was toward increasingly large political units. In this respect, the American Revolution was a reversal of the trend toward consolidation, but it was still too early to decide

Dummer's "Defense" was not sufficiently convincing, however, to stop the agitation in Britain to rescind the charter. In
1723, the Lords of Trade reminded the Lords Justices that
Massachusetts was growing rapidly in population, trade, and

whether the Revolution meant progress or reaction or merely a temporary step
backward in preparation for future advance. Future developments might be such,
he continued, that the Revolution, losing its significance, would eventually appear
merely as a temporary separation of two kindred peoples whose similarities were
obscured by superficial differences (pp. 315–16).

The Beer "thesis" came to final fruition during World War I with the publication of *The English-speaking Peoples, Their Future Relations and Joint International Obligations* (New York, 1917). As the author stated, the object of the
book was to explain the advisability and necessity of a co-operative democratic
alliance of all the English-speaking peoples. Earlier suggestions, he claimed, had
been premature, presumably including his own which he had voiced at the conclusion of *British Colonial Policy, 1754–1765*. But what had once been impractical
and academic had now become practical and urgent.

At least part of the Beer thesis—that colonial history should be written from a
British rather than an American point of view—was adopted by Charles McLean
Andrews. Andrews believed that colonial society was undemocratic (*Colonial
Background of the American Revolution* [New Haven, 1924], p. 201, and *Colonial
Period of American History*, IV, 423n.). But he also thought that the proper
perspective for writing colonial history was from Great Britain rather than the
colonies (*ibid.*, I, preface; "Colonial Commerce," *American Historical Review*, XX
[Oct. 1914], 43–63), and that American colonial history should be placed in the
larger history of the world of its time ("On the writing of Colonial History,"
William and Mary Quarterly, 3d ser., I [Jan. 1944], 27–48).

Meanwhile, the first mover in this interpretation, Herbert L. Osgood, appears
to have changed his mind about the proper place from which to view early American history. In 1924, Andrews wrote one of the chapters in the book, *George
Louis Beer: A Tribute to His Life and Work in the Making of History and the
Moulding of Public Opinion* (New York, 1924) in which he praised the work of
Beer as an historian and pointed out that Beer had started under the guidance
of Osgood, who emphasized the English point of view. That same year and the
following one, 1924–1925, Osgood's *The American Colonies in the Eighteenth
Century*, 4 vols. (New York, 1924–1925), came from the press. In these four volumes, Osgood reverted to an American emphasis, showing that colonial history
became more American with each decade. These volumes were reviewed by
Andrews (*American Historical Review*, XXXI [April 1926], 533–38), who charged
Osgood with failure to deal with the whole empire or with the British side of
events. Osgood, said Andrews, wrote from an American viewpoint, failed to understand fully British policy before 1763, and did not fully grasp the meaning of
mercantilism.

While it is necessary to present much that was occurring in Great Britain, a
predominantly British point of view might well fail to explain what the Americans were doing and why. Americans acted as they saw events and policies, not as
the British saw them, so perhaps an American approach is justified if we would
explain what Americans did.

military power. At the same time, the governor, though appointed by the king, was "without any salary but such as the people are pleased to give him, and that from year to year only," and the House of Representatives far outnumbered the Council. Said the Lords:

From so unequal a balance in their constitution daily inconveniences occur. And Your Excellencies may perceive by the several facts mentioned in this report, that the inhabitants, far from making suitable returns to His Majesty for the extraordinary privileges they enjoy by their charter, are daily endeavouring to wrest the small remains of power out of the hands of the Crown, and to become independent of their mother kingdom. . . . Hence Your Excellencys will be apprized of what importance it is to His Majesty's service that so powerful a colony should be restrained within the due bounds of obedience to the Crown, and be more firmly attached to the interest of Great Britain, than they at present seem to be; which we conceive cannot effectually be done without the interposition of the British legislature, wherein in our humble opinion no time should be lost.[7]

The first effort to restore British authority in Massachusetts—a proposal that the governor be given a fixed salary to make him independent of the legislature—failed completely. In ordering the governor to get a fixed salary, the Lords of Trade said that this was essential for preserving the dependence of the colony on Great Britain and for securing obedience to the laws of trade and navigation.[8] The General Court refused the demand, however, on the ground that it had not been done previously, that it was their right to raise and dispose of money without compulsion, that it would lessen the dignity of the House of Representatives and destroy the balance in the government, and that it might open the door to future encroachments.[9] Under Governor Belcher, the British threatened that if the General Court did not grant a fixed salary the king would lay the undutiful behavior of the colony before Parliament for action. On this occasion the assembly was accused of attempting to weaken if not cast off altogether the obedience they owed the Crown and

[7] Hardwicke Papers, DLX, 89–91.
[8] *Boston Gazette,* July 29 and Aug. 5, 1728, Sept. 1, 1729.
[9] *Ibid.,* Sept. 23, 1728.

"the dependence which all colonies ought to have on their mother country." [10]

Both the British and their governors might better have saved their energies for more profitable undertakings, for they were never able to get the General Court to grant a fixed salary. The colonists fully understood the importance of salary control in their dealings with a colonial governor.

Paper money provided another issue for revealing differences of principle and interest between Britain and Massachusetts. Having an unfavorable balance of trade with England, the colony found itself constantly drained of its gold and silver. To meet the problem, the General Court issued paper bills which were to be loaned to the people on land security.[11] Realizing that paper money hurt British trade with the colonies, the British ordered the colony to call in all outstanding paper money by 1741 except £30,000 to run the government. All future paper money bills were to contain suspending clauses to insure their approval in England before they became effective.[12] When the colony petitioned both king and Commons for relief on the ground that paper money was the only colonial currency and that its withdrawal without a substitute would hurt the colony, the House of Commons declared that the colonial complaint was *"frivolous and groundless, an high insult upon His Majesty's Government, and tending to shake off the dependence of the said colony upon this Kingdom,* to which by law and right they

[10] Hutchinson, *History,* II 280–82.

[11] *Acts and Resolves,* II, 61–63, 189–94. Andrew McFarland Davis has done the most comprehensive work on paper money in Massachusetts. Davis tended to treat paper money as a currency problem rather than as a manifestation of economic imperialism. Use of the terms "wild plunge," "recklessness of the provincial legislature," "sound money," and "financial heresy" indicate Davis' orthodox economic views. He did not seem to realize that the silver money which was so eminently respectable in 1740 had itself become "financial heresy" when Davis was writing in 1900 (*Currency and Banking,* I, 51–52). For a similar orthodox approach, see Charles J. Bullock, *Essays on the Monetary History of the United States* (New York, 1900), ch. iv. Joseph Barlow Felt, in *An Historical Account of Massachusetts Currency* (Boston, 1839), included much valuable source material on the money problem.

[12] Leo Francis Stock, ed., *Proceedings and Debates of the British Parliaments Respecting North America,* 5 vols. (Washington, 1924–1941), V, 48–49; *Boston Gazette,* June 5, 1727, Sept. 8, 1728; *House Journals,* X, 104–05.

are and ought to be subject." [13] The General Court, on the other hand, refused to pass any appropriations except in paper money. Furthermore, the appropriations did not contain suspending clauses, as the British demanded, and the paper money was to circulate beyond the 1741 deadline. [14]

From the controversy over paper money emerged the famous Massachusetts Land Bank or Manufactory Scheme of 1740. [15] As the name implies, and as the promoters admitted, the scheme had the dual purpose of furnishing a currency to replace public bills of credit and of stimulating colonial manufacturing. [16] The plan called for a private company which would lend its notes on land security, with borrowers to repay their loans either in company bills or certain specified manufactured articles. [17]

[13] *House Journals*, XVII, 149–55; *The General Magazine and Historical Chronicle of All the British Plantations in America* (1741), pub. by Benjamin Franklin; republished (New York, 1938), pp. 10–11.

[14] *Boston Gazette,* July 17, 1727; *Boston Town Records*, XII, 199, 222–29; Leonard Woods Labaree, ed., *Royal Instructions to British Colonial Governor, 1670–1776*, 2 vols. (New York, 1935), I, 220–44; Mass. Arch., CII, 37; *House Journals*, XVII, 82–83.

[15] I have discussed the Land Bank in much more detail in my unpublished dissertation, "The Road to Revolution in Massachusetts," University of Wisconsin, 1946. Andrew McFarland Davis wrote many articles on various aspects of the Land Bank: "Legislation and Litigation Connected with the Land Bank of 1740," in American Antiquarian Society, *Proceedings*, n.s., XI, 86–123; "The General Court and Quarrels between Individuals Arising from the Land Bank," *ibid.*, pp. 351–68; "Land Bank Mortgages in Worcester County," *ibid.*, XVI, 85–90; "Certain Considerations Concerning the Coinage of the Colony and the Public Bills of Credit of the Province of Massachusetts Bay," in American Academy of Arts and Sciences, *Proceedings*, XXXIII, no. 12 (Feb. 1898); "Boston Banks, 1681–1740; Those Who Were Interested in Them," *New England Historical and Genealogical Register* (July 1903); "Currency Discussion in Massachusetts in the Eighteenth Century," *Quarterly Journal of Economics*, XI (Oct. 1896; Jan. 1897). For the best factual account of the Land Bank, see Davis, *Currency and Banking*, II, ch. vii–xi. Davis did not emphasize imperialism, manufacturing, or democracy in his discussion of the bank. His interpretation was based on the orthodox views of contemporaries Thomas Hutchinson and Dr. William Douglass. See also Theodore Thayer, "The Land Bank System in the American Colonies," *Journal of Economic History*, XIII (Spring 1953), 145–59.

[16] Mass. Arch., CII, 45.

[17] Colonial Society of Massachusetts, *Publications*, 33 vols. (Boston, 1895–1940), IV, 135–42. This writer disagrees almost entirely with the widely accepted interpretation of the Land Bank presented by John C. Miller in "Religion, Finance, and Democracy in Massachusetts," *New England Quarterly*, VI (March 1933), 29–58. Miller presented the Land Bank as an internal class conflict rather than an

That the Land Bank or Manufactory Scheme demonstrated the effectiveness of democracy there can be little doubt. As I have said in Chapters III and IV, Hutchinson, in referring to the Land Bank, declared that the vote of a poor man was worth as much as that of a rich man, and that the partners and their supporters in the scheme had complete control of both the House and the Council in the General Court. Without the intervention of Britain, there is no question but that the company would have gone into operation. So popular was the scheme that its suppression almost caused a revolution in the colony.

The suppression of the Land Bank further demonstrated some differences of principle between the colony and the mother country. To understand colonial reaction, one must remember that previous proposals for a similar scheme as well as this particular

---

imperial problem of colonial currency and its relation to British trade. He said the colony was in the midst of an economic depression, although most writers present a picture of prosperity, and he contended that the rift between the rich and the poor was steadily widening, but he neither presents any evidence to this effect nor any evidence which would refute that presented in Chapter I above. Miller also links religion and class conflict by saying that the Great Awakening came along just in time to divert attention away from the Land Bank, thus implying that the religious revival brought an end to political turmoil. The facts are that the religious revival had started several years before the Land Bank episode and had actually reached its peak before the Land Bank trouble broke in 1741, that popular resentment was aimed at Parliament as well as at a few merchants, and that it was the political sagacity of Governor William Shirley rather than the Great Awakening that helped to calm the storm. Miller appears to accept without question the views of such anti-Bank writers as Thomas Hutchinson and William Douglass, even though the other side refuted these views with good arguments and evidence.

The sources do not show that the Land Bank and the Great Awakening were at all connected. For example, Miller said that the clergy felt that George Whitefield had succeeded in shelving the Land Bank question (p. 35). But the evidence which he quoted made no connection whatever between Whitefield, the Land Bank, and the Great Awakening. As a matter of fact, the big controversy over the Land Bank did not really get under way until after Whitefield had left Massachusetts in 1740.

Neither Perry Miller, in *Jonathan Edwards* (New York, 1949) nor Ola Elizabeth Winslow, in *Jonathan Edwards, 1703–1758: A Biography* (New York, 1940) related the Great Awakening to class conflict or the Land Bank. In fact, Miller shows that both Jonathan Edwards and Charles Chauncy, the chief spokesmen for the opposing sides in the Great Awakening, conducted their debate with practically no reference to social theories. The issue was wholly religious ("Jonathan Edwards' Sociology of the Great Awakening," *New England Quarterly*, XXI [March 1948], 50–77).

scheme had been declared legal by the attorney general of Great Britain.[18] The attorney general had also declared that an earlier act of Parliament (6 Geo. I, c.18) against stock companies did not apply to the colonies.[19] Yet in spite of these legal rulings, Parliament not only declared that the earlier act did apply to the colonies, but also declared that any partner in the scheme, even though he paid back his subscription, could still be sued by anyone who held manufactory notes.[20] Hutchinson called this passage of what amounted to an ex post facto law "an instance of the transcendent power of Parliament." He said that the company was dumbfounded at the action of Parliament, and he declared that Parliament was probably not interested in seeing justice done.[21]

There is no doubt, either, that suppression of the Manufactory Scheme caused a major crisis in the colony. Men resigned their commissions as civil and military officials, declaring that they favored the scheme because it would benefit their "native country." [22] There were threats of a general uprising to force acceptance of manufactory notes regardless of Parliament.[23] The General Court refused to do anything in the way of appropriations or defense that the governor requested.[24] There were open threats that the people would defy Parliament and claims that they had grown so "brassy and hardy" that they were combining to raise a rebellion.[25] Speaking of the Parliamentary act in later years, John Adams declared: "The act to destroy the Land Bank Scheme raised a greater ferment in this province, than the Stamp-Act did, which was appeased only by passing province laws directly in opposition to it." [26]

[18] Board of Trade *Journal,* VII, 57–58, 76; *Acts of the Privy Council, Colonial Series,* ed. by W. L. Grant and James Munro, 6 vols. (Hereford and London, 1908–1912), III, 683–85.

[19] Stock, *Debates,* V, 97–99.

[20] *Statutes at Large,* ed. by D. Pickering, 46 vols. (Cambridge and London, 1762–1814), XVII, 459–61. 14 Geo. II, c.37.

[21] Hutchinson, *History,* II, 301.

[22] Mass. Arch., CII, 88–90; *Boston Weekly News-Letter,* Jan. 1, 1741.

[23] Colonial Society of Massachusetts, *Publications,* IV, 18–20.

[24] *Belcher Papers,* II, 357.

[25] *Ibid.,* p. 388; Shirley, *Correspondence,* I, 40.

[26] Adams, *Works,* IV, 49. In "The Conservative Attitude toward the Great Awakening," *William and Mary Quarterly,* 3d ser., I (Oct. 1944), 331–52, Leonard

What would have happened if this ex post facto law had been allowed to take full effect in Massachusetts we will never know, for as Adams said, the General Court prevented its intended effect. In the first place, William Shirley, who replaced Belcher as governor, was politician enough to realize the danger of allowing the act to take its course. Shirley needed the backing of the legislature and the people at large, and to get this backing, he joined with the legislature "to do equal justice to all parties," and to see that no one suffered by the act of Parliament.[27] By September 1742, Shirley declared that not one honest man would suffer much by the suppression of the Land Bank.[28] Both House and Council thanked the governor for conducting the affair with great moderation, thus preventing distress to partners in the company.[29] Eventually the General Court set up a commission, first to collect from delinquent partners, then to spread the £2,318 loss in outstanding notes among all the partners, and finally to set up a lottery to raise funds for closing the account of the scheme.[30] The affairs of the Land Bank or Manufactory Scheme dragged out for many years until its close in 1770, leaving much bitterness in its wake.

The Land Bank episode was of particular interest to one of the mainsprings of the Revolution, Samuel Adams, whose father was a director of the company. In later years, John Adams, in defending his own part in the Revolution, declared that Samuel Adams' efforts in the cause of his country dated from about

---

W. Labaree designated the opponents of the Great Awakening as conservatives. He defined a conservative as one who wishes to preserve the *status quo*, which is true only if the *status quo* is what the conservative desires. A conservative in a Communist country would probably want to change the *status quo*. Eugene E. White, "Decline of the Great Awakening in New England: 1741–1746," *New England Quarterly*, XXIV (March 1951), 35–52, assumes that the Great Awakening occurred in an undemocratic society but that its net result was to stimulate democratic sentiment.

27 Mass. Arch., LIX, 326–29; CII, 111–12, 225, 243–45, 262; *Acts and Resolves*, XIII, 120, 154; *Boston Weekly News-Letter*, Jan. 20, 1743.

28 Shirley, *Correspondence*, I, 91.

29 *Boston Weekly News-Letter*, Sept. 15, 1743.

30 *Acts and Resolves*, III, 318, 521, 551; IV, 288; Mass. Arch., LIX, 346; CII, 382–84, 681; Davis, *Currency and Banking*, II, 203, 234; Shirley, *Correspondence*, I, 107–11; Hutchinson, *History*, II, 308.

1741.[31] In 1743, Adams in his master's thesis at Harvard had argued in the affirmative that it was lawful to resist the supreme magistrate if the commonwealth could not otherwise be preserved.[32] His father seems to have suffered little loss in the Land Bank affair except, of course, that he had to, and did, repay his subscription.[33] After his death, however, the commissioners of the General Court who were appointed to settle the affairs of the company tried unsuccessfully to collect his share of the general assessment from his son Samuel. Adams protested the injustice of his father's being assessed £219 while other directors were assessed as little as £10.[34] And when the sheriff attempted to sell the son's estate to satisfy the assessment, Adams blocked the sale.[35] Hutchinson claimed that Adams' actions both gained him attention in Boston and also prevented collection of the Land Bank debt.[36]

In addition to the difficulties growing out of the Land Bank, Governor Shirley inherited other problems arising from British imperialism. He received instructions which summed up rather clearly some of the reasons for discord between the colony and the mother country. On the mercantilist side, the governor had orders to prevent passage of paper money bills without suspend-

[31] Adams, *Works,* II, 295.

[32] "Subjects for Master's Degrees, 1655–1791," in Mass. Hist. Soc., *Proceedings,* XVIII (1880), 125.

[33] Suffolk County Probate Records, XLI, 64–66. Unfortunately, the inventory of the Adams' estate is missing from the original papers.

[34] *Boston Gazette,* March 1, 1756.

[35] *Ibid.,* Aug. 14, 1758; *Boston Weekly News-Letter,* Aug. 14, 1758.

[36] Hutchinson, *History,* III, 212. An interesting story has grown up around Samuel Adams and the Land Bank. In his *History of the United States,* III, 505, Edward Channing made the unsupported statement that the Land Bank brought financial ruin to Samuel Adams, Sr. John C. Miller, *Sam Adams, Pioneer in Propaganda* (Boston, 1936), p. 5, asserted that the elder Samuel Adams lost his money in the Land Bank, with the result that Samuel Adams, Jr., had to serve as a waiter for the lower table at Harvard. On page 9, however, Miller said that Adams graduated from Harvard before the Land Bank project even got under way and before the elder Adams could have lost his fortune. If Adams waited on tables after he returned to Harvard for his master's degree, the reason is shrouded in the mist of ignorance, for the younger Adams still had his father's brewery and house in 1758. Unfortunately, the inventory of the estate, which would show what property Samuel Adams, Sr., had when he died, is missing from the probate records.

ing clauses and to veto laws which injured the property of British subjects and the trade and shipping of Great Britain or which placed colonials in a more advantageous position than British subjects. He had to enforce the coinage act, aid the surveyor of the woods, report any trade or manufacturing in the colony that would affect the interests of Great Britain, encourage British merchants—especially the Royal African Company—to trade in Massachusetts, and prevent colonial trade with Britain's enemies. On the imperial side, the governor had orders to stop the colonial practice of putting two unrelated matters in the same law, that is, of adding riders which would benefit the colonists. He also had to veto laws which reduced the king's revenue or weakened the king's prerogative, get a fixed revenue for government, and secure the king's approval for any special colonial grant to an official. Furthermore, he was to insist that the legislature grant the governor a fixed salary of £1,000, or at least grant £1,000 before it passed any other legislation, and that it stop the colonial practice of raising money and supplies by resolve instead of an act. In the appointment of councilors, sheriffs, judges, and other officials, the governor was to be sure to select "men of good life, and well-affected to His Majesty's government, and of good estate and abilities, and not necessitous persons." [37]

That Shirley got along with the legislature as well as he did is to be attributed mainly to the fact that he did not carry out the king's instructions. He allowed the legislature to circumvent the act of Parliament killing the Land Bank; then he defended his actions by telling the Lords of Trade that the colonial law would carry out the real intentions of Parliament by spreading losses over the whole company, not just a few individuals, and that it would "correct several abuses of the act of Parliament." [38] When he tried to get suspending clauses attached to money bills, he

[37] Shirley, *Correspondence,* I, 43–76.
[38] *Ibid.,* pp. 108–11. The standard biography of Shirley (George Arthur Wood, *William Shirley, Governor of Massachusetts, 1741–1756: A History* [New York, 1920]) shows Shirley as a successful governor because he was willing to compromise with the assembly or even to relinquish some of the prerogative on occasion. Wood did not discuss the Land Bank in connection with Shirley's appointment (chs. iv and v) but did discuss it later in his book (pp. 104–08).

found such a "settled aversion" to suspending clauses in the House of Representatives that he "thought it most prudent . . . to give them a short recess." He also warned the British that if trouble developed with the French, his refusal to consent to a money bill without a suspending clause might be fatal.[39] Shirley had to violate his instructions in order to carry on preparations for a West Indian expedition,[40] and soon the British had to relax this instruction.[41] The British also had to back down on their demand for a fixed salary for the governor.[42]

Some of these controversies clearly showed the effectiveness of democracy in the colony. Shirley said the people had a strong aversion to a fixed salary, which made the question so unpopular among the representatives that even those who favored it dared not vote for it because they were extremely dependent on their constituents. If the salary were ever to be secured, it would have to be done by Parliament at some unexpected time when the legislature was well disposed toward the governor so that a precedent could be set.[43] As we have seen in Chapter IV, Shirley did inaugurate the policy of restricted representation to cut down the power of the democratic part of the legislature, but this proved ineffective, as the House was already sufficiently large to dominate the General Court.[44]

Shirley was not much more successful in getting restrictions on paper money than he was in carrying out his other instructions, and again democracy was in part the reason for his failure. When he attempted to persuade the legislature to pass an act prohibiting circulation of Rhode Island bills in Massachusetts, he encountered much opposition in the Council and could get only one vote for the bill in the House. Even if it had passed, he said, it could never have been enforced.[45] He did succeed in having the General Court pass a law providing for adjustments in depreciated paper money so creditors would not suffer losses.[46] But Hutchinson said popular opinion was so opposed to this

[39] Shirley, *Correspondence*, I, 76–79, 80.   [40] *Ibid.*, p. 78.
[41] *Boston Weekly News-Letter*, Jan. 21, 1742; *Pennsylvania Gazette*, Feb. 10, 1742.
[42] Shirley, *Correspondence*, I, 79.   [43] *Ibid.*, pp. 88–89.
[44] *Acts and Resolves*, III, 70. Also see Chapter IV.
[45] Shirley, *Correspondence*, I, 88–89.
[46] *Ibid.*, p. 77; *Boston Weekly News-Letter*, Jan. 28, 1742.

law that those who were to determine the depreciation never had the courage to do their duty.[47] Although he was a royal governor and a strong imperialist, Shirley realized that under British mercantilist policies Massachusetts had to have a paper currency to continue its normal economic life.[48] A war against France in 1745 brought British need for colonial assistance and with it a temporary end to restrictions on paper money.[49]

The Anglo-French war in America, 1745–1748, a concomitant of the War of the Austrian Succession in Europe, was as noteworthy for the controversies it generated between the British and the colonists as it was for the exploits of either the British or the French. These controversies started with the capture of Louisbourg, a French fortress near the St. Lawrence, and lasted through the peace treaty ending the war.

Difficulties at Louisbourg grew out of a situation in which a colonial army under a colonial general, William Pepperrell, had collaborated with a British naval unit under Commodore Peter Warren. The army had captured Louisbourg after a siege, and according to accounts, the navy had not fired a shot in the entire maneuver. Nevertheless, Warren assumed that his commission from the king gave him the right to take supreme command on shore. The result was strong resentment both in the colonial army at Louisbourg and in Massachusetts proper. Men talked about this as a design against their "native country" and declared that Massachusetts would back its general to the limit.[50] The Reverend Charles Chauncy, one of the leading Boston ministers, wrote that Warren's actions were "indeed *highly resented by every New-Englandman in Boston*," and he declared that if the *"High Admiral of England had been there, he would not have had the least right to command anywhere but in his own ships."* [51]

Trouble also developed at Louisbourg over British treatment

<hr />

47 Hutchinson, *History*, II, 306–07.   48 Shirley, *Correspondence*, I, 104–07.
49 Hutchinson, *History*, II, 315.
50 Shirley, *Correspondence*, I, 232, 235–36, 245; *Pepperrell Papers*, in Mass. Hist. Soc., *Collections*, 6th ser., X, 325, 330. For more detailed accounts of the Louisbourg expedition see William C. H. Wood, *The Great Fortress: A Chronicle of Louisbourg, 1720–1760* (Toronto, 1915) and J. S. McLennan, *Louisbourg from Its Foundation to Its Fall, 1713–1758* (London, 1918).
51 Mass. Hist. Soc., *Collections*, 1st ser., I, 50–51.

of colonial troops. The British never understood colonial soldiers, who, as one American officer said, were freeholders and
freeholders' sons who fought well because they fought for liberty
and their country.[52] They were volunteer militia—civilians in
the army—enlisted under officers who were granted commissions
chiefly because they were popular among the people and could
raise their own troops. Governor Shirley said the soldiers would
not enlist unless they knew their officers and had confidence in
their fitness.[53] Colonial soldiers also enlisted for short terms,
usually a summer campaign, and expected to be discharged at
the termination of their enlistment. At Louisbourg, the British
first replaced colonial with British officers, causing much discontent among both American officers and soldiers. The officers
felt that they had been ill used by the British, and the men were
dissatisfied because they had expected to be commanded by
American officers.[54] In addition, the British decided to keep
colonial troops at Louisbourg over the winter to do garrison
duty. The result was a threatened mutiny. Serious trouble was
averted only when Governor Shirley went to Louisbourg to
settle differences between Pepperrell and Warren and to pacify
the soldiers by advancing wages and promising discharges the
following spring.[55] Warren called the soldiers' demand for release "absurd," but the soldiers themselves obviously did not
think so.[56] The keeping of American soldiers beyond the term
of their enlistment was to result in repeated clashes between
the British and their colonists.

To climax an already unpleasant situation, many soldiers
died in Louisbourg because they had not come prepared to spend
a severe winter there. Warren reported in January that out of
2,000 troops they had buried nearly 500 and at that time had
1,100 sick. Seamen fared better than soldiers because they were
inured to a salt diet, he said, whereas the soldiers at home were
accustomed to plenty of roots, milk, and other wholesome food.[57]

[52] *Pennsylvania Archives*, 1st ser., II, 127.
[53] Shirley, *Correspondence*, I, 193. [54] *Ibid.*, p. 315.
[55] *Ibid.*, pp. 257, 266–68; II, 2; *Pepperrell Papers*, p. 415.
[56] To Corbett, Nov. 23, 1745, Library of Congress Transcripts, Public Record
Office, Admiralty 1, Admirals' Dispatches, CDLXXX.
[57] To Corbett, Jan. 18, 1746, *ibid.*

That the Louisbourg episode left a lasting impression on some colonists is attested by a statement of John Adams. Writing in later years, Adams said he had listened to the conversation of his father and his father's friends during the Louisbourg expedition and had received "very grievous impressions of the injustice and ingratitude of Great Britain towards New England in that whole transaction." [58]

Further unpleasantness developed during the war over British treatment of British and American sailors. British sailors were constantly deserting in American ports because, as Shirley said, of the way they were treated. British officers complained that they were mobbed if they tried to retake deserters, but Shirley said the mobbing had occurred because the officers had wantonly killed two British sailors in Boston, thus incensing the people of the town. [59] In addition, the British caused a riot when they attempted to impress colonial seamen into the British navy. A crowd in Boston captured some British officers and refused to release them until the impressed men had been freed. The British commander, Knowles, threatened to move up his ships and fire on the town unless his officers were returned to their ships. In the riot, a sheriff was wounded, a deputy sheriff was put in the stocks, stones were thrown through the windows of the Council chamber, and Governor Shirley sought the protection of the fortress, Castle William, when the militia refused to put down the riot. Order was restored when Knowles released the impressed seamen. [60]

The impressment incident, which brought a further statement of democracy in Boston, generated hard feelings all around and was not quickly forgotten by the colonists. First it resulted in a head-on clash between Shirley and the Boston town meeting. Shirley blamed the democratic constitution of the town and declared that the lower orders ran town affairs. [61] The town, in

[58] Adams, *Works,* IX, 611. On the importance of Louisbourg for later developments, see R. H. Haley, "Louisbourg—Prelude to Revolution," *National Historical Magazine* (Jan. 1940).
[59] Warren to Townsend, Aug. 8, 1746, Townsend to Shirley, Aug. 17, 1746, Shirley to Townsend, Sept. 12, 1746, Public Record Office, Admiralty 1, CDLXXX.
[60] Shirley, *Correspondence,* I, 406–14; Hutchinson, *History,* II, 330.
[61] Shirley, *Correspondence,* I, 418.

turn, demanded an apology from the governor for casting unfounded reflections on the town.[62] Later a Boston paper carried a reminder of the extreme hardships arising from what the writer called the insolent and abusive behavior of some military men among them, and especially for their contempt of the constitution, fortunes, and lives of the colonists. Mr. Knowles was the latest to distinguish himself this way, continued the writer, but he had been punished by the resentment of a brave and injured people.[63]

Relations between colony and mother country were little improved by Britain's decision at the end of the war to restore Louisbourg to the French in exchange for territory captured by the French in India. Immediately after the fall of Louisbourg, Governor Shirley had urged the British to keep the fortress, and his reasons were most interesting. He contended that Louisbourg under British control would serve as a restraint on the principal colonies "if ever there should come a time when they should grow restive and dispos'd to shake off their dependency upon their Mother Country. . . ." Shirley believed that such action was further off than some gentlemen in England seemed to think, but he still thought Louisbourg would be good insurance.[64] Parliament thought otherwise, however, looking on the restoration of the fortress to the French as an act strictly in the best interests of Great Britain.[65] In Massachusetts, there was much resentment over British policy, especially since the colony had expended a great deal of money and had lost many men in the expedition.[66]

At the same time that Shirley favored retention of Louisbourg by the British to insure colonial dependence, he opposed a proposal that Louisbourg be made a free port to encourage settlement there. The reason was the same—colonial dependence. The acts of trade, he said, were designed for Britain to benefit by colonial commerce. To make Louisbourg a free port would not only defeat this purpose, but would also "break the main ligament, whereby the British colonies are made dependent on their

---

[62] *Boston Gazette,* Jan. 15, 1748. [63] *Independent Advertiser,* Aug. 21, 1749.
[64] Shirley, *Correspondence,* I, 244. [65] Stock, *Debates,* V, 382.
[66] Hutchinson, *History,* III, 1; *Independent Advertiser,* April 17, May 29, and Oct. 2, 1749.

mother country." Shirley thought the granting of free trade privileges to Louisbourg would have "dangerous consequences" in the colonies, where the "spirit of illicit trade" already prevailed too much.[67] In short, Shirley saw a close connection between enforcement of the acts of trade and colonial dependence on Great Britain.

The end of the French war brought much evidence that colonial and British interests and principles were not as harmonious as might be desired.

For one thing, there was a good deal of dissatisfaction in Massachusetts with British restrictions on colonial trade. Hutchinson said that under British policy Massachusetts was not expected to increase her wealth by her trade with Great Britain. But the colony's trade with the West Indies also suffered from restrictions. By the Molasses Act of 1733, the British attempted to confine colonial trade to the British West Indies. These islands, however, could not absorb all the surplus products of the northern colonies, so the latter sought additional outlets in the French and Dutch islands. If the Molasses Act had been enforced, said Hutchinson, Massachusetts would have suffered severely.[68] The *Independent Advertiser* in Boston carried on a campaign against unprofitable commerce which created an unfavorable balance of trade and drained the colony of its gold and silver. The *Advertiser* declared that any trade which would not supply its own medium was "pernicious and detrimental" to the country.[69] The implication in the article was that trade with

[67] Shirley, *Correspondence*, I, 246.

[68] Hutchinson, *History*, II, 338–44. See Lawrence A. Harper, "The Effect of the Navigation Acts on the Thirteen Colonies" in Richard B. Morris, ed., *The Era of the American Revolution: Studies Inscribed to Evarts Boutell Greene* (New York, 1939), pp. 3–39. Harper attempted to weigh the costs of mercantilism as well as the benefits to the colonies. He concluded that mercantilism hurt the colonies in some ways but helped in others, that the aim was to benefit Britain, not the colonies, but that the colonies could have fared worse. As Harper pointed out, the extreme views on mercantilism are represented by Beer, who praised the British system, and Bancroft, who condemned it.

[69] *Independent Advertiser*, Feb. 27, 1749. The subject of smuggling has been treated by William Smith McClellan, *Smuggling in the American Colonies at the Outbreak of the Revolution* . . . (New York, 1912), who concluded that interference with colonial smuggling by the British would have entailed commercial disaster for the colonies.

Britain was pernicious and detrimental because it resulted in an unfavorable balance for the colony.

There was also much agitation in the colony to promote local manufacturing instead of importing British goods. Again the *Independent Advertiser* led the attack. It proclaimed the advantages to the colony of producing and manufacturing all the items it needed for its consumption as well as the gain to be made by exporting manufactured products. There was the proposal that the colony place heavy duties on imported luxuries and use the tax to pay bounties on local manufactures.[70] Hutchinson declared that the people generally wanted to reduce their trade with Britain and manufacture articles usually imported from the mother country.[71]

The colony did not stop with mere talk, but actually took steps to promote local manufacturing. The General Court appointed a committee to consider ways of improving the natural advantages of the colony, of imposing duties on unnecessary imports, and of encouraging settlement of foreign Protestants to increase manufactures.[72] Protestants were actually imported to carry out the proposal.[73] The General Court then attempted to tax tea, coffee, arrack, snuff, and china ware, only to have the act disallowed as a violation of instructions prohibiting colonial acts which taxed British products.[74] In addition, the General Court

[70] *Independent Advertiser,* Feb. 27, 1749. On manufacturing in general, see Victor Selden Clark, *History of Manufactures in the United States, 1607–1860* (Washington, 1916) and on wool manufacture, Arthur H. Cole, *The American Wool Manufacture,* 2 vols. (Cambridge, 1926). Arthur Cecil Bining, *British Regulation of the Colonial Iron Industry* (Philadelphia, 1933), contended that British regulations of the colonial iron industry were not dictated by an intelligent plan to build up a self-sufficient empire but resulted from a conflict of interests in England between the iron masters who made raw iron and the iron manufacturers. The Iron Act of 1750 failed either to promote the production of raw iron for British mills or to prevent the development of rolling and slitting mills in the colonies.

[71] Hutchinson, *History,* II, 343. In *Household Manufactures in the United States, 1640–1860: A Study in Industrial History* (Chicago, 1917), Rollo Milton Tryon distinguished between household manufacturing for home use and handicraft manufacturing of salable commodities. He considered household manufacturing as extremely important in colonial days and in the fighting of the Revolution.

[72] *Independent Advertiser,* July 17, 1749.

[73] *Acts and Resolves,* III, 557; Hutchinson, *History,* III, 8–9.

[74] *Acts and Resolves,* III, 495, 508–09.

agreed to lend one Isaac Potter £125 interest free if he would use the money for manufacturing pottery.[75] Later the General Court and the town of Boston both contributed funds for a building in Boston where linen manufacturing would be carried on and where people throughout the province could come to learn the linen trade.[76]

While the colony was exhibiting some restiveness under British mercantilist policies, the British were also expressing dissatisfaction with conditions in the colonies. A comparison of British manufactures sent to the colonies for the years 1721–1730 and 1739–1748 showed an increase in New England of only 3.8 per cent compared with a range of from 58 per cent in Virginia and Maryland to 215 per cent in Carolina.[77] West Indian planters also attempted to get action against illicit trade by northern colonies with the Dutch and French. One London merchant justified the actions of the northern colonies by saying that at an earlier date lumber had been £7 per 1,000 (board feet?) and rum 15d. a gallon at Antigua, but that now lumber was only £4 or £5 per 1,000 (board feet?) while the price of rum had doubled to 2s.6d. a gallon. The colonies, he said, could not afford to trade with the British islands.[78] Other traders, however, took the view in 1750 that the northern colonies, acting as though they were independent of Great Britain, were ignoring their duty to the king and their mother country and were carrying on an illicit trade with the foreign islands. If anything endangered the dependence of the northern colonies on Great Britain, they declared, it was allowing this trade to continue.[79] Sugar refiners in England attempted to prevent sugar refining

[75] *Ibid.,* p. 69.

[76] American Statistical Association, *Collections,* I, 347; *Boston Town Records,* XIV, 234–35; Mass. Arch., LIX, 381–84; *Acts and Resolves,* III, 680. Curtis P. Nettels developed the thesis of the importance of colonial manufacturing in the British mercantile system in "The Menace of Colonial Manufacturing," *New England Quarterly,* IV (April 1931), 230–69.

[77] Library of Congress Transcripts, Public Record Office, Colonial Office 5, XXXVIII, appendix 3. See also Curtis P. Nettels, "The Place of Colonial Markets in the Old Colonial System," *New England Quarterly,* VI (Sept. 1933), 491–512. Nettels differed with Beer, who believed that colonies until about 1750 were valued as sources of raw materials rather than as markets.

[78] Pickering, *Statutes,* XX, 97; Stock, *Debates,* V, 391–92.

[79] Public Record Office, Colonial Office 5, XXXVIII; Stock, *Debates,* V, 460.

in the colonies on the ground that it injured British interests. Agent Bollan said this attempt was merely an indication of a too-prevalent inclination among important men in England to restrain manufactures in the colony.[80]

In addition to dissatisfaction with British mercantilist policies, there were complaints in Boston that the British had too much political authority in the colony. Newspaper articles in 1749 stressed the excessive powers of the governor and the threat to liberty posed by corrupt officials.[81] A few weeks later a pamphleteer asked the people to consider well in the coming election. He said their ancestors had settled in Massachusetts on principles of liberty and had left England because of religious tyranny and an attempt to raise the prerogative above the laws and liberties of the people. He reminded them that under the Dominion of New England their fathers had been stripped of their rights by Governor Andros and that when they pleaded English privileges, they were told that these things did not follow them to the ends of the earth. Present circumstances were dark, this writer said, and must be surveyed with the fortitude of Englishmen, "or rather *New-England* men." The people must choose "a free, honest and independent House of Representatives" which would not permit their pockets to be turned inside out or the power of the House to be subservient to that of the governor.[82] After the election, the same writer urged the representatives to elect councilors who were not afraid to introduce truth into the presence of a governor—men who were bold friends of liberty, independency, and truth.[83] This was the election in which Thomas Hutchinson was defeated and in which he lamented that the colony was "govern'd not by weight but by numbers." [84]

[80] Mass. Arch., XXI, 86–110; Shirley, *Correspondence,* II, 11. Eleanor Lord, *Industrial Experiments in the British Colonies of North America* (Baltimore, 1896), shows how the British tried to promote industries connected with the production of naval stores. The aim was to relieve Britain from dependence on Norway, Sweden, and Russia, and at the same time to provide the colonists with the means for purchasing British manufactures.

[81] *Independent Advertiser,* Jan. 23 and March 6, 1749.

[82] "Letter to the Freeholders," *ibid.,* May 8, 1749.

[83] *Ibid.,* May 29, 1749.

[84] To Williams, May 19, 1749, Israel Williams Papers, II, 140.

One of the clearest analyses of the perpetual discord between Britain and her colonies was made by Peter Kalm, the Swedish scientist who traveled through the colonies about 1750. Kalm explained how the mercantilist system promoted British interests and how the colonists reacted to that system. In the first place, he said, the colonists were increasing so rapidly in numbers and wealth that they almost vied with Old England. To keep up the authority and trade of the mother country, he continued, the colonies were forbidden to establish manufactures which would be disadvantageous to Britain or to carry on free trade with other countries. Instead, they had to buy all sorts of English and foreign goods from England, and though they sent all their specie to pay for these goods, they never had enough specie to pay the balance. England, and especially London, profited immensely by the colonial trade, he declared, showing how well-regulated colonies contributed to the welfare of the mother country. These and other restrictions caused the inhabitants "to grow less tender for their mother country"—a coldness that was augmented by the many foreigners who settled in the colonies and who had no particular attachment to Old England.[85]

Kalm then went on to explain one of the chief causes of discord between the colonies and the mother country—the threat of colonial independence. Said he:

I have been told by Englishmen, and not only by such as were born in America but also by those who came from Europe, that the English colonies in North America, in the space of thirty or fifty years, would be able to form a state by themselves entirely independent of old England. . . . The English government has therefore sufficient reason to consider means of keeping the colonies in due submission.[86]

The Swedish scientist also saw the importance of the French in Canada as a restraint on the colonies:

It is however of great advantage to the crown of England that the North American colonies are near a country, under the government of the French, like Canada. There is reason to believe that the king never was in earnest in his attempts to expel the French from their

[85] Peter Kalm, *The America of 1750: Peter Kalm's Travels in North America*, ed. by Adolph B. Benson, 2 vols. (New York, 1937), I, 134, 138–40. Published by permission of Mrs. Rufus Rockwell Wilson.   [86] *Ibid.*, pp. 139–40.

possessions there; though it might have been done with little difficulty.

These dangerous French neighbors, Kalm concluded, were "sufficient to prevent the connection of the colonies with their mother country from being quite broken off." [87] Perhaps this explains the statement in Parliament that the return of Louisbourg to the French would, "when duly considered, appear to have been the effects of necessity, prudence, and a strict regard to the true interests of this nation." [88]

Incidents during the period before the outbreak of the French and Indian War continued to furnish evidence that all was not harmonious between the colonies and Great Britain. In Massachusetts, the House of Representatives rejected a proposal by the Lords of Trade that a revised code of laws be drawn up in the colony. The members feared some hidden design, especially against the ecclesiastical part of the constitution. Part of the plan, considered "very necessary" by the British, was a suspending clause in every law, and the people had long been opposed to suspending clauses.[89] In Britain, there was a proposal to lower duties on goods coming to the colonies from the French West Indies so that a fixed salary under British control could be paid to governors of northern colonies.[90] The project was not carried through at this time but it continued to be considered as one method of re-establishing British authority in America.

British and American principles again came into conflict when in 1754 the British proposed to extend their Mutiny Act to regulate colonial soldiers. Undoubtedly the riots and threatened mutiny during the previous war were responsible. At any rate, the colonial agent protested against the move on the ground that colonial soldiers were freeholders and men of property, not the type of men who made up the British army. If they were subjected to strict discipline, they would refuse to enlist in the king's service.[91] Members of Parliament also used the argument that American soldiers were economically independent and could

[87] *Ibid.*
[88] Stock, *Debates,* V, 382.
[89] Hutchinson, *History,* III, 10–11.
[90] Mass. Arch., XXI, 86–110.
[91] Petition of William Bollan to House of Commons, 1754, Mass. Arch., CCCIII, 275.

not be forced into service. They had to be induced to serve, and harsh punishment would hardly be an inducement.[92] The opposition showed its lack of understanding of colonial conditions first by saying that the extension of the Mutiny Act was of no importance to the colonies, then by proposing that the British could give the gentlemen and better sort in America special privileges while applying the Mutiny Act to common soldiers. One member declared there was no principle involved because the king would never think of abusing his prerogative.[93]

More controversies arose when the British attempted to secure an effective military union of the colonies by calling a colonial congress to meet at Albany for the purpose of forming a colonial union. The Albany Plan, drawn up by Benjamin Franklin, provided for a colonial administration about midway between British imperialism and colonial independence.[94] Yet neither the Americans nor the British wanted any part of the plan. One objection in the colonies was that the British would grant all military commissions and that freeholders and freeholders' sons would not enlist under British officers.[95] In Boston, the Albany Plan was called "a scheme for destroying the liberties and privileges of every British subject upon the continent." [96] The Boston town meeting instructed its representatives to prevent adoption of the plan and to oppose any other plan which endangered the liberties and privileges of the people.[97] Franklin said his plan was rejected in Britain because it gave too much power to the democratic part of the constitution, that is, to the people, and in the colonies because it gave too much power to the prerogative.[98] Shirley, on the other hand, advised the British to reject the plan because it was too much like the constitutions of Rhode Island and Connecticut, both of which considered themselves practically independent. The Albany Plan, he declared, was unfit for establishing "a general government and *imperium* over all the colonies," for the prerogative was so weakened that it did not "appear well calculated to strengthen the dependency of the

[92] *Parliamentary History*, XV, 378–82, 390–94.
[93] *Ibid.*, pp. 382–90.　　[94] Franklin, *Writings*, III, 207–26.
[95] Mass. Hist. Soc., *Collections*, 1st ser., III, 203–10.　　[96] *Ibid.*, IV, 85.
[97] *Boston Town Records*, XIV, 266.　　[98] Franklin, *Writings*, III, 226–27.

colonies upon the Crown; which seems a very important article in the consideration of this affair." [99]

If Britain and her colonies both considered the compromise Albany Plan a device for the complete benefit of the other, it is obvious that British and American principles were becoming widely separated indeed.

Additional differences between British and American principles were brought out in an exchange of ideas between Franklin and Shirley over a colonial union. Both Shirley and the Lords of Trade had plans for colonial union which would have permitted a British-dominated colonial government either to draw unlimited funds from colonial legislatures or to get funds from England by way of a tax to be raised by Parliament in the colonies.[100] John Adams said that Shirley had told Franklin in 1754 "the profound secret, the great design of taxing the colonies by an act of Parliament." [101] Franklin then defended the colonial position, that the colonists must be granted an important part in any plan of union. He declared that the colonists could not be excluded from the choice of representatives to a union government or taxed without their consent. To tax them without their consent, he said, showed a suspicion of their loyalty to the Crown and would be treating them like conquered people, not like British subjects. Then Franklin went on to show that Britain benefited by restricting colonial trade and manufacturing, in effect taxing the colonies for Britain's benefit.[102] He even proposed a parliamentary union of the colonies with Great Britain, provided the colonies were given a reasonable number of representatives and also provided all restrictive colonial legislation was first repealed. Franklin thought that such a union would "strengthen the whole, and greatly lessen the danger of future separations." [103]

By 1755, there was renewed suspicion that Parliament was

[99] Shirley, *Correspondence*, II, 111.

[100] *Documents Relative to the Colonial History of the State of New York*, ed. by E. B. O'Callaghan, 15 vols. (Albany, 1853–1887), VI, 901; Hutchinson, *History*, III, 17–18.

[101] Franklin, *Writings*, III, 232–33; Adams, *Works*, IV, 18–20.

[102] Shirley, *Correspondence*, II, 103–04; Franklin, *Writings*, III, 231–38.

[103] Franklin, *Writings*, III, 338–41.

planning to tax the colonies and to take additional measures to strengthen British imperial authority. Governor Shirley wrote the ministry that failure of colonial assemblies to defend the king's dominions showed a need for parliamentary taxation of the colonies.[104] From agent Bollan in England came word that the British intended to govern the colonies as they governed Ireland—to keep a standing army there and to curtail the legislative powers of colonial assemblies so that acts would have to be sent to England for approval even before they were passed by the colonial assemblies. Bollan warned that the times required great caution, circumspection, and secrecy, especially so that he could continue to get important information about British designs.[105] During the summer of 1755, Bollan reported that the question of whether to stop colonial trade with the foreign West Indies or to allow the trade and collect a lower duty to be used in the colonies was again being considered. He said there was strong sentiment for raising a colonial revenue.[106]

Colonial uneasiness about Britain's designs against the colonies in 1755 is apparent from articles in the *Boston Gazette*. One writer extolled the virtues of democracy by insisting that the common people had natural qualifications for making sound judgments, that honesty and common ability were sufficient talents for running government, and that the people, unlike ambitious and intriguing great men, desired only the security of their persons and property. First principles of power are in the people, said this writer, and the aim of men in power should be the good of the people. People of Asia could be ruled, but where the people were free it was madness to hope to rule them against their will. Liberty, he said, meant government executed for the good of all with the consent of all. Massachusetts' liberties were secured, for the colony had a constitution in which the people elected one branch of the legislature, had sole power over money, and had representatives who would always act for their country's interests. But, this writer asked, what if their representatives should not be allowed to meet or should be compelled by force

[104] Shirley, *Correspondence*, II, 123.
[105] Mass. Hist. Soc., *Collections*, 1st ser., IV, 129.
[106] Mass. Arch., XXI, 324–40, 498.

to betray their trust? It had happened before and could happen again, he said, but of course it would never happen under His Majesty's just and gentle reign.[107] During July and August 1755, the *Gazette* ran a series of articles on the dangers of tax collectors.

Between 1691 and 1755 there is ample evidence of "perpetual discordance" between American and British interests and principles. On the colonial side, there was the ever-present threat that the British might take away some of the political and religious liberties which the colonists claimed. The General Court guarded its prerogatives jealously, refusing to attach suspending clauses to its laws or to grant the governor a fixed salary. At the same time, there was much evidence of dissatisfaction with British mercantile regulations which were designed to benefit Britain at the expense of the colonies. On the British side, there were accusations that the colonists violated the acts of trade to the detriment of British interests and that violations of the trade acts weakened British authority. The British attempted to strengthen their administration by fruitless efforts to get suspending clauses on all laws and to get fixed salaries which would make officials independent of the colonial legislature. Particularly significant were the repeated fear of colonial independence and the proposals that Britain keep troops in the colonies and raise funds which would be used by Parliament to pay the salaries of colonial governors.

This brief sketch of "perpetual discordance" before 1755 is essential if we would understand many of the incidents which occurred during and after the French and Indian War. Policies which the British adopted after the defeat of the French were not merely the result of events during the war or the acquisition of a vast new empire which required reform of the imperial machinery. Plans such as those to establish Parliamentary taxation of the colonies in order to re-establish authority over colonial officials, to station troops in the colonies as they were in Ireland, and to insure both economic and political dependence of the colonies on Great Britain had all been thought of before the French and India War occurred. Whether the war hastened imperial reform or postponed it is a moot question, but it seems

[107] *Boston Gazette,* June 23, 1755

quite obvious that many measures adopted after the war would have been attempted had there been no war.

With this background, clashes between the British and Americans during the French and Indian War and reforms in the colonial system inaugurated by the British when the fighting was over have an understandable logic, particularly when viewed in the light of a democratic colonial society.

CHAPTER VIII

Perpetual Discordance
and War, 1755–1763

THE French and Indian War brought a temporary suspension of British plans for an army stationed in the colonies and for a colonial revenue controlled by Parliament, but the war did not in any way decrease the discord between mother country and colony. British need for colonial aid against the French precluded the inauguration of unpopular reforms in colonial government. But even the experience of fighting a common enemy was not sufficient to prevent continued clashes of interest and principle during the fighting of the war. In fact, the war merely served to emphasize, if such emphasis were needed, how far apart these two English-speaking people had grown. One might easily contend that the French and Indian War was more important for its effects on British-colonial relations than it was in determining whether Britain or France would be the dominant imperial power in America.

These British-American controversies, as we shall see, were in large part the direct outgrowth of colonial democracy, and in turn they had important implications for the future of democracy in the colony. At times the issues involved what the colonists considered the rights and privileges of a democratic assembly in opposition to the prerogative as exercised by a British general or governor. On other occasions, the problem was the treatment of colonial soldiers by British officers, a problem that a democratically elected legislature could not have ignored even if it had been so inclined. Now and again colonists were incensed by a haughty attitude which appeared to relegate a colonist to an inferior social station, or by British practices of impressing and enlisting sailors and soldiers—practices which ran counter to accepted colonial custom. Given the long period during which the colonists had guarded their rights, privileges, and customs from British encroachments, it is not surprising that they insisted on maintaining, or even enlarging, these same rights and privileges regardless of the consequences.

British-American differences began to appear in the preliminary conflicts of the French and Indian War before the war itself even became official. Following the rejection of the Albany Plan, the British in 1755 decided to conduct their own military operations in the colonies rather than to depend on a colonial military union. John Adams said that the British began to fear a colonial union and that many people believed that the colonies could defend themselves better and could even conquer Canada without the British if Britain would allow the colonies to unite.[1] Adams must have been thinking in terms of a colonial union which would exclude Great Britain, since the colonists opposed the Albany Plan as strenuously as the British did. Franklin expressed the problem even more succinctly than Adams:

The British government, not chusing to permit the union of the colonies as propos'd at Albany, and to trust that union with their defense, lest they should thereby grow too military, and feel their own strength, suspicions and jealousies at this time being entertained of them, sent over General Braddock with two regiments of regular British troops for that purpose.[2]

[1] Adams, *Works*, IX, 591. It has been popular to criticize the colonies for their failure to unite for their own defense and to say that they often acted from narrow, selfish interests rather than for the interests of the empire. But many writers forget that the issue was often "who is to control the union," and undoubtedly both sides operated from selfish motives. See Miller, *Origins of the American Revolution*, ch. ii; Adams, *Revolutionary New England*, pp. 226–27; Gipson, *The British Empire*, IV, *passim;* Beer, *British Colonial Policy, 1754–1765*, pp. 20–22.

[2] Franklin, *Writings*, I, 393. The military side of the war has been dealt with often, but seldom from the standpoint of democracy. Osgood, *The American Colonies in the Eighteenth Century*, is still one of the standard works for events before

General Braddock was hardly the man to eliminate differences between the British and the Americans, and his defeat by the French in western Pennsylvania did little to cement friendlier relations between the two people. Braddock had little understanding of American conditions or of the American people. He had to be told first by colonial governors that colonial assemblies would never set up a common fund for his use as the British demanded.[3] He seems to have had little but contempt for American troops and Indians, both those Indians who were collected to accompany his expedition and those who would oppose him. He also refused to heed colonial warnings that he would be defeated if he attempted to fight the French and Indians by accepted European methods. In addition, British troops were accused of plundering and insulting colonists in the areas through which they marched.[4] The crushing rout of Braddock's army, in which Braddock was killed, brought this analysis from Franklin: "The whole transaction gave us Americans the first suspicion that our exalted ideas of the prowess of British regulars had not been well founded."[5]

1763. See vol. IV, *passim*. Interesting accounts are those by George M. Wrong, *The Conquest of New France* . . . (New Haven, 1918), and *The Rise and Fall of New France*, 2 vols. (New York, 1928). Francis Parkman wrote the most complete account of British-French relations, and still the most interesting to read, but he did not relate the war to internal politics. See *A Half-Century of Conflict*, 2 vols. (Boston, 1892), for the period to 1748 and *Montcalm and Wolfe: France and England in North America*, 2 vols. (Boston, 1910), to the end of the war in 1763. Sir John William Fortescue, *A History of the British Army*, 13 vols. in 14 (New York, 1899–1930), II, *passim*, took a great deal of his account from Parkman but did not show much insight into internal conditions in the colonies which governed their relations with the British. Gipson, *The British Empire*, vols. VI and VII, covering in great detail the period from 1754 to 1760, is mainly concerned with military affairs from a British viewpoint. Gipson was strongly influenced in his approach to American history by George L. Beer and Charles McLean Andrews. See Gipson, *Charles McLean Andrews and the Re-orientation of the Study of American Colonial History* (Bethleham, Pa., 1935).

[3] Keppel to Cleveland, April 25, 1755, Library of Congress Transcripts, Public Record Office, Admiralty 1, CDLXXX. In "The Politics behind Braddock's Expedition," *American Historical Review*, XIII (July 1908), 742–52, Thad W. Riker attributed the Braddock expedition to personal animosities between the dukes of Cumberland and Newcastle rather than to imperial strategy.

[4] Franklin, *Writings*, I, 400–03; Shirley, *Correspondence*, II, 311; Mass. Hist. Soc., *Collections*, 1st ser., VII, 94; *Annual Register*, 1758, p. 4.

[5] Franklin, *Writings*, I, 403. Stanley M. Pargellis, in "Braddock's Defeat," *Amer-*

Braddock's defeat received full and highly unfavorable coverage in the *Boston Gazette*. The "melancholy defeat" was generally "charged upon the cowardice of the British troops," who were then compared unfavorably with New England troops. This writer said that New England led in all military matters, that New England troops alone justified confidence, and that it was to be lamented that British regulars were not used for garrison duty and that New England militia, who fought from principle and always succeeded, had not been sent to the Ohio.[6] There was also sharp criticism of British methods of training troops in European tactics when they were going to fight the French and Indians, who did not fight European style.[7] Later the *Gazette* declared that "whoever depends on a general whose friends and countrymen are in an interest diametrically opposite to theirs, will depend on a broken reed." When *New England* men took *Cape Breton* [Louisbourg], they had a *New England* general, said the *Gazette*.[8]

A second campaign in 1755, this one against Nova Scotia, raised three points of conflict between Britain and Massachusetts. Colonial soldiers, remembering their retention beyond their enlistment at Louisbourg, received certificates to insure their discharge at the end of their enlistment. On this occasion the British attempted to get the Massachusetts soldiers to enlist in British regiments by subjecting them to inconveniences not inflicted on British regulars. News of this treatment aroused the whole province, resulting in a demand by the House of Representatives that the men be discharged and sent home. Colonial soldiers would not remain even under their own officers.[9] The General Court then petitioned the king that colonial troops did not make good regular soldiers and that they grew uneasy when they reflected on their folly of placing themselves in a

---

ican *Historical Review*, XLI (Jan. 1936), 253–69, contended that Braddock failed to follow fundamental rules of war as laid down in British military manuals and therefore never gave his soldiers a fair chance to demonstrate the effectiveness of Old World military methods. In contrast, J. T. Adams said Braddock's failure was due to obstinate assemblies and dishonest colonial contractors who seemed bent on delaying and ruining the expedition (*Revolutionary New England*, p. 233).

6 *Boston Gazette*, Aug. 11, 1755.   7 *Ibid.*, Sept. 1, 1755.
8 *Ibid.*, Nov. 10, 1755.   9 Shirley, *Correspondence*, II, 464.

state of subjection when they might have remained free and independent.[10] A second difficulty arose over the relative rank of colonial and British commissioned officers. The British maintained that all British commissions ranked above any colonial commission whenever British and colonial forces were joined in an expedition, but for the sake of the king's service they finally agreed that on this particular occasion ranks should be equal.[11] A third controversy arose when Halifax merchants congratulated the British on the capture of French forts. A Boston newspaper declared that these forts were captured by New England troops under New England officers, not by regulars, and that the action of the Halifax merchants was the more to be deplored because they were said to be *"New-England men"* and should have had "greater regard to the *credit* of their native country." [12]

After the war was finally declared in 1756, British failures during its early stages continued to arouse much criticism in Massachusetts. Even though Braddock was dead, an article in the *Boston Gazette* criticized him as unqualified by training or temperament to carry through the campaign he was assigned. Shirley, who succeeded Braddock in command, was labeled a worn-out lawyer who had never seen a siege nor a battle. Webb succeeded Shirley, Abercrombie succeeded Webb, and Loudoun succeeded Abercrombie, said the *Gazette;* the general who should have come first to study the problems he would face was the last to arrive. The paper also criticized the British policy of sending cannon in one ship, cannon balls in another, and powder in a third, so that loss of any one ship would ruin an expedition.[13]

Trouble began in 1756 during a campaign against Crown Point. Massachusetts had been dissatisfied with a campaign conducted by William Johnson of New York in 1755 and had

10 *Ibid.*, p. 287.   11 Mass. Hist. Soc., *Collections,* 4th ser., IX, 214.
12 *Boston Gazette,* July 14, 1755.
13 *Ibid.*, Nov. 15, 1756. On British-colonial conflicts, see Eugene Irving McCormac, *Colonial Opposition to Imperial Authority during the French and Indian War* (Berkeley, 1911). McCormac developed the thesis that British measures which followed the war were largely the result of disputes which arose during the war. Colonial claims between 1765 and 1776 had already been stated before 1763.

finally consented to send troops for the campaign of 1756 only on condition that a Massachusetts man would command the expedition.[14] There was also the old problem of joining colonial militia and regulars, for the king had regulated rank so that regulars ranked ahead of provincials, and rank was a touchy point with New Englanders.[15] The *Boston Gazette* reported the plan by which a colonial army under John Winslow of Massachusetts would do the fighting, with regulars to follow up to garrison forts and passes and to aid the provincials if necessary. Perfect harmony existed between the two, said the *Gazette,* and doubtless the wise and prudent behavior of British officers would gain the affections of the Americans and greatly promote the common cause.[16]

Harmonious relations between regulars and provincials ceased, however, when the British decided to combine the two forces in the campaign. As Winslow later explained the controversy, General Abercrombie (who was still in command) changed plans and decided to join provincials and regulars in spite of previous plans. When Winslow so informed his officers, many of them protested, for in the union of the two forces colonial officers would lose rank and command. Privates also contended that they had enlisted under terms of serving with their own officers, and this principle was so strong, said Shirley, that it was not in the power of man to remove it.[17] Winslow also said he feared that the men would desert and that New England would refuse to raise men for future expeditions if regulars and provincials were joined.[18] Loudoun, who succeeded Abercrombie during the fracas, maintained that Winslow and other pro-

[14] Hutchinson, *History,* III, 32–34. One of the most influential books on this phase of colonial history has been Beer's *British Colonial Policy, 1754–1765.* Beer developed the general thesis that imperial defense was the rock on which the old empire shattered itself. The chief question during the war, he said, was to secure support from the colonies and to force them to subordinate local to empire interests. Beer asserted that plans for colonial union and Parliamentary taxation before 1756 were intended for a permanent military establishment in the colonies in time of peace, but that the ultimate objective was to effect the security of the colonies in time of war. Beer gave the British side and thus failed to explain why the colonists followed the policies that they did. See pp. 20–22, 30–31, 50, 58, 71.

[15] Shirley, *Correspondence,* II, 515.   [16] *Boston Gazette,* July 26, 1756.
[17] Shirley, *Correspondence,* II, 497.   [18] *Ibid.,* p. 493.

vincial officers had declared that if regulars joined them Winslow would withdraw his troops and return home.[19]

Loudoun, who was about as little qualified to win the good will of a democratic colony as any man the British could have sent, was furious about the whole affair. He said that he was sorry to find provincial troops so little inclined to obey the king's commands. In a council of war, he declared, they not only refused obedience but also they had taken it upon themselves to direct the king's troops.[20] When Shirley wrote a long letter to Loudoun explaining the whole affair, Loudoun marked passages of Shirley's letter as false, implicated Massachusetts officers as the ringleaders, and then sent the letter on to England.[21]

Loudoun's relations with civil authorities in Massachusetts were no more successful than his relations with provincial troops and officers. Apparently he ordered Shirley to conscript soldiers for him in Massachusetts, for Shirley had to inform him that a governor could not conscript men for service outside the colony without the consent of the assembly.[22] Then there was trouble over quartering troops. Loudoun planned to send a regiment to Boston to be quartered over the winter. Governor Thomas Pownall, who succeeded Shirley, asked the assembly to provide quarters, saying that otherwise the soldiers would provide for themselves. The House provided quarters on two islands in Boston harbor but denied that anyone had the right to demand that the province quarter soldiers.[23]

---

[19] *Ibid.*, p. 492.   [20] *Ibid.*, p. 495.

[21] *Ibid.*, p. 501. One of the best accounts of the French and Indian War is that by Stanley M. Pargellis, *Lord Loudoun in America* (New Haven, 1933). Pargellis was concerned not merely with Loudoun's military career but also with his relations to civil governments in the colonies. Pargellis also attempted to show *why* things happened as well as *what* happened, for example, that the colonists objected, not to assuming a share of the cost of war, but to assuming it under the conditions imposed by Great Britain. Although he was more charitable toward Loudoun than the colonists were, the author well understood the issues involved in the conflicts between Loudoun and the colonists. See especially pp. 27–28, 42, 84, 89, 91, 101, 104–31, 167–86, 187–210. Pargellis' account is in contrast with Beer's, which gives mainly the British side. See footnote 14 above.

[22] Shirley, *Correspondence*, II, 526.

[23] *Acts and Resolves*, IV, 112. Two sympathetic studies on Pownall are William Otis Sawtelle, "Thomas Pownall, Colonial Governor," in Mass. Hist. Soc., *Proceedings*, LXIII, 233–87, who believed that Pownall understood Americans better

The quartering question also raised the highly controversial issue of Crown rights versus assembly rights. In getting the quartering act passed, Pownall said that as usual he had been forced to waive a very essential right of the Crown by allowing the vote to pass in the form it did. But he considered getting the act passed more important than arguing unsuccessfully about regaining Crown rights which his predecessor had given up for so many years. Pownall recognized the influence of democracy when he told Loudoun that it would help if Loudoun would send an officer with orders to require quarters from town magistrates. The people of the towns would then petition the General Court and the Court, "acting upon a petition coming from the people would go into measures that they never could be induced to come into from a governor's recommendations[.] [I]n the one case they act to relieve the people and in the other they would look upon it as giving up a point to the governor." [24]

A heated controversy over quartering developed between Loudoun and the General Court when, on Pownall's advice, Loudoun sent recruiting officers to Boston. To be effective in recruiting, they had to be stationed in Boston rather than on the islands where quarters had been provided. Pownall told them to request quarters from Boston magistrates, but the magistrates refused the request. When the governor asked advice of the speaker of the House, the Boston representatives, and the Council, he was told by all that soldiers could not be quartered on the people except by law, that there was no law, and that any magistrate who quartered troops would be sued. Pownall told Loudoun that the people were mistaken on this point, but he assured the general that they had the king's service at heart.[25]

---

than any other Englishman did; and John A. Schutz, *Thomas Pownall, British Defender of American Liberty* . . . (Glendale, Calif., 1951), who called Pownall a constructive imperialist whose views were not appreciated in England. Schutz did not deal especially with democracy in Massachusetts, but occasionally he indicated indirectly an understanding of the democratic society that existed. Pownall was a mercantilist who differed from other mercantilists in his belief that the colonists as well as the British had rights. See pp. 166, 188–92, 199.

[24] Pownall to Loudoun, Sept. 2, 1757, Library of Congress Transcripts, Public Record Office, War Office 34, Amherst Papers, XXV, 1. Hereafter cited Amherst Papers.

[25] *Ibid.,* p. 85.

Loudoun, on the other hand, contended that the British Quartering Act extended to America, making a colonial act unnecessary, and he threatened to use force if the colony persisted in its views. Said he:

And as nothing more is wanted to set things right, but the magistrate or justice doing their duty, for no act of the assembly is necessary or wanted for it, I have ordered my messenger to remain but forty eight hours in Boston, and if on his return I find things not settled I will instantly order into Boston the three battalions from New York, Long Island, and Connecticut, and if more are wanted, I have two in the Jerseys at hand besides those in Pennsylvania.

Loudoun also informed Pownall that he had kept troops beyond their enlistment period—always a sore spot in British-colonial relations—but would leave it to Pownall to fix this affair with the assembly.[26]

When the General Court did pass a quartering act, however, Loudoun was even more unhappy than before. The issue now changed from quartering to the question of whether or not the assembly had the right to pass a quartering act. Loudoun considered the colonial contention that a colonial law was necessary for quartering troops as a dangerous doctrine that had to be quelled.[27] He believed that the act passed by the General Court made it necessary to settle the point of right once and for all; the assembly, he declared, had no concern with the king's right to quarter troops, for this matter was settled by an act of Parliament. Peacetime rules, he said, must give way to rules, necessities, and customs of war.[28] This was a position that was sure to arouse a democratic assembly which had long held the civil above the military.

Loudoun countermanded his orders for troops to march on Massachusetts after the General Court provided quarters, but he closed the incident with another threat: "As to the dispute the gentlemen seem willing to enter into of the necessity of a Provincial Law to enforce a British Act of Parliament, I shall not enter into it at all, as the Administration is wise and powerful and will take their own methods of settling affairs of that na-

---

26 *Ibid.,* XXVII, pt. 1, 59–67.   27 *Ibid.,* p. 69.
28 *Ibid.,* p. 83.

ture." [29] These were the methods which culminated in the disintegration of the old empire.

The democratic House of Representatives had the last word, however, as it stuck by its guns in its contention that a colonial act was necessary before troops could be quartered. The assembly insisted that the British act did not apply to the colonies and that the colonies had always acknowledged all British acts which did include the colonies. At the same time, it denied Loudoun's accusations that Massachusetts was attempting to become independent. Declaring that the colonists "never had a desire or thought of lessening" their dependence on Parliament, the assembly "utterly disavowed" the principles Loudoun accused them of holding.[30] The House declared that the charter granted them the rights of Englishmen and the powers of civil government, that they would resist an invading enemy to the last breath in defense of their rights, and that any threat to these rights from any other source tended to deject and dispirit them.[31]

So both Loudoun and the assembly closed the incident with veiled threats: the one that Parliament would eventually deal with colonial claims of rights and powers, the other that it would resist any encroachments on these same rights and powers. Both threats proved only too true.

No sooner had the difficulty between Loudoun and the assembly been settled than Governor Pownall encountered trouble with the House over a question of the king's prerogatives. In providing for defense of the frontiers, the House restricted the use of troops to certain posts. Pownall considered this a usurpation of the governor's powers, but the House refused to vote any defenses unless the governor agreed to their stipulations. Because of the circumstances, Pownall signed, but he protested the violation of Crown rights to England. There the Lords of Trade declared that the dependence which the colony should have on the mother country stood on a "very precarious foot" and that unless some effective remedy was applied it was "in great danger of being totally set aside." The Lords said that the

29 *Ibid.*, p. 87.   30 *Ibid.*, pp. 85–87.
31 *Acts and Resolves,* IV, 113–16.

House, by votes and resolves, controlled almost every legislative and executive power but that they doubted that the time was propitious for changing practices of long standing.[32] Hutchinson was obviously wrong when he said that "no notice was taken of this in England, where there was no disposition to contend with the colonies, nor any apprehension of serious consequences from the advances made by the people upon the prerogative." [33]

Perhaps this incident was responsible for the searching analysis of colonial government and of colonial relations to Great Britain which Pownall wrote in 1757. As lieutenant governor of New Jersey, Crown agent to the Albany Congress, and governor of Massachusetts, Pownall had had some opportunity to become acquainted with the colonies. His analysis and suggestions certainly deserved more attention than they apparently received.

It had often been remarked, wrote the governor, that Britain should take care in the administration of her colonies lest in some future day the colonies should become independent of the mother country. Everyone acknowledged that caution was necessary, yet they supposed colonial independence was a remote event and therefore did nothing about it. If at any time the colonies, either through disinclination or disaffection, should decide to oppose the king's commands and act under their own governor, they would do so as independent states, and it would be high time to inquire how the colonies had arrived at this state of independence. Pownall then declared that the colonies were not thinking of revolt, but that perhaps they had formed practices unknown to and unsuspected by the mother country. In the future, the colonies might take advantage of British weaknesses at home or involvement in Europe to engage in independent action. Under these circumstances, said the governor, "perhaps it may be thought now high time, and perhaps the only that will ever offer, to apply some remedy, while the Government of Great Britain has a power in these countries, to carry it into execution." [34]

[32] *Ibid.*, pp. 95–96.　　　　　　　　[33] Hutchinson, *History*, III, 48.

[34] Thomas Pownall, "The State of the Government of Massachusetts-Bay as It Stood in the Year 1757," Library of Congress, Massachusetts Miscellaneous MSS., 1757.

Pownall then went on to enumerate the colonial practices which in effect made Massachusetts independent of British authority—practices which, with little change, he said, applied to most of the colonies. The colonists had "a settled point" that no commands from the Crown or other British agencies were binding unless the colonists acquiesced in them. Instead of passing acts which were subject to veto in England, they conducted most of their business by votes and orders which did not have to be sent to England or, if they were sent, would have taken effect before the British could veto them. They rejected any effort to get suspending clauses attached to acts. Money was generally disbursed by the General Court, not the governor and Council, and the treasurer gave bonds, not to the Crown, but to the three eldest councilors. The acts of trade and navigation, designed to secure the dependence of the colonies on the mother country, were seldom obeyed, and it was almost impossible to convict anyone who violated them. The governor was dominated in his actions by the Council, which was "little other than an annually elected committee of the General Court." The General Court, rather than Crown courts, acted as a court of equity, and it transacted its business by orders rather than acts. Even the direction of military affairs, reserved in the charter to the governor, had been usurped by the General Court, so all that was left to the governor was to sign his name. Thus, said Pownall, were the colonies actually becoming independent of British authority.[35]

Early in 1758, another incident occurred in Boston to mar relations between Britain and the colony. The issue was British methods of enlisting colonial soldiers. Pownall said that he wished enlistment officers would avoid imprudences that hurt the service. "To see a drunken man lugged through the streets on a soldier's back guarded by others . . . must certainly give a strange impression of the method of enlisting & certainly have an ill effect on an inflamed mob," he declared.[36] The *Boston Gazette* also protested against British methods of recruiting drunk men. New England men were instructed from the cradle

35 *Ibid.*
36 Pownall to Loudoun, Feb. 6, 1758, Amherst Papers, XXV, pt. II.

that the law protected them, said the *Gazette*, as it "warmly" upheld the dignity of the civil law.[37]

By early 1758, there was a good deal of dissatisfaction in the colony not only over enlistment methods but also with the general conduct of the war. The *Boston Gazette* printed a letter to the effect that the colonies were successful when they did most of the fighting but that as soon as British forces arrived under British generals "things took a different turn" and got progressively worse.[38] John Adams also expressed the idea of general dissatisfaction with the conduct of the war. As early as 1755, he voiced the opinion that eventually the center of the empire would shift to America, for ample resources and a rapidly growing population would make the colonists more numerous than the English and then not even all Europe could subdue them. The only way to keep the colonies from setting up for themselves, he declared, was to divide and rule them.[39]

Adams later expressed sharp criticism of the British and their conduct of the war. He said he had long heard stories in this country praising colonial soldiers and condemning British policies. Loudoun's "ridiculous" conduct made him wish that Britain would leave the colonies to defend themselves. He was not alone, he said, in wishing that the colonies were unshackled from the British, for he believed they could do better without than with the aid of the mother country. In the course of the war, he said, "I heard such relations from our provincial officers of the treatment they received from the regulars as made my blood boil in my veins. . . . As early as this, I thought seriously of American independence; and if the conduct of Britain was not altered, I thought I should wish for it." [40]

With the return of Louisbourg to the French in 1748 still fresh in mind, Israel Williams of Hatfield, who later became a Tory, expressed the fear that even successful operations against the French would not bring permanent benefits to the colonies. Louisbourg was taken again in July 1758, but there was some doubt in his mind as to whether the fortress would be retained.

---

37 *Boston Gazette*, March 6, 1758.   38 *Ibid.*, April 2, 1758.
39 Adams, *Works*, I, 23–24.
40 *Ibid.*, IX, 592, 612; Mass. Hist. Soc., *Collections*, 5th ser., IV, 338.

Williams wrote to Hutchinson that he hoped the conquered territory would be kept to insure universal peace, as bloody wars for the past hundred years, he said, had been due to French occupation of Canada. Wars would be protracted if the French were left there, pessimistically concluded Williams, "which I expect will be the case, notwithstanding all our acquisitions elsewhere, and with a political view to keep us dependent." [41]

So once again there was expressed the belief that the presence of the French in Canada was closely associated with colonial dependence in the eyes of British policy-makers.

With Pitt, Wolf, and Amherst in command, the fortunes of war improved markedly in 1759 and 1760, but controversies continued to plague the associations of British and provincials. The British did make an important concession in preparation for a concerted effort against Canada. To get co-operation between regulars and colonials and to entice the best gentlemen and freeholders into the service, the king finally ordered that British and American officers were to have equal rank, except that within each rank, British officers were to be considered senior officers. [42] Governor Pownall seems to have had premonitions that all might not be well during the Canada campaign. He warned Amherst about the American practice of short enlistments and discharge of soldiers at the end of their service. During the Shirley period, he said, there had been "a most violent flame in the country" when troops had been retained at Louisbourg beyond their enlistment period. Pownall feared a similar incident and warned Amherst to guard against it. [43]

For one thing there was the difficulty of raising troops. In 1758, the colony had furnished 7,000 men, but apparently the conduct of the campaigns of that year made the General Court reluctant to provide soldiers in 1759. [44] In April, the Court agreed

---

[41] Israel Williams Papers, II, 145.   [42] Amherst Papers, XXV, pt. III, 451.

[43] *Ibid.,* p. 567. Two favorable biographies of Amherst are Lawrence Shaw Mayo, *Jeffery Amherst: A Biography* (New York, 1916), and John Cuthbert Long, *Lord Jeffery Amherst, a Soldier of the King* (New York, 1933). Both writers accepted the estimate of Fortescue, *History of the British Army,* that Amherst was the greatest English general between Marlborough and Wellington, although the evidence which they used does not always substantiate this claim.

[44] Hutchinson, *History,* III, 50.

to raise only 1,500 and to pay a £10 bounty for each enlistment. Pownall objected on the ground that an £18 bounty had previously been paid and that all who would enlist had already done so.[45] Later Pownall proposed a solution for getting troops each spring—pay them during the winter so that they would be ready to return to service when the spring campaign began. The drawback to this, however, was that the assemblies had raised troops and supplies at the requisition of the Crown only and under promises of being compensated by the British.[46] Presumably the British government would object to the expense of paying troops while they were at home during the winter.

In spite of Pownall's warning against retention of troops beyond their enlistment period, Amherst invited serious controversies by keeping troops in Nova Scotia over the winter of 1759–1760. One colonial soldier graphically portrayed the reactions of the provincials to this act in his journal: "Although we be Englishmen born yet we are debarred Englishmens liberty, therefore we now see what it is to be under martial law and to be with the regulars who are but little better than slaves to their officers; and when I get out of their [power] I shall take care how I get in again." On November 1, the men all "stood to it" that they would not serve any longer and were sent to the guardhouse. The next day the regiment was turned out to hear its doom for refusing to do duty and for sending a "round robin" letter to the colonel demanding that the men be sent home according to the terms of their enlistment.[47] Further trouble was averted temporarily when the General Court extended the enlistment period six months and paid a £4 bounty for each man kept beyond the promised time of discharge.[48] What would have happened if officers had carried out their threat to shoot mutinous soldiers is difficult to say.[49]

Nothing that the British could do, however, sufficed to keep the disgruntled soldiers in Nova Scotia when spring came and they were able to depart. The commanding officer wrote that

[45] Amherst Papers, XXV, pt. III, 469.   [46] *Ibid.*, p. 597.

[47] "Extracts from Gibson Clough's Journal," Essex Institute, *Historical Collections*, III, 99–105.

[48] Amherst Papers, XXVI, pt. I, 13–16, 57–59.

[49] *Ibid.*, XXV, pt. III, 647–49.

the soldiers had informed him of their unanimous decision to leave the fort on May 1 and that not a single man among them would re-enlist for the coming campaign.[50] The General Court also refused to extend the enlistment period of the men, pointing out that further retention would endanger later attempts to raise soldiers.[51] The men did not even wait to be relieved by reinforcements which were to be sent. Some seventy or eighty of them commandeered a ship which had arrived in the harbor and departed on it for Massachusetts. The remainder threatened to follow their example at the first opportunity.[52] Wrote one officer in despair: "Not one soldier in the garrison will stay on any acct whatsoever, but will force any vessel that may arrive here to carry them off." [53] Some of the men even threatened to leave by land if they could not get ships.[54] The General Court resolved to raise 500 men to replace those in Nova Scotia, but it also requested Amherst to discharge all men who would not re-enlist.[55] Amherst, accustomed to the discipline of the British army, could hardly believe that soldiers would do what the Massachusetts militia had done. He expressed the hope that they would receive punishment commensurate with their offense,[56] but of course under the democratic militia regulations of Massachusetts they received no punishment whatever.

The conquest of Canada in 1760 by British and American troops brought an end to major military operations, but this did not mean a cessation of hostilities between the British and the colonists. British policies during the war, especially their treatment of American soldiers, had generated a good deal of resentment in Massachusetts. Two incidents will suffice to show American opinion.

First, the Massachusetts assembly was extremely reluctant to raise the requested number of troops for General Amherst in his campaign to drive the remaining French out of the Ohio valley. Opposition in the assembly was due both to the destination of the troops and the fear that they would be kept beyond their

50 *Ibid.*, XXVI, pt. I, 39, 41.
52 *Ibid.*, pp. 95–96.
54 *Ibid.*, XXVII, pt. II, 393.
56 *Ibid.*, XXVII, pt. II, 393–95.

51 *Ibid.*, pp. 57–59.
53 *Ibid.*, p. 97.
55 *Ibid.*, XXVI, pt. I, 65.

enlistment time. To satisfy the assembly, Governor Francis Bernard, who had replaced Pownall, had to promise that the men would be used for defense only, that they would not be sent beyond the Delaware River, that they would be paid a £6.15.0 bounty, and that they would be discharged on July 1, 1762, as the assembly proposed.[57]

Under the circumstances, Bernard thought he had done well to get the assembly to vote troops, but Amherst was highly displeased with Massachusetts' actions. The colony had agreed to furnish only 3,000 men instead of the general's requisition for 4,000. Amherst believed that the assembly was motivated purely by a spirit of opposition, for he apparently did not believe that British actions had been just cause for colonial complaint. He called the assembly's reasons "frivolous pretenses," and he regretted that Bernard had been "obliged in order to quiet those restless spirits, to give them assurances to which they were not entitled." Amherst then complained that being tied down by conditions as to where troops could be used and how long they would serve made his command very difficult and might cause a failure to comply with the king's instructions.[58] Bernard insisted, however, that he had done as well as he could and that if he had not given the promises he did he could not have raised the men.[59] The British commander simply never understood the philosophy of a democratic colonial assembly.

Nothing untoward appears to have occurred during this 1761–1762 year's enlistment, but at the end, Bernard offered a bounty of £10.15.0 for provincial soldiers who would join the British regular army after their enlistment expired July 1, 1762.[60]

A final controversy over treatment of colonial soldiers came in 1763. Provincial troops had been enlisted to serve at Halifax until May 1, 1763. When May 1 came, they asked to be dismissed, but were refused. The men, in turn, refused to do duty. As a result, the officer in command stopped the issuance of all provisions for both colonial officers and men, and since he would not let the men go home, they were forced to buy their

[57] *Ibid.*, XXVI, pt. I, 179–83.
[59] *Ibid.*, XXVI, pt. I, 185.
[58] *Ibid.*, XXVII, pt. II, 429.
[60] *Ibid.*, pt. II, 335.

own provisions. As it turned out, Amherst had ordered an extension of the provincials' service without consulting the General Court.[61] This was a violation of the colonial charter, since
troops could not be forced to serve outside the province without the consent of the General Court, but Amherst merely
praised the actions of the officer at Halifax and called the actions of the troops "very irregular." [62] The General Court saw
things differently, however. It passed a resolve to the effect that
soldiers had been kept at Halifax beyond the date of their enlistment by an officer of the regular army; then it passed another
resolve for Bernard to write to Amherst demanding that the
men be released.[63]

The results of the French and Indian War and its relation to
democracy in Massachusetts will be discussed at a later time.
Suffice to say here that the war merely accentuated the "perpetual discordance" between mother country and colony which
had existed before the fighting started. The two people, Americans and British, simply had differences of interest and principle too fundamental to permit amicable relations. Perhaps
the most charitable thing one can say about the interests involved was that both sides were looking out for themselves as
one might expect them to do. The conflict of principles, which,
of course, also involved interests, chiefly concerned the inevitable clashes between a democratic society and a democratic way
of life in opposition to an aristocratic philosophy as exemplified
by British governors, generals, and officers. British officials were
unwilling to concede either the independent position in the
empire which the Massachusetts assembly so stubbornly claimed
or the rights to which it adhered. Accustomed as British officers
were to class differences in the British army, they could not conceive of granting the democratic demands of colonial soldiers.
So strong is custom in the shaping of human affairs that the
British might well have found their task much easier had American society been as aristocratic as we have been accustomed to
consider it.

[61] *Ibid.*, p. 475.   [62] *Ibid.*, XXVII, pt. II, 581.
[63] *Ibid.*, XXVI, pt. II, 487–89.

[CHAPTER IX]

Democracy and Imperial Rule, 1760–1763

THE French and Indian War had interrupted British plans for reform in the colonial system, but neither the need nor the desire had been abated as far as British officials were concerned. In all probability, the war had forced a postponement of suggestions that an army be kept in the colonies and that the colonies be taxed to support this army, as was done in Ireland. Experiences in connection with the conduct of the war merely reinforced previous opinions that some changes needed to be made. But as long as the fighting continued, nothing drastic could be done, for as governors often pointed out, the colonists could and would withhold necessary military aid if the occasion demanded.

The years between the fall of Montreal in 1760 and the Treaty of Paris in 1763 were not merely years in which British colonial officials marked time. Many things could be, and were, done during this time, and although they were not sufficiently novel or startling enough in scope to elicit violent colonial reaction, they caused considerable uneasiness in Massachusetts and forecasted more drastic reforms to follow. During these years, Britain's imperial problem, possible solution for that problem, and what reaction could be expected from the colonists were all made abundantly clear. In all this, colonial democracy played the lead role, not as a condition to be achieved but as an element already far too much in evidence from a British point of view.

One of the best statements of the situation which faced the British when the fighting ended in 1760 was made by the British customs official Comptroller Weare. Weare not only told the British what their problems were, but he also suggested what Britain should do to resolve them. This account is worth a lengthy summary, for it shows the influence of economic democracy on political democracy and especially the significance of the latter on Britain's failure to enforce her mercantile system.

Weare first pointed out the importance of the colonies to Britain's future commercial greatness. Commerce, he said, was the source of British power, and it had been to increase commerce that colonies had been established. These colonies, established under adverse circumstances by private adventurers, had increased tremendously to their present size. Rivals to British commercial power had arisen, however, and these rivals were rapidly restricting British commerce to her colonial possessions. To preserve the commercial lead she had hitherto enjoyed, Britain must take measures, "and that very speedily," for British commerce depended for its support and extension on *"securing the dependency and improving the advantages"* of the American colonies.

But these colonies, so important to Britain's future, were growing at a rate dangerous to British interests, Weare continued. First there was the natural increase brought about by economic opportunity. The means of life were so easily attainable that no one avoided marriage because of the expense of a family. As a result, the present stock in the colonies would produce a population exceeding that of Great Britain in less than a century. Add to this the people from Europe who were attracted to America by economic opportunity, and the time required for the colonial population to pass that of the mother country would be cut to less than half a century.

There was little doubt in Weare's mind that Europeans would eventually be attracted to America in great numbers, where they could enjoy advantages of democracy never dreamed of in the old countries. The lower classes would learn that the climate of America was temperate and healthful, that the soil produced necessities of life in great abundance, and that an easy living or even wealth could be gained there by industry and economy. They would also learn "that under the forms of a democratical government, all mortifying distinctions of rank [were] lost in common equality; and that the ways to wealth and perferment [*sic*] [were] alike open to all men." When the "useless" classes of Europe discovered these facts, Weare prophesied, they would abandon their "necessitous and servile condition" in Europe for one of "property and independency" in America.

With ample resources at hand, Weare continued, what was to keep these colonists from thinking of independence once their population surpassed that of the mother country? Said he:

An event so fatal to the British empire, might the less be apprehended, did a single instance remain of any colony, that ever continued in subjection, after it could assert its liberty, or could the desire of independency be thought irradicable from the human heart; or that a thousand leagues distance from the eye and strength of government should never suggest *to a people accustomed to more than British liberty,* a thought of setting up for themselves. . . .

Economically, the customs officer said, the colonies were already moving in the direction of independence from the mother country. They were extremely offended whenever their dependence on Britain was questioned, yet they endeavored by all possible means to establish manufactures among themselves and they sent their money to foreign countries to buy the things they needed. The colonies would remain a market for British goods only if Britain stopped both smuggling and the development of competing colonial manufactures. Instead of trying to enlarge her holdings in America, Britain should improve what she already had and "consider in time how most effectively to secure the future *dependency"* of the colonies on the mother country.

One of the chief hindrances to colonial dependence on Great Britain, according to Weare, was the presence of democracy in the colonies. Given the fact that the colonies were violating the mercantile system, he said, it was surprising that they had been suffered to remain to this day under these little factions, *democracies,* which had their first rise in the republican ideas of licentious times; instead of introducing such political systems and establishments, as might, agreeable to the genius of the British constitution, have formed them upon rational principles of subordination, as well as liberty, and have prepared a people so remote for that just submission to the crown, which can admit of no departure from it, without weakening in every instance, the very foundation of their dependency.

In Massachusetts, the House of Representatives chose the Council, making the latter "a very insignificant part of the legislature." But even in the royal colonies, where the king appointed both governor and council, "the authority of the crown [was] not sufficiently supported against the licentiousness of a republican spirit in the people," who were extremely jealous of any power not immediately derived from themselves.

The chief method by which these colonial democracies circumvented British authority was through control of the salaries of colonial officials, Weare continued. The colonists considered Britain as a friend and ally, rather than as the country to which they belonged and should be subordinated. They elected artful and factious representatives who met as so many tribunes, with opposition to the government their chief motive. These representatives fully realized the advantage of having the governor dependent on them for his salary, and when conflicts arose, the governor was forced to reject or modify the king's instructions for the sake of his salary. All this prejudiced the king's authority, overturned all ideas of good government in the minds of the people, for the representatives purposely adapted their measures to please popular prejudices and sapped the very foundation of that dominion over the colonies to which Great Britain had so unquestionable a right.

Weare believed that immediate reform in the colonial system was imperative and that this reform should be carried through while Britain still had an army in the colonies. If his analysis of the colonies was correct, he declared, much remained to be done before they were sufficiently digested into the state of subordination and improvement which their interests as well as those of the mother country required. Then Weare followed with this revealing statement, which he underlined for emphasis:

For which happy purpose never could a more favourable opportunity, than the present have offered, and if an effectual reformative be not introduced before those troops are withdrawn which could have been thrown in upon no less occasion without giving a general alarm, one may venture to pronounce it impossible afterwards, and also to add, that the northern colonies ripened by a few, a very few more years to maturity, must, agreeable to nature's ordinary laws, drop off from that stock whence they originally sprung; which policy may long retard, though perhaps not finally prevent.

Weare obviously did not subscribe to the view held by many historians that British troops were necessary for colonial defense after the war ended.

Above all else, Weare advocated a check on colonial democracy as one of the most fundamental of all reforms. He said that he would not enter on vain speculation about the natural rights of mankind, which the most ignorant colonial assumed to understand and was extremely tenacious of, but which was contrary to the very idea of government. To Weare, nothing seemed clearer than the fact that the rights and liberties of the American people ought to be adapted to the genius of that government to which they belonged. Colonies were not planted to found new empires but to promote trade, and those who had the expense of founding and protecting them should give law to them. Their interests must give way to the general good, "the *salus imperii.*" American charters were necessary expedients at first, but they had answered their ends and had *"now become nuisances pregnant with mischief.* But into whatever new systems those people shall be formed," he continued, "it will be necessary to check licentiousness of a democracy, by reducing the present exorbitant power of assemblies."

Weare declared that Britain should never again think of uniting the colonies into one government or forming confederacies among them. While they remained divided, their jealousies and antagonisms would serve as a great security against any attempts at independence. But even so, the time would most certainly come when even these colonial antagonisms would cease to serve that purpose.

What specific proposals did Weare offer to cut down colonial democracy, to insure that the colonies would not eventually seek their independence, and to fit the colonies more securely into the British mercantile system?

To eliminate as many colonial democratic institutions as possible, Weare advocated reforms that would transfer much power of government from the colonies to the king. The king should pay the salaries of all governors and should appoint his own council or upper house of the legislature in each colony. Only counties and trading towns should choose representatives, with elections not to be held more often than once in three years. Chief justices and attorney generals should be sent from England, then orders from the king would not be treated with insolence and disrespect. At the same time, said Weare, Britain must govern her colonies justly. The colonies all favored officials and laws of their own, so that British authority would depend on the wisdom of British policies and the caliber of British officials sent to the colonies. A people as far away as America might well revolt if they saw public officials using their power for private gain.

To keep the colonies dependent on England, the customs official warned that Britain should avoid any policy which tended to lessen colonial need for the protection of the mother country. Men always sought independence as soon as they were able to take care of themselves. In particular, Britain should give Canada back to the French in order to keep the French threat as an influence on the colonies. The colonies were urging Britain to keep Canada as a means of preventing future wars, of increasing consumption of British manufactures, and of perpetuating the dependence of the colonies on the mother country. But Britain should not heed these colonial arguments. A people who doubled their population every sixteen years already had too much territory in which to grow, and Weare said he feared this growth. If from their remoteness and long inattention by the mother country the colonies gave proof of an untractable temper and spirit, they would not become more tractable if Britain enlarged their boundaries and removed the French threat. In short, the best way to keep the colonies dependent was to keep them in need of British protection.

Finally, Weare advocated reforms which would insure that the colonies fulfill their intended purpose under the British mercantile system. The fact that Americans used such small amounts of British goods, yet lived much better than similar classes in England, was ample proof that the colonies smuggled or manufactured their own products. They did both, and both must be stopped, for the colonies were worthless to Britain unless she directed their work and prevented smuggling. Smuggling, which was the worst fault and needed immediate attention, was made possible by the long seacoast, laxity of officials, inclination of the people for it, disregard of the acts of Parliament, jealousy of English officials, insufficiency of existing trade acts, and licentiousness of charter governments. All demanded a speedy remedy. This involved reforms in the customs service, constant inspection of colonial conduct, and removal of Crown servants from the mercy of colonial assemblies.

Weare believed that the British should repeal such inequitable acts as the Sugar Act, meaning, of course, the Molasses Act of 1733. He said there was not a man in America that did not consider the Sugar Act as a sacrifice made by the northern colonies to West Indian planters in Parliament. This imperious preference for one colony over others did little to improve the affections of the northern colonists for the mother country.

And finally, the customs official urged the British to take advantage of the present opportunity which favored a thorough reform in the colonial system. No difficulty should be an obstacle, for the colonies were infinitely important to the commerce and the future of the British Empire. No man could perform a more patriotic service than directing the labor of the colonies into the right channels, preventing smuggling, and establishing, as far as possible, "the perpetual subordination and dependency of those very remote and growing provinces, on the British Empire." [1]

[1] Comptroller Weare, "Observations on the British Colonies on the Continent of America," in Mass. Hist. Soc., *Collections,* 1st ser., I, 67–82.

Weare was not the only one who understood the significance of the French and Indian War. Another imperialist, Thomas Hutchinson, also saw the implications of the conquest of Canada to the future of British power in the colonies. He said that men had speculated on an American empire at some future date, but that the presence of the French had been a restraint. After the defeat of France, however, "a new scene opened." Expansion was rapid, population increased tremendously, and it was evident that the colonies would soon be larger than the parent state. These considerations did not bring immediate desires or plans for independence, he said, but they did produce a greater sense of the importance of the colonies. Men questioned the advantages enjoyed by Englishmen over colonists and they inquired more carefully into the relations between mother country and colony. Arguments favoring removal of distinctions were well received, and men were prepared to think more favorably of independence.[2]

In Massachusetts, when the fighting ended, there was some apprehension that the British planned some drastic changes in the Massachusetts government. John Adams said that after the fall of Montreal "rumors were everywhere spread, that the English would now new-model the colonies, demolish the charters, and reduce all to royal governments." One morning, Adams met his friend Jonathan Sewall, who had also heard the rumors. Said Sewall: "These Englishmen are going to play the devil with us. They will overturn everything. We must resist them and that by force."[3] Adams said that the colonies were too important in the conduct of the war for the British to make any open attempts against their liberties while the war was in progress.[4] In Boston there were more rumors that an attempt would be made to overthrow the town meeting because it was "popular and mobish."[5] Warnings to the people to vote more than doubled the number of votes cast in 1760 over those cast in 1759.[6]

2 Hutchinson, *History*, III, 62.   3 Adams, *Works*, IV, 6.
4 *Ibid.*, p. 21.
5 *Boston Gazette Supplement*, May 5, 1760; *Boston Gazette*, May 12, 1760.
6 *Boston Town Records*, XVI, 23, 40.

Perhaps this colonial apprehension of British intentions accounts for a controversy which took place between Bernard and the assembly. In a speech to the General Court following the conquest of Canada, Bernard reminded the colonists of "the blessings they received from their *subjection* to Great Britain," without which they could not have been a free people. In answering Bernard, the Council urged Britain to retain Canada in order to keep the colonies tranquil, for the greatness of Great Britain would depend on the tranquility of the colonies. The Council also substituted a word for subjection: "To our *relation* to Great Britain we owe our present freedom." [7]

The House of Representatives, however, refused to allow Bernard's implication of subjection to pass unchallenged. The assembly said it was

sensible of the blessings derived to the British colonies from their subjection to Great Britain; and the whole world must be sensible of the blessings derived to Great Britain from the loyalty of the colonies in general, and from the efforts of this province in particular; which, for more than a century past, had been wading in blood, and laden with the expenses of repelling the common enemy; without which efforts, Great Britain, at this day, might have had no colonies to defend.

Hutchinson said that Bernard could only have meant the same subjection owed to the supreme legislative authority by the people in England, but that some people in the colony used the occasion to alienate colonial subjects from those of Great Britain.[8]

That reform in the colonial system was to be in the making after the war was over there can be little doubt. While the fighting was still in progress, Governor Bernard spoke of the ap-

[7] Hutchinson, *History*, III, 60–61; Amherst Papers, XXVI, pt. I, 167.

[8] Hutchinson, *History*, III, 60–61. Writers of the pro-British school have emphasized the extent to which Britain expended men and money in defense of the colonies and the laxity of the colonists in carrying their share of the burden. But obviously the colonists did not look on their contributions as insignificant. See Beer, *British Colonial Policy, 1754–65, passim;* Miller, *Origins of the American Revolution*, p. 48; Fortescue, *History of the British Army*, II, 265; Adams, *Revolutionary New England*, pp. 226–27, and *Building the British Empire*, p. 374; Gipson, *British Empire before the Revolution*, vols. VI–VIII.

pointments of governors being "settled by Parliament so as to make them independent of the people (which has been much talked of & cannot be done too soon)." Bernard also revealed one of the reasons for the perpetual discord between Britain and her colonies. He said that he took much pleasure in serving his country whenever his own interests were not involved, and except for defending the colonies, the greatest service he could perform would be to settle disorders, heal divisions, and balance the constitutions of the colonial governments.[9] Later Bernard said that if there was a general discussion of colonial constitutions after the peace treaty, "as it is much expected," he would be glad to be of assistance.[10] The governor did not believe any of the colonial governments should serve as a model, for he said that royal governments were as faulty as popular governments. If the North American governments were to be established "upon a true English constitutional bottom," there would need to be a new plan. The New England charter governments would offer the most difficulty to reform, but Bernard did not anticipate insuperable obstacles. In fact, he believed that Massachusetts would be better disposed to a perfect establishment than any other colony, and that therefore New England was the place to start reform. In offering his services, however, he warned the British that it would be best not to let the news of reform be known in Boston until after June of any year, for that was when the assembly voted funds for the support of government.[11] The governor was soon to understand how mistaken he was about reform in Massachusetts.

Before the year 1760 had run its course, there was evidence that the British government intended to carry out some of the suggestions it had received. One item involved writs of assistance which were to aid customs officials in the enforcement of the acts of trade. Enough has already been written about writs so that the details need not be repeated here. Suffice it to say that writs had been issued in 1755, but apparently because of the war, little notice had been taken of them. When they had

---

[9] *The Barrington-Bernard Correspondence and Illustrative Matter, 1760–1770,* ed. by E. Channing and A. C. Coolidge (Cambridge, 1912), p. 4.
[10] *Ibid.,* p. 35.   [11] *Ibid.,* pp. 42–45.

to be renewed at the death of George II in 1760, however, a question was raised as to their legality.[12]

One of the first important results of the writs controversy was the appointment of a chief justice of the Massachusetts Superior Court. Thomas Hutchinson, the lieutenant-governor, received the appointment instead of James Otis, Sr., who had been promised the post by two former governors, Shirley and Pownall. Hutchinson claimed that James Otis, Jr., had threatened dire consequences if his father failed to get the appointment. Although he did not ask for the position, Hutchinson said that his appointment created a personal animosity which was the spark that started the Revolution.[13] John Adams later claimed that Hutchinson was appointed chief justice specifically to hand down a favorable decision on writs or any other cause in which the British government was interested.[14] Whether or not Adams was correct, the fact remains that the British later attempted to control judges through the payment of salaries.

If we can believe John Adams, the hearing before the Massachusetts Superior Court on writs of assistance brought out a great deal of colonial animosity toward British trade laws and the threat of other British imperial regulations. The government argued that the need for revenue was more important than was the liberty of any individual, and Hutchinson added that special warrants would seldom be used because of an informer's fear of the rage of the people.[15] Obviously the trade acts

---

[12] Emily Hickman, in "Colonial Writs of Assistance," *New England Quarterly,* V (Jan. 1932), 83–104, says that the contest over writs lasted for fifteen years and involved all British colonies, island as well as continental. In "Writs of Assistance as a Cause of the Revolution," in Richard B. Morris, ed., *Era of the American Revolution,* pp. 40–75, Oliver M. Dickerson contended that the controversy over writs in Massachusetts was a local incident of little significance, but that writs became important with the passage of the Townshend Acts. Dickerson also claimed that writs were not search warrants, for customs officials had the power to search in their commissions. But the commission which he cited on p. 45 shows that customs officials could search only ships with a commission, but could search other places with a writ. If the writ was not a general search warrant itself, it was certainly necessary to make the commissions general search warrants. A commission was not a general search warrant without a writ.

[13] Hutchinson, *History,* III, 62–64.   [14] Adams, *Works,* X, 182–83.

[15] "Substance of Mr. Gridley's Arguments in Favor of Writs," Joseph Hawley Papers, New York Public Library; Hutchinson, *History,* III, 68.

were not popular with the people. James Otis, who argued against the writs, placed individual liberty above government expediency. Special writs issued under oath were unobjectionable, he said, but a blanket search warrant was "the worst instrument of arbitrary power, the most destructive of English liberty and the fundamental principles of law, that ever was found in an English law-book." There was an implied threat in Otis' statements that previous attempts to exercise this kind of arbitrary power had "cost one king of England his head, and another his throne" and in his hope that his patriotism would never be put to a practical test.[16]

Otis also had other things to say about the trade acts which might well have served as a warning to the British. He agreed that the regulatory navigation act of 1660 was permissible but that revenue acts such as the Molasses Act of 1733 were unconstitutional. All security for life, liberty, and property would vanish if the Molasses Act were enforced by writs of assistance in admiralty courts before dependent judges and without juries or open examination of witnesses. In fact, Otis continued, the Molassas Act and similar laws could never be enforced even if the king in person encamped on Boston Common with 20,000 men and had his whole navy at his command. As for restrictions on manufacturing, there was a note of resentment in Otis' statement that one member of Parliament had said "that a hobnail should not be manufactured in America" and another "that Americans should be compelled by act of Parliament to send their horses to England to be shod." [17]

John Adams saw in the conflict over writs much more than the mere collecting of a tax to help pay for colonial defense. He said that Otis exposed the designs of the British "in taxing us, of destroying our charters and assuming the powers of our government, legislative, executive, and judicial, external and internal, civil and ecclesiastical, temporal and spiritual." To

16 Hutchinson, *History*, III, 68; Adams, *Works*, II, 521–25; X, 314–17. See also William Tudor, *The Life of James Otis of Massachusetts* (Boston, 1823), and Charles Frederic Mullett, *Fundamental Law and the American Revolution, 1760–76* (New York, 1933). Mullett showed how Otis used fundamental law to justify specific claims (pp. 80–82).

17 Adams, *Works*, X, 345, 348–50.

Adams, the writs case brought the prospect of revolution nearer than he had seen before, for he saw a haughty, powerful nation, contemptuous of the colonies, bent on a policy that could lead only to civil war and separation.[18]

While the case on writs of assistance was still pending, another controversy arose which gives both some indication of colonial feeling toward the imperial system and the conflict between imperialism and democracy. Under the Molasses Act of 1733, forfeitures for seizure were divided three ways—one part for the governor, one for the informer, and a third for the king, the king's share to be used in the colony. Hutchinson said that the assembly had always considered the Molasses Act a grievance and consequently had never collected the third which was to go to the colony. Now the House and Council decided to sue for this money, which had been used by the admiralty court to pay informers. Governor Bernard tried to prevent the suit, but both assembly and Council refused to change their votes. Bernard had to consent to the suit, for he discovered that refusal to do so would make him extremely unpopular, though giving his consent would be considered a victory for the popular party. The governor also failed in an attempt to have the crown-appointed attorney general instead of the treasurer bring suit. The House insisted that it might be a dangerous precedent to entrust such business to a man who was not elected by the people and could not be sued by the colony, for precedents never slept once used, whereas it would be safe to entrust the treasurer who was annually elected by the people and was under bond.[19]

Although there have been statements to the effect that the acts of trade did not cause much resentment before 1763,[20] this cannot be said of John Adams. Adams apparently did not believe that revenue was designed for colonial defense, for he said later that the Molasses Act, if it had been enforced, would have raised enough to pay the salaries of all governors and judges of ad-

[18] *Ibid.*, IX, 418; X, 182–83, 233, 247, 317; Mass. Hist. Soc., *Collections*, 5th ser., IV, 340.

[19] Hutchinson, *History*, III, 64–66, 331.

[20] Oliver M. Dickerson, *The Navigation Acts and the American Revolution* (Philadelphia, 1951), pp. xii, 140, 149; Lawrence Henry Gipson, *The Coming of the Revolution, 1763–1775* (New York, 1954), p. x.

miralty.[21] Furthermore, he believed that anyone who wanted to understand "the causes, feelings, and principles of the Revolution" must study the acts of trade. He obviously did not subscribe to the view that British regulations were mutually beneficial to colony and mother country alike. Was there, he asked, "in this preamble or in any statute of Great Britain, in the whole book, the smallest consideration of the health, the comfort, the happiness, the wealth, the growth, the population, the agriculture, the manufactures, the commerce, the fisheries of the American people?" Then he answered himself: "All these are sacrificed to British wealth, British commerce, British domination, and the British navy, as the great engine and instrument to accomplish all." Adams said that he never turned over the leaves of these British statutes without pronouncing a hearty curse on them and without feeling humiliation, degradation, and disgrace for his country and for himself as a native of it.[22]

The controversy over writs and admiralty courts also reveals a considerable amount of evidence on colonial democracy and on the connection between democracy and the imperial system. The Loyalist Peter Oliver pointed out both economic and political democracy when, in discussing the appointment of Hutchinson rather than Otis as judge, he said that Otis had started as a cordwainer and became a prosperous lawyer. Otis was able to influence country jurors "who were too commonly drovers, horse jockies, & other lower classes in life," and he had a wide

---

21 Adams, *Works*, X, 348.

22 *Ibid.*, pp. 320–21, 340. George Louis Beer was one of the first to develop the thesis that the British imperial system "as a whole was thus based on the idea of the mutual reciprocity of the economic interests of mother country and colony." To show that the system was designed to benefit the colonies, Beer declared that British and Irish farmers were prohibited from growing tobacco and that this restriction entailed far greater sacrifice than did the British restrictions on colonial manufacturing (*British Colonial Policy*, pp. 195–96). Other writers have followed Beer in using restrictions on British tobacco as an example of reciprocal benefits of the empire. See Arthur Meier Schlesinger, *The Colonial Merchants and the American Revolution* (New York, 1918), p. 18; Andrews, *Colonial Period*, IV, 426. Said Andrews: "The old colonial system, as the ruthless destruction of tobacco-growing in England demonstrated, was far from being one-sided." Given the climate in Great Britain and the need for warm weather in growing tobacco, one wonders how much tobacco could have been grown in England if Parliament had forced all farmers to produce tobacco.

influence in the House of Representatives, "too great an ingredient of which composition consisted of innkeepers, retailers, & yet more inferior orders of men." [23] Popular sentiment against the writs also had its influence. Hutchinson, according to Adams, did not dare give a judgment in favor of them, so he sent to England before making his decisions.[24] Otis became so popular as a result of his part that he was elected a representative by Boston.[25] Governor Bernard became unpopular when he vetoed an act to substitute a different kind of writ for writs of assistance. He condemned the Council for failure to kill the bill, but admitted that it was a "very popular subject." [26] And Hutchinson pointed out that the writs and admiralty court cases had increased popular opposition to government. The people, he said, were taught that innovations, incompatible with English liberties, were confirmed under pretense of law by judgments of colonial courts and that the power of admiralty courts and customs officers, always deemed grievous because unconstitutional, were now established by judges devoted to the king's prerogative.[27] Adams' view that Hutchinson was appointed to hand down favorable decisions for the British must have been pretty widely accepted.

Two significant statements on possible reforms of the colonial system resulted from the episode over writs and admiralty courts. Governor Bernard said that the importance of America to England was now well known and that as soon as the war was over "its politicks must also undergo the examination of the British councils." He still believed the people of Massachusetts were loyal, but they were "jealous of their liberties (of which they form high & sometimes unconstitutional ideas) to a great degree." [28] Hutchinson wrote that his stand on writs and currency had alienated a great number of his friends. The House of Representatives not only reduced the allowance for the Superior Court, but refused to make any provision whatever for Hutchinson as chief justice. Concluded Hutchinson: "We wish for a good

---

[23] Egerton MSS., 2671, pp. 48–52.   [24] Adams, *Works*, X, 233.
[25] *Ibid.*, pp. 247–48; Hutchinson, *History*, III, 69.
[26] *Barrington-Bernard Correspondence*, p. 51.
[27] Hutchinson, *History*, III, 69.
[28] *Barrington-Bernard Correspondence*, p. 53.

peace with foreign enemies it would enable us to make a better defense against our domestic ones." [29]

Hardly had the commotion over writs died down when British-colonial relations were again stirred up over what appeared to be a British threat against the Congregational church as well as against colonial democracy. This was the proposal, made on various occasions, for sending an Anglican bishop to the colonies. Early in 1762 fear was expressed in Massachusetts that Britain intended to send an Anglican bishop to the colony, and that Governor Bernard, a strong Churchman, was deeply involved in the plot. James Otis said that there were some worthy persons among American Episcopalians, but too many of them were very "high" in their religious and political principles, that is, believed in an authoritarian church and monarchy. These Episcopalians, combined with a few dissenters who also had high notions of government, he declared, had formed a party whose plans for power were diametrically opposed to the rights of mankind. For the sake of their offices, these few dissenters were as high in their political ideas as were the Churchmen. Otis accused Thomas Hutchinson of being the head of this prerogative party, of recommending himself to governors by intrigue, subservience, and preaching arbitrary measures, and of holding many important appointive offices besides getting others filled with relatives and friends.[30]

The importance of religion in politics, as reflected by the fear that a bishopric might be established, also resulted in the change of colonial agents in England. The current agent was William Bollan, son-in-law of former Governor Shirley, who was ac-

[29] To Bollan, March 6, 1762, Mass. Arch., XXVI, 8–9.

[30] April 6, 1762, Mass. Hist. Soc., *Collections,* LXXIV, 29, 30n., 76. For a full discussion of the bishop controversies, see Cross, *The Anglican Episcopate in the American Colonies.* Cross said that the move for an Anglican bishop was primarily religious at first, but that gradually political motives entered in and that this came at a time when tendencies in the colonies were toward separation of church and state (pp. 111–12, 137–38). Claude H. Van Tyne, in "The Influence of the Clergy, and of Religious and Sectarian Forces, on the American Revolution," *American Historical Review,* XIX (Oct. 1913), 44–64, expressed the belief that economic causes of the Revolution had been overdone and that religion was much more important than has been assumed. The same view is expressed in Alice M. Baldwin, *The New England Clergy and the American Revolution* (Durham, N.C., 1928).

cused of being the agent for the "Shirley faction," a "motley mixture" of high Churchmen and dissenters. Bollan had been very watchful for any encroachments on colonial rights. It was he who had written earlier that the British planned to keep an army in the colonies, to tax the colonies for its support, and to rule the colonies as they ruled Ireland. Later he had warned that the times were precarious, that there were strong reasons for establishing colonial rights on a firm foundation.[31] But Bollan belonged to the Church of England. With the threat of a colonial bishop and of church interference in colonial political and religious life, dissenters in Massachusetts were afraid that a Churchman would never defend colonial rights if these came into conflict with those of the church. So Bollan was dismissed, in spite of his good work, and Jasper Mauduit, a dissenter in England, was chosen instead. Otis informed Mauduit that his selection was carried by "the friends of liberty civil and religious." [32] Otis also declared that a dissenting agent was a bitter pill for a colonial governor whose favorite plans were to fill his own pockets, push the prerogative of the Crown as far as possible, and propagate high church principles.[33] As did Otis, the Reverend Jonathan Mayhew said that the choice of Mauduit was made by the steady friends of liberty and all the friends of the dissenting interest, an apparent indication that he believed both liberty and religion were involved.[34]

In the change of agents, Massachusetts democracy again demonstrated its effectiveness. Thomas Hutchinson said that he opposed the election of Mauduit as strenuously as he could in the Council, "but the terror of election which [was] just at hand prevailed over all other considerations," so the Council voted to concur with the decision of the House.[35] The fear of coming elections was to prove a great moderating factor in both the

---

[31] Mass. Hist. Soc., *Collections,* LXXIV, 28.

[32] *Ibid.,* p. 29. On colonial agents, see Edwin P. Tanner, "Colonial Agencies in England during the Eighteenth Century," *Political Science Quarterly,* XVI (March 1901), 24–49; Beverley W. Bond, "The Colonial Agent as a Popular Representative," *ibid.,* XXXV (Sept. 1920), 372–92; James J. Burns, *Colonial Agents of New England* (Washington, 1935).

[33] Mass. Hist. Soc., *Collections,* LXXIV, 76.   [34] *Ibid.,* p. 37.

[35] April 24, 1762, Mass. Arch., XXVI, 12.

House and the Council as the British-colonial controversy increased in intensity.

Fear as to what was in store in the way of imperial reform as well as prophecy on future colonial actions are to be found in the instructions which the House of Representatives sent to its new agent, Jasper Mauduit. Citing Bollan's letter about the need for placing colonial rights on a firm basis, the House declared that the natural rights of the colonists were the same as those of all other British subjects. The most important of these rights was for a man to be "free from any superior power on earth, and not to be under the will or legislative authority of man, but to have only the law of nature for his rule." Then the House went on to say that the liberty of all men in society was to be under no legislative power except that established by consent in the commonwealth and under no laws or restraints except those established by this legislature. There was no reason to abridge a man's liberty just because he had moved to America. In fact, there were good judges who would contend that Britain's strength was due to the growth of her plantations. The mutual happiness of colony and mother country depended on their mutual support, the House continued, and nothing tended more to the destruction of both than sowing seeds of dissension between them. Massachusetts had always supported the king loyally: in fact, New England had long defended itself from the French and Indians without any help from England. Then, after defending the right of the General Court to pay salaries, levy taxes, and legislate without suspending clauses, the House told the agent to use this letter if any attempt were made to abridge or control the legislative power of the General Court.[36] Whatever the belief of present-day historians, it is obvious that the House did not believe that Britain had always defended the colonies at British expense.

Some of the prevailing atmosphere of apprehension for religious and political rights is to be found in the writings of John Adams. A fellow lawyer expressed the conservative opinion that the people should be superstitious, should follow their minister,

[36] Instructions to Jasper Mauduit, June 12, 1762, Mass. Hist. Soc., *Collections*, LXXIV, 39–41.

and not know what they believe. He also believed that they should be ignorant, and in this respect, the free schools in Massachusetts were the very bane of society, for they made the lowest of the people infinitely conceited. Adams, who is generally pictured as a conservative, had only contempt for his colleague's views. He said that such words would come naturally from a tyrant, or a king or minister about to introduce arbitrary power, or from an ambitious ecclesiastic, but a man who would have the people as ignorant as beasts was no friend of liberty.[37]

In all probability, the controversies over writs, admiralty courts, and bishops was responsible for the following statement in which John Adams expressed his confidence in democratic education and its connection with democratic religion and politics:

The English constitution is founded, 'tis bottomed and grounded, on the knowledge and good sense of the people. The very ground of our liberties is the freedom of elections. Every man has in politics as well as religion, a right to think and speak and act for himself. No man, either king or subject, clergyman or layman, has any right to dictate to me the person I shall choose for my legislator and ruler. I must judge for myself. But how can I judge, how can any man judge, unless his mind has been opened and enlarged by reading? A man who can read will find in his Bible, in his common sermon books that common people have by them, and even in the almanac, and the newspapers, rules and observations that will enlarge his range of thought, and enable him the better to judge who has, and who has not that integrity of heart and that compass of knowledge and understanding which forms the statesman.[38]

Probably any one of the incidents during this time would have been quickly forgotten if it had occurred alone, without reinforcement from other incidents. But since they followed each other in rapid succession, the effect was cumulative. Before 1762 had run its course, three other events were to add more fuel to the colonial fire. Again came the apprehension of imperial reform and the forecast of the stand the colonists would take.

In September 1762 the House became involved in a dispute

[37] Adams, *Works*, II, 97.
[38] *Ibid.*, p. 131.

with the governor and Council over who should have the power to levy taxes. During the summer, when the General Court was not in session, the governor and Council had outfitted an armed ship to protect the fisheries. When the General Court met, the House drew up a remonstrance condemning the action of the governor and Council as one which would take from the representatives "their most darling privilege, the right of originating all taxes." The remonstrance then went on to say that "it would be of as little consequence to the people, whether they were subject to George or Louis, the king of Great Britain or the French king, if both were as arbitrary as both would be, if both could levy taxes without parliament." Then the House warned the governor not to repeat the offense in the future, regardless of the advice of the Council. Bernard objected to the references to the king, and they were removed. In relating this incident, Hutchinson said that the purpose was to arouse feeling against the Council, of which Hutchinson was president.[39]

In defending the stand taken by the House of Representatives, Otis wrote a pamphlet in which he revealed many colonial opinions about the imperial structure. For one thing, he declared that the colonies had been blamed for failures which were due to the British—that the colonies were used as pawns in British politics. He also maintained that if the governor and Council could spend money without the consent of the House, they could eliminate the House altogether. Otis then quoted Locke on government by consent and on his belief that kings and governors should exist for the good of the people. Some people, Otis said, believed that inferiors should avoid offending their superiors and that if the superior was a governor he should have all the prerogatives ever exercised by the most absolute prince in Great Britain. Such men were informers and seekers of office, who considered principles of right and wrong as mere vagaries of a weak and distempered imagination. It was well known that the least "patriotic spark" disqualified a candidate from all further preferment among such men. To prevent future encroachments by the governor and Council, Otis suggested remonstrance, then refusal to supply the treasury, and finally the stop-

[39] Hutchinson, *History*, III, 71.

page of all salaries. As a last resort, Parliament had been known to appeal to heaven and the longest sword: God forbid there should ever be need for such again. But the worst that could happen would be for the people to lose the privilege of taxing themselves, "upon which single privilege evidently depends all others, *civil and religious.*" [40]

Within a short time, another controversy developed over whether the General Court or the king had the authority to issue charters of incorporation. The House had passed a bill to establish a college in western Massachusetts, but the Council rejected it. The promoters then applied to Governor Bernard for a charter, and Bernard ordered the charter to be granted. This caused a great outcry that such an act was injurious to the rights of the people. Bernard believed that the right to grant charters belonged to the king, but he also realized that insistence on the right might interrupt important legislative matters. So while he stopped the issuing of the charter, he nevertheless insisted on the right of the king to grant charters.[41] The Reverend Charles Chauncy believed the governor's power to grant charters would be harmful to religious as well as civil affairs, and he thought such an act would be too unpopular for Bernard to carry out unless he were encouraged from England.[42]

Differences between Congregationalists and Churchmen flared up again late in 1762 and early in 1763 to show that the religious issue had not been settled by any means. Congregationalists believed that the Society for the Propagation of the Gospel in Foreign Parts was supporting the Church of England party in Massachusetts and attempting to undermine the Congregational church while promoting Episcopacy. To combat this influence, men in the colony asked the General Court to charter a rival society, ostensibly to propagate the gospel among the Indians. The act was disallowed in England, but it did have the effect of touching off a pamphlet war involving Jonathan Mayhew, the Archbishop of Canterbury Thomas Secker, and the Reverend East Apthorp, minister of the Society in Cambridge, Massa-

[40] James Otis, "A Vindication of the Conduct of the House of Representatives of the Province of Massachusetts Bay (1762)," in *Some Political Writings of James Otis,* ed. by Charles F. Mullett (Columbia, Mo., 1929), IV, *passim.*

[41] Mass. Hist. Soc., *Collections,* LXXIV, 68; *Acts and Resolves,* IV, 562.

[42] Mass. Hist. Soc., *Collections,* LXXIV, 71.

chusetts. Mayhew accused Secker of first being disgusted with the colonies, then hating them and sending Apthorp to spy on them, and finally scheming to establish an archbishop in America.[43]

As the French and Indian War was coming to a close, additional evidence appeared that colonial apprehensions about British measures were not unfounded. Governor Bernard stressed two items for reform in a report to the ministers. Like Pownall, he pointed out the importance of salaries in the British imperial system. Salaries of British officials were disgracefully low, he declared, simply because salaries were fixed yearly by the General Court. Unpopular judgments by courts were often successfully used as a means of lowering judges' salaries, he said, while the attorney general had received no salary for several years because the assembly claimed the right to elect him. Great harm resulted from the fact that the chief officers of the Crown had such a precarious income, Bernard continued, and there would be no relief until a sufficient and independent civil list was established. The king could then pay his officials' salaries commensurate with the dignity and duty of their offices.[44]

Bernard's second suggestion was one which would curtail popular control in the Massachusetts legislature. He said the election of the Council annually by the representatives of the people made the Council much too popular a body. The desire to be re-elected influenced councilors, as was well known, so that whenever any popular business was to be carried through, contrary to the sentiments of the government, it was brought up just before an election. Bernard considered it "highly indecent" that councilors should be publicly threatened with defeat for what they did in the Council, and he urged the creation of an independent council as a reform which should accompany an independent civil list.[45] Apparently Bernard agreed with Hutchinson that the fear of popular elections had a moderating influence on the views of councilors.

In 1763, also, British officials were complaining that both the House and the Council were too democratic to serve British interests. In a report to the king, the ministers declared that

[43] *Ibid.*, pp. 74, 104ff.; *Acts and Resolves*, IV, 562.
[44] King's MSS., CCV, pt. I, pp. 413–14.   [45] *Ibid.*, p. 414.

the House of Representatives, chosen by the people, refused to pay due regard to the king's instructions or to provide an adequate salary for the governor, especially when the governor tried to carry out the king's orders, and on all occasions affected "too great an independence on their mother kingdom." Continued the ministers: "The assembly is generally filled with people of small fortunes and mean capacities, who are easily led into any measures, that seem to enlarge their liberties and privileges, how detrimental soever the same may be to Great Britain, or to Your Majesty's royal prerogative." [46]

When the end of the war came in 1763, this problem of a democratic assembly having "too great an independence on their mother kingdom" received official attention when the long-simmering question of whether to keep Canada or the sugar island of Guadeloupe came to a climax. The main issue revolved about whether it was important to keep Canada in French hands as a restraint on colonial ambitions for independence.

The Canada question was one of long standing. We have already seen that the British, considering their action strictly in British interests, had restored Louisbourg to France in 1748. We have also seen that Peter Kalm recognized the importance of the French in Britain's colonial policy. He had commented in 1750 that the British had never really been anxious to defeat the French in Canada.[47]

When Montreal fell in 1760, there was a vigorous pamphlet war in England over the retention of Canada and its relation to colonial dependence. One writer offered two arguments for restoring France to her possessions. First, removal of the French threat would permit colonial expansion into the interior, where the people, being too far from British merchants, would manufacture for themselves and thus become useless to Britain. Secondly, removal of the French would be dangerous, for the colonists would expand rapidly, and being a hardy, independent

---

[46] *Ibid.,* pp. 22–23.

[47] Kalm, *Travels,* I, 138–40. In developing his thesis that British policy really favored the colonies as much or more than it did Britain, George Louis Beer failed to give Kalm's views of colonial reaction to British regulations and policies. He mentioned Kalm, but merely said that the accuracy of Kalm's observations was open to question. See *British Colonial Policy, 1754–1765,* p. 207.

people, would eventually break their ties with the mother country. Leave the French in Canada, said this writer, then prevent the colonies from expanding beyond the mountains, thus keeping them under British commercial and military influence. Others pointed out that Britain should keep the sugar island of Guadeloupe instead of Canada, then keep an army over the colonists to prevent any moves toward independence.[48]

Others in England, including Benjamin Franklin, argued just the opposite—the best way to insure colonial dependence was to retain Canada. Unlimited expansion would keep the colonies agricultural and thus in need of British manufactured goods, Franklin declared, for the colonies could never manufacture for themselves until they had poor people to do the work, and there would not be poor people as long as there was cheap land. On the other hand, if the colonists were confined to the coastal area, as suggested, they would soon develop a surplus population and be forced to manufacture for themselves.[49] But whatever the arguments on both sides, the core seemed to be colonial dependence as one important facet of Britain's imperial problem.

The controversy which was in progress in England over whether to keep Canada or Guadeloupe was both well known and fully understood in the colonies. Hutchinson said that the Americans were completely aware that the people of England as well as the administration were divided over the expediency of keeping Canada or the islands. They also knew, he said, that the objection to Canada was due to the belief that elimination of the French would in time cause the separation of the colonies from Great Britain.[50]

Probably as a result of the experience of 1748, when the British had restored Canada to France, there was a good deal of skepticism in the colony as to what Britain would do with Canada at the end of the war. Israel Williams of Hatfield, who later became a Tory, had voiced the fear that the British would restore Canada to French control "with a political view to keep us de-

---

[48] Franklin, *Writings*, IV, 45–46, 51–53; William Lawson Grant, "Canada versus Guadeloupe," *American Historical Review*, XVII (July 1912), 735–43.

[49] Franklin, *Writings*, IV, 47–49, 52–53, 75–77.

[50] Hutchinson, *History*, III, 73.

pendent." [51] As late as February 1763, some Americans still expected Canada to be restored to the French. John Adams recorded the following in his diary: "The anecdote of Mr. Erving. He had prophesied so long, and with so much confidence, that Canada would be returned to the French, that, because he begins to see his prediction will not be fulfilled, he is now straining his invention for reasons why we should not hold it." [52] If such a fear were as current as these sources indicate, it is not surprising that the colonists were sometimes reluctant to vote men and money for campaigns against the French.

At the Treaty of Paris, 1763, the British decided to keep Canada. The question, then, is why? Why did they choose Canada instead of Guadeloupe, why did they not restore the French in Canada as they had done in 1748, if they believed that French control of Canada would be a surer means of keeping the colonies dependent than British control of Canada? Unless we are willing to concede that the British wanted the colonies to become independent—and nobody has ever even suspected that —the answer must be that the British had changed their minds about the value of the French as a restraint on their rapidly growing colonies.

The answer to British policy lies both in events preceding and following the treaty. We must remember that Britain had long feared colonial independence, that the colonies had continually violated the mercantile system, that colonial governors and other officials had never been able to enforce British policy because of democratic assemblies. Before the French and Indian War, proposed remedies had been, first, to have Parliament levy a tax on the colonies so that British colonial officials would receive salaries from Britain, not the colonies, and, second, to station troops in America so that the colonies could be ruled as Ireland was ruled. British need for colonial aid against the French had postponed these suggested measures, just as British need for colonial aid during the war had forced governors to surrender

[51] Israel Williams Papers, II, 145. Although the emphasis is different, a general account of events and issues in this chapter can be found in Channing, *History of the United States*, III, chs. i and ii, and Curtis P. Nettels, *The Roots of American Civilization* (New York, 1939), chs. xxi and xxii.

[52] Adams, *Works*, II, 140.

some of their authority from time to time. Then, in 1760, we have Weare's suggestion that Britain must enforce the mercantile system if she would make it effective, that she must take steps to secure the dependence of colonies that were already thinking too much of independence, that she should keep troops in the colonies while reform was in progress, for once removed, there would never be any cause to send them back, that she must raise a revenue to pay the salaries of colonial officials, and that above all, she must cut down on the power of democratic assemblies.

After the war, Britain attempted to carry out many of these suggested reforms. She left troops in the colonies as had been proposed before the war started, she did numerous things to make mercantilism more effective, she attempted to raise a revenue to pay salaries of officials, she eventually decided to pay these salaries regardless of a revenue, and she finally took steps to curtail democracy in Massachusetts.

In view of this background, it seems logical to assume that the British government had changed its views about the value of the French in Canada. As we look back on it now, war or threat of war between Britain and France had always forced the British to make concessions to the colonists in return for assistance. Instead of the French keeping the colonies dependent on Britain, they had actually kept Britain dependent on the colonies. If the British intended to reform the colonial system after the war, as all the evidence indicates, could she do it best with the French in or out of Canada? Would the British have attempted the measures they did after 1763 if a hostile France had been poised in Canada ready to take advantage of any difficulty between Britain and her colonies? With the British fully aware of the importance of their colonies and of the connection between the French and colonial dependence, we can only conclude that they kept Canada because they believed that previous policy had been wrong. Now they could enforce the mercantile system and secure the dependence of the colonies without the necessity of making concessions to the colonists in some future war.[53]

[53] Various reasons have been suggested for the retention of Canada. In "Canada versus Guadeloupe," *American Historical Review*, XVII (July 1912), 735–43,

In Parliament there seemed to be little controversy over the retention of Canada by 1763.[54]

The peace treaty of 1763 was greeted by a somewhat curious incident in the Boston town meeting. James Otis, the moderator, took the occasion to express the gratitude of the colonists for the results of the war and to praise the British constitution as the greatest the world had ever seen. But then Otis went on to declare that the colonists were entitled by common right, acts of Parliament, and the laws of God and nature to all the essential privileges of the people in Britain. He deplored the jealousies which had arisen in the past and declared that the true interests of Britain and her colonies were mutual. Concluded Otis: "What God in His providence has united, let no man dare attempt to pull asunder." [55]

Perhaps the measures already inaugurated by the British and the threat of future reforms had given Otis some premonition of troubles to come. As long as the war was in progress, the Brit-

---

William Lawson Grant saw the issue as one between a mercantilist empire and a free empire, and he realized that the army was concerned with colonial independence, not merely defense. George Louis Beer developed the thesis which has been widely accepted that colonies were valued as sources for raw materials until about 1750, then were considered primarily as outlets for manufactured goods. The retention of Canada marked a victory for the manufacturers (*British Colonial Policy, 1754–1765*, pp. 134–35). For an opposing point of view, see Curtis P. Nettels, "The Place of Colonial Markets in the Old Colonial System," *New England Quarterly*, VI (Sept. 1933), 491–512. Clarence W. Alvord, in *The Mississippi Valley in British Politics . . .* , 2 vols. (Cleveland, 1917), I, 45–54, followed Beer in saying that the merchants favored Guadeloupe for raw materials but that the farmers and manufacturers favored Canada for markets. In contrast, Lawrence H. Gipson believed that the British kept Canada, not for mercantilist, imperial, or strategic reasons, but for the altruistic reasons of the security and welfare generally of the older American colonies. See "The American Revolution as an Aftermath of the Great War for the Empire, 1754–1763," *Political Science Quarterly*, LXV (March 1950), 90, and also *The British Empire before the American Revolution*, VIII. Max Savelle, in *The Diplomatic History of the Canadian Boundary, 1749–1763* (New Haven, 1940), pp. 105–06, said that Pitt wanted Canada for long-range mercantilist reasons. He quoted a Board of Trade recommendation that Britain should retain Canada "as a security to our other dominions in America, and as a means of wealth and power of Great Britain," but did not say whether the board meant to secure the colonies from foreign threat or to secure their dependence on Great Britain.

[54] *Parliamentary History*, III, 73.

[55] Hutchinson, *History*, III, 73–74.

ish did nothing drastic, but the end of the war brought with it an end to the old colonial system.

Events from 1760 to 1763 make it abundantly clear that colonial democracy was at the heart of Britain's imperial problem and that one of the most urgent of the reforms proposed was the curtailment of democracy. Democracy prevented the enforcement of the mercantile system; democracy contributed heavily to the threat of colonial independence. In all this, there was no hint of a controlling aristocracy in Massachusetts opposed to a disfranchised and underprivileged lower class; in fact, the British would have been much happier than they were if such an aristocracy had existed. What was needed was some way to curtail the overabundance of democratic customs which already existed, so that Britain could enforce her mercantile system and secure the dependence of the colonies on the mother country.

[CHAPTER X]

Democracy and the "New" Policy, 1763–1766

CONFRONTED with rapidly growing colonies which the British believed to be on the way to independence and plagued because their mercantile and imperial policy had been largely vitiated by the effective actions of democratic assemblies, Britain adopted what might well be called the "new" colonial policy in 1763. What was new was not the *purpose* but some of the *methods* to be used for achieving that purpose. Mercantilism was still the guiding principle: colonies should exist primarily for the benefit of the mother country and should be regulated in the interests of the mother country. The difficulty lay in the imperial structure which had been designed to make mercantilism effective. Failure rested with the imperial organization, not with mercantilist objectives, and so it was to the imperial structure that the British turned their attention.[1]

1 Historians have treated this crucial period in the British imperial system from two interacting points of view: (1) that the colonies were not democratic, and (2) that changes in British policy after 1763 marked a shift away from mercantilism and toward imperialism. In "Colonial Commerce," *American Historical Review*, XX (Oct. 1914), 43–63, Charles McLean Andrews, in stating his well-known position that colonial history must be viewed from England rather than from the colonies, said the colonists would not have understood and did not want modern democracy. Terms such as freedom, liberty, and independence did not have the same meaning then as now. In his *Colonial Background of the American Revolu-*

Britain in 1763 was in a favorable position for the first time to enforce her colonial policies, which had always combined mercantilism and imperialism. With the French eliminated from Canada, there would be no need to make concessions to the colonies in exchange for colonial military and financial assistance. The accession of George III to the throne of England in 1760 effectively neutralized the Stuart pretenders as a threat in British politics. The prospect of war in Europe to divert British attention appeared remote; 1763 seemed to be propitious for inaugurating the new policy.

Since most students of American history are familiar with British measures after 1763, it is not necessary here to repeat these in great detail. The essential problem is to discover the relationship between British measures and colonial democracy as it existed in Massachusetts—to see whether an aristocratic or democratic society existed and whether in its origins the war from 1775–1783 was an "American Revolution" or a "War of Independence." [2]

Almost before the ink was dry on the Treaty of Paris, 1763, there was ample evidence of important innovations in adminis-

---

tion, pp. 125–26, and *Colonial Period of American History,* IV, 426, Andrews maintained that a new and untried imperialism was added to a tried mercantilism, but that "mercantilism and imperialism had nothing in common." Lawrence Henry Gipson, who continued the Beer-Andrews approach to colonial history (*Charles McLean Andrews and the Re-orientation of the Study of American Colonial History*), claimed that the colonies were much like the British in many ways, including the fact that the electorate, as in England, was composed of a political aristocracy made up of qualified males "as against the great mass of the disfranchised." Unfortunately, Gipson also used McKinley, *The Suffrage Franchise,* as his source of information. See *The Coming of the Revolution,* pp. 2, 27n. Beer (*British Colonial Policy,* p. 227) and Gipson (*Coming of the Revolution*) both emphasized defense rather than mercantilism as the British motivation after 1763. Apparently they did not believe that an effective imperialistic system was essential to an effective mercantilist system in British eyes.

2 There are many available accounts of *what* happened after 1763. Most of the authors have assumed, however, that these events occurred in an undemocratic society and had an important bearing on class conflicts within the colonies. See Miller, *Origins of the American Revolution,* ch. iii; Gipson, *The Coming of the Revolution,* ch. i; Claude H. Van Tyne, *The Causes of the War of Independence . . .* (Boston, 1922); J. T. Adams, *Revolutionary New England;* Channing, *History of the United States,* III; Nettels, *Roots of American Civilization,* chs. xii–xiv.

trating the colonies. Some of these simply involved a stricter enforcement of already-existing laws; others indicated changes in the imperial system. To prevent smuggling, additional ships were sent to patrol colonial waters and ships' crews were to receive an increased share of all forfeitures of illicit goods.[3] Governor Bernard had strict orders to enforce the trade acts, which included the obnoxious Molasses Act of 1733, and to have a census taken in the colony.[4] And although it does not appear to have affected Massachusetts directly, the Proclamation Line of 1763 stopped westward migration at the very time when it would have been greatest, at the end of a long war.[5]

One innovation deserves special attention because of its later significance and because of the interpretations which have been placed upon it. This was the stationing of a standing army in the colonies during peacetime. This move by the British has generally been justified on the ground that the colonies would

[3] Pickering, *Statutes,* XXV, 345. Clarence W. Alvord, in *The Mississippi Valley in British Politics,* developed the thesis that the West was the key to British policies after 1763. Whenever British ministers soberly and seriously discussed the American problem, he said, the vital phase to them was not the disturbances of the maddening crowd in Boston or New York, but the development of the vast western region acquired by the Treaty of Paris. What to do with Canada and the West was the first and last question asked of ministers between 1763 and 1776, and every ministry realized that this was the most important of all American problems. The decisions to tax the colonies by the Stamp and Townshend Acts, he declared, were only subordinate parts of the western problem (pp. 13–16).

This thesis can be maintained only by ignoring a mountain of contradicting evidence. Alvord himself said that the strife which stirred up Parliament and the colonies frequently obscured the real issue, even in the eyes of the ministers (p. 16), which would not indicate that the West was the dominant issue. Throughout his two volumes, Alvord shows that the West was relegated to a secondary position when more important issues were at stake. The late Carl Becker gave a fairly accurate evaluation of the Alvord thesis when he pointed out that Alvord himself admitted that the problem of the West was overshadowed by other more important problems and that, while the western issue was important at times, it was in fact largely obscured by the other conflicts and must occupy a strictly subordinate place (*American Historical Review,* XXII [April 1917], 671–73).

[4] Bernard, *Select Letters,* p. 1; King's MSS., CCV, pt. 1, pp. 390–93.

[5] On the Proclamation Line, see Max Farrand, "The Indian Boundary Line," *American Historical Review,* X (July 1905), 782–91; Clarence W. Alvord, "The Genesis of the Proclamation of 1763," in Michigan Pioneer and Historical Society, *Historical Collections,* XXXVI (1908), 20–52. Both writers looked on the Proclamation Line as a measure to solve the Indian problem rather than as a temporary restraint on westward expansion pending imperial reform which would give the British better control over the colonies.

not contribute sufficiently to their own defense. There was another possible motive for stationing troops, however, which a few modern writers have mentioned but have played down—the use of troops in effecting imperial reform.[6]

The suggestion to station troops in the colonies to keep the colonists in subordination was neither new nor a result of the French and Indian War. We have already seen that Governor William Shirley wanted the British to keep Louisbourg in 1745 as a possible restraint on the colonies if they should ever become disposed to shake off their dependence. In August 1755, before the French and Indian War was officially started, Shirley again reminded British officials that a British army of 7,000 troops would have a very salutary effect on the colonists if the troops were stationed in the western areas.[7] It was the following year, 1756, that agent Bollan warned of a plan to station an army in the colonies so that the colonies could be governed as was Ireland. Comptroller Weare was most emphatic in urging that the army be kept until reforms were achieved, for he said that there would be no excuse to bring an army back to the colonies once it was removed. In 1762, a plan for keeping troops in America gave as one reason "to retain the inhabitants of our ancient provinces in a state of constitutional dependence on Great Britain." [8] Even granted that one purpose for the troops was defense, this second purpose must be kept in mind if we would understand colonial reaction.[9]

[6] Gipson, *The Coming of the Revolution*, ch. i; J. T. Adams, *Revolutionary New England,* p. 392; Fortescue, *History of the British Army,* III, 26, said that Grenville probably saw the advantage of troops to enforce law in a new country where the people from long habit and tradition opposed restraint, but he did not mean any injustice to the colonies. Beer, *British Colonial Policy,* 261n., 266, after saying that troops were necessary for defense, conceded that it was generally recognized in England that the colonies were tending toward independence and a standing army as a counteracting agency was not ignored. But if this was a motive, said Beer, at most it was a distinctly subordinate one. In note 1, p. 261, Beer cited the letter from William Bollan in 1756 that the British were going to keep troops in the colonies, but Beer did not point out that Bollan said the purpose of the troops was to help govern the colonies as Ireland was governed, not to protect the colonists from Indians.

[7] Cited in Beer, *British Colonial Policy,* 266n.   [8] *Ibid.*

[9] Beer blamed the colonists for Pontiac's Revolt, which he said showed that the colonists could not be depended on to defend themselves, *ibid.,* 252–60. This raises the question of whether the colonists were responsible or whether the revolt

In addition to troops, there was also present the threat of the long-recommended policy of Parliamentary taxation of the colonies. A letter by Thomas Hutchinson of November 17, 1763, gives us a preview of what was intended: "A revenue from the colonies will certainly be attempted the next Parliament sufficient at least to support the troops to be kept up here. The molasses duty is to be enforced and a general stamp duty private letters say is also determined upon." Obviously Hutchinson had premonitions that this news was not going to be popular when it became known, for he added this note of warning: "This I would not have mentioned from me." [10] Hutchinson's early knowledge of a proposed stamp tax later became an integral part of the Stamp Act controversy.

Popular resentment did not need a stamp tax to arouse it, however, for news that the Molasses Act was to be enforced was sufficient. Governor Francis Bernard declared that this bit of information alarmed New England more than did the fall of Fort William Henry to the French during the French and Indian War.[11] James Otis had already predicted trouble when he said during the hearing on writs that the Molasses Act, if enforced, was a revenue act, and that the king and 20,000 soldiers, stationed on Boston Common, could not enforce it. It was natural for merchants involved in the molasses trade to object, for they looked on the Molasses Act of 1733 as an obvious discrimination favoring the sugar islands.[12] But not only merchants made objections. Hutchinson said that the people became more antagonistic toward Crown officials, especially customs officers, whom they accused of restricting the natural rights and liberties of the people. The term Tory came into common use, and many towns throughout the province refused to take a census on the suspicion that it was intended for sinister purposes.[13]

Opposition to enforcement of the Molasses Act began in the General Court late in 1763 or early 1764. A large committee

was due to Amherst's contempt for the Indians and his refusal to continue gifts and supplies of rum, guns, and powder.

[10] Israel Williams Papers, II, 158.
[11] Bernard, *Select Letters*, p. 9. See also *Boston Gazette*, Jan. 16, 1764.
[12] Mass. Hist. Soc., *Collections*, LXXIV, 135; Bernard, *Select Letters*, pp. 4–9.
[13] Hutchinson, *History*, III, 74–75; *Acts and Resolves*, IV, 790–92.

of both houses considered the question and came to the conclusion that the act was being enforced vigorously at this particular time in order to obtain the colony's consent for other taxes. The committee considered this dangerous, as it would concede Parliament the right to tax colonial trade, which they could not do, for it would be contrary to the fundamental principle of the Massachusetts constitution, that all taxes should originate with the people. As Massachusetts was not represented in Parliament, Parliament could not tax the colony. On January 27, 1764, the house appointed a committee to instruct the colonial agent, Jasper Mauduit. In the midst of these events, rumor had it that the ministers intended new regulations, such as those to place troops on the frontier posts—to be supported by taxes on colonial trade—and to levy a stamp tax. The agent had orders to oppose any such projects.[14]

Thomas Hutchinson did not believe that the proposed revenue or Sugar Act of 1764 was sufficient to cause trouble, but the proposed stamp tax, which was a threat to democracy, was a different matter. There was a general alarm, he said, when the colonial agent informed the province that the ministers intended to raise by a stamp duty a sum sufficient to free colonial governments from colonial control. This, of course, would mean the payment of officials' salaries as had often been proposed. Hutchinson went on to say that the House sent a letter to the agent, written by James Otis and without the usual consultation with the Council, and at the same time appointed a committee of correspondence with Otis at its head to send copies of the agent's instructions to other colonial assemblies.[15] But of course this action came too late to be effective in preventing the passage of the Sugar Act.

Before further controversy occurred over the Sugar Act, a book by former Massachusetts governor Thomas Pownall, which reached Massachusetts early in 1764, explained in great detail what the new colonial policy should do and how it was a threat to colonial democracy.

Pownall first pointed out the divergence which had developed

14 Mass. Hist. Soc., *Collections*, LXXIV, 145–46.
15 Hutchinson, *History*, III, 79–80.

in the interests of the colonies and mother country. The shift in colonial possessions had given a general impression of impending changes, he said—some revolutionary event, some new crisis. This crisis centered in the emerging dominance of Britain as the leading commercial power, a power which should not merely have colonies, but which should weld her possessions into one grand maritime dominion. Mercantilist Pownall did not believe, however, that the colonies should or could be completely subordinated to the interests of Great Britain. Colonies were supposed to exist for the benefit of the mother country, he said, but under existing conditions the American colonies had been forced to violate this maxim in order to have either trade or subsistence. As a result, the colonies had developed a commercial interest distinct from that of the mother country, he contended, and this distinct interest would eventually dissolve artificial bonds of government. Britain should, therefore, set up an administration for the colonies based on these existing realities.[16]

The former governor did not agree with many Englishmen that the colonies were aiming at a separation from Great Britain, but he did think that the British should consider the problem of colonial independence. "It has been often suggested," he said, "that care should be taken in the administration of the plantations; lest, in some future time, these colonies should become independent of their mother country." Although he believed that nothing was further from their minds, still he thought that it was time to discover how far the colonies had actually become independent in their government and laws, how much advantage they had taken of Britain's weakness at home and distraction abroad to gain this actual independence, and what remedial measures should be taken.[17]

To Pownall, there was no doubt whatever that imperial reform and colonial democracy were inextricably interwoven. On one occasion he declared that in popular governments, where every executive officer was dependent on the representatives of

[16] Thomas Pownall, *The Administration of the Colonies* (London, 1764), pp. 1–9. A good analysis of Pownall's views on imperial relations is to be found in Schutz, *Thomas Pownall*. Schutz was aware of colonial democracy but did not emphasize it in his work.

[17] Pownall, *The Administration of the Colonies*, pp. 25–35.

the people for his pay, the rights of the Crown received short shrift when opposed to the spirit of democracy.[18] And again he contended that Crown officials should be independent of the legislature for their salaries, especially in popular governments where the legislature itself was so much influenced by the passions of the people.[19]

So among the many reforms proposed by Pownall, the ones to curb the powers of democratic assemblies received his first consideration. He wanted all colonial affairs concentrated in the office of a secretary of state who would have complete power to appoint and dismiss all colonial officials. He also proposed revision and enforcement of those trade acts which he did not consider just or prudent in their effect on the colonies. In particular, he urged the raising of a British-controlled revenue in the colonies. Said the ex-governor: "I will further venture to suggest, that, whatever revenues are raised, the *first and special appropriation of them ought to be to the paying the governors, and all other crown officers independent of the legislatures of the colonies.*" [20]

Pownall also put his finger on the difficulties which the British were to experience in carrying out the many suggested reforms. He said there were two great points which the colonists labored to establish. One was to exercise their several rights and privileges as founded in the rights of Englishmen. The other was to retain the command of revenue and the payment of officials' salaries in their own hands as security for the conduct of those officials.[21] The British would discover that Pownall's analysis of the obstacles to imperial reform was only too accurate.

That the British were determined to reform the colonial system and to curtail colonial democracy was clearly evident with the passage of the Sugar Act.[22] When George Grenville in-

---

18 *Ibid.*, pp. 75–80.   19 *Ibid.*, pp. 49–54.
20 *Ibid.*, pp. 9–22, 66–68, 113–28.   21 *Ibid.*, p. 36.
22 The most complete analysis of the Sugar Act is to be found in Oliver M. Dickerson, *The Navigation Acts and the American Revolution*, pp. 161–86. Dickerson recognized that the Sugar Act was not a mere revenue act, but was designed to reform the whole colonial constitutional system. Dickerson saw it not as a reform to curtail colonial democracy, insure colonial dependence, and enforce the mercantile system, but primarily as a means of laying the legal foundation for planned

troduced the bill, he said that the purpose was to support government in the colonies and to encourage the trade of the sugar islands.[23] He also declared at the time that the money was not to be used to help liquidate the British national debt which had been incurred during the French and Indian War. All he desired was that the tax provide funds for colonial government and defense, nothing more.[24] This emphasis on the support of colonial governments, when the colonists already paid for the cost of their governments, was especially significant.

The Sugar Act itself not only lowered the tax on molasses from 6*d.* to 3*d.* a gallon to make it a revenue rather than a prohibitive tax, but also taxed coffee, indigo, wine, East India goods, calico, linen, pimento, and sugar. Then there was a whole host of restrictive regulations which were particularly obnoxious to a democratic people—admiralty courts without juries, British-appointed judges who received a percentage of all forfeitures, provisions making recovery of damages by colonists or prosecution of British officials almost impossible, and especially the provision that proof of innocence rested with the accused, not the accuser. Furthermore, in view of repeated urgings that Britain take measures to "secure" the dependence of the colonies on the mother country, the statement that funds raised by the Sugar Act were to be kept separate and used by Parliament to protect, defend, and secure the colonies should be noted.[25]

If we would understand events after 1764, we must realize that the British and the Americans interpreted past events and imperial relations in 1764 from two diametrically opposed, and perhaps irreconcilable, points of view. The British argued that the original colonies had been founded and protected at great expense to the mother country, that the mother country had expended much blood and treasure during the French and Indian War, that this war was started because of solicitations for aid

changes in the empire and of providing "fat pickings" for an army of placemen soon to be sent from England (p. 183). He also said that money raised under the Sugar Act could not be used to pay salaries, as could the taxes under the Townshend Acts, but in view of the stated purpose of the act, it is difficult to see why this was so if the king decided to use it for salaries.

[23] *Parliamentary History*, XV, 1426–34.
[24] Mass. Hist. Soc., *Collections*, LXXIV, 142–43, 146n.
[25] Pickering, *Statutes*, XXVI, 33–52.

from the colonists and was conducted solely for colonial benefits. As the colonists had not borne their fair share of imperial
expense, Britain was justified in taxing them.[26] Colonists, on the
other hand, denied this version of colonial developments. They
claimed that the original colonists had settled at their own expense, had left England because of persecution, and had always
defended themselves at a time when British aid could have been
used. They looked on the French and Indian War primarily
as an offensive war by Great Britain for British interests, and
pointed out that British remittances during the war were evidence that they had paid their share. Furthermore, they had always paid for their own government. Why was there a need to
tax the colónies for the support of government, and now that
France no longer controlled Canada, why were troops needed to
protect and defend Americans? [27]

Thomas Hutchinson furnishes a good example of the way in
which a man's interests at the time could shape his interpretation
of events. In 1764, before he had become completely pro-British,
Hutchinson argued this way: In future wars the only defense
necessary would be the British navy and colonists would contribute their share just as they had done in the last war. There
was no justification for keeping troops in America, he declared,
as the colonists had fought the French and Indians for a hundred years without British aid and were perfectly capable of defending their frontiers from the Indians. Hutchinson then went
on to say that the French and Indian War was fought to protect British trade, not to save the colonists from French domination, and that Britain, not the colonies, would reap the benefits
of the war. He also declared that if the British had paid taxes
during the war in the same proportion that the Americans had,
there would not have been a large debt at the end of the war.[28]
After he became a Loyalist, however, Hutchinson had this explanation: "The amazing increase of the national debt, by a war
engaged in at the solicitations, and for the protection of the colonies seems to have caused this new attention." [29]

British taxation of the colonies was not due to the fact that the

26 Mass. Arch., VI, 283–88. These arguments can be found in numerous documents of the period.
27 Ibid.   28 Ibid., XXVI, 90–96.   29 Hutchinson, History, III, 75.

colonists had not defended themselves or paid for their own government. They had done both, but they had not always done them as the British desired. As we have seen, they used appropriations during the French and Indian War to wrest concessions from British officials, concessions that weakened British authority in the colonies. Time and again they did the same with civil officials through salary payments. A parliamentary tax was designed to remedy both evils, a fact which does much to explain colonial resistance.

Passage of the Sugar Act resulted in another pamphlet by James Otis in which he denied Parliament's right to tax the colonies and pointed out the threat of a parliamentary tax to colonial democracy. Otis conceded that Parliament could regulate in the interests of the whole empire—a concession he soon retracted as it cost him much popularity in Boston. But Parliament could not tax the colonists without their consent, either internally or externally, for a tax was a tax, whatever its nature, and if property could be taken without consent, so could liberty. Government came from the people, wrote Otis, must operate in the interests of the people to protect life, liberty, and property, and could be overthrown if it violated these natural rights. Otis stated that the colonies had been settled and defended with little or no aid from Britain. He condemned juryless admiralty courts, unjust restrictions on colonial trade, Negro slavery, and treatment of colonial soldiers during the late war. In particular, Otis denied accusations made by Thomas Pownall in his *Administration of the Colonies* that the colonies were committing treason and aiming at independence. He also called attention to Pownall's statement that any colonial revenue must be raised without colonial consent and that the first use for such revenue was to pay the salaries of governors and other Crown officials.[30]

Since the General Court was not in session, opposition to the Sugar Act was soon taken up by the democratic Boston town

[30] James Otis, *The Rights of the British Colonies Asserted and Proved* (Boston, 1764), in C. F. Mullett, ed., *Some Political Writings of James Otis* (Columbia, Mo., 1929), pp. 50–90. On the extent to which Otis fluctuated in his point of view on colonial rights see Ellen Elizabeth Brennan, "James Otis: Recreant and Patriot," *New England Quarterly*, XII (Dec. 1939), 691–725.

meeting.[31] On May 15, 1764, the town elected, as its representatives to the House, Royal Tyler, James Otis, Thomas Cushing, and Oxenbridge Thacher, two of whom, Otis and Thacher, had opposed writs of assistance. The town also elected a committee of Richard Dana, Samuel Adams, John Ruddock, Nathaniel Bethune, and Joseph Green to instruct these representatives.[32]

These instructions by the town politicians, and written by Samuel Adams, leave little doubt of the general fear that political rights were being threatened by the Sugar Act. After expressing the strongest testimony of confidence in the choice of representatives, the town urged these men to use their utmost influence to guard the invaluable rights and privileges of the province. They were to preserve the independence of the House of Representatives by getting a law passed to force anyone to stand for re-election if he accepted a post of profit from the Crown or governor. Judges should be given a sufficient salary, "as long as they, having in their minds an indifference to all other affairs," devoted themselves wholly to their duties and studies as judges. This was doubtless aimed at Thomas Hutchinson and other judges who held multiple appointments.

Then the instructions attacked the Sugar Act, both as a restraint on trade and as a tax that threatened democratic govern-

31 In this and following chapters, I have not followed the widely accepted interpretations of Arthur M. Schlesinger, *The Colonial Merchants and the American Revolution, 1763–1776,* and Charles McLean Andrews, "The Boston Merchants and the Non-Importation Movement," in Colonial Society of Massachusetts, *Publications,* XIX (1918), 159–259. Schlesinger's thesis is based on two assumptions, (1) that merchants were the dominant element in colonial society and a merchant aristocracy controlled the seaport towns, and (2) that there was little democracy for the lower classes as the artisans and workers, who depended for their living on the merchants, were for the most part unenfranchised and unaware of their political power (pp. 27–28). I have already shown that farmers and artisans could vote and were overwhelmingly dominant in Massachusetts politics. Both Schlesinger and Andrews assumed that the merchants started the agitation against the British to protect their economic rights but that "radicals" later took control for purposes of political rights. But as the *Boston Town Records* show, the politicians and elected leaders were behind the opposition and political rights were involved from the Sugar Act on. Furthermore, a comparison of the times at which the merchants and others took actions will show that the merchants were almost invariably second when it came to promoting opposition.

32 *Boston Town Records,* XVI, 116. Notice of the Sugar Act appeared in the *Boston Gazette,* May 10, 1764.

ment. The representatives were to join any proposals for promoting the better cultivation of land and improving husbandry, as well as for supporting the commerce of Boston. Commerce had long operated under many difficulties, for as colonial trade centered in Great Britain, the colonies already paid revenue to Britain. Especially the town expressed surprise that nothing had been done about proposed new taxes, though the agent had sent notices of these proposals. The General Court had not been called to consult on this problem until the evil was beyond easy remedy. Obviously Boston blamed Governor Bernard for not calling a session of the General Court soon enough to do any good.

Boston was particularly fearful of setting a precedent for further taxes which would pose a threat to the colony's right to govern and tax itself. The town looked on these taxes as possible preparations for other taxes, for if trade could be taxed, why not lands, the produce of lands, or anything else the colonists possessed or used. This annihilated their charter rights to govern and tax themselves, for if taxes could be laid without their consent, they were no longer free subjects. The colonial agent should be instructed to assert the colony's just rights and privileges, at the same time assuring the British of Massachusetts' unshaken loyalty, unrivaled exertions to support the crown, acknowledged dependence upon and subordination to Great Britain, and the merchants' ready acquiescence in all necessary regulations of trade. In carrying out these instructions, the House of Representatives should get the co-operation of other colonies, as they were involved, and should cut expenses, especially military expenses, as peace prevailed and there was no threat from the French or Indians.[33]

When the General Court met in the spring of 1764, the stand of the colony against taxation was definitely fixed. One of the first orders of business was to form a committee, with Otis as chairman, to instruct agent Mauduit. This committee based its instructions on Otis' *Rights of the Colonies* and on information from the agent about passage of the Sugar Act and Grenville's

---

[33] *Boston Town Records*, XVI, 119ff.; Samuel Adams, *The Writings of Samuel Adams*, ed. by H. A. Cushing, 4 vols. (New York, 1907), I, 1–7; *Massachusetts Gazette*, May 31, 1764.

proposal for a stamp tax unless the colonies could propose a substitute. In its instructions, the House declared that Grenville had postponed the stamp tax to consult the ease, quiet, and good will of the colonies. But, said the House to Mauduit, "If the ease, the quiet, and the good will of the colonies are of any importance to Great-Britain, no measures could be hit upon, that have a more natural and direct tendency to enervate those principles, than the resolutions you inclosed." Grenville's kind offer of suspending the tax amounted only to the threat that if the colonies would not tax themselves, Parliament would tax them. Mauduit had orders to remonstrate, to obtain repeal of the Sugar Act, and to prevent the imposition of any further duties or taxes on the colonies.[34] If the agent did inform British authorities of these instructions, they had no reason to be surprised at the reception of the Stamp Act some months later.

Out of the opposition by the House to the Sugar Act came an interesting statement by Bernard as to the source of this opposition and its relation to democracy. The governor said he had studied the policy of several governments in America and had endeavored to acquire a true idea of their relation to Great Britain. These he had committed to writing in the spring, but he wished he had done it sooner, "for the late proceedings in Parliament had given such a rouse to the politicians in this country" that publication of something of this nature might be of service.[35]

Governor Bernard also suggested reforms which would curtail colonial democracy and strengthen British authority. He contended that Britain could tax and legislate for the colonies even though the colonies were not represented, an anticipation of colonial arguments against parliamentary taxation. The money thus raised should be used to support British officials in

[34] Mass. Hist. Soc., *Collections*, 1st ser., IX, 270; Tudor, *Life of James Otis*, pp. 166–69. The evidence does not support John C. Miller's statement that Samuel Adams was almost alone in protesting against the Sugar Act on the ground that Parliament was overstepping its authority. See *Sam Adams, Pioneer in Propaganda*, p. 44. On the postponement of the Stamp Act, see Edmund S. Morgan, "The Postponement of the Stamp Act," *William and Mary Quarterly*, 3d ser., VII (July 1950), 353–92.

[35] *Barrington-Bernard Correspondence*, p. 76.

America, especially since some colonies had been remiss in the payment of salaries. The governor expressed the fear that colonial charters might check British authority and thus contribute to the dismemberment of the British Empire. He proposed a consolidation of the dominions into several large and respectable governments with balanced powers. Bernard believed that the councils were not effective as a balance against the popular assemblies, and that what the colonies needed was a nobility or aristocracy to check popular government. A hereditary nobility was not feasible, but the king might establish a nobility appointed for life. The time for reform was now, the governor urged, as postponement would only make the job more difficult.[36]

Democratic action against the Sugar Act and proposed Stamp Act continued to be a factor during the summer of 1764. After the spring session of the General Court, the governor attempted to head off agitation against the Sugar Act by refusing to call another meeting of the General Court. But Hutchinson said that the people were dissatisfied and that Boston's representatives feared popular opinion would be against them unless they continually instructed the agent in England on so important a matter. So Bernard yielded to popular pressure and called the General Court into session again.[37]

During the fall session of the General Court, a breach between the democratic House and the Council, which had been in evidence since taxation became an issue, showed definite signs of increasing and eventually culminated in the complete domination of the Council by the House. Previously the House had sent instructions to agent Mauduit without consulting the Council as was customary. Now a rift appeared over the philosophical basis for colonial claims. The House and Council agreed that the Sugar Act was not just a commercial act but that it affected civil rights as well. But they could not agree on whether to demand the exclusive *right* of colonial assemblies to tax, as the House demanded, or the *privilege* of taxation, as the prerogative party in the Council, led by Thomas Hutchinson and Andrew Oliver, insisted. House and Council compromised on the word *liberties,* but the House informed the agent that

[36] Adams, *Works,* IV, 22–28.   [37] Hutchinson, *History,* III, 81–82.

as far as the House was concerned, its stand was still based on *rights,* not *privileges* or *liberties.*[38] This rift eventually brought the elimination of Hutchinson and Oliver from the Council.

Colonial resistance to the Sugar Act soon took a more practical turn than mere instructions and petitions, however, as popular opinion became directed against British economic interests. As early as January 16, 1764, a writer in the *Boston Gazette* talked of bounties on cloth, stockings, and hardware, and there were rumors of bounties on foreign sugar and molasses which were purchased with colonial products.[39] In June 1764, *Americanus* advocated a bounty of sheep's wool to encourage wool manufactures.[40] There were notices of thread stockings, with AMERICA in the clock, being made in Maryland and proposals from several colonies for introducing manufactures into the country as a method of expressing patriotism.[41] By September 27, according to the *Massachusetts Gazette,* people had stopped using mourning dress at funerals, used country-made instead of imported white gloves, and tradesmen had agreed to wear leather clothes made in the colony.[42] Boston formed an association—the papers were signed by some councilors and representatives and by many people in Boston—to prevent the importation of British manufactures and to advocate abstention from eating lamb. Hutchinson said that these measures united the people against Parliament, which they considered unqualified to legislate for both countries because their interests were different and Parliament was biased. Advocates of parliamentary legislation soon lost favor in Massachusetts.[43]

What Massachusetts would have done eventually about the Sugar Act if the Stamp Act had not been passed is, of course, a moot question, but certain it is that the colony, as represented by the lower house, had taken a strong stand against parliamentary taxation by early 1764.[44] Perhaps this preliminary opposi-

38 *Ibid.,* p. 82; Mass. Hist. Soc., *Collections,* LXXIV, 167, 170.
39 *Boston Gazette,* Jan. 16, 1764.   40 *Ibid.,* June 25, 1764.
41 *Massachusetts Gazette and Supplement,* Sept. 13, 1764.
42 *Massachusetts Gazette,* Sept. 27, 1764.
43 Hutchinson, *History,* III, 82; *Boston Gazette,* Jan. 3, 1765.
44 Again the evidence does not support Miller's view (*Sam Adams,* p. 41) that Otis and Adams did not have much popular support and that Otis lost control

tion was essential as a preparation for the stand soon to be taken against the Stamp Act, for the lower house by 1765 had aroused or reflected public opinion in Massachusetts and had taken the first steps toward a colonial union by approving a committee to send information to other assemblies concerning the instructions to Mauduit.

Given this background, the British should have expected what the Stamp Act in fact produced, especially as the declared purposes of the tax was to reform democratic government.[45] As is so well known, the Stamp Act provided for a stamp tax on a host of items, some of which, such as ships' clearance papers, were designed to aid in enforcing the navigation acts. There were many obnoxious provisions in the act, especially to a democratic people. No newspaper or pamphlet could be printed without the name of the author or printer, presumably a device to stop anonymous attacks on government. Violations were to be tried in courts of record or admiralty, where there were no juries and where judges held office at the pleasure of the British government. Officials were safeguarded in enforcement by the provision that any official who was sued because of the Stamp Act merely had to present the act itself as evidence to recover treble damages. And then, of course, the act would provide a fund, over which the colonists had no control, to carry out proposed reforms in colonial government.[46]

---

of the House of Representatives. Miller cites a letter of Dec. 22, 1766, describing events after the Stamp Act was repealed, to prove that all was quiet in Massachusetts before the Stamp Act. On the early position taken by the colonies against Parliament's right to tax or regulate trade, see Edmund S. Morgan, "Colonial Ideas of Parliamentary Power, 1764–1766," *William and Mary Quarterly*, 3d ser., V (July 1948), 311–41.

[45] Dickerson, in *The Navigation Acts and the American Revolution*, pp. 190–95, emphasized the impact of the Stamp Act on commerce but did not stress the threat which the act posed to democratic government. Gipson stressed imperial defense as the motive behind the Stamp Act, not the possible use of troops in effecting reforms to reduce the power of democratic assemblies, but he does show that Grenville was perfectly aware of the threat of colonial independence when he discussed the Stamp Act (*The Coming of the Revolution*, pp. 70–81).

[46] Pickering, *Statutes*, XXVI, 179–204. The most complete account of the Stamp Act is that by Edmund S. and Helen M. Morgan, *The Stamp Act Crisis: Prologue to Revolution* (Chapel Hill, 1953). The Morgans contended that the colonies did not distinguish between internal and external taxation, but opposed any Parlia-

The Stamp Act again brought out those differences between British and American views of the empire which had so often caused trouble between the two peoples. There were reports from London, vigorously denied in the colony, that the colonists were attempting to gain their independence.[47] In Parliament, there was the pro-British view expressed by Charles Townshend that the colonies had been planted by Britain and nourished to strength and opulence by British indulgence. Isaac Barrè countered with the pro-American view that the colonies were planted by British oppression and tyranny, nourished by neglect, and had not only not been protected by British arms but had actually taken up arms in Britain's defense.[48] In Boston, Governor Bernard told the General Court that changes in colonial administration had long been proposed and would be pushed to completion. Some regulations would probably appear disagreeable, but he was convinced that they would operate for the benefit of the colonies and that they should submit respectfully to the decrees of Parliament. Bernard assured them that Parliament was the sanctuary of liberty and justice, that the king was a patriot king, and that the colonies could submit in perfect confidence that their rights would be safe.[49]

It is a little difficult to believe that Bernard expected the House of Representatives to follow his advice. As Hutchinson had said, the people had long believed that British and American interests conflicted and that Parliament could not be trusted to legislate for both people. Instead of "submitting respectfully," the House ignored Bernard's speech and called for a colonial congress which would consolidate colonial opposition. This move had already been forecast by the committee which had been set up to notify other assemblies of the strongly worded House instructions to agent Mauduit.

As is well known, the Stamp Act resulted in riots in Boston

---

mentary tax from the first (pp. 114–15). These authors differ from the present account in their statement that Parliament's "right" to tax was not emphasized at the time of the Sugar Act and that the Sugar Act was considered more as a regulation of trade than a revenue act (p. 39). The Morgans did not discuss the relation of the Stamp Act to democracy.

47 *Massachusetts Gazette*, May 23, 1765.   48 *Ibid.,* May 30, 1765.
49 *Boston Gazette,* June 3, 1765.

during the summer of 1765, but these were not just mob actions by disfranchised lower classes against aristocratic upper classes and led by such "radical" leaders as Samuel Adams and James Otis.[50] Governor Bernard attempted to picture the disturbances as a leveling movement to eliminate all distinctions between rich and poor. But in the same letter he effectively refuted his own charge by saying that leading men in Boston publicly justified the attack on stamp distributor Andrew Oliver's house and that the Stamp Act merely revived popular discontent which had been present for years.[51] The fact is that attacks were made only on the property of men engaged or believed to be engaged in enforcing British colonial policy—Lieutenant Governor Hutchinson, stamp distributor Oliver, deputy register of admiralty court William Story, and comptroller of customs Benjamin Hallowell.[52] The property of even more wealthy men on the popular side, such as John Hancock and James Bowdoin, was not molested.

Lest there should be exception taken to this view, a special word needs to be said about the destruction of Hutchinson's home. Word got out that Hutchinson had known about the Stamp Act and had encouraged the British to pass it "by recom-

[50] This interpretation is to be found in J. T. Adams, *Revolutionary New England*, pp. 304–322, and John C. Miller, *Sam Adams*, pp. 51–69. Adams maintained that the Boston town meeting was not democratic, that the franchise was rigidly restricted so that not all men were represented in the colony (Adams cites McKinley), that many who shouted loudest about no taxation without representation would have been the least willing to put this practice into operation in America, that the outcry against England taught the unenfranchised classes in America a lesson, thereby helping to arouse a genuinely revolutionary movement, and that leaders of the lower classes organized the unenfranchised classes into Sons of Liberty while the upper classes were passing resolutions in assemblies. The Stamp Act raised not only the question of maintaining colonial rights but the more important question, by whom and by what methods. "In other words," said Adams, citing the famous statement by Carl Becker, "to the question of home rule was added that of who was to rule at home." Miller followed the Adams interpretation to a large extent. Radical organizations such as the Sons of Liberty were not founded spontaneously to resist the Stamp Act, he said, but had been in existence for many years, not to resist British tyranny but to combat the colonial aristocracy and give the underprivileged classes a share of political power. Miller depicted Samuel Adams as a conniving backstair and garret politician who both instigated and controlled mob action against the upper classes.

[51] Bernard to Lords of Trade, Aug. 31, 1765, *Parliamentary History*, XVI, 129.

[52] *Massachusetts Gazette*, Aug. 29, 1765.

mending it as an easy method of gulling the people of their liberty and property." [53] Hutchinson was given twelve days and several opportunities to deny the accusations, but he refused on the ground that this was an indignity to which he would not submit.[54] The letter to Israel Williams in November 1763 showed that he did have previous information, so that he could not truthfully say otherwise. A simple denial would have cleared Hutchinson, for the crowd had quietly dispersed the first time it met merely on the assurance of Hutchinson's friends that Hutchinson was not connected with the Stamp Act.[55] On the day his property was attacked, he was given a final chance to assert his innocence, but again he failed to do so.[56] As a result, Hutchinson shared the fates of the stamp distributor and the customs officials.

There seems to be little doubt that the Stamp Act riots were the work of a cross section of Boston society, not a lower-class uprising. Jonathan Mayhew, one of the leading ministers, was accused of instigating the trouble by an inflammatory sermon,[57] and merchant John Rowe acknowledged that the merchants were behind the whole affair.[58] One of the ringleaders, shoe-maker and cordwainer Ebenezer Mackintosh, had to be released by the sheriff when some of the leading merchants and men of property threatened to withdraw the town watchman and leave the town unprotected unless this was done. So general was the discontent that Bernard did not even dare to enlist soldiers to

[53] Israel Williams Papers, II, 159; *Boston Evening Post,* Aug. 19, 1765.

[54] *Boston Evening Post,* Aug. 19, 1765; Hutchinson, *History,* III, 88.

[55] *Boston Evening Post,* Aug. 19, 1765. In commenting on the fact that the crowd had dispersed at Hutchinson's house on being told that Hutchinson was not responsible for the Stamp Act, the *Evening Post* said, "God grant they may not have occasion to meet again."

[56] *Boston Gazette,* Aug. 26, 1765; Mass. Arch., XXVI, 146. In "Thomas Hutchinson and the Stamp Act," *New England Quarterly,* XXI (Dec. 1948), 459–92, Edmund S. Morgan contended that Hutchinson was innocent of charges that he had helped foster the Stamp Act, but Morgan did not explain Hutchinson's early information about the Stamp Act, the newspaper warnings that his innocence should be established, and his refusal to heed these warnings.

[57] Mass. Hist. Soc., *Collections,* 4th ser., IV, 206.

[58] Thomas Hutchinson, *The Diary and Letters of His Excellency Thomas Hutchinson* . . . , ed. by Peter Orlando Hutchinson, 2 vols. (Boston, 1884, 1886), I, 67.

guard the stamps.[59] Hutchinson said that he himself had for some time been the principal object of "popular" resentment and called the opposition "the rabble." [60] But later he said that the attack on two such prominent officials as himself and Oliver brought terror to the people of the lower rank, who saw the danger of popular power, but feared reprisals if they opposed it.[61] The day after the riots, Hutchinson admitted that he had mistaken the extent of popular feeling and was now convinced that the people throughout the continent believed they were no longer considered by the English as fellow subjects entitled to English liberties.[62]

John Adams, who was certainly no leveler, fully recognized the danger to colonial democracy if Britain enforced the Stamp Act. While he deplored violence, he also thought that Hutchinson had demonstrated "a very ambitious and avaricious disposition" and that he and his relatives had grasped a dangerous number of offices in the government.[63] He called the Stamp Act "that enormous engine, fabricated by the British Parliament, for battering down all the rights and liberties of America," and he wondered that there was not more violence.[64] Then Adams made this significant statement:

If there is any man, who from wild ideas of power and authority, *from a contempt of that equality in knowledge, wealth, and power, which has prevailed in this country,* or from any other cause, can upon principle desire the execution of the Stamp Act, those principles are a total forfeiture of the confidence of the people. If there is anyone who cannot see the tendency of that act to reduce the body of the people to ignorance, poverty, dependence, his want of eyesight is a disqualification for public employment. Let the towns and the representatives, therefore, renounce every stamp man and every trimmer next May.[65]

Adams' statement was not merely evidence of the existence of democratic equality in education, wealth, and politics; it was a call for democratic action against anyone who would jeopardize this democracy.

[59] Hutchinson, *History,* III, 90–91.
[60] Mass. Arch., XXVI, 146; XXVII, 489.
[61] Hutchinson, *History,* III, 89.
[62] Mass. Arch., XXVI, 145 a and b.
[63] Adams, *Works,* II, 150–51.
[64] *Ibid.,* pp. 154–55.
[65] *Ibid.,* p. 167. Italics mine.

The Stamp Act also furnished the occasion for Adams' famous analysis of Massachusetts democracy as it related to civil, religious, and educational institutions and of the threat to this democracy posed by the Stamp Act. This analysis was contained in his "Dissertation on the Canon and on the Feudal Law," which was published both in the colony and in England.

In the "Dissertation," Adams first stressed the part that education had played in the establishment of religious and civil liberty in the American colonies. Before the Reformation, nobles and clergy had combined to exercise feudal and ecclesiastical tyranny over the people, mainly through keeping them in ignorance, which deprived them of any knowledge of their rights and wrongs. The Reformation, by restoring knowledge to its rightful place, broke the power of the church and the nobility. As knowledge among the people increased, ecclesiastical and civil tyranny declined. The struggle between the people, on one hand, and canon and feudal tyranny, on the other, reached a climax under the Stuarts; and this struggle, to which knowledge had contributed so much, helped to people America. It was not simply religion alone, according to Adams, but a love of universal liberty and a dread of the infernal union of church and state that brought people to America. Puritans, persecuted for their knowledge and freedom of inquiry, left England and established their plan of civil and ecclesiastical government in direct opposition to the feudal and canon systems.[66] Perhaps Adams was presenting the Puritan background more as it was later interpreted than as it actually was.

Adams then went on to show how the Puritans' civil and religious principles promoted democratic education and were in turn protected by democratic education. Said Adams:

They were convinced, by their knowledge of human nature, derived from history and their own experience, that nothing could preserve their posterity from the encroachments of the two systems of tyranny, in opposition to which, as has been observed already, they erected their government in church and state, but knowledge diffused generally through the whole body of the people. Their civil and religious principles, therefore, conspired to prompt them to use every measure

[66] *Ibid.*, III, 448–51.

and take every precaution in their power to propagate and perpetuate knowledge. For this purpose they laid very early the foundations of colleges, and invested them with ample privileges and emoluments; and it is remarkable that they have left among their posterity so universal an affection and veneration for these seminaries, and for liberal education, that the meanest of the people contribute cheerfully to the support and maintenance of them every year, and that nothing is more generally popular than projections for the honor, reputation, and advantage of those seats of learning. But the wisdom and benevolence of our fathers rested not here. They made an early provision by law, that every town consisting of so many families, should be always furnished with a grammar school. They made it a crime for such a town to be destitute of a grammar schoolmaster for a few months, and subjected it to a heavy penalty. So that the education of all ranks of people was made the care and expense of the public, in a manner that I believe has been unknown to any other people ancient or modern.[67]

Whatever we may think of Puritan education, there was no doubt in John Adams' mind that it was the best system for the common people that the world had ever known and that its roots stemmed directly from a determination to eliminate religious and civil tyranny.

Having given the historical background of Massachusetts' educational system, Adams proceeded to show the effects of a democratic education on the people at large and its relation to democracy in general:

The consequences of these establishments we see and feel every day. A native of America who cannot read and write is as rare an appearance as a Jacobite or a Roman Catholic, that is, as rare as a comet or an earthquake. It has been observed, that we are all of us lawyers, divines, politicians, and philosophers. And I have good authorities to say, that all candid foreigners who have passed through this country, and conversed freely with all sorts of people here, will allow, that they have never seen so much knowledge and civility among the common people in any part of the world.

It is true, Adams continued, that an imported party of high Churchmen and high statesmen censured the provision for educating youth as a needless expense, an imposition on the rich

67 *Ibid.,* pp. 451–52, 455–56.

to help the poor. They said it produced idleness and vain speculation among the people, who ought to devote their time to
labor, not to examining the conduct of their superiors. But,
said Adams, the colonists had a right to liberty, "and liberty
cannot be preserved without a general knowledge among the
people." The people had a right to knowledge, especially the
most dreaded and envied knowledge about the character and
conduct of their rulers. Rulers were no more than trustees for
the people, and if this trust is insidiously betrayed, the people
have the right to revoke the authority of their rulers and to
constitute abler and better trustees. "And," concluded Adams,
"the preservation of the means of knowledge among the lowest
ranks, is of more importance to the public than all the property
of all the rich men in the country." [68]

In the prevailing controversy with England, Adams placed
knowledge in the forefront among the weapons which the colonists had for defending their rights against encroachments. He
urged them to guard a free press, one of the chief means of information, and he praised the free colonial press for promoting
freedom of expression and for combating efforts to destroy
freedom of thinking, speaking, and writing. Spirit, however,
meant little without knowledge:

Let us tenderly and kindly cherish, therefore, the means of knowledge. Let us dare to read, think, speak, and write. Let every order
and degree among the people rouse their attention and animate their
resolution. Let them all become attentive to the grounds and principles of government, ecclesiastical and civil. . . . Let the colleges
join their harmony in the same delightful concert. . . . In a word,
let every sluice of knowledge be opened and set a-flowing.[69]

Adams looked on the Stamp Act as a part of British designs
to impose the canon and feudal law on America, especially
through the suppression of knowledge. He said there seemed
to be a direct and formal design on foot to enslave America by
degrees, the first step of which was the entire subversion of the
colonial system by the introduction of the canon and feudal
law. The Stamp Act itself, he said, made it manifest "that a
design is formed to strip us in a great measure of the means of

[68] *Ibid.*, pp. 456–57.   [69] *Ibid.*, pp. 457–59, 462–63.

knowledge, by loading the press, the colleges, and even an almanack and a newspaper, with restraints and duties. . . ." [70]

Others besides John Adams were fully aware of the relationship between democracy and the Stamp Act. In his account of events at the time of the Stamp Act, the later Loyalist, Peter Oliver, declared that the country representatives in the assembly were generally men of very inferior understanding and "were ever to be charmed by the word patriotism, which in the dictionary of this province was translated Republicanism." [71] Thomas Hutchinson explained how this republicanism worked in practice. There was a proposal to compensate the men who had suffered losses in the Stamp Act riots, but many of the towns instructed their representatives not to grant compensation. As a result, said Hutchinson, twenty or more of his friends were instructed to vote against him. Concluded he: "Instructions to restrain a representative from voting according to his judgment, however popular, always appeared to me unconstitutional and absurd." [72] Absurd to Hutchinson, perhaps, but woe to the representative who failed to obey his constituents' commands.

A British officer traveling in the colonies during the Stamp Act controversy also saw the conflict between colonial democracy and British imperialism. First he commented on the extent of social and economic democracy—that the common people here had names associated with the aristocracy in England, that any pretty girl here could attend a dance and be well received because there was "no sort of distinction of persons," that "the levelling principle here, every where operates strongly and takes the lead, everybody has property & everybody knows it." Then he pointed out how this democracy hindered British policies. The "better sort," he continued, lamented their plan of government because the popular branch had too much power, a condition which could be remedied only by a thorough alteration of the charter to allow the king to appoint the Council. For

[70] *Ibid.*, p. 464. Arthur M. Schlesinger, in "Colonial Newspapers and the Stamp Act," *New England Quarterly*, VIII (March 1935), 63–83, pointed out that newspapers became important in propaganda at the time of the Stamp Act.

[71] Egerton MSS., 2671, pp. 82–89.   [72] Mass. Arch., XXVI, 248.

without such change and an adequate force to support civil government, he concluded, "that ancient rugged spirit of levelling, early imported from home, and too successfully nursed, and cherished, will, in the four New England governments never be got the better of." Palliatives might postpone the danger, but the malady was radical, he said, and could be cured better now than later, especially while there was peace in Europe.[73]

Instructions and resolves of the towns, the General Court, and eventually the Stamp Act Congress show clearly that democracy was preparing itself for a strong stand against any encroachments. Not only did these resolves claim that colonists could not be taxed without representation but they also declared that the colonies could not be represented in Parliament. Hence only colonial legislatures could ever tax the colonists. Some of the towns admitted that the trade acts had always been considered a grievance. In all instructions and resolves, the rights of property held a conspicuous place beside personal rights, which would be natural in a society where most men owned property. In particular, there was complaint over extension of the powers of admiralty courts. Cases concerning colonial property were to be tried without benefit of jury by one judge, appointed at pleasure by the British and given a percentage of all convictions. After stating their position in no uncertain terms, the towns ordered their representatives to suppress all riots but not to assist in the collection of stamp taxes. In addition, the resolves were to be printed in the public records so that all the world would know that the people had not tamely relinquished their rights and liberties.[74]

Letters of the time explain the purpose of the Stamp Act as it affected democracy and show the extent of popular opposition. One writer said that the act of Parliament for collecting internal taxes in the colonies and paying all officers of the government would destroy the great influence of the assembly over the

[73] "Journal of an Officer," King's MSS., CCXIII, 123–25.
[74] *Boston Town Records*, XVI, 152–57; *Braintree Town Records*, pp. 404–06; *Massachusetts Gazette*, Oct. 10, 1765; *Plymouth Town Records*, III, 161–69; Andover Town Records, Sept. 11, 1765; Malden Town Records, II, 8.

administration, which influence prejudiced the king's prerogative in the colonies. It was chiefly for this reason, he said, that popular leaders so violently opposed the Stamp Act.[75] Hutchinson declared in March 1766 that popular control was complete and that Britain should postpone any external provision for the future support of government until popular feeling died down.[76] In short, taxes were obviously designed for more than the mere payment of expenses in defense of the frontier.

In turn, troops could have other uses than frontier defense. In letters to colonial officials, Secretary Conway said that the tumults in Massachusetts struck at the very being of all authority and subordination in the colony. He was greatly surprised that the Council had refused to call in the aid of regular troops to support the civil magistrate and expressed the hope that the lack of confidence in the tenderness and justice of the mother country came from the lower classes. The better sort would know that decency and submission would serve better than violence in obtaining grace and favor. Conway ordered Britain's military and naval officers, Gage and Colvil, to use leniency if possible in restoring peace, but if this failed, to use all force necessary. They must not allow the authority of Parliament and the king's dignity to be trampled on by force and violence.[77]

Out of the Sugar and Stamp Act controversies there emerged one of the most influential leaders of a democratic society—Samuel Adams. Adams had written the strong Boston resolves against the Sugar Act, was elected to the legislature to replace Oxenbridge Thacher when he died, then directed the opposition in the General Court while James Otis was at the Stamp Act Congress. Adams also wrote the resolves of the assembly which were used as a model for the Stamp Act Resolves.[78]

[75] *Parliamentary History*, XVI, 125.   [76] Mass. Arch., XVI, 203–06.
[77] Oct. 14, 1765, *Parliamentary History*, XVI, 114–16.
[78] Hutchinson, *History*, III, 94–96. Unfortunately, the significance of Samuel Adams as a democratic leader of a democratic society has been missed by writers who consider colonial society undemocratic. Conservative writers have naturally condemned Adams for his views and actions largely because they have depended on Thomas Hutchinson as a main source. There is no evidence whatever to justify the story of Samuel Adams as a tax embezzler with a prison sentence hanging over his head. See Miller, *Sam Adams*, pp. 58–60. Miller (p. 60, n. 24) cited

The emergence of Adams as a popular leader is further proof that the issues were between the British and Americans, not between lower- and upper-class Americans over the problem of internal democracy. Adams was known for his anti-British views, not for being opposed to upper classes in America. Hutchinson said that the resolves which Adams wrote reflected the view which Adams acknowledged without reserve in private—colonial independence.[79] Adams denied that the colonies were aiming at independence, but insisted that the only way to preserve colonial rights was to leave the colonies with the powers they had previously possessed.[80] The Loyalist, Peter Oliver, claimed that Adams followed policies to win the votes of Boston artisans, and that "such men chiefly composed the voters of a *Boston Town Meeting*." [81] If Boston artisans elected Adams, a champion of colonial independence, the problem could not have been one of internal democracy, and, as we shall see, Adams was to play a stellar part in the conflict between colonial democracy and British imperialism.

After the passage of the Stamp Act, there was simply no question that democracy was in the saddle in Massachusetts, not only in the assembly, but also in what should have been the "aristocratic" Council. Governor Bernard said that the colony was democratic in all respects except the appointment of a governor

---

William Gordon, *The History of the Rise, Progress, and Establishment of the Independence of the United States of America*, 3 vols. (New York, 1801), I, 348 as evidence for his story, but Gordon on page 348 discussed Washington, not Samuel Adams. A careful perusal of the *Boston Town Records* would have revealed much of the truth about Adams as a tax collector. Despite many faults, William V. Wells's *The Life and Public Services of Samuel Adams . . .* , 3 vols. (Boston, 1865), I, 35–38, has most of the salient facts about the Adams episode as tax collector in Boston. The psychological approach to Adams is that by Ralph V. Harlow, *Samuel Adams, Promoter of the American Revolution: A Study in Psychology and Politics* (New York, 1923). Harlow attempted to depict Adams as a neurotic with an inferiority complex, a man whose political activity was always irrational because it was the product of emotions rather than reason. Harlow also claimed that England had ruined Adams' father in the Land Bank. A more rational and successful politician than Samuel Adams would be difficult to find in the eighteenth century.

79 Hutchinson, *History*, III, 94–96.   80 Adams, *Writings*, I, 38.
81 Egerton MSS., 2671, p. 74.

and was especially democratic in the appointment of the Council. The recent commotions, he declared, had demonstrated how the preponderance of the popular part of the government tended to defeat the principal ends of government, meaning, of course, British ends. The governor believed that the issue was no longer a stamp tax but subjection to Great Britain. Royal government in the colony could never recover its authority without British aid, he continued, for the people had felt their strength and would never submit to anything they disliked.[82] Governor Bernard said that colonial governments should have been changed and strengthened before Parliament tried to tax the colonies. Now much time and money would be necessary to reduce America to the degree of submission required by Parliament. The colonies, he said, should have an upper house appointed for life, a fixed civil list, and a revised law code to conform with English laws.[83]

In a letter to former governor Thomas Pownall, Hutchinson, in detailing the events incident to the Stamp Act, pointed out what Pownall knew so well from experience—the complete control of democracy, especially in the Boston town meeting. First, Hutchinson conceded that Pownall was right when he had often suggested that the colonies were aiming at independence. Then he went on to show the utter inadequacy of British authority: "In the capital towns of several of the colonies & of this in particular, the authority is in the populace, no law can be carried into execution against their mind." He was not sure but that the trade acts would be considered as grievous as the Stamp Act. Government, he continued, operated at several levels, with the town meeting at the top. First, there was the rabble of the town under Mackintosh to burn effigies and pull down houses. These were somewhat controlled by the master masons, carpenters, and other artisans of Boston. More important tasks, such as opening the customs house, were carried out by the merchants under John Rowe. But all really important decisions were made in the Boston town meeting, where Otis prevailed without opposition. The town decided what was to be done, then petitioned the governor and Council to do it, and, said

82 Bernard, *Select Letters*, pp. 42–43.   83 *Ibid.*, pp. 93–102.

Hutchinson, "it would be a very extraordinary resolve indeed that is not carried into execution." [84]

Hutchinson believed that the British government should realize the extent of democracy in the colony before making any future attempts to recover its authority by raising a colonial revenue to support government. In his discussion of the completeness of popular control and the impotence of the government, meaning, of course, the British side of government, Hutchinson gave this advice:

I do not mention this as a sufficient argument against external provision for the future support of government, but it may possibly be a reason for deferring for a short time at lest [sic] in degree any measures for that purpose until the minds of the people are somewhat calmed, and the effect of the repeal if that should be [the] case shall appear. [85]

The extent of democratic influence was also made evident during the discussions over whether or not the courts should proceed without using stamps in legal transactions. Boston requested that the courts of law be opened regardless of the Stamp Act, and the assembly resolved, with not more than a half-dozen dissenting votes, that this be done. Hutchinson blocked the move in the Council and was accused by Otis of saying that the House resolve was impertinent and beneath the notice of the Council. Hutchinson asked the Council to take action against Otis, but the Council would only go so far as to declare that Hutchinson had not made the statement attributed to him. This appeased the rabble, said Hutchinson, but was so dishonorable of the Council that he withdrew from Council meetings as a protest. Hutchinson believed that the majority of the House were friendly to government but were afraid to vote their convictions because Otis threatened to print the names of anyone who voted against his proposals. Popular control, Hutchinson declared, was complete. [86]

Even the Anglican clergy felt the sting of popular influence as a result of the Stamp Act. The Reverend William Agar of Cambridge wrote: "I am not surprised that the clergy in Eng-

[84] March 8, 1766, Mass. Arch., XXVI, 199–206.   [85] Ibid., p. 203.
[86] Ibid., pp. 206–13; Boston Gazette, Feb. 3, 1766.

land should be so backward to take missions; for the people here are of a very capricious temper, & this Stamp Act, has made it dangerous to preach up loyalty & subjection. Especially here where presbytery has the superiority." [87]

One of the major objectives of the Stamp Act—more British control over colonial governments—is revealed in the debates concerning the repeal of the Stamp Act, which colonial opposition and the resulting economic loss to British merchants soon effected. In these debates, the statement was made that the colonies had become too large to be governed by their original laws and charters. They had run into confusion, and it would be the policy of Great Britain to form a plan of laws for them.[88] Parliament also passed the Declaratory Act, basing repeal on the expediency that the Stamp Act hurt British trade but not abdicating the right of Parliament to tax the colonies. In the Declaratory Act, nothing was said about Parliament's right to tax the colonies for their defense. But Parliament did say that the colonies had been, were, and ought to be subordinate to and dependent on Great Britain, that king and Parliament had the power to make laws for the colonies in all cases, and that any act or resolve denying the authority of Parliament was utterly void.[89]

In effect, Parliament was attempting to do by words what it had failed to do by acts. The new policy was designed to raise a revenue which would restore British authority in the colonies. The failure of the tax did not eliminate the purpose for which the tax had been levied. Neither did repeal mean that the British would not try again.

Repeal of the Stamp Act brought great rejoicing in the colony and was looked on as a victory by the "friends of liberty." There were fireworks and open houses by such popular leaders as Otis and Hancock.[90] Hutchinson said he did not think that the people would ever submit to internal taxes and that he was afraid for other regulations, as he had heard that Otis told the town meeting that the merchants were fools for submitting to

[87] SPG Archives, XXII, 20.
[88] *Parliamentary History*, XVI, 163–228.
[89] Pickering, *Statutes*, XXVII, 19.
[90] *Boston Gazette*, May 26, 1766.

duties and other restraints on trade.[91] He believed that repeal
of the Stamp Act was necessary, since the madness of the people
might have led them to commit almost any action.[92]

The Declaratory Act, on the other hand, met with a mixed
reception. Some thought it was merely a face-saving device by
Parliament and signified nothing; others believed that the colonists should oppose any declaration of British right to legislate
for the colonies as strenuously as they had resisted the Stamp
Act.[93] Thomas Paine later said that the Stamp Act usurped
Americans' most precious and sacred rights, but "the Declaratory Act left them no rights at all." It contained the seeds of the
most despotic government ever exercised in the world, made all
charters subject to repeal, and was the only instance in which
tyranny had been established by law.[94] A writer in the *Boston
Gazette* warned his readers that failure to protest against the
Declaratory Act might have serious consequences, but nothing
was done.[95]

Hutchinson, however, injected a sinister and prophetic note
in the midst of the rejoicing. It was necessary to quiet the minds
of the people first, he said, then they would "be better prepared
to receive such regulations as are absolutely necessary in order
to restore & support authority." [96] He also stated that future rule
in America would be the same as that used in Ireland.[97] Had
the people known of these expressions, their jubilance might
have been more restrained.

Hutchinson also confirmed the view presented thus far that
the trouble in Massachusetts had nothing to do with an internal
revolution for more democracy. Said he:

Had our confusions, in this province, proceeded from any interior
cause we have good men enough in the country towns to have united
in restoring peace and order and would have put an end to the
influence [of] the plebeian party in the town of Boston over the rest
of the province. In the town of Boston a plebeian party always has

[91] To Pownall, May 11, 1766, Mass. Arch., XXVI, 231.   [92] *Ibid.*, p. 227.
[93] *Ibid.*, Hutchinson, *History*, III, 106.   [94] Paine, *Writings*, II, 217–18.
[95] *Boston Gazette*, Aug. 18, 1766.   [96] Mass. Arch., XXVI, 227.
[97] *Ibid.*, p. 230.

and I fear always will have the command and for some months past they have governed the province. *But as our misfortunes come from a cause without us,* many of those persons who in the other case would have been friends to government are now too apt to approve of measures inconsistent with government & unite with those whom they would otherwise abhor under a notion of opposing by a common interest a power which they had no voice in creating, & which they say has a distinct and separate interest from us.[98]

Certainly there is no idea here of an internal revolution for more democracy or of a controlling merchant aristocracy in Boston.

If more evidence were needed that the popularly elected part of the government held the driver's seat, the election of 1766 furnished it. This election showed why representatives were afraid to have their names published as opponents of popular measures and what happened to what John Adams called "stamp men" and "trimmers" at election time.

The purge of pro-British legislators started with the election of representatives in the spring election. A writer in the *Boston Gazette* urged that the Sons of Liberty elect the right representatives and give them proper instructions. This writer suggested that appointed officials, especially judges, should not be elected to the Council, and he advocated open meetings of the General Court with the vote recorded so that the people could reward or punish legislators as they saw fit. He also wanted a revised table of fees, no monopoly of offices, and liberty of the press. Under this article was a list of representatives and the towns they represented.[99] A later item explained the list: If the political conduct of these men merited it, they should be honored in the coming election; if not, they should be accounted enemies of their country, especially if they approved the Stamp Act.[100] In the election, twenty of the thirty-two men on the list were purged.[101] Samuel Adams demonstrated his political popularity by receiving the highest vote among the four Bos-

[98] To Jackson, April 21, 1766, Mass. Arch., XXVI, 227. Italics mine.
[99] *Boston Gazette,* March 31 and April 14, 1766.
[100] *Boston Evening Post,* April 28, 1766.
[101] *Acts and Resolves,* XVIII, 112–13.

ton delegates—Adams, Thomas Cushing, James Otis, and John Hancock.[102]

The purge continued when the General Court met in May 1766 and elected a Council. Many towns followed the advice of the *Gazette* writer, sending strongly worded instructions, especially that representatives elect as councilors men of integrity and wisdom, lovers of liberty, and defenders of their civil and ecclesiastical constitution.[103] Samuel Adams was elected clerk and James Otis was elected speaker of the House, but was negatived by Bernard. Thomas Cushing, second highest vote getter in Boston, was then elected speaker, a post he was to hold without interruption until he went to the First Continental Congress in 1774.[104] Then the House cleansed the Council of men considered unworthy of public office. Out went Hutchinson, Peter and Andrew Oliver, Judge Trowbridge, Benjamin Lynde, and George Leonard, which included the lieutenant governor, the secretary, two judges, and the attorney general.[105] "What a change!" exclaimed John Adams. "The triumph of Otis and his party are complete." [106] Governor Bernard, after vetoing new councilors chosen by the popular party, accused the House of depriving the province of its best and most able servants whose only crime was their fidelity to the Crown.[107] Peter Oliver, one of those purged, accused the assembly of trying to destroy all attachment with Great Britain and of "swallowing down all legal government, and substituting a democracy in its place." [108] Hutchinson, another purged councilor, called the newly elected councilors "little better than the scum." The House assumed the powers of government, the Council acquiesced, and the governor was helpless to prevent it, he declared.[109]

The popular party, not satisfied with simply winning an election, gave the governor a sharp lecture on the way democratic and constitutional government worked. Replying to the gov-

---

[102] Rowe, *Diary*, p. 93; *Boston Gazette*, May 26, 1766.

[103] *Boston Town Records*, XVI, 183–84; *Worcester Town Records*, IV, 138; *Boston Gazette*, June 2, 1766.

[104] *Acts and Resolves*, XVIII, 112, 224, 330, 372, 464, 528, 616, 708, 798.

[105] *Ibid.*, p. 3; *Boston Gazette*, June 2, 1766.   [106] Adams, *Works*, II, 195–96.

[107] *Boston Gazette*, June 2, 1766.   [108] Egerton MSS., 2671, pp. 101–06.

[109] Mass. Arch., XXVI, 233, 254.

ernor's charge of depriving the colony of its best servants, the House said it was their constitutional right to choose councilors and the governor's constitutional right to negative those chosen. It had not deprived the province of its best and ablest servants, the House said; it had just released the judges from the cares of politics to give them "opportunity to make still farther advances in the knowledge of the law" and had left other gentlemen off the Council to give them more leisure to discharge their various duties as officials. They were merely correcting a dangerous union of executive and legislative officials, as they had been instructed to do by their constituents, and they hoped to see the time come when no Crown official sat in the Council. The House said it could not see how it had violated the charter by doing as the charter directed, and it expressed the hope that the governor was not threatening them with the loss of their charter. Bernard tried in vain to get the House to restore the purged councilors, since they were about the only men who were willing to back the British government.[110]

From this time on, the Council, which should have been the "aristocratic" part of the government, was just as much dominated by the popular or democratic party as was the House. The Council backed the house in its dispute with Bernard over the purged councilors.[111] Then, as Hutchinson explained it, wealthy merchant James Bowdoin succeeded to Hutchinson's dominant position in the Council and obtained greater influence over that body than Hutchinson had exercised. Said Hutchinson of Bowdoin: "Being united in principle with the leading men in the house, measures were concerted between him and them; and from this time the council, in matters which concerned the controversy between the Parliament and the colonies, in scarce any instance, disagreed with the house." [112] Being elected by the

110 *Boston Gazette,* June 9, 1766; Hutchinson, *History,* III, 110–11.

111 *Boston Gazette,* June 16, 1766.

112 Hutchinson, *History,* III, 113. Francis G. Walett, "James Bowdoin, Patriot Propagandist," *New England Quarterly,* XXIII (Sept. 1950), pp. 320–38, treats James Bowdoin as an aristocratic propagandist on the popular side. Walett also recognized that the Council became the instrument of the popular party after 1766, but he did not relate this as having been the result of the action of a democratic society. See "The Massachusetts Council, 1766–1774: The Transforma-

House on instructions from the voters, how could the council do otherwise?

Although the people of Massachusetts were happy at repeal of the Stamp Act, repeal did not materially affect the attitude of the popular party. Bernard wrote in July 1766 that he was still obliged to "maintain political warfare with the popular party." The kindness of the king and Parliament had not produced its deserved results, he said, for the House, "with great imprudence as well as ingratitude," had treated the king's authority "with fresh indignity." [113] British Secretary Conway had suggested the use of troops, but Bernard was afraid to bring troops to Boston. He said the faction declared that they would not allow troops to enter the town.[114] The House also consulted its constituents about compensating the Stamp Act riot sufferers, and when it did pass a compensation bill, it included a provision to pardon anyone implicated in the riots. This act was vetoed in England through fear of setting a bad precedent, but the compensation was paid and nothing more was said.[115] In recommending compensation, the town of Plymouth declared that there was a very material difference between those men who had suffered from their attachment to an act of Parliament and those who had suffered from a lack of due attachment to the constitution of their native country.[116]

Thus did the British fail in their first attempt at the new policy. Instead of procuring a revenue which would strengthen British authority in the colonies and prevent much-feared colonial independence, the British came out of the experiment with less authority and prestige than before. Once the Stamp Act was repealed, all became quiet again in the colony, indicating that the trouble was caused by British measures, not by internal friction.[117] If anything, democracy emerged from the controversy stronger than ever. The House acquired more power, especially over the Council, it had a standing committee

tion of a Conservative Institution," *William and Mary Quarterly*, 3d ser., VI (Oct. 1949), 605–27.

[113] *Barrington-Bernard Correspondence*, p. 110.   [114] *Ibid.*, pp. 113–14.
[115] Hutchinson, *History*, III, 109, 113.
[116] *Plymouth Town Records*, III, 181–82.   [117] Adams, *Works*, II, 203.

of correspondence to keep other colonies informed, and it built a gallery for spectators so that House debates would have a wide influence. In particular, Boston, the most underrepresented town in the province, emerged as the most influential.[118]

So the "new" policy which was designed to curtail democracy succeeded only in strengthening it.

[118] Hutchinson, *History*, III, 119–22.

CHAPTER XI

Democracy and the
Townshend Taxes, 1767–1770

WITH the repeal of the Stamp Act and the passage of the Declaratory Act, the "new" policy failed its first test, but this was by no means an indication that the policy had been permanently abandoned. The British still recognized the threat in the rapid growth of the colonies, in the violations of mercantilism, in the colonial democracy which thwarted British regulations, and, worst of all, in the possibility of colonial independence. Parliament's strong statement in the Declaratory Act concerning colonial independence was indicative that such a prospect still worried British legislators. The equally strong statement of Parliament's right to legislate for the colonies in all cases was certainly no concession to colonial claims of exclusive right of taxation. What would happen when Parliament attempted to make these claims effective remained to be seen.

The story of the three years from 1767 to 1770 has been told many times in great detail—the passage of the Townshend Acts, the setting up of a Board of Customs Commissioners in Boston to collect taxes and enforce the trade acts, the opposition to these commissioners resulting in the Massachusetts circular letter of 1768 calling for united efforts of all the colonies, the sending of warships to Boston harbor, the seizure of John Hancock's ship, the *Liberty*, the calling by Boston of an extralegal convention in 1768, the sending of troops to Boston, the nonimportation agreements, the Boston Massacre, and the partial repeal of the Townshend Acts in 1770.[1] But these events have been explained in terms of a society in which democracy was still to be achieved, not in terms of a society in which democracy had already arrived. The purpose in this chapter, therefore, is not to give the events of these three years in great detail, but to show how these events and democracy were related.

Charles Townshend, author of the Townshend Acts, gave the clearest hint of what was being contemplated and how it would affect colonial democracy. In Parliament, Townshend said it had long been his opinion that America should be regulated and deprived of its militating and contradictory charters. In addition, governors, judges, and attorneys should be supported so that they would be independent of the people.[2] Lord Shelburne also wanted to know what each colony spent on government and how the money was provided.[3] And to show that mercantilism was not forgotten, colonial governors had orders from the Lords of Trade to send reports on all colonial manufacturing from 1734 to 1766 and annual reports thereafter.[4]

Governor Francis Bernard was very explicit in pointing out how democracy operated in Massachusetts and why Townshend's proposals were so much needed there. Writing to Shelburne on March 2, 1767, the governor complained that the democratic General Court kept salaries low and used its power over salaries to influence public officials. Said he: "Envy of superior qualities, false frugality, and the spirit of levelling, will always prevent the higher officers of popular governments being properly supported whilst the determination of the quantum shall lie with the people." The House refused to pay the salaries of officials which it did not appoint and drastically cut the salaries of others that it disliked, especially Hutchin-

[1] Channing, *History,* III; Miller, *Origins of the American Revolution;* Dickerson, *The Navigation Acts and the American Revolution,* Schlesinger, *The Colonial Merchants and the American Revolution,* and Gipson, *The Coming of the Revolution,* all have detailed accounts of the period, though their interpretations differ.

[2] Bancroft, *History,* VI, 9–10.

[3] Shelburne to colonial governors, Dec. 11, 1766, King's MSS., CCVI.

[4] *Ibid.,* Aug. 1, 1766.

son's and Oliver's. There had been for some time past an expectation that these evils would be remedied, he continued, and the measure most needed in the regulation of the American governments was a fixed civil list, "especially in a democratical state, where the King's service is continually laboring and suffering for want of it." [5]

In England, the Connecticut agent, William Samuel Johnson, heard that Parliament and the ministers were unfriendly toward the colonies; that repeal of the Stamp Act had been a mistake; that the colonies were still in rebellion and were working for independence; that more troops were being sent to America, whether to relieve other troops or to carry out new designs against the colonies was not certain; that there should be heavy taxes and better regulations for America; and that severe measures were needed to regulate the colonies and reduce them to order. Johnson said that Lord Townshend urged the British not to deliberate longer—they should act with vigor while they could still call the colonies their own and could secure them to Britain. If not, the colonies would soon be gone forever. [6]

Charles Townshend in particular was determined on strong measures according to agent Johnson. Townshend intended to regulate trade in such a way as to raise a revenue in the colonies. When he was told that the army might be withdrawn with safety from America, which would eliminate the need for a revenue, he refused to listen and declared peremptorily that the moment a resolution was taken to withdraw the army, he would quit public affairs. He proposed taxes on glass, paper, lead, and paint, with a Board of Commissioners of Customs in America to prevent smuggling. Salaries of governors and judges were to be raised to £2,000 and £500 respectively, to be paid out of the American revenue, so that these officials would be independent of colonial legislatures. According to Johnson, the plan was to attack the colonies one at a time, to prevent the formation of a common union, and by degrees to reduce them

[5] *Ibid.*, March 2, 1767.
[6] *Trumbull Papers* (Mass. Hist. Soc., *Collections*, 5th ser., IX and X), I, 214, 224–25, 484–87. Hereafter cited *Trumbull Papers*.

to the desired state of subordination and humble obedience. He warned that while Connecticut was not in immediate danger, general regulations might eventually endanger the universal liberties of America, and by degrees the charters and assemblies would be superseded and made useless.[7]

In Massachusetts, the overwhelming dominance of the democratic party should have warned the British as to the kind of reception any new reform measures would receive. Governor Bernard tried without success to get Lieutenant Governor Hutchinson restored to a place on the Council, but the House agreed that Hutchinson could not sit with the Council, even though he had no vote, unless he were elected a councilor.[8] A "Freeborn American" wrote in the *Gazette* that unfortunately, in the present depraved state of human nature, a Bernard could always find a Hutchinson, an Oliver, and a Ruggles (who had opposed the Stamp Act Resolves) to support him, but a people who had a Henry, an Otis, and an Adams to counteract their pernicious designs should account themselves happy indeed.[9] March 18 was celebrated as the first anniversary of the repeal of the Stamp Act, as a large copper plate was placed on the Liberty Tree to commemorate the occasion.[10] The Reverend Andrew Eliot denied accusations that the people desired independence, but he predicted further controversies between the governor and the assembly. The governor had lost the confidence of the people, if he ever had it, Andrews declared, but at present the people were so completely agreed, and so many were on watch, that no one would care to attempt any encroachments.[11]

And well they might have been watchful, for by early May 1767 British plans for a revenue to pay salaries and the importance of such plans were well known and fully appreciated in Massachusetts. Thomas Cushing, one of the Boston representatives, was alarmed at talk of troops for America and at efforts on both sides of the ocean to drive a wedge between colony and

[7] *Ibid.*, pp. 229–33.
[8] *Boston Gazette Supplement*, Feb. 9, 1767, and *Boston Gazette*, March 9, 1767.
[9] *Ibid.*, March 9, 1767.   [10] *Ibid.*, March 30, 1767.
[11] To Thomas Hollis, May 13, 1767, Mass. Hist. Soc., *Collections*, 4th ser., IV, 404.

mother country. Troops to enforce acts of Parliament would push the colonies into a fatal disaffection for Britain, he warned, forcing them to live on their own production. Cushing conceded duties for regulation—if they affected all parts of the empire equally—but duties for revenue which would be used to establish a civil list in America, with salaries of British colonial officials to be decided and paid by Great Britain—that was something else. Such a plan would be considered unconstitutional, he declared, and could not be put into effect except by annulling the charter and overthrowing the present constitution.[12]

Agitation for colonial rights was not simply confined to Boston or the propaganda tactics of "radicals" such as Samuel Adams, as has sometimes been pictured.[13] Typical of the support for Boston from most of the country towns were the instructions of Worcester to its representative, Joshua Bigelow. Bigelow was to use his influence to maintain harmony and good will between Britain and Massachusetts by a steady and firm attachment to English liberty and the charter rights of the province. He should not allow any innovations whatever—evidence that the colony was trying to keep what it had, not change things—and if he found any encroachments on charter rights, he was to use his utmost abilities to obtain constitutional redress. Worcester wanted a law against slavery, and the town ordered Bigelow to vote against any councilor who would not support such a law or who had not distinguished himself in defense of liberty. In addition, the town wanted an effective militia, freedom of the press, and English rather than Latin schools, so that the people could attain the English learning necessary to retain the freedom of any state.[14]

12 Cushing to DeBerdt, May 9, 1767, *ibid.*, 248ff.
13 See Miller, *Sam Adams*, pp. 103–12. Miller claimed that all was peaceful after the repeal of the Stamp Act, leaving "radicals" Adams and Otis nothing to agitate about, that Adams and the Whigs on many occasions were about to suffer defeat at the hands of conservatives, and that Adams was saved by British measures. Miller also said that Adams and Otis had difficulty getting elected in Boston. He did not support these statements with evidence, and the evidence presented here certainly does not bear out the Miller thesis.
14 *Worcester Town Records,* IV, 148–49.

As had been true in 1766, the election of the Council in 1767 showed that the popular party was still in command in spite of the fact that there appeared to be no major issues such as the Stamp Act. Bernard tried to bargain with the opposition for the restoration of Hutchinson and other pro-government councilors, but to no avail. The House refused, since it controlled the Council anyway, the party elected its own men, and of course Bernard rejected their choices.[15] Hutchinson said that the assembly was no better than the previous one had been and that it left Colonel Williams, "almost the only supporter of government they had amongst them," off the Council.[16] Hutchinson declared that the continued ill usage from his countrymen had affected his nerves, causing him to take a vacation. "The party opposed to me increases in the general court," he complained, as he was able to get only fifty votes out of some 138. A majority of the members said they were attached to him personally, but contended that it would "not do to strengthen the prerogative interest in the general court." [17] This was further evidence that the conflict was external rather than internal.

By early June 1767, there were rumors that Parliament intended to regulate the governments of the colonies, rumors which led Hutchinson to suggest that if Parliament interfered it should be on particular points, not on general items which would arouse all the colonies.[18]

Such was the general climate of opinion in Massachusetts when Parliament passed the Townshend Acts. In the resolutions submitted to Parliament, there was the statement that the duties were to be applied in making a more certain and adequate provision for the expenses of administration of justice and the support of civil government in the colonies. Any residue remaining after this purpose was accomplished was to be paid into the king's exchequer to be disposed of by Parliament for defending, protecting, and securing the colonies.[19] This purpose of the tax—to pay the salaries of judges, governors, and

[15] Hutchinson, *History*, III, 128–29; *Acts and Resolves*, XVIII, 223.
[16] To ?, June 2, 1767, Mass. Arch., XXVI, 278.
[17] To Bollan, June 2, 1767, *ibid.*, p. 238.
[18] To ?, June 2, 1767, *ibid.*, 276, 278.   [19] *Parliamentary History*, XVI, 375.

other civil officials—was incorporated in the preamble of the Townshend Act itself so that the colonists had no doubt about how the resulting revenue was to be used. The act was to levy taxes on several items imported into the colonies, and it was to be enforced by a separate Board of Customs Commissioners under provisions of the Sugar Act, and with writs of assistance specifically legalized.[20]

There was no pretense in the Townshend Acts that the money was for defense of the colonies and was justified by failure of the colonies to provide for their own defense. This act was frankly a move to recapture control over colonial governments, so long considered necessary in order to enforce the mercantile system effectively and to insure the dependence of the colonies on Britain. There was no pretense, either, that the colonists had not always paid for the support of their own governors and judges. As Hutchinson said, the British believed that it was necessary to free civil officers from the restraints which colonial assemblies exercised through control of salaries, but the colonists were to continue to pay the bills.[21]

How the Townshend Act would affect colonial democracy was clearly pictured by colonial agent Johnson. Aside from the heavy taxes and strict regulations of trade, Johnson said all "hearty Americans" would consider as most dangerous that part of the act which allowed the king to use the revenue for paying officials' salaries. Governors would become independent of the people, he said, and needing no support from them, would have little inducement to call meetings of the assemblies. In time, governorships could become sinecures to support friends of the administration (as was true in Virginia), and an American governor would not even need to know where his government was. Judges would be completely dependent on the Crown, as their commissions were during pleasure, not good behavior.[22]

How the new taxes would free British officials, especially

---

[20] Pickering, *Statutes*, XXVII, 505ff.

[21] Hutchinson, *History*, III, 130; Gipson, in *The Coming of the Revolution*, pp. 169–75, looked on taxes as designed for defense. Although he cited the preamble and its purpose, he did not explain why it was necessary for Britain to raise money to pay salaries, since the colonies already paid them.

[22] To Pitkin, July 13, 1767, *Trumbull Papers*, I, 239.

those who had upheld British authority, is clearly evident from the correspondence at the time. There was a proposal, which never materialized, that Hutchinson would receive the lucrative post as first commissioner of the customs [23] and a handsome salary as chief justice as soon as the revenue provided the money.[24] Secretary Andrew Oliver also heard that he was to receive a more certain and adequate support. As the secretary was the king's servant, said Oliver, he could see no impropriety in having the king pay his salary. If the support depended entirely on the people, "it would be in effect giving them a negative on the King's appointment." [25]

For future reference, when we turn to the Tea Act of 1773, it should be noted here that the Townshend Acts helped to carry out a complicated bargain between Parliament and the East India Company. There was talk in Parliament of interfering in East India Company management of India. To retain a free hand in India, the company agreed to pay the British government £400,000 a year, and in return the government agreed to aid the company in recapturing the American tea market by lowering taxes on tea.[26] This bargain between Parliament and the East India Company was an important factor in events from 1767 to 1773.

[23] Pownall to Hutchinson, Aug. 8, 1767, Mass. Arch., XXV, 191.

[24] *Warren-Adams Letters* (Mass. Hist. Soc., *Collections*, vols. LXXII and LXXIII), I, 6n.

[25] To Jasper Mauduit, Oct. 30, 1767, Andrew Oliver Letter Book, I, 5–6. Dickerson, in *The Navigation Acts and the American Revolution*, developed the thesis that the new taxes were designed primarily for patronage purposes by the king and his friends, not as a check on colonial democracy to enforce mercantilism and preserve colonial dependence. Dickerson considered the Townshend Acts as thoroughly antitrade, not as a device to raise a revenue on a few British products in order to insure future British trade in the colonies. See pp. 195–98. Undoubtedly patronage and the desire of colonial officials for lucrative salaries were factors. Dickerson also characterized the British decision to set up a separate Board of Customs Commissioners in America as "England's Most Fateful Decision," *New England Quarterly*, XXII (Sept. 1949), 388–94, for it divided the colonial empire administratively and permitted the customs racketeering which followed.

[26] Miller, *Origins of the American Revolution*, pp. 244–45; *Parliamentary History*, XVI, 375; Pickering, *Statutes*, XXVII, 7 Geo. III, c.41, 46, 56, 57. On the tea tax, see also Max Farrand, "The Taxation of Tea, 1767–1773," *American Historical Review*, III (Jan. 1898), 266–69.

Given the background presented thus far, reaction in Massachusetts to the Townshend taxes was a foregone conclusion. Hutchinson said that the people considered that the Townshend Acts were a mere prelude to heavier taxes, that a standing army was to enforce obedience, and that the legislative power of the colonies was to be taken away.[27] With these threats in the offing, there was bound to be a strong reaction in a colony where democracy had long been the accepted rule. Payment of salaries and control of military expenditures would deprive colonial legislatures of their most effective weapons in dealing with British officials and policies.

It was in connection with the rising opposition to the Townshend taxes that Hutchinson had occasion to show the middle-class character of colonial society and its connection with British imperialism:

Property is more equally distributed in the colonies, especially those to the northward of Maryland than in any nation in Europe. In some towns you see scarce a man destitute of a competency to make him easy. They have as high notions of liberty as any part of the globe, but then they are as tender of their property & see the importance of enjoying their estates in quiet. I find no argument so successful as urging to them that under the notion of obtaining their liberty they are pursuing measures which will deprive them of their property as well as liberty or render it of little value.

Hutchinson used the argument that since the colonies could not be represented it was necessary for Parliament to tax them and that they should submit to this tax rather than break the connection with England. He said the people would bear this kind of reasoning patiently, but tell them that an army was being sent to compel obedience, and they flew into a passion and rage. Despite his conciliatory efforts, however, he would not guarantee that there would be no disorders.[28]

Once again it was the democratic Boston town meeting which took the lead in promoting opposition to British taxation. At a meeting on October 28, 1767, the town voted to prepare a subscription for promoting local manufacturing and preventing the importation of British goods. This subscription was to be cir-

---

[27] Mass. Arch., XXV, 205–08.   [28] *Ibid.*, p. 207.

culated in Boston, and copies were to be sent to all towns in Massachusetts as well as to other principal towns in other colonies. The town also voted to revive linen manufacturing and to ask the governor to call a special session of the General Court. Later meetings on November 20 and 22 asserted the town's determination to preserve order and drew up strong instructions to the town's representatives expressing the constitutional rights of the colonies.[29] Most of the towns backed Boston, some of them heaping the highest praise on the "metropolis" for taking the lead on this occasion.[30]

It was the action of Boston in initiating opposition measures which caused Hutchinson, as we have seen in Chapter V, to condemn town-meeting democracy in no uncertain terms. In telling about the Boston resolves, Hutchinson declared that every town in Massachusetts was an "absolute democracy." Even though the law required that a man "pay a small tax" to be a voter, he said, it was not one time in twenty that any check was made. "The town of Boston is an absolute democracy," he lamented as he told how constant use of this democratic form of town government had taught the people to think that any other form was unnecessary.[31] Hutchinson would have many occasions to regret the extent of democracy in Massachusetts before he left the colony in 1774.

Peter Oliver, who, with Hutchinson, had been left off the Council, also described the resistance to the Townshend taxes

[29] *Boston Town Records,* XVI, 221–28. Schlesinger, *Colonial Merchants,* pp. 91–114, emphasized the leadership of the merchants and the merchants' fear of the lower classes. Experiences from 1764–1766, he claimed, had warned the merchants that they had overreached themselves in calling to their aid the unruly elements and "underprivileged classes" and showed them the need for more orderly and constitutional processes. According to Schlesinger, the merchants wanted reform, not rebellion; but having used the lower classes for their own purposes, they found that when they wished to terminate their propaganda they were confronted with forces too powerful to control. The records show, however, that Boston was several months ahead of the merchants in taking action, and that the merchants were controlled by the democratic town meeting, not the reverse.

[30] See for example Andover Town Records, March 7 and May 23, 1768; Malden Town Records, II, 32; *Braintree Town Records,* p. 416; *Watertown Records, 1745–69,* pp. 336–37; *Muddy River and Brookline Records,* p. 218; *Plymouth Town Records,* III, 190–92.

[31] Mass. Arch., XXV, 226–27.

in terms of economic and political democracy. Oliver believed that Boston's efforts to promote manufacturing would fail because wages were too high in America. "A manufacturer who works for six to eight pence a day can undersell him who will not work under two shillings per day; and that is the case between Great Britain and America," he wrote. As for the disturbances, men of sense could do nothing, "for the government was in the hands of the mob, both in form & substance." Oliver also connected this democracy with independence, for he said that the colonies had repeatedly demonstrated a determination to throw off the supremacy of the British Parliament.[32]

There was little doubt that Boston, and not the merchants, received full credit in England for initiating resistance to British policy. Franklin wrote that the "resolutions of the Boston people" made "a great noise" in England, and while Parliament had taken no action, the newspapers were "in full cry against America." [33] Boston was also accused of promoting independence, as the resolves on manufacturing convinced many people in England that the Americans were determined to have as little connection with Britain as possible and to separate from the empire the moment they were able.[34]

As if the Townshend taxes were not enough, the old threat of sending an Anglican bishop to the colonies again raised its head late in 1767 to add religious fears to the fears already present. The Reverend Andrew Eliot expressed concern that a bishop would increase the Anglican faction, extend episcopal influence, subject American dissenters to their yoke, and tyrannize over those who stood fast in liberty. Eliot said that the people of New England were greatly alarmed and that the arrival of a bishop would raise a storm as quickly as any other measure. He reported that the assembly, sitting at the time, was "greatly warmed" over the late taxes, and he expressed the doubt that the dispute between Britain and her colonies could ever be settled amicably.[35]

[32] Egerton MSS., 2671, pp. 106–18.   [33] Franklin, *Writings*, V, 74–75.
[34] Mass. Arch., XXV, 241.
[35] To Thomas Hollis, Nov. 13, 1767 and Jan. 5, 1768, in Mass. Hist. Soc., *Collections*, 4th ser., IV, 408, 421. For the bishop controversy, see again Cross, *The Anglican Episcopate in the American Colonies*, ch. VII.

Urged on by Boston, Governor Bernard had called a meeting of the General Court, where the "greatly warmed" representatives, delegates from the "absolute democracies," took over the agitation where Boston had stopped. The result was the famous Massachusetts circular letter of February 1768, calling for united resistance against Britain and pointing out the threat to democracy implicit in the Townshend taxes. The House contended that a people could not be free if the king, who appointed governors and judges to serve at pleasure rather than during good behavior, could also grant these officials salaries which would be paid by the people without their consent.[36] For its troubles, the General Court was quickly dissolved.

Popular opposition had another opportunity to assert itself in February 1768. The *Boston Gazette* carried an article accusing Governor Bernard of misrepresenting the election of 1767, in which Hutchinson and other councilors were defeated. Bernard wanted to sue the *Gazette* for libel, but the assembly refused to take action; and the Council, though it condemned the article, advised Bernard not to carry out his suit. Bernard called the annual election of councilors "the canker-worm of the constitution . . . which will always weaken this government so that the best management will never make its weight capable of being put in the scales against that of the people." [37] Bernard then failed in an attempt to get a grand jury to bring in a libel bill, even though Chief Justice Hutchinson told the jury they could depend on being damned if they failed to do so. As a result, the grand jury became the toast of the popular party, Hutchinson declared, and the claim to be independent of Parliament in whole or in part became almost universal. "Either my brain is turned inside out or all the brains of most people about me are so," concluded Hutchinson as he bore witness to the strength of the popular party.[38]

Governor Bernard used the libel incident as an occasion for showing the British how completely democracy controlled government in Massachusetts and what Britain should do to recover her authority. In writing to Lord Shelburne, he said:

[36] Adams, *Writings*, I, 184ff.
[37] Bernard to Shelburne, March 5, 1768, Bernard Letters, 1768–1769.
[38] Mass. Arch., XXVI, 296–97.

If the opposition was directed only against persons and measures a reconciliation might and soon would take place and all might be well again. But men and measures are only nominal defendants: The authority of the King the supremacy of Parliament the superiority of government are the real objects of the attacks and a general levelling of all the powers of government and reducing it into the hands of the whole people is what is aimed at and will at least in some degree succeed, without some external assistance.

The Council, formerly revered by the people, was now generally "timid and irresolute, especially when the annual election draws near." This fatal ingredient in the constitution was "the bane of the whole," and royal authority would never be balanced with that of the people except by "making the council independent of the people." Bernard again lamented the fact that councilors had to face the threat of defeat in elections whenever they opposed the demagogues.[39]

Others besides Bernard were fully aware that the Council had become the instrument of the popular party just as the House was. In a letter, probably to Pownall or Jackson, Hutchinson said he knew how tender his correspondent was of any abridgment of the people's rights, but the popular part of the constitution had taken the whole government very much into their hands. At least one other branch had lost much of the power intended for it by the charter, he continued, "and that was full little." [40] Peter Oliver said that the Council, formerly called His Majesty's Council, had now become known as *"the people's Council."* The general assembly was a pandemonium—Otis talked of treason, the "rest of the house grinned horribly their ghastly smile; the council felt pleased, & the people loved to have it so." [41]

Bernard also confirmed the interpretation presented thus far that the conflict was imperial rather than internal—a War for Independence rather than an American Revolution. To the question of what protection he could give the customs commissioners, Bernard had this to say: "I answer none in the world. For tho' I am allowed to proceed in the ordinary business of the government without interruption; in the business of a popular

---

[39] Bernard to Shelburne, March 12, 1768, Bernard Letters, 1768–1769.
[40] Mass. Arch., XXVI, 288.   [41] Egerton MSS., 2671, pp. 120–21.

opposition to the laws of Great Britain founded upon pretensions of rights and privileges, I have not the shadow of authority or power." Why did he not ask for troops? He needed the advice of the Council but could not get it, he said, "for considering the influence they are under from being the creatures of the people and the personal danger they would be subject to in assisting in the restraining them, it is not probable that the utmost extremity of mischief and danger would induce them to advise such a measure." [42]

Thomas Hutchinson likewise expressed the idea that the conflict was not an internal lower-class movement for more democracy. The authority of Parliament to make any laws for the colonies was now denied as freely as Parliament's right to tax had previously been, he declared. This was a new doctrine which spread every day.[43] To another correspondent he observed that there had been no new actions during the winter to show the people in England that the colonies were more inclined to independence than they had been. But to an observer in the colonies it was easy to perceive that independence was a principle which continued to spread and would before long be universal. "It is the lowest part of the vulgar only who have not yet been taught that if they are to be governed by laws made by any persons but themselves or their representatives they are slaves," Hutchinson wrote. Things were quiet, he continued, but the people never looked more discontented than at present, for many had suffered during the hard winter for lack of work. "They think every difficulty they feel is owing to acts of Parliament, custom house officers, etc." [44]

According to Governor Bernard, popular pressure was responsible for placing the merchants behind the popular cause for the first time in 1768. This came about when one Malcolm, a small trader, unloaded a ship noisily and publicly one night, then came to the customs and later called a meeting of the merchants in March 1768. Bernard wrote:

This may be said to be the first movement of the merchants against the acts of Parliament: all the proceedings before were carried on

[42] Bernard to Shelburne, March 19, 1768, Bernard Letters, 1768–1769.
[43] Mass. Arch., XXVI, 298.   [44] *Ibid.*, p. 297.

at town meetings and were rather upon refinements of policy than concern for trade. However the merchants are at length dragged into the cause; their intercourse and connection with the politicians and the fear of opposing the stream of the people have at length brought it about against the sense of an undoubted majority both of numbers property and weight.[45]

Bernard's interpretation would certainly run counter to the view that merchants originated the opposition to British measures, then backed down when they saw the dangers of popular control.

Practical results of the new revenue-salary policy became apparent in 1768 with the payment of part of Hutchinson's salary from the Townshend taxes. Hutchinson, who had recently expressed the hope for a colonial government like that in Ireland,[46] had been promised the first salary from the Townshend revenues after the commissioners of the customs had been paid.[47] On receiving a warrant for £200 a year in addition to his regular salary, he wrote, "I am more than ever obliged to exert myself in His Majesty's service." This he thought he could best accomplish by convincing the people that their imagined fears of oppression and slavery were without foundation.[48] There was little doubt that a colonial official who received a salary from the British became a better official in British eyes.

The election of 1768 was an even more complete demonstration of popular power in Massachusetts than was the election of 1767, and the latter had certainly been convincing as far as Bernard and Hutchinson were concerned. There was an unsuccessful attempt to discredit Samuel Adams, who had been a leading force in both the town meeting and the General Court, over his previous failure to collect taxes when he was tax collector.[49] Instead of treating Adams as an embezzler, the town expressed confidence in him by giving him 432 out of 440 votes, and as usual it elected popular leaders Otis, Cushing, and the wealthy

45 Bernard to Shelburne, March 21, 1768, Bernard Letters, 1768–1769.

46 Mass. Arch., XXVI, 289–90.   47 *Ibid.*, XXV, 236–39.

48 *Ibid.*, XXVI, 300, 301.

49 Boston inhabitants' petition to selectmen, March 16, 1768, and H. Gray to Boston Committee, March 23, 1768, Library of Congress, Massachusetts Miscellaneous MSS., 1759–1768.

Hancock as his colleagues.[50] Bernard explained to the British how this popular faction, "bankrupts in reputation as well as in property" as he called them, could rule other inhabitants who had many times as much wealth. The town was "governed by the lowest of the people," he said, and from the time of the Stamp Act had been in the hands of the mob. The faction influenced the legislature, ruined the reputations of representatives with their constituents, and thus excluded a great many of the best men of the province from the House.[51] Again, this is not evidence of a merchant aristocracy in control of Boston and Massachusetts.

In the election of the Council, the popular party still dominated, thwarting the continued efforts of Bernard to get prerogative men restored to the Council. Otis and Adams had learned that Hutchinson was receiving part of his salary from the British government, a fact which they used effectively against him. Except for his negative of councilors, the governor said, government would have been completely in the hands of the faction who were "endeavouring to separate themselves from Great Britain in regard to all civil power." Just before the election the faction put out handbills designed to make all Crown officials appear as obnoxious as the customs commissioners and thus exclude them from the Council. "The whole purpose of these proceedings," Bernard wrote, "is to divest the Crown of all its natural and constitutional power in this government and fling all real power into the hands of the people." [52] Obviously the king's governor was the only obstruction to complete rule by the democratic forces.

Shortly after the elections of 1768, Boston's democratic sentiments were inflamed by the British seizure of John Hancock's sloop *Liberty*. There was a riot, not only because of Hancock's popularity but also because of animosity against the Townshend taxes, the customs commissioners, and the British for attempting to impress seamen for the British warship *Romney*. There was also resentment against what one historian has characterized as

[50] *Boston Town Records*, XVI, 244–53.
[51] Bernard to Hillsborough, May 19, 1768, Bernard Letters, 1768–1769.
[52] Bernard to Hillsborough, May 30, 1768, *ibid.; Acts and Resolves*, XVIII, 329.

customs racketeering.[53] As a result, the customs commissioners sought safety aboard the *Romney,* and the Council, fearing popular resentment, refused to back Bernard's suggestion that British troops be called in to enforce the law. Some of the Council said that they "did not desire to be knocked in the head," while Bernard maintained that if he acted alone in so unpopular a measure he would be forced to leave the colony.[54]

The *Liberty* episode brought that "absolute democracy," the Boston town meeting, back into action again. At a huge meeting which had to move from the town house, Faneuil Hall, to Old South Church for accommodations, the town, after "very cool and deliberate debates," drew up a strongly worded petition to the governor complaining about taxation, impressment, armed force, and the customs commissioners. When Bernard gave an unsatisfactory reply to demands that the *Romney* be removed from Boston harbor, the town petitioned the General Court for action, declaring that more ships and troops were expected to force compliance from Boston.[55]

Unfortunately for Governor Bernard, whatever chance he had of exerting any influence in the General Court—and at best that was very little—was completely nullified by a letter from Hillsborough to Bernard demanding that the House rescind its strongly worded circular letter of February 1768. In spite of the arrival of another warship and rumors that more ships and troops

[53] See Dickerson, *The Navigation Acts,* ch. ix, for the best account of the *Liberty* episode and the interpretation of the American customs as a racket. For a standard interpretation of the *Liberty* seizure, see George Gregerson Wolkins, "The Seizure of John Hancock's Sloop *Liberty,*" in Mass. Hist. Soc., *Proceedings,* LV, 239–84. The administrative side of the Customs Board is presented by Dora Mae Clark, "The American Board of Customs, 1767–1783," *American Historical Review,* XLV (July 1940), 777–806. Lorenzo Sears, *John Hancock, The Picturesque Patriot* (Boston, 1912) and Herbert S. Allan, *John Hancock, Patriot in Purple* (New York, 1948), are the best biographies of Hancock, but greatly underestimate Hancock as an astute politician. A good account of the Hancock business affairs, but a poor account of Hancock and the history of the time, is W. T. Baxter, *The House of Hancock: Business in Boston, 1734–1775* (Cambridge, Mass., 1945).

[54] Bernard to Hillsborough, June 11 and 14, 1768, Bernard Letters, 1768–1769; Hutchinson, *History,* III, 137–41.

[55] Bernard to Hillsborough, June 16, 1768, Bernard Letters, 1768–1769; *Boston Town Records,* XVI, 253–58.

were coming to reduce the recalcitrant port of Boston to order, the House took a strong stand against rescinding. In the debates, James Otis countered with the demand that Britain rescind her acts before it was too late.[56] Encouraged by approval of the circular letter in other colonies, the House, at a "very full meeting" and by "a very great majority," refused to rescind, 92-17. The "92" became the toast of the colony; the "17" became as odious as the customs commissioners. Hutchinson predicted defeat in the next election for the "17," while Bernard predicted that two more years like the last two would see the British empire at an end.[57] As for the popularity of the actions of the House, Hutchinson wrote: "The people seem to me to be in a state of absolute dementation. Some of all orders, not many, disapprove the late measure, but in general it is supposed that all we have done is quite regular." [58]

Bernard was perfectly aware of the helplessness of a colonial governor caught in the vice of colonial democracy and British imperialism. Before the change of British policy, he said, he had had no trouble, but now everything he did was condemned both in England and the colony. It was impossible to reconcile his duties as governor with the people's demands, he lamented, for nothing less than a general sacrifice of the rights of the sovereign state could make him popular in Massachusetts under prevailing conditions.[59]

Although the governor could take no action unless approved by popular sentiments, he recognized that there was an effective government in Boston even if it was not the king's government. On one occasion the Boston selectmen ordered the return of some smuggled molasses which had been taken after being seized by customs officials. No British officer could have found the molasses, Bernard declared, "but to serve the purpose of the people the selectmen in a summary way can do the business in a trice. So we are not without a government: only it is in the

---

[56] Mass. Hist. Soc., *Collections*, 5th ser., IX, 289; Bernard to Hillsborough, June 16, 17, and 25, Bernard Letters, 1768–1769.

[57] Hutchinson, *History*, III, 141–44; Hulton, *Letters*, p. 11.

[58] Mass. Arch., XXVI, 315.

[59] Bernard to Hillsborough, July 18, 1768, Bernard Letters, 1768–1769.

hands of the people of the town, and not of those deputed by the King or under his authority." [60]

Shortly after writing the above letter, Bernard gave a clear explanation of the purpose of the Townshend taxes and why the colonies opposed them so strenuously. The present question between Great Britain and her colonies, he said, "is whether Great Britain has a right to take care that the governments of the colonies be properly supported so as to maintain the political balance between the Crown and the people which is necessary for the safety of both." [61] Necessary for the Crown, perhaps, but the people of Massachusetts well understood what would happen to democratic government if the people lost all checks on their officials.

Historians have sometimes assumed that the troubles of the time were the work of a few "radical" leaders, but the above statement by Bernard, as well as others, indicate that opposition to Britain had wide popular support. Customs Commissioner Henry Hulton saw things pretty clearly. He believed that "inherent republican, & levelling principles" were responsible and that the colonies were advancing "toward a state of independency." Hulton warned that the defection had been falsely represented in England as the sedition of a dying faction, but this was not so. It was too general, and most of the other colonies were only waiting to see what happened in Boston.[62] Marblehead voted that when lawful attempts to unite the people for redress of grievances were pictured as the efforts of a desperate faction which did not represent the sentiments of the people, the people should interfere and let their sentiments be known to the world. So that no one would mistake Marblehead's sentiments, the town voted unanimously to thank the "92" for refusing to rescind.[63]

During the summer of 1768, the threat that troops were to be

[60] *Ibid.*, July 9 and 11, 1768.
[61] *Ibid.*, July 16, 1768. Gipson, *The Coming of the Revolution*, p. 193, insisted that the Townshend taxes were passed to alleviate the burdens of British taxpayers.
[62] Hulton, *Letters*, p. 11.
[63] July 15, 1768, Marblehead Town Records, IV, 62–63.

sent to Boston did not appear to restrain popular sentiment in the least. A grand jury, called to investigate the *Liberty* riot, found nothing against the rioters. Bernard complained that this happened because the jury was elected, not appointed by the sheriff as it was in England.[64] The governor had been forced to circumvent the Council to get troops sent to Boston, for as he said, councilors were looking out for their own interests by joining "the prevailing party of the people." And again he urged the British to change the Massachusetts constitution so that the Council would support the Crown. When he called a few councilors to discuss the arrival of troops, he found the "popular spirit" higher among them than ever before. And he could not expect help from the dissolved assembly, for he said a new election would only result in the exclusion of the few representatives who had supported government.[65]

Again the democratic town meeting took the lead as the town faced the prospects of British troops in its midst. After Bernard refused to call a meeting of the General Court at the town's request, the town passed a set of resolves worded in no uncertain terms. Stressing the threat to civil and religious liberty, Boston contended that the first principle in civil society was the democratic one that no law was binding on any individual without his consent or the consent of his freely elected representative. Taxing the colonies without their consent was therefore unconstitutional, and trying to enforce an unconstitutional act by keeping a standing army over them without their consent was even more unconstitutional. And since the governor could not call a General Court without consent from England, the town decided to summon a convention of delegates from all the towns to consider proper measures. Elected as the Boston delegates were representatives Otis, Cushing, Adams, and Hancock. Furthermore, the town made a thinly veiled threat to use force against the expected troops by voting that all inhabitants should obey the law that every householder and listed soldier should be armed.[66] From this town meeting Bernard expected any ex-

[64] Bernard to Hillsborough, Sept. 9, 1768, Bernard Letters, 1768–1769.
[65] *Ibid.,* July 9 and 30, 1768.   [66] *Boston Town Records,* XVI, 260–64.

tremes of action, for he said some people advocated "a system of politics exceeding all former exceedings." [67]

Efforts by the governor to procure quarters for the expected troops in Boston merely furnished additional proof that the popular party had complete domination. Bernard was afraid to quarter troops in small parties "in a town where there was so public and professed a disaffection to His Majesty's British government." He also expressed surprise "that so many persons of consideration and property" backed a scheme to start an insurrection by forcing officers to seize quarters. Boston's selectmen refused to authorize quarters, as did the Council, where one councilor replied pleasantly to Bernard's argument, "What can you expect of a council that is more afraid of the people than they are of the King." Another said he had talked to many of the "middling people" and was convinced that if the Council supported the governor, there would "soon be no government." Only one of the ten councilors who voted on quartering supported the government, causing Bernard to call this "the greatest blow" yet given to the king's government.[68]

In spite of the fact that Boston's call for a convention was considered illegal by some people, the town received wide popular support throughout the province when the towns elected and instructed their delegates.[69] A few towns either refused to send delegates—as Sheffield and Hatfield did unanimously and Northampton did by a vote of 66-65—or perhaps received notice too late to act. Although he had been left off the Council in 1768, Hutchinson's friend Israel Williams was still a powerful influ-

---

[67] Bernard to Hillsborough, Sept. 16, 1768, Bernard Letters, 1768–1769.

[68] *Ibid.*, Sept. 23, 26, and 30, 1768.

[69] For a different interpretation, see John C. Miller, *Sam Adams*, pp. 151–64, and "The Massachusetts Convention: 1768," *New England Quarterly*, VII (Sept. 1934), 445–74. Miller assumed that radicalism was centered in Boston because of Adams and had to be pushed by force into the agricultural towns. He said the towns sent conservative politicians who refused to follow Adams' radical ideas. Miller also gave a long account of Hatfield's refusal to send a delegate but failed to point out that Hatfield was one of a small minority. The facts are that most of the towns which had received notice of the convention sent delegates, that most of these delegates were the same men who had previously been representatives and had caused the governor so much trouble, and that many of the towns sent strong instructions of support for Boston.

ence in Hatfield, where the town considered the convention as unconstitutional and blamed Boston for policies that justified troops.[70] But most of the towns sent delegates, some of them elected unanimously, with instructions resembling those given to the Boston delegates. Braintree suggested that the province send a petition to the king, voted on by every town, to show the king how strong the popular party was.[71]

From available records, it is difficult to tell just what the convention of 1768 intended to accomplish, so that it is impossible to gauge its success. If Adams and others really expected it to foment armed rebellion against the landing of troops, as seems unlikely, it was a failure. But as a gesture in defiance of authority and in the face of an approaching army, it must be considered a popular victory. In effect, the convention was just another meeting of the House of Representatives without authority from the governor, for it elected as chairman and clerk the speaker and the clerk of the House—Cushing and Adams. The convention was also a precedent for later provincial congresses in which the colony set up a government without British authority. At any rate, the Reverend Andrew Eliot said that the people had great confidence in the convention and were ripe for anything.[72]

Troops landed in Boston on September 28, 1768, under the protecting guns of the fleet, and the convention dissolved on September 29; but with all that, the British government still could not dominate the democratic forces in the province. Hutchinson declared that the design of Parliament was utterly frustrated by the refusal of the selectmen and council to comply with Parliament's quartering act.[73] For safety's sake, the customs commissioners were at Castle William, the island fortress in Boston harbor, but when asked about their return to Boston, one of

[70] Hatfield Town Records, IV, 191–93; Northampton Town Records, II, 143–44; Sheffield Town Records, Sept. 15?, 1768; Hadley Town Records, Sept. 23, 1768.

[71] *Plymouth Town Records*, III, 200–202; *Braintree Town Records*, p. 419; *Fitchburgh Town Records*, p. 56; *Watertown Records, 1745–69*, p. 351; Malden Town Records, II, 34; Andover Town Records, Sept. 21, 1768. Andover sent Samuel Phillips, Esq., the wealthiest man in town, and other towns also sent their most prosperous citizens.

[72] Mass. Hist. Soc., *Collections*, 4th ser., IV, 426–28.

[73] Hutchinson, *History*, III 153–57.

them remarked that while there were troops in Boston to protect them, what civil officer would request their use? Neither
Bernard nor Hutchinson, present at the time, would give any
assurances. General Thomas Gage, who had come to Boston as
a result of the troubles there, said that even the few magistrates
who might have supported government desired to be popular
and feared to do anything contrary to the general sentiments of
the people. The governor could not dismiss magistrates without
the consent of the Council, and the Council also refused to do
anything that was unpopular. According to Gage, the constitution leaned so much on the side of democracy that the governor
had no power to remedy disorder.[74] With the "common people"
"in a frensy" and talking "of dying in defense of their liberties,"
the popular party still had the upper hand.[75]

   Thus did British troops fail to restore British authority in
Massachusetts or diminish in any way the strength of democracy.
The king might accuse Massachusetts and Boston of desiring independence, and Chancellor of the Exchequer North might declare that he would not repeal the Townshend taxes *"until he saw
America prostrate* at his feet," but the desired ends of colonial
reform still remained unachieved.[76] Conflicts between troops
and civilians in Boston forced officers to relax their rigid military rules. Out of this situation came the story of a sentry who
refused to stop a burglary because he had orders "to do nothing
which might deprive any man of his liberty." [77] When Bernard
accused the Council of "servility in regard to the people," one
councilor replied that "he liked to be concerned in public business and did not choose to quit his place in the Council; and
therefore must be content to hold it upon such terms as he could."
Again Bernard urged the British to recapture control of the
Council.[78] The Council made the "humoring of the people their
chief object" and received "cooly" the appointment by the gov-

[74] Gage to Hillsborough, Oct. 31, 1768, *Letters to the Right Honourable the
Earl of Hillsborough from Governor Bernard, General Gage,* . . . (Boston, 1769),
p. 33.
[75] Mass. Arch., XXV, 281.
[76] *Parliamentary History*, XVI, 422, 466; *Trumbull Papers*, II, 301.
[77] Hutchinson, *History*, III, 161–62.
[78] Bernard to Hillsborough, Nov. 12, 1768, Bernard Letters, 1768–1769.

ernor of a "fit person" for office because the appointee "was not popular," leading Bernard to say that the man would never have been appointed if he had been popular. If a justice "acts in a popular cause," he said, "the council who are themselves the creatures of the people will never join with the governor in censuring the *overflowings of liberty*." [79]

Governor Bernard was particularly emphatic about the effect of democracy on the Council. He had no expectation of reversing the Council on one of its decisions, he said, "for the council is brought under such an awe of their constituents by the frequent removal of the friends of government; that there is very little exercise for private judgment in popular questions." [80]

There were naturally many suggestions that Parliament take more drastic action to check colonial democracy. Early in 1769, Hutchinson penned the hope that such measures would be taken. His words were to rebound with devastating effect when his letter was later sent back to Massachusetts. He wrote:

This is most certainly a crisis. I really wish that there may not have been the least degree of severity beyond what is absolutely necessary for maintaining I think I may say to you *the dependence* which a colony ought to have upon the parent state but if no measures shall be taken to secure this dependence or nothing more than some declaratory acts or resolves it is all over with us. The friends of government will be utterly disheartened and the friends of anarchy will be afraid of nothing be it ever so extravagant. . . . I never think of the measures necessary for the peace and good order of the colonies without pain. There must be an abridgment of what is called liberty. . . . I doubt whether it is possible to project a system of government in which a colony 3000 miles distant from the parent state shall enjoy all the liberties of the parent state.[81]

In considering ways to curtail democracy, quite naturally the old proposal of altering the charter came up many times, but just how effective this would be was not certain. There was talk in England that the colony would never be allowed to elect another Council, as it was now called "the upper house of convention," and that a *quo warranto* would deprive the colony of its

[79] *Ibid.,* Nov. 14, 1768.   [80] *Ibid.,* Dec. 5, 1768.
[81] Hutchinson to ?, Jan. 20, 1769, Mass. Arch., XXVI, 338.

charter.[82] In spite of his statement that there must be an abridgment of liberty, Hutchinson doubted the efficacy of changing the constitution. Said he: "Altering our constitution will not alter the principles of the people & I fear it will not alter their temper for the better." [83] Hutchinson often misjudged the people, but he was probably right on this occasion.

Former governor Thomas Pownall had a solution—to go back to the colonial system used before the reforms were started—but Pownall did not get much of a hearing in England. He insisted that all would be well if Britain would just return "to that *old safe ground of administration*"—another way of saying, of course, that the trouble was imperial and not internal. Then Pownall proceeded to explain why Americans objected to the Townshend taxes. The British, he said, had passed a law, independently of the colonial people, to raise a revenue for the support of civil government in the colonies. This deviated from the old way, destroyed the checks on government which the colonists had, and should never have been done.[84]

With popular opposition so strong, even customs officers backed by troops were not sufficient to stop smuggling in Boston. Hutchinson claimed that the reduction in the price of tea effected by the Townshend taxes had increased rather than lessened the importation of Dutch tea. So much was imported in the fall of 1768 that his merchant sons in Boston could not sell lawfully imported tea, he said, for Dutch importers sold it more cheaply than English tea could be bought in England.[85]

Neither customs commissioners nor troops had been able to prevent the adoption of the weapon that had been effective during Stamp Act times, nonimportation. And again the influence of the popular party was discernible. Months after both Boston and the House of Representatives had taken strong action, the merchants began to organize. Bernard reported on August 9, 1768, that for the past week a nonimportation subscription had been agitated among the merchants. It was started by two of the

82 Hutchinson to Williams, Jan. 26, 1769, Israel Williams Papers, II, 162.
83 Mass. Arch., XXVI, 340.
84 Pownall to Cooper, April 19, 1769, King's MSS., CCII.
85 To Jackson, Jan. 24, 1769, Mass. Arch., XXVI, 339.

leading merchants who had always abetted the purposes of the popular faction, and though the move had little success at first, ways and means were used to insure its adoption. By August 8, 1768, a sufficient number had signed to go ahead with plans, although forty merchants refused to sign but agreed to abide by nonimportation, and thirty-five would neither sign nor agree. Bernard presumed that the thirty-five would be brought to reason by mob law, since thirty-five recalcitrants would defeat the scheme.[86] After nonimportation went into effect on January 1, 1769, all but a few merchants were forced into compliance by popular pressure.

Just before the spring elections of 1769, another incident involving democracy "aroused a rage" throughout the province. Letters of Governor Bernard, condemning the Council as too democratic and suggesting that a royal council be established, were sent from England and published in April. The Council demanded Bernard's recall, but Hutchinson defended the governor on the ground that he had the impossible task of attempting to carry out measures opposed by the whole continent. Changes in the Council were due to the times, he said, for the Council also feared the resentment of the people.[87]

When the spring elections of 1769 did come, the popular party simply carried all elective offices. Boston protested the presence of troops during an election, then elected popular leaders Otis, Cushing, Adams, and Hancock by the almost unanimous votes of 502, 502, 503, and 505 out of 508 votes cast. Strongly worded instructions to these representatives, instructions which were ordered to be published in the newspapers, condemned the British on many counts, while at the same time the town expressed approval of the merchants for adherence to nonimportation.[88] The Reverend Samuel Cooper of Boston sent these instructions to Pownall in England with the warning that they represented the disposition of the whole province, in the country as well as in Boston. This new assembly would be as firm as ever, he declared, with the Council "more than ever united with the house & the

---

[86] Bernard to Hillsborough, Aug. 9, 1768, Bernard Letters, 1768–1769.
[87] Hutchinson, *History*, III, 163–65.
[88] *Boston Town Records*, XVI, 277–88.

people." [89] Instructions by other towns more than confirmed Cooper's statement that the country had the same ideas as Boston.[90]

Cooper's predictions of unanimity in the legislature proved all too true as the popular party dominated both Council and House. Bernard accused the Council of merely echoing the views of their intimate friends in the Boston town meeting.[91] Then the House purged the Council of four men who had not opposed the governor and elected four others "strongly attached to the cause of liberty." [92] Bernard expressed it this way:

The faction had previously declared that they would clear the council of Tories: by this denomination they signify all those who are disposed to support the King's government, to acknowledge the authority of Parliament, and to preserve the people from a democratical despotism. . . . These gentlemen [defeated councilors Flucker, Ropes, Paine, and Worthington] were flung out by such large majorities, and the others, excepting the new ones and one or two more, elected so nearly unanimously, that it afforded a strong instance of the absoluteness of the faction as well as their disposition to abuse their power.[93]

Except for British influence, and despite Bernard's negative of eleven councilors, the triumph of the democratic party was complete. Wrote Andrew Oliver despairingly:

There is apparently but one party now in either house of assembly, Brigadier Ruggles had not attended the court this session nor is there any gentleman however well disposed that seems inclined to share the fate of those 17 [rescinders] who were proscribed the last year so that every measure that is proposed is carried without opposition.[94]

89 May 11, 1769, King's MSS., CCII.

90 Malden Town Records, II, 38; Marblehead Town Records, IV, 73; *Boston Gazette,* June 5, 1769.

91 Bernard to Hillsborough, May 15, 1769, Samuel Adams Papers, Colonial Document 381.

92 Hutchinson, *History*, III, 166–69.

93 Bernard to Hillsborough, June 1, 1769, Samuel Adams Papers, Colonial Document 385.

94 *Acts and Resolves,* XVIII, 371; to Mauduit, July 10, 1769, Oliver Letter Book, I, 106.

The House unanimously passed resolves condemning Bernard, standing armies, admiralty courts, customs commissioners, and particularly General Gage for "impertinently" meddling in civil affairs by letters to the ministers branding the constitution of Massachusetts as so democratic that government was powerless to remedy disorders. The trouble, contended the House, was arbitrary government, not too much spirit of democracy.[95]

Thus had relations between colonial democracy and British imperialism reached an impasse by the summer of 1769. Governor Bernard was recalled in July, unable to please both the British and the colonists. The House had voted 109 to 0 for his recall. As there was not much violence, two of the four British regiments in Boston were sent to Halifax.[96] But from England came persistent rumors that British ministers had not conceded defeat. Pownall said that they would not give up the maxim that Parliament "should raise a revenue for the support of civil government independent of the people" in the colonies. He warned that repeal of some of the Townshend taxes were a "Trojan Horse" to mislead and divide the colonies.[97] A letter, purportedly from London, also warned that the ministers planned to alter the Massachusetts constitution, a view reflected by Andrew Eliot's statement that the ministers intended "to new-model our constitution." [98]

In spite of the outward calm which seemed to prevail, the popular party still retained its position of power. Hutchinson, who replaced the departed Bernard as governor, said that the government was powerless because "the body of the people are of one mind," and he warned that repeal of the Townshend Acts would not suffice, as many would demand the repeal of all tax acts and the removal of all restraints on trade. But unless Britain enforced her policies, he said, she would lose her colonies, for the designs of many were to cast off all subjection to acts of Parliament.[99] Andrew Oliver hoped that the people would remain quiet to make Hutchinson's administration easy, but he

[95] *Boston Gazette,* July 10, 1769.
[96] Hutchinson, *History,* III, 170, 182–83.
[97] Pownall to Cooper, May 25, 1769, King's MSS., CCII.
[98] *Boston Gazette,* Aug. 21, 1769; Mass. Hist. Soc., *Collections,* 4th ser., IV, 442.
[99] Mass. Arch., XXVI, 366.

feared otherwise "unless they are allowed to have their own way." [100]

The Sons of Liberty, 350 strong, had a celebration on the anniversary of the Stamp Act riots, where forty-five toasts and denunciations were drunk to almost everything and everybody, including a toast to the "Massachusetts 92" and *"Strong Halters, Firm Blocks,* and *Sharp Axes* to all such as deserve them." John Adams said that Otis and Samuel Adams promoted these festivals to tinge the minds of the people, impregnate them with sentiments of liberty, and render them fond of their leaders in the cause and bitter against their opponents. Adams said he "did not see one person intoxicated, or near it"—and this after forty-five toasts.[101]

The Boston town meeting warned that the only solution for the impasse was for Parliament to repeal every act raising a revenue without colonial consent, to recall customs commissioners and troops, and to restore conditions as they had formerly been.[102]

Troops proved to be useless mainly because British officials, fearful of popular reaction, refused to call them to the support of civil government. Hutchinson wanted to use troops when a large crowd caught a customs informer, but refrained when the Council, justices of the peace, and sheriff advised against it.[103] Troops proved of little aid to John Mein, Boston bookseller and publisher of the progovernment *Boston Chronicle,* which was supported by and was mainly the mouthpiece for the customs commissioners.[104] Mein, refusing to abide by the nonimportation agreement, was accused of firing on a crowd that gathered, fled to the troops for protection, and finally had to leave the colony. He condemned Hutchinson bitterly for failure to use troops to protect supporters of government, as the ministers intended they should be used. Hutchinson defended his

---

[100] *Ibid.,* XXV, 325. [101] Adams, *Works,* II, 218.

[102] *Boston Town Records,* XVI, 309–24.

[103] To Gage, Oct. 29, 1769, Mass. Arch, XXVI, 398.

[104] Oliver M. Dickerson, "British Control of American Newspapers on the Eve of the Revolution," *New England Quarterly,* XXIV (Dec., 1951), 453–68. On the influence of propaganda see Philip Davidson, *Propaganda and the American Revolution, 1763–1783* (Chapel Hill, 1941). Unfortunately the word "propaganda" does not always carry the connotation in popular usage which Davidson's definition ascribes to it.

failure by saying that troops could be used in Ireland but not in the colonies and that Mein did not use good judgment in attacking "so many of the heads of the populace when they have all the power in their hands." [105]

In all this, there continued to be ample evidence that the issues were British-American, not that radical leaders were stirring up the underprivileged masses against aristocratic merchants or that the merchants were simply using the lower classes for their own ends. According to Hutchinson, an objection to a motion in the Boston town meeting on the ground that it implied independence of Parliament received this retort from Samuel Adams: "Independent we are and independent we will be." [106] Harvard College, which should have been aristocratic, allowed debates among the students which "breathed the spirit of liberty," and the choice of a president was made on the political principle that he be "a friend of liberty." [107] The Reverend Samuel Cooper pointed out that all the "body of the people" desired was to go back to the "old establishment upon which they have grown and flourished." They did not want independence; they just wanted the removal of innovations.[108] And another "popular" minister, Andrew Eliot, warned that Hutchinson "must not attempt anything against our liberties"—an implication that the colonists were merely trying to keep what they had, not to get something they did not have.[109]

All this is not to say, of course, that the merchants were not important. They undoubtedly were. Andrew Oliver called their committee which enforced nonimportation "the grand assertors of liberty" and the movement itself the greatest threat yet to British authority. The committee carried all before it, he declared, and their inspectors worked as though they were acting from authority.[110] But the merchants' resistance was only a part of the much greater popular opposition.

Tension mounted rapidly in Boston when the nonimporta-

[105] Hutchinson, *History*, III, 186–87; Mass. Arch., XXV, 403, 457–59.
[106] Hutchinson, *History*, III, 190.
[107] *Ibid.*, p. 188; Mass. Hist. Soc., *Collections*, 4th ser., IV, 445.
[108] To Pownall, Jan. 1, 1770, King's MSS., CCIII.
[109] Mass. Hist. Soc., *Collections*, 4th ser., IV, 445.
[110] Oliver Letter Book, I, 117–19, 129.

tion agreement expired on January 1, 1770, and the progovernment party attempted to prevent its renewal. Some half-dozen
merchants, including Hutchinson's sons Thomas and Elisha,
tried to scuttle the agreement, but popular pressure forced the
Hutchinsons into line. The governor, anxious to end nonimportation, attempted to break up the mass meetings which were
called to force the compliance of recalcitrant merchants, but the
Council and justices of the peace refused to act and the sheriff
had no success whatever.[111] Reports had it that the ministers had
sent orders for governors to use troops if necessary to protect
anyone who imported. Andrew Oliver saw that this protection
would be futile.[112] But Hutchinson decided to back the few importers, as the minister suggested, although he realized that, with
the Council, representatives, justices of the peace, selectmen, and
other town officials mixing with the multitude which was "ripe
for anything," he sat on a powder keg to which the use of troops
might set a spark.[113]

As many people at the time had predicted, importation finally
led to violence and bloodshed. Almost every day, large crowds
gathered in front of the shops of importers, sometimes resorting
to more persuasive methods than talk. One day in February an
informer named Richardson, attempting to stop the crowd, was
driven inside his house with the use of rocks and other missiles.
Richardson fired into the crowd, killing a small boy, and was
almost hanged on the spot. As a result, one importer left town,
another had soldiers as a guard, and still others slept with loaded
guns near by. The funeral procession for the dead boy, some
two miles long, was considered perhaps the largest ever seen in
America.[114]

With the exceptions that Hutchinson was still governor and
that a few merchants continued to import, the will of the people
held complete sway. The principle of independence increased
every day, said the governor, for the Council denied the power
of Parliament and the leading men in the House demanded the

[111] Mass. Hist. Soc., *Collections*, 4th ser., IV, 445; Hutchinson, *History*, III,
191–93.
[112] To Bernard, Jan. 10, 1770, Oliver Letter Book, I, 135–36.
[113] Mass. Arch., XXVI, 434–36.   [114] *Ibid.*, pp. 446, 450.

removal of all restraints on trade. He quoted a New York councilor as writing that Britain must eventually set up a lord-lieutenant and an American Parliament, "for the spirit of democracy [was] so persevering that they will be obliged at last to come into it." [115] Because all officials except himself joined the body of the people in popular measures, Hutchinson could do nothing. But, said the governor, "in all other matters which have no relation to this dispute between the Kingdom and the colonies government retains its vigor and the administration of it is attended with no unusual difficulty." [116]

With tempers flaring and tension mounting over nonimportation and the use of troops, the final episode, the Boston Massacre, might well have been predicted. Clashes between troops and civilians on March 2 and 3 resulted in British complaints and retorts by the Council that the only solution was withdrawal of troops. Predictions of serious consequences proved all too true —on March 5, troops fired on a crowd, killing several people.[117]

So great was popular feeling over the Massacre that the Revolution might well have started in 1770 had not the British removed their troops from Boston. A tremendous town meeting on March 6 unanimously demanded evacuation, refused to accept an evasive answer from the governor, and set up a watch to see that the removal was carried out. The Council unanimously backed Boston. These meetings were characterized by Hutchinson as being composed of "all the inferior people" without "any qualification of voters," where gentlemen no longer met with common civilities.[118] There was also little doubt that Boston would have received ample aid had it been needed.

[115] *Ibid.*, p. 440. [116] *Ibid.*, p. 446.

[117] *Ibid.*, p. 452; Hutchinson, *History*, III, 194–96. There have been many accounts of the Boston Massacre. Samuel A. Green, "The Boston Massacre, March 5, 1770," in American Antiquarian Society, *Proceedings*, n. s., XIV, 40–53, favored the American side. Randolph G. Adams, "New Light on the Boston Massacre," *ibid.*, XLVII, gives a pro-British account. In "The Commissioners of Customs and the 'Boston Massacre,'" *New England Quarterly*, XXVII (Sept. 1954), 307–325, Dickerson presents evidence that the customs commissioners or their employees probably fired on the crowd from a window in the customs house and that judges and others were rewarded with salaries for their efforts in freeing the accused.

[118] Mass. Arch., XXVI, 464.

There was almost unanimous agreement that Boston, aided by the country, would remove the troops by force if necessary. In fact, the alarm went out and armed men began to march on Boston until stopped by Boston inhabitants.[119] From New Hampshire came word that ten thousand men would have marched from that province if the occasion had demanded.[120]

The Boston Massacre made it evident, if such a demonstration were needed, that the great mass of the people and most of the elected officials in the province were supporting the popular party. It was not just a question of a few "radical" leaders fomenting trouble. Hutchinson said that a very great part of the people were in a perfect frenzy, that selectmen, councilors, and justices of the peace all warned that the people could not be restrained unless the troops were removed. The authority of government was gone "in all matters wherein the controversy between the kingdom and the colonies is concerned," he declared; war would result if the troops remained. "The great proportion by far of the members of every branch of the legislature or executive power join in supporting the people in this measure," the governor continued, "and the few which remain are obliged to submit." [121]

The only group who could thwart popular opinion were the judges of the Superior Court, officials appointed by the governor and momentarily expecting to receive their salaries from Great Britain rather than from the democratic assembly. But popular demands were felt even by the judges, for they yielded to pressure and tried and convicted Richardson, the informer who had shot the small boy. Richardson's execution was not effected, however; he was imprisoned until the court could get orders from England. The British pardoned him, and he was released at a time when most of the people were in town meeting, so he escaped even though he was pursued. Trial of the Massacre soldiers was postponed for several months, however, because the judges knew that "the democratick thermometer" was "some degrees above boiling heat." [122] Peter Oliver, one of the judges, wrote:

119 *Ibid.*, XXV, 380–82.
121 *Ibid.*, XXVI, 452.
120 *Ibid.*, pp. 369–70.
122 Egerton MSS., 2671, pp. 153–62.

Government was now pretty thoroughly dissolved: the lower house of assembly coincided with the measures of the faction out of doors; His Majesty's council, some from timidity and the most part from inclination, coincided with the house; & the clergy had changed their usual form of prayer, & prayed for the ruling powers; and the governor was left alone to fill up the gap against any further inundation.

The judges remained firm, but only at the risk of their lives, Oliver continued, for the son of a councilor posted a notice on the assembly door calling for the people to kill the judges.[123] Eventually, even the judges were forced to yield to the wishes of the people.

On the very day of the Boston Massacre, March 5, 1770, Parliament was taking steps to repeal the Townshend Acts. Lord North, who had now become head of the government, proposed partial repeal on grounds of expediency, but he was determined to keep the tax on tea, and he refused to withdraw the preamble, which he saw as an assertion of right. Total repeal, he declared, would bring demands for repeal of other colonial regulations. Former governor Pownall, on the other hand, demanded total repeal. He had long contended that the Townshend Acts had not kept the colonies more dependent on Great Britain but had actually shaken that dependence to its very foundation. But North won easily, and the Townshend taxes were repealed except for the preamble and the tax on tea.[124]

Throughout the controversy over the Townshend Acts, there was not the slightest indication that democracy was restricted or that a ruling aristocracy governed the colony. Quite the contrary. The difficulties, as men of the time reiterated again and again, were due to British attempts to alter the status quo, not to efforts by a disfranchised lower class to gain political rights. These British measures threatened colonial democracy, for if the British could raise a revenue to control the salaries of colonial officials and to pay other expenses, the assembly would soon lose

[123] *Ibid.*, pp. 169–70.
[124] *Parliamentary History*, XVI, 610ff., 853ff.; Johnson to Trumbull, March 6, 1770, *Trumbull Papers*, I, 421.

all power. The colonists understood this fully and had no intention whatever of permitting the British to levy taxes.

Thus ended a chapter in Britain's "new" policy, a policy which was thwarted in Massachusetts by the force of democratic action which even the presence of British troops could not restrain. But it was a chapter only, not a book, for the new policy was not to be abandoned, nor had colonial democracy retreated from its position.

[C H A P T E R   X I I]

"Period of Quiet,"
1770–1772

HISTORIANS in general have either ignored the period imme-diately following partial repeal of the Townshend Acts as being of little significance, or they have interpreted it as a period of quiet in which there were no real grievances and in which the people would have been contented except for the "agitation" carried on by "radicals" such as Samuel Adams. According to some writers, conservatives recovered much power in Massa-chusetts and might have broken Samuel Adams' influence had not the British rescued Adams by another blunder in policy.[1]

Events during the period do not bear out these interpreta-

---

[1] Channing, *History*, III, 120–22, passed over the period almost without comment, and Gipson, *The Coming of the Revolution*, pp. 203–04, 210–11, has a very short summary. J. T. Adams, *Revolutionary New England*, pp 372–74, said the merchants were motivated by interests and feared that the movement which they had in-itiated was getting beyond control. They did not like the tendencies toward social and political revolution which their own propaganda had fostered. Schlesinger, *Colonial Merchants*, p. 240, called the period one of material prosperity and political calm. Merchants, who had previously controlled the agitation against Parliament, feared the strengthening of nonmercantile interests in provincial politics and were generally satisfied with the concessions Parliament had made. Between 1770 and 1773, however, the alliance of merchants and radicals was broken. But Schlesinger cited Adams to show that the popular party had in reality used the merchants for popular ends (p. 254). Both Schlesinger, p. 254, and Miller, *Sam Adams*, ch. ix, presented the thesis that Adams was saved by the British from declining influence and perhaps ultimate defeat.

tions, however, for there was more doing than meets the eye at a cursory glance. There is no doubt that affairs were quieter in Massachusetts than they had been for many years, but as we shall see, it was a quiet tempered more by resentment than contentment.

What happened after 1770 marked a change in British tactics rather than in purpose. The problem still remained of how to recover authority over democratic assemblies in order to enforce the mercantile system and to head off anticipated future attempts at colonial independence. Apparently the ministers decided to heed the advice of colonial officials to effect reform a little at a time so that the colonies would not be united in a common cause. Hampered somewhat by the threat of war in Europe, but aided immeasurably by the political maneuvering of Thomas Hutchinson, the British attempted a system of gradual reform in Massachusetts. How successful it was, and how democracy was involved, is the meat of this chapter.

Evidence was not long in forthcoming that partial repeal of the Townshend Acts had not solved many of the fundamental problems. Troops and customs commissioners had left Boston, and the town was quiet, but the news that the tea tax had been retained "set the town mad again." Hutchinson claimed that the General Court opposed him because of Parliament's acts rather than from personal motives, but with the whole force of government in the colony united against him, he asked to be replaced. His position was not improved any when he carried out Hillsborough's orders to move the General Court to Cambridge in order to eliminate the influence of the democratic Boston town meeting upon the legislature.[2] This move started a bitter wrangle between House and governor which lasted for three years.

When in his opening speech at Cambridge Hutchinson did not mention the Massacre but asked for a renewal of a riot law to punish offenders for tarring and feathering a Gloucester customs officer, the House gave a biting answer which set the tone for relations between governor and House. Present laws were suf-

[2] Mass. Arch., XXVI, 448, 451, 460, 473; Cooper to Pownall, March 26, 1770, King's MSS., CCIII.

ficient, said the House. Additions might give the civil magistrate dangerous powers. The governor should inquire into the real cause of the riots, and if they arose from oppression, removal of the cause would stop the riots. The governor could not expect patience from a people accustomed to liberty; their resentment would express itself in ways naturally unpleasant to oppressors. The House said it could not understand why the governor mentioned this particular case but did not mention much worse offenses, such as the presence of a standing army designed to subjugate the people to arbitrary measures. The House called the army an unlawful assembly which assaulted subjects, beat and wounded magistrates, rescued prisoners, and committed a massacre. Surely his honor the governor had heard of these things, the House concluded sarcastically.[3]

Looking on the assembly's statement as another long stride toward independence and especially as an assumption of power over military forces which was the last resort of all governments in maintaining supreme authority, Hutchinson decided to send this message to the king, then he dissolved the General Court.[4]

Retention of the tea tax and the preamble of the Townshend Acts quickly led to opposition throughout the province. One after another, various towns voted to support the "patriotic" merchants in Boston, to force any merchant to reship any goods imported from England, and especially to stop all use of India tea until the tea tax was repealed. At the same time, they agreed to promote local manufacturing as a method of obtaining their ends.[5] Hutchinson wrote that the agreement, backed by the people, had all the force of law, as merchants did reship their goods to England. "I have so often represented that this is not a combination of a party only but of the whole body of the people justified and favored by every part of the authority of government which by the constitution has power to suppress it," Hutchinson explained to Pownall.[6] In Marblehead, one Robert Jameson, a teacher and a government man, lost all his pupils because

---

[3] Hutchinson, *History*, III, 203–05; app. P, p. 368.   [4] *Ibid.*

[5] Malden Town Records, II, 42; Marblehead Town Records, IV, 90; Milton Town Records, March 12, 1770; Andover Town Records, May 21, 1770; *Topsfield Town Records*, II, 289.

[6] Mass. Arch., XXVI, 481, 484 (May 10 and 18, 1770).

he refused to sign the agreement against tea and had his house threatened "by a rabble at unseasonable hours of the night, calling out with a loud voice kill that dog Jameson he is a Governor's man and a Bastard of Liberty." [7]

When the general election was held in May, Hutchinson had little reason to hope that the democratic party had lost any of its power. Out of 513 votes in Boston, Hancock received 511, Adams 510, and Cushing 510. James Otis was replaced by James Bowdoin, a perennial thorn for Hutchinson in the Council. Otis had had an attack of insanity; it is not known whether this insanity was hereditary or whether it resulted from a blow on the head by a customs officer. Bowdoin received 439 votes, and Otis, who was in the country at the time, was sufficiently popular, as Hutchinson said, to get seventy or eighty despite his "lunacy." [8] John Adams replaced Bowdoin when the latter returned to the Council, which was not much of a net gain for the governor.[9]

Boston's instructions to these representatives lent further grounds for suspicion that democracy was very much in evidence and that the influence of the democratic Boston town meeting had not been eliminated by moving the General Court to Cambridge. The town warned that the times were perilous—that there was a plot afoot to destroy colonial liberty and to undermine the constitution by subtle means. Then the town declared unequivocally that as the people had always expected to be the judges of their own rights and liberties, so they rejected the pretended right of any Crown lawyer or any exterior authority on earth to determine, limit, or ascertain in any way their constitutional, charter, natural, civil, political, or sacred rights, liberties, privileges, or immunities. At one time the king's prerogative had been considered too delicate and sacred to be questioned, perhaps because it would not bear inspection, said the town, but the time had long passed. Such statements as that by James I that a good subject would be content with the king's will as revealed in his law was called by the town "mystical jar-

[7] Jameson to Hutchinson, May 30, 1770, *ibid.*, XXV, 409.
[8] *Boston Town Records*, XVIII, 21; Mass. Arch., XXVI, 482.
[9] *Acts and Resolves*, XVIII, 464.

gon," "absurd and infamous rant." The king's prerogative was *"solely governed by the laws of the land"*—laws which limited the rights of the king and maintained the rights of the people.[10]

The town then ordered its representatives to maintain the rights of the people at all costs. They should investigate the decayed state of the militia. When every effort was made to enslave them, when they were denied their constitutional rights, and when high-handed invasions were made on their property, certainly the constitutional watchmen of their liberties were asleep at their stations—or traitors—if they did not rise against these plots. Promote an increase in population, encourage industry and local manufacturing as pacific devices, but these salutary measures should never exclude or supersede the more open, manly, bold, and pertinacious exertions for freedom. The town urged its delegates to maintain a firm and lasting union as an effective method of thwarting their enemies. It was repugnant to the idea of free government that a government three thousand miles away and often having different interests should be allowed to proscribe citizens, fix the residence of the assembly—"our parliament," the town called it—forbid the colony to improve its own produce, force it to purchase British merchandise, and with sword in hand demand colonial property. So the representatives must at all hazards act as the faithful emissaries of a free-born, awakened, and determined people, who were impregnated with a spirit of liberty in conception and nurtured on principles of freedom from their infancy.[11]

Hutchinson fully expected the views of Boston to be representative of the views of the colony. He said that he had only a shadow of power without the concurrence of the Council and that he had never been able to obtain their advice for any proposal he made to prevent the usurpation of governmental powers by the town of Boston. He was convinced that it was impossible to suppress measures in which the people were so generally engaged unless he had outside help. The longer things continued as they were, "the farther the infection spreads," he said, for "the Boston principles obtain more and more in the remote parts of

10 *Boston Town Records*, XVIII, 26–30.   11 *Ibid.*, pp. 30–31.

the province."[12] Hutchinson sent a copy of the Boston instructions to Lord Hillsborough with the comment that they appeared to be the "ravings of men in a political frensy" but that the people believed them, and the same flame was raised as if they were really so. He told Hillsborough that while these instructions were only the work of Boston, yet the influence of Boston extended to all other towns and many would follow Boston's example.[13] The instructions were evidence of what he had often observed—if they were ignored by England, the colonies would go step by step until they were independent.[14]

If democracy still reigned supreme in the Boston town meeting, it was also effective in keeping the merchants of Boston in compliance with popular demands. There was an attempt by a few merchants to get approval of the town to import everything except the taxed tea, since the British had backed down on all taxes except the tea tax. But the vast majority of the people were opposed, and approval was not granted.[15] Then came notice, apparently false, that Philadelphia merchants had voted to import everything but tea. The Boston merchants decided to do as Philadelphia merchants did, but again the town meeting forced continuation of the nonimportation agreement until all taxes were repealed.[16] Hutchinson said that the merchants had called on the people to aid them and now the people were forcing the merchants to continue nonimportation against the merchants' desires. He urged Crown servants to make every effort to spread dissension in order to break the agreement.[17] In July another attack on the customs officers sent them all scurrying to Castle William for protection, but the crack in the nonimportation wall was getting larger in spite of popular feeling.[18] Word came that New York merchants had agreed to import everything except tea, but the lowest classes still ruled Boston, Hutchinson said, and would not allow a vote to be taken.[19] Actually

[12] To Hillsborough, April 27, 1770, Mass. Arch., XXV, 391.
[13] May 18, 1770, *ibid.*, XXVI, 485.　　　[14] To ?, May 22, 1770, *ibid.*, p. 489.
[15] *Ibid.*, p. 492.
[16] Hutchinson to Hillsborough?, May 27, 1770, *ibid.*, p. 495.
[17] To ?, June 2, 1770, *ibid.*, p. 498.
[18] Hutchinson to Robinson, July 24, 1770, *ibid.*, p. 520.
[19] Hutchinson to Hillsborough?, July 26, 1770, *ibid.*, p. 522.

only some nine or ten merchants wanted to follow New York's lead, for popular spirit in Boston was still very strong, but pressure to import was beginning to build up.[20]

Hutchinson looked on nonimportation and colonial independence as practically one and the same thing, and for both he blamed democracy. The people, he said, were determined to continue nonimportation regardless of what New York did, and though such a move was "perfect madness," he did not doubt in the least that they would carry out their threat.[21] "Independence is more and more the aim," he declared. One member of the Council had said that all the colonies had to do was to order a good stock of goods, then enter into a new combination to order no more goods until the Molasses Act and every other British act was repealed.[22] Hutchinson accused the popular party of threatening to appeal to heaven as a last resort, of hinting downright revolt, and of holding principles incompatible with the idea of colonial dependence.[23]

By the summer of 1770, affairs in Massachusetts had reached what might be called a state of uneasy equilibrium. Because of his unpopularity in the colony and his conviction that he could be of little service to England, Hutchinson continued his efforts to resign as governor.[24] The people complained about postponement of the Massacre trial, Andrew Eliot reported, but were as quiet as they were likely to be. But there was talk that the British officer, Captain Preston, who had been in command of the Massacre troops, would be pardoned even if he were convicted, and this would cause trouble. As a matter of fact, Hutchinson had orders from the king to pardon Preston and the soldiers, though he said he would have done so even without orders. Eliot said that independence was nearer than he had once thought, unless conditions changed.[25]

In both the General Court and the newspapers, the popular

20 Hutchinson to ?, July 26, 1770, *ibid.,* p. 523.

21 To McKay, July 27, 1770, *ibid.,* p. 526.

22 To ?, July 26, 1770, *ibid.,* p. 524.

23 To ?, August 4, 1770, *ibid.,* p. 530.

24 Hutchinson to Williams, June 30, 1770, Israel Williams Papers, II, 164.

25 Eliot to Hollis, June 28, 1770, Mass. Hist. Soc., *Collections,* 4th ser., IV, 449–53; Hutchinson to Hillsborough?, June 26, 1770, Mass. Arch., XXVI, 508.

party had things its own way. Governor and assembly were dead-locked in Cambridge over the right of the Crown to determine where the Court should sit. Despite Hutchinson's strategy of proroguing the Court and then calling it back into session, the House unanimously refused to do business until it was moved back to Boston, and it denied that British officials could say where the General Court should sit or even that the king in council could decide a dispute between governor and assembly.[26] The governor accused Samuel Adams of altering Hutchinson's speech to the legislature and printing it in the popular newspa-per, the *Boston Gazette*. Hutchinson had the correct version printed in the government paper, but the correction did no good, he said, for "the misfortune is that seven eights [*sic*] of the peo-ple read none but this infamous paper [the *Gazette*] and so are never undeceived." [27]

While the governor and House were deadlocked over colonial rights, the British, with the aid of Hutchinson, completed a second reform, both the manner and intent of which posed a threat to colonial democracy. In August, Hutchinson had word from General Gage for British troops to replace provincial troops as the garrison at Castle William. Hutchinson, afraid of arous-ing suspicion, desired to prevent the plan from being known until it was ready to be put into effect.[28] The governor real-ized that a change of the garrison would cause trouble, for the fort had been built and maintained at province expense and the people would consider it their property. For this reason, everything was to be done in secret.[29] Hutchinson then received direct orders from the king to change the garrison. The governor called a Council meeting, swore the Council to secrecy, told them what was intended but did not either ask the advice of the Council or allow the Council to question his motives. Then before word could spread of his intentions, he went to Castle William and carried out his orders. The next day he went to his country home in Milton, but the word of what he had done

---

[26] Hutchinson, *History*, III, 218 and appendix S, p. 388.
[27] Hutchinson to ?, August 12, 1770, Mass. Arch., XXVI, 532–33.
[28] Hutchinson to Hillsborough?, Aug. 28, 1770, *ibid.*, p. 542.
[29] Hutchinson, *History*, III, 221–23.

got out, and when he received repeated messages of the rage of the people over his actions, he decided to go back to Castle William.[30]

That British control of Castle William was a prelude to changes in the Massachusetts constitution there seemed little doubt. In a letter to England, Hutchinson said the transfer of troops "seems intended as a preparatory to further measures with which I am not yet fully acquainted and rather think you will have a voice in determining in Parliament." [31] Hutchinson realized that he was treading on dangerous ground. He had cooperated at every step with the British officer concerned, but he said that he had difficulty in convincing the people that only a change of garrisons was involved and that he had realized that the least slip in the secret plans might have been fatal.[32] Later Hutchinson said that the king had a perfect right to take over the fort and that such a move would "facilitate any further measure which shall be judged necessary." [33] At the same time, there was talk in England of spirited and effectual measures to be taken against Massachusetts, especially for the purpose of altering the Massachusetts constitution.[34]

The plan for change involved the elimination of the elected Council, which had become merely the instrument of the people, and the substitution of a mandamus council which would carry out British policies. Hutchinson proposed to send a list of men who would serve British interests, particularly those men who had been removed from office because of their attachment to government. It was difficult to say how many men would refuse to serve on a mandamus council because of their fear of the people. Hutchinson said that he had asked one man, who desired reform and who understood the people, how the change in councils would be received. The man replied that a mandamus council would be as obnoxious and unsafe as the commissioners of customs, but it had to come to a trial sometime, and the present was as good as any. Whatever was done should be done

---

[30] Hutchinson to Bernard, Sept. 15, 1770, Mass. Arch., XXVII, 1–3.
[31] To Whately, Oct. 3, 1770, *ibid.*, pp. 11–12.
[32] To Gage, Sept. 25, 1770, *ibid.*, XXV, 431.
[33] To Bernard, Oct. 20, 1770, *ibid.*, XXVII, 34–35.
[34] Johnson to Trumbull, June 25, 1770, *Trumbull Papers*, I, 439.

the same way the garrison was changed—quickly, before the people had a chance to prevent it—but this man doubted that the House of Representatives would work with a mandamus council.[35]

News that Hutchinson had secretly turned over the garrison at Castle William to British troops naturally caused an uproar in the colony. The assembly abandoned its determination not to do business until it returned to Boston; instead it sent Hutchinson an angry message accusing him of violating the charter, then chose Benjamin Franklin and Arthur Lee as its agents in England.[36] The governor tried to convince everyone that the change of garrisons meant nothing, that Castle William was still under the governor's command. "The General," he said privately, "has aided me much to keep up this appearance." [37] The House then printed its correspondence with its agents in the newspapers, a device which Hutchinson said would keep the people "in a perpetual flame." He accused Samuel Adams of writing these letters, of being one of the greatest incendiaries in the king's dominions, and of desiring "the destruction of every friend of government in America." These letters really contained the doctrine of independence, he said—a doctrine which was spreading every day.[38] Hutchinson also declared that Samuel Adams had proposed that the colony raise twenty thousand men to seize Hutchinson and to retake Castle William.[39]

While the storm over the garrison raged, Hutchinson suggested other moves to cut down on democratic government in Massachusetts. He told Hillsborough that the people were rapidly accepting the doctrine that Parliament not only could not tax but could not legislate for the colonies. These ideas would be difficult to eradicate.[40] Changes needed to be made, he said, and he advocated repeated strict measures to bring the colonies back under British domination. Hutchinson would have a house of lords, laws to punish anyone who denied Parliament's author-

[35] To Hillsborough?, Oct. 6, 1770, Mass. Arch., XXVII, 13–14.
[36] Hutchinson, *History*, III, 223.
[37] To Bernard, Oct. 20, 1770, Mass. Arch., XXVII, 21.
[38] To ?, undated, *ibid.*, XXV, 437.
[39] To ?, Nov. 30, 1770, *ibid.*, XXVII, 60.
[40] To Hillsborough, Oct. 9, 1770, *ibid.*, XXV, 441.

ity, trial of offenses in England instead of in the colonies, appointment of all officials to serve at pleasure, and forfeiture of the charter in case of refusal to comply.[41] Said the governor: "We know by experience that the present form of government in this province gives too great a share both of legislative and executive power to the people to consist with the interest of the parent state or the welfare of the colony itself." [42]

The transfer of Castle William to British hands was not to be the only British move to strengthen its military power in the colony. James Bowdoin had a letter from Pownall containing a detailed account of the ministers' plans, which included delivery of Castle William to the King's troops, making Boston the rendezvous of the British navy, taking and fortifying Fort Hill in Boston, and sending regiments to Boston.[43] Hutchinson also contended that possession of Castle William and the stationing of the navy in Boston harbor, which the British had done, were excellent measures as they prepared the way for later policies. He said he still kept up the pretense that he commanded Castle William because it made the people easier.[44]

All this was merely indicative that the British were the ones who desired changes in the status quo, not the lower classes in Massachusetts. At the very time that the British were inaugurating reforms, two popular leaders were demanding a return to the system in effect before 1763. Thomas Cushing said he feared the results if Britain arbitrarily altered the Massachusetts charter. He also denied that the colonies would demand repeal of the navigation acts if conditions existing before the revenue acts were restored. If the ministers were wise, he said, they would go back to the old system by repealing revenue acts and removing customs commissioners and troops, for then the people would be satisfied and would not want independence. But if the British continued to use severe methods, Cushing would not predict the consequences.[45] And despite Hutchinson's repeated

[41] To Bernard, Oct. 20, 1770, *ibid.*, XXVII, 28; to Hillsborough?, Oct. 26, 1770, *ibid.*, p. 38.

[42] To Hillsborough?, Dec., 1770, *ibid.*, pp. 74–75.

[43] Hutchinson to ?, Oct. 25, 1770, *ibid.*, p. 36.

[44] Hutchinson to Hillsborough?, Oct. 26, 1770, *ibid.*, p. 38.

[45] To Stephen Sayer, Nov. 6, 1770, Mass. Hist. Soc., *Collections,* 4th ser., IV, 356–57.

accusations, Samuel Adams insisted that the colonies would not aim at independence if the British would just go back to relations existing before the Stamp Act.[46]

British plans to curtail democracy in Massachusetts had to be shelved temporarily, however, because of the threat of war with Spain. William Samuel Johnson, the Connecticut agent, reported that the possibility of war forced the British to desire harmonious relations with the colonies. There was still talk of securing Britain's commercial interests in the colonies, and there were threats that the British intended something drastic against Massachusetts; [47] but Franklin wrote that the project to abridge the charter rights of Massachusetts had been laid aside.[48] This was the same type of situation, of course, that had occurred so often while the French possessed Canada.

Meanwhile, Governor Thomas Hutchinson was doing everything in his power to break the power of the popular party over the colony. He was aided in this respect by the collapse of the nonimportation agreement. Whenever possible he rewarded by appointments to office men who had opposed the popular party, promoted dissension among members of the popular party, and called meetings of the General Court at times most convenient for the few "friends of government." The governor praised the seizure of Castle William and the stationing of ships in Boston harbor as a "humbling stroke" against the popular party.[49]

But these measures were not enough, according to Hutchinson. The British should take advantage of the comparative lull to curb democracy even more, although there might be some difficulty. Better pay for judges to secure their loyalty and actions similar to the seizure of Castle William would do much to secure the colonies to Great Britain, he believed. The constitution should be changed because it gave the people too great a share of both executive and legislative power. "Great discretion will undoubtedly be necessary," he warned, "& it will be prudent to retain all forms and usages in the administration of government as far as may be for some time & whatever altera-

46 To Sayer, Nov. 16, 1770, Samuel Adams Papers, II.

47 Johnson to Trumbull, April 14, Oct. 12, and Nov. 15, 1770, Trumbull Papers, I, 429, 454, 461; Parliamentary History, XVI, 1036.

48 Franklin, Writings, V, 283–84.

49 Mass. Arch., XXVI, 531–33, 546; XXVII, 64, 68.

tions are requisite for maintaining the authority of government should be made gradually and almost insensibly." Knowing popular opinion as he did, Hutchinson added this precaution: "It will be best that I should not be suspected by the people here of having suggested any alterations." [50]

That the British still considered complete control of colonial officials as the most effective alteration is evident in a letter from Benjamin Franklin to Samuel Cooper and Thomas Cushing. "There is no doubt of the intention to make governors and some other officers independent of the people for their support," he wrote, "and that this purpose will be persisted in, if the American revenue is found sufficient to defray the salaries. Many think this so necessary a measure, that, even if there were no such revenue, the money should issue out of the treasury here." [51]

Instead of levying taxes to pay salaries, since taxes had resulted in organized colonial resistance, the British apparently decided to pay the salaries themselves. This would free colonial officials from the domination of democratic assemblies and in turn lead to better enforcement of British mercantile and imperial regulations. Strict enforcement would yield more revenue for additional salaries, and the preamble of the Townshend Acts would become a reality instead of a mere objective.

But as long as the British took no steps to pay salaries, the people in Massachusetts were quiet, despite some dissatisfaction over the acquittal of Captain Preston and the Massacre troops.[52] Colonial unrest seemed to be directly proportional to British activities.

Hutchinson, meanwhile, continued to use the lull to win support for the government and to divide the popular party. He postponed the meeting of the General Court as long as he could, for every day enabled him "to take off one or another [of the representatives] from their attachment to the Boston faction." [53] He urged attractive salaries for government officials to win converts to the government side, and he believed that the lull offered as good a time as any to change the Massachusetts con-

[50] *Ibid.,* pp. 70, 74–75, 87–88.   [51] Franklin, *Writings,* V, 286–87, 296.
[52] Eliot to Hollis, Jan. 26, 1771, Mass. Hist. Soc., *Collections,* 4th ser., IV, 454–57.
[53] To ?, Jan. 7, 1771, Mass. Arch., XXVII, 91.

stitution. Unlike his superiors in England, who tried to avoid trouble with the colonies when the prospects of war appeared, Hutchinson believed that a war would show the colonists how dependent they were on the British. But even if the British were unable to institute reforms, they should still leave the impression that more reforms were to come. "The wise step of changing the garrison at the Castle began our cure," he declared, as he urged that Parliament pass some colonial measure every session to familiarize the colonists with Parliament's authority.[54] Confident of his success against the popular party, the governor, however, still wished to hedge a little on future events by investing some of his money in England.[55]

The only ripple on otherwise calm waters was an oration commemorating the first anniversary of the Boston Massacre. At a meeting organized by Adams and Hancock, the oration appeared to rekindle some flame, but not much. Hutchinson looked on the oration as treason, however, as he urged Parliament to stop such denials of British authority, "which first or last must be done or you will lose the colonies." [56]

In connection with the Massacre Oration, Hutchinson revealed still another proposal under consideration in England for curtailing colonial democracy—the alteration of the democratic town meeting. The lower classes were still under the influence of their leaders, he wrote to John Pownall, and would be until Parliament altered the town's constitution "as some time ago you gave me a hint of." [57] Writing to Hillsborough, he said that such events as the oration tended to confirm the people in their disrespect for Parliament and their belief in their own independence. Then he explained just how democratic the Boston town meeting was: "In these votes and in most of the public proceedings of the town of Boston persons of the best character and best estates have little or no concern. They decline attending town meetings where they are sure to be outvoted by men of the lowest order, all being admitted and it being very rare that any

[54] To ?, Jan. 8, 1771, *ibid.,* p. 92; to North?, Jan. 22 and 30, 1771, *ibid.,* pp. 99, 110.
[55] To Palmer, Feb. 7, 1771, *ibid.,* p. 116.
[56] To John Pownall, April 18, 1771, Mass. Arch., XXVII, 149; *Boston Town Records,* XVIII, 47–48.
[57] To John Pownall, April 3, 1771, Mass. Arch., XXVII, 143.

scrutiny is made into qualifications of voters." [58] No controlling merchant aristocracy here—but Hutchinson forgot to mention that such men as Hancock, Bowdoin, and Cushing did very well indeed in the Boston town meeting.

Instead of attempting to reform the town meeting, which attempt came at a later date, the next move by the British in what might be called "creeping imperialism" was to pay all of Hutchinson's salary and thus remove the influence of the assembly over him. As an added incentive, the British increased the stipend from £1,000 to £1,500 a year. The governor had long insisted that an adequate salary which was not contingent upon the whims of a democratic and often hostile House of Representatives would encourage colonial officials to carry out orders. On this occasion, he informed Hillsborough that his best thanks would be a faithful discharge of his trust.[59]

Hutchinson's leading opponent, Samuel Adams, was perfectly aware that a governor's salary paid by the British posed a grave threat to democracy in Massachusetts. He called this a "perfect despotism" on one occasion, and on another, wrote as follows:

I have long thought that a design has been on foot to render ineffectual the democratical part of this government. . . . The plan is still carried on tho in a manner somewhat different; and that is by making the governor altogether independent of the people for his support; this is depriving the house of representatives of the only check they have upon him.[60]

The importance of an independent salary is attested by Hutchinson's statement that the taking of Castle William, the stationing of warships in Boston harbor, and the payment of the governor's salary were of about equal value in checking colonial democracy. He doubted whether altering the constitution would have produced better results, for these three together had sunk the spirit of the opposition. All that was now needed was a plan to punish those who denied the authority of Parliament—a necessary prelude to an effective change in the constitution.[61] The governor was aghast at the suggestion that Castle William be restored to colonial control so that the assembly

---

[58] To Hillsborough, April 19, 1771, *ibid.*, p. 151. [59] *Ibid.*, pp. 128, 296.
[60] To Sayer, Jan. 22, 1771, Samuel Adams Papers, III; Adams, *Writings*, II, 165.
[61] To Bernard, April 25, 1771, Mass. Arch., XXVII, 153–54.

would vote needed repairs, which it had refused to do.[62] A proposal to shift the fleet base from Boston to Halifax, probably because of desertion, met a similar response. The shift would strengthen the opposition, he declared, for two capital ships in the harbor struck more awe in the town than two regiments of soldiers.[63]

Just why the payment of the governor's salary did not cause a greater immediate stir than it did is difficult to explain. Perhaps the lull after a long period of agitation was the cause, or perhaps the charter could have been construed as permitting it. As we have seen in an earlier chapter, the General Court in 1692 claimed the right to pay all salaries, but the act was disallowed in England. On this occasion, when Hutchinson refused to sign two bills providing for his salary, the House asked what other provision had been made "independent of His Majesty's commons"—meaning themselves. The governor corrected the House in its assumption that it was "His Majesty's commons," then told the House that the British government had decided to provide a certain and adequate support for civil government in the colonies.[64]

Still the lull continued, but there was something ominous about it. Samuel Adams recognized that Hutchinson was trying to undermine the popular party, but Adams, who had great confidence in the people, did not expect the governor to succeed. The people were quiet, he said, but it was a "sullen silence" which did not prove that the spirit of liberty was dead.[65] Hutchinson, noting the lack of controversy among the people and in the General Court, indulged in some wishful thinking that the election of 1771 would favor the government. But he also admitted that all but two or three members of the House were anti-government, making it prudent for a governor not to raise controversial issues.[66] The governor favored the abolition of yearly elections so that he could continue "a house of representatives that should be well disposed."[67]

62 To Pownall, Feb. 4, 1771, *ibid.*, p. 114.
63 To John Pownall, April 5 and 8, 1771, *ibid.*, pp. 146–48.
64 Hutchinson, *History*, III, 239–42.   65 *Warren-Adams Letters*, I, 8.
66 To Hillsborough, April 19, 1771, Mass. Arch., XXVII, 151; Hutchinson, *History*, III, 243.
67 To Hillsborough, May, 1771, Mass. Arch., XXVII, 157.

Believing that he had won out over the popular party, Hutchinson still expressed the belief that the trouble was too much democracy, especially in Boston. He thought the faction was dying, though it died hard, and that its future success depended on events in England. Boston was the source of trouble, he contended, but considering the town constitution, it could not be otherwise while the majority which conducted all affairs was a group which would be called a mob anywhere else, "there being no sort of regulation of voters in practice." Men of weight and value wished to suppress this mob, but could not be induced to do it for fear not only of being outvoted but affronted and insulted. There was no hope for a cure from internal legislation, Hutchinson continued—the people would not do anything that would lessen their importance. Parliament would have to force the people "to swallow" a remedy before the trouble would be cured.[68]

The election of 1771 did not fulfill the governor's expectations, however, for it indicated little diminution in the strength of the popular party. James Otis had recovered from his mental illness and was back in politics after a year's absence, but according to Hutchinson he "really would have been a more fit representative while his lunacy was upon him." The "Sons of Sedition," as he called the Sons of Liberty, fearing that many towns would change their representatives, made a strong effort in the newspapers to keep the same men in office.[69] Apparently they succeeded, for of the 410 votes cast in Boston, Otis received 399, Cushing 410, Hancock 410, and Adams 403.[70] Hutchinson reported after the election that the assembly was in a better temper even though four-fifths of the members were the same as in the last assembly.[71] Andrew Oliver was not so optimistic. He wrote to Thomas Whately in England:

The times are indeed turbulent, but matters have now been carried such a length, as I think must unavoidably bring on a crisis. I wish it may be such a one as shall break the force of the distemper the state

[68] To ?, May 24, 1771, *ibid.*, pp. 171–73.
[69] To Bernard, May 10, 1771, *ibid.*, pp. 163–64.
[70] *Boston Town Records*, XVIII, 53.
[71] To ?, June 5, 1771, Mass. Arch., XXVII, 178.

labors under. Posterity will account the politics of the present day as the madness of enthusiasm: we are not a whit behind you, & altho' there is an intermission of acts of violence at present, yet the leaders of the people were never so open in asserting our independence of the British legislature which possibly may be productive of more serious consequences hereafter.[72]

In the General Court of 1771, sparring for advantage continued between Hutchinson and the House, with the popular party still in control of affairs on major issues despite the prevailing lull. The governor appeared to have won over James Otis when the latter defeated Samuel Adams' motion not to do business until the governor returned the General Court to Boston.[73] There were hints that Hancock wanted to break with Adams and that the governor should accept Hancock into the Council to end his influence in the House, but Hutchinson expressed confidence that he could win Hancock without concessions.[74] The governor vetoed a law against importation of slaves on the ground that it violated his instructions, then, when the news of the governor's salary became known publicly, the House passed strong resolves against government by instruction, removal of the General Court to Cambridge, and payment of the governor's salary.[75] The governor also won the displeasure of the House by vetoing a bill which would have taxed the salaries of Crown officials. Another instruction against taxing officers of the Crown "raised a great ferment" and brought a sharp message from the House denying the king's right to establish customs commissioners, to raise revenue, or to instruct the governor.[76]

These strong resolves and messages were a gentle reminder to the governor that the popular party still dominated the General Court whenever a major issue was at stake. Hutchinson had thought he was making progress in winning converts, yet at the first provocation, he said, the assembly could pass resolves by

[72] May 15, 1771, Oliver Letter Book, II, 17.   [73] Adams, *Works*, II, 266.
[74] Hutchinson to John Pownall, May 30, 1771, Mass. Arch., XXVII, 174; to ?, June 5, 1771, *ibid.*, p. 180.
[75] Hutchinson to Hillsborough, May, 1771, *ibid.*, p. 159; Hutchinson, *History*, III, 245, appendix T, p. 400.
[76] Hutchinson, *History*, III, 347–49.

a two-thirds majority. He accounted for his defeat by saying that the Boston delegates misled the poor country representatives.[77] Andrew Oliver, on the other hand, was not blinded by wishful thinking as was Hutchinson. Said Oliver of the popular leaders:

Their influence is still so great in the general court that they can demand a majority on any question: some who vote with them there do not scruple in private to disavow the part they take in public, owning that they do it to preserve their places and influence: while others disdaining to hold their seats on such base and ignominious terms retire from public life.

Oliver said that he did not envy the governor, for as long as these same men had the lead, Hutchinson could not please the people and at the same time be faithful to his trust.[78]

It was perfectly clear at this point that British measures had neither diminished the power of democracy nor eliminated the threat of colonial independence. The attempt to exempt Crown officials from colonial pressure by exempting them from taxes caused widespread resentment and brought a statement from the Reverend Samuel Cooper that this touched the pocket of the farmer, who would be aware of this fact.[79] Warships, sent to Boston "for a purpose far from agreeable to the people," said Hutchinson, were regarded "with an evil eye" by the Sons of Liberty, who understood their purpose only too well.[80] The governor was pleased that trouble with Spain was being settled, for the "mad sons of liberty" hoped to see Britain embroiled in a war. "We are become more orderly in our actions," he declared, "but our principles are as bad as ever. Independent, it is said we are [quoting Adams] and independent we must be." [81]

Although Hutchinson believed that he had quieted the

[77] To Hillsborough, June 22, 1771, Mass. Arch., XXVII, 188; to Bernard, July 8, 1771, *ibid.*, p. 191; to Pownall, June 22, 1771, *ibid.*, p. 189.

[78] To Bernard, July 20, 1771, Oliver Letter Book, II, 30; To Whately, July 8, 1771, *ibid.*, pp. 27–28.

[79] To Franklin, July 10, 1771, Franklin, *Writings*, V, 353–54.

[80] To Bernard and Pownall, Aug. 14 and 15, 1771, Mass. Arch., XXVII, 214.

[81] To Pownall, Aug. 14, and to General Mackay, Aug. 15, 1771, *ibid.*, p. 216. See also pp. 246 and 253.

people, who had been misled by their leaders, in his less emotional moments he recognized that popular sentiment had not changed much and that any incident might touch off a violent reaction. Things were remarkably quiet and had been for months, he wrote to his son in September 1771, but he doubted that there was "much more of a disposition to good humor" than there had been since the Stamp Act. "A sullen discontent has succeeded to a furious rage," he declared, and for once agreed with Samuel Adams, who had called it a "sullen silence." [82]

In a letter to Thomas Pownall, the Reverend Samuel Cooper also warned that the British should not be misled into thinking that the prevailing lack of agitation meant a change in disposition among the people. Reports to Britain that the people and the assembly were ready to give up the point of right tended only to deceive and mislead the government, he said. The tone of the House was as firm as ever on every point of privilege, and while a high ferment could not be maintained among the people, their inward sentiments were not altered. To prove his point, Cooper cited a late incident of the governor's Thanksgiving proclamation calling on the people to thank Heaven "for the *continuance of our privileges.*" The people considered this such mockery and an insult that whole congregations threatened to walk out of church if the ministers read the proclamation. "Had the ministers inclined it was not in their power to read it, a circumstance which never before took place among us," Cooper continued. And he accused Hutchinson of deliberately inserting the clause, omitted since the Stamp Act, to convince the government in England that the people in Massachusetts had changed. Cooper said that he mentioned this in confidence to show the temper of the people, even though they appeared quiet.[83]

If nothing spectacular occurred, there was still an undercurrent of feeling that the lull was only temporary. Thomas Cushing believed that the colonies should revive their union, continue to assert their rights, and above all be ready to take

82 To his son, Sept. 30, 1771, *ibid.,* p. 236.
83 Cooper to Pownall, Nov. 14, 1771, King's MSS., CCIII.

advantage of a probable war in Europe.[84] From agent Benjamin Franklin came the warning that Hillsborough acted as though he knew of some approaching trouble with the colonies. He tried to impress Franklin with assertions of friendliness toward the colonies, but Franklin said he would believe the colonial secretary only when he ordered the withdrawal of troops and customs commissioners, repealed all duties, restored Castle William to the colony, canceled offensive instructions, and restored control of the governor's salary to the General Court.[85]

From the following quotation it is not difficult to understand why the colonists opposed instructions to the governor, why they considered these a threat to democracy, and how a democratic legislature would react to them. Franklin quoted Lord Granville:

Your American assemblies slight the King's instructions, pretending that they are not laws. The instructions, sent over to your governors, are not like the pocket instructions given to embassadors [sic], to be observed at their discretion as circumstances may require. They are drawn up by grave men learned in the laws and constitution of the realm; they are brought into council, thoroughly weighed, well considered, and amended if necessary by the wisdom of that body; and when received by the governor, are the law of the land; for the King is the *legislator of the colonies.*[86]

As already noted in Chapter I, it was during this apparent lull that Franklin made his tour through Ireland and Scotland, where he noted the great differences between the class-ridden societies of those countries and the middle-class, democratic society of New England. There society was composed of the few rich and the many poor, but in New England, every man was a freeholder and voter, living in comfortable circumstances. Franklin believed that the Indians in America lived better than did the poor people of Ireland and Scotland.[87]

Perhaps Americans were thinking of these things when they

[84] To Roger Sherman, Jan. 21, 1772, Mass. Hist. Soc., *Collections*, 4th ser., IV, 358.

[85] To Cushing, Jan. 13, 1772, Franklin, *Writings*, V, 363.

[86] To Bowdoin, Jan. 13, 1772, *ibid.*, pp. 358-59.   [87] *Ibid.*, pp. 362-63.

opposed British restrictions and regulations, and when they talked about dying for their liberties.

In Massachusetts, meanwhile, Hutchinson continued his efforts to break the solidarity of the popular party, but was never quite sure of his success. He believed that he had separated Hancock and Adams, yet both declared they would not abandon the cause of liberty.[88] As governor, he apparently was ready to change from the Congregational to the Episcopal church, but for political reasons he had to work both sides of the religious street. "It is my opinion & I find it to be the opinion of the Episcopal clergy," he wrote to Bernard, "that I can do more good in the way I am in at present than by wholly going over from the way of worship which is so universal in the province & which will always be the prevailing way in America until the inhabitants have other notions of civil government than they have at present." [89] On one hand Hutchinson would express confidence in his tactics, but then he would say that he was postponing a meeting of the General Court until prospects looked better.[90] Sure that he had broken the faction beyond repair, he contradicted himself by hoping for a better assembly next time as the late disorders "brought not only into the house but the council the lower orders of the people" from whom he did not expect much.[91]

The Boston election of 1772 appears to have been Hutchinson's supreme effort to divide the party and to eliminate his most inveterate antagonist, Samuel Adams. The number of voters jumped from 410 in 1771 to 723, an indication that something unusual was afoot at a time when everything seemed so peaceful. Of these, Cushing received 699, Hancock 690, William Phillips (who replaced Otis) 668, and Adams only 505.[92] A clue to what happened is to be found in a letter of Andrew Oliver, who should have known:

88 To Gage, Dec. 1, 1771, Mass. Arch., XXVII, 258; to Hillsborough, Jan. 31, 1772, *ibid.,* p. 290.
89 To Bernard, Dec. 24, 1771, *ibid.,* p. 265.
90 To Bernard, March 14, 1772, *ibid.,* p. 302.
91 To ?, April 8, 1772, *ibid.,* p. 319.
92 *Boston Town Records,* XVIII, 53, 77.

I think our friend the governor will get the better of the faction which has been so long in opposition to government. We had our election of representatives in Boston this week. Mr. Adams who has been so long the idol of the populace wanted near 200 votes of the number which each of his brethern [sic] had who were chosen with him: this shows he is not invulnerable. He is no longer supported by Mr. Hancock, who appears inclined to be very civil to the Governor.[93]

Given Hutchinson's previous activity, in all probability he mustered the "gentlemen" and "better sort," who usually avoided the town meetings, in his concerted effort to oust Adams. It was one way to make Adams appear as unpopular, but if this was his intention, it failed in its objective.

Although at times Hutchinson was optimistic, at this time he was under no illusions about his success in conquering the party, regardless of Oliver's optimism. He said that government had few supporters in the legislature and even those few would not appear when they were most needed. In urging his friend Israel Williams of Hatfield to attend and to bring his colleague Partridge, the governor expressed the hope that "every good town" would send two representatives. "But remember," he warned Williams, "you don't live in the Commonwealth of Plato but in the dregs of Romulus." [94]

The dregs of Romulus were soon dredging up the issue of salaries for British officials paid by the British instead of the colony—an issue which would shatter the peace and quiet that had long prevailed. Boston, as so often happened, assumed the lead. In its instructions to guide its representatives "in the Assembly of the Commons," the town declared that the very being of the constitution was endangered. An exterior power claimed the right to govern and tax them, the governor refused an honorable support from the people, and the town believed that part of the money unjustly taken from them by taxes was used to make the governor independent of the people. The same committee which instructed the representatives on the governor's salary also had orders to bring instructions on the

93 Oliver to Gambier, May 8, 1772, Oliver Letter Book, II, 82–83.
94 To Williams, May 9, 1772, Israel Williams Papers, II, 170.

appointment and salaries of Superior Court judges, but could not agree on the report. Apparently the town had heard that judges' salaries were to be the next reform. In strong words, the town condemned the governor as well as the British, then ordered its representatives to seek redress of grievances when the General Court met.[95]

Boston's instructions again brought a condemnation of colonial democracy from Hutchinson as he explained to Hillsborough how complete that democracy was. He sent the *Boston Gazette* with the instructions. These were criminal but were looked upon as a matter of course, he said,

the meetings of that town being constituted of the lowest class of the people under the influence of a few of a higher class but of intemperate and furious dispositions & of desperate fortunes. Men of property & of the best character have deserted these meetings where they are sure of being affronted. By the constitution forty pounds sterl.—which they say may be in cloaths household furniture or any sort of property is a qualification & even into that there is scarce ever any inquiry & anything with the appearance of a man is admitted without scrutiny.[96]

If this is not democracy, democracy cannot be defined, and it was obviously a democracy which was seriously interfering with British imperialism.

At the time the General Court met, Hutchinson wrote to Bernard that he hoped to move the legislature back to Boston where he could entertain members at his table every day and thus "provide an antidote for the poison of that white liverd [*sic*] fellow that [Bernard] used so much to detest." [97] Perhaps the desire to counteract the influence of Samuel Adams led the governor to accept an ambiguous House message which he could construe as meaning that the king's right to determine the place of meeting of the General Court was not questioned. He had held out, he said, to show the people that he intended to obey the king's instructions.[98] At any rate, the General Court

95 *Boston Town Records,* XVIII, 77–87.
96 May 29, 1772, Mass. Arch., XXVII, 339.
97 To Bernard, May 29, 1772, *ibid.,* p. 340.
98 June 15, 1772, *ibid.,* p. 344.

moved to Boston after a three-year sojourn in Cambridge, but it remained to be seen whether Hutchinson and his dinner table would have more influence on the assembly than "that white liverd fellow," Samuel Adams.

Immediately on its return to Boston, the House appointed a committee to report on the Boston instructions about the governor's salary, but still Hutchinson did not seem to be concerned. Instead of worrying, the governor merely condemned democracy in no uncertain terms. "Can anything be more absurd," he wrote, "than for the representatives of a people to declare that all power is to be exercised for the good of the people & they are to judge when it is so exercised and submit or not submit accordingly." [99] It was a statement, not a question. To Hillsborough he expressed confidence that the friends of government would prevent any justifiable resolves or votes, especially those designed to "raise a clamor" about the salary. He did not fear the reaction among the people, for he was sure that they wanted peace and would be quiet except for the actions of a few wicked men.[100]

As so often happened, Governor Hutchinson proved to be wrong: Samuel Adams had more influence than he had and the friends of government could not prevent resolves about the salary. The committee which reported on Boston's instructions stated that the assembly, under the charter, had the right to tax for defense and support of government, including the governor's salary. Any other provision was unconstitutional as it made the governor independent of the people, leaving them no checks on him. So strong were the resolves that government men, such as Israel Williams, John Worthington, and John Murry walked out of the House, but the House passed them 85-19 after deciding to publish the vote.[101] Hutchinson accused the House of attempting to alter the constitutional dependence of the colony on Britain. The king, he said, had the *right* to appoint the governor, had granted the people the *privilege* of electing the House and the House the *privilege* of electing the Council.[102] Then he prorogued the general court.

[99] To Pownall, June 22, 1772, *ibid.*, p. 346.   [100] June 25, 1772, *ibid.*, p. 350.
[101] Hutchinson, *History*, III, 257.   [102] *Ibid.*, app. W, p. 406.

As the summer of 1772 wore on, Hutchinson's confidence in his position relative to that of the popular party was further shaken. Soon after the House made its resolves on the salary question, he wrote to Hillsborough that these resolves would really benefit the government, for the position taken by the House was so ill founded that his own answer would quiet rather than arouse the people.[103] The governor accused a few crafty leaders of agitating the people, but he had to admit that even the "good men" in the House opposed acts of the British ministers. He fully realized that the threat of defeat for those who supported the government made the holding of a new election fruitless. Laws could not be executed, he lamented, and trade acts were disregarded because customs officials did not care to hazard their lives by seizures. Hinting that the colony might lose its charter as a result of the House resolves on the salary question, he expressed the view that if there were less frequent meetings of the legislature his hand would be strengthened.[104]

In his letters to England, Hutchinson continued to urge action by the British government, especially the payment of judges' salaries, which apparently had been postponed awhile but which he considered fundamental if the British expected to recover their authority. He blamed the "levelling constitution" of Massachusetts for the inadequate salaries, urged Britain to compensate these officials for their loyalty, then added: "It will increase the clamor here but it can't be helped." [105] The governor even thought that the British could rely on the middle-class structure of Massachusetts society to make their reforms successful. Said he: "The demagogues who generally have no property would continue their endeavors to inflame the minds of the people for sometime but the inhabitants in general have real estates which they would not run the hazard of forfeiting by any treasonable measures." [106] Apparently the governor forgot that two of the "demagogues" throughout the entire con-

---

103 July 15, 1772, Mass. Arch., XXVII, 363.
104 To ?, July 21, 1772, ibid., p. 361, 365–66.
105 To ?, Aug. 22, 1772, ibid., p. 373.
106 To ?, Aug. 27, 1772, ibid., pp. 377–79.

troversy had been John Hancock and James Bowdoin, two of the wealthiest men in the province.

Andrew Oliver wrote to Bernard:

If the report be true which has begun to circulate since the arrival of the last ships from London, that the judges of the superior court are to receive their salaries out of the revenue duties the newspapers will presently sound a fresh alarm. I have heard that one of the demagogues has said that this will bring matters to a crisis, & that they shall now effect their purpose. What that is I can't say.[107]

"The salaries of the law officers made a great noise." [108] Thus did Thomas Hutchinson verify Oliver's prediction and signify the end of an era—the period of quiet had been shattered. Statements by Samuel Adams, Samuel Cooper, Andrew Oliver, and on occasion, Hutchinson himself, that the people's silence was a "sullen silence" which could be broken by renewed activity of the British government proved only too true. Payment of judges' salaries was all that was needed to arouse a latent animosity toward the mother country. Castle William, warships, the meeting of the General Court in Cambridge, the king's instructions, exemption of customs officers from taxes, a governor's salary paid out of what were considered unconstitutional revenues—these and other irritants had been instrumental in creating an atmosphere which needed only a spark to cause an explosion. That spark was the issue of judges' salaries.

The period from 1770 to 1772 was not simply one in which agitation was maintained by Samuel Adams and his "radical" cohorts to arouse the underprivileged and unenfranchised classes to action against the "aristocrats." Adams was a politician, and there is no question whatever about the fact that he engaged in all kinds of political maneuvers to gain advantages over the Hutchinson party. But no one can read Hutchinson's letters without reaching the conclusion that the governor was also a politician who intrigued to the best of his ability to defeat the Adams party. If Massachusetts had possessed an aristocratic society and a limited franchise Hutchinson probably would have won out over his popular rival. Samuel Adams de-

---

[107] Aug. 31, 1772, Oliver Letter Book, II, 96.
[108] To Bernard, Oct., 1772 Mass. Arch., XXVII, pp. 392–93.

feated the governor because, as Oliver said, he was the "idol of the populace" in a democratic society where the populace rendered the verdict. The people had long exercised the right to choose between Adams and Hutchinson, and they had chosen Adams. The only "aristocracy," if such existed, was a small group of appointed officials, such as the Hutchinsons and Olivers, who held office only because of the British and who could never have won an elective office in the colony.

CHAPTER XIII

Collapse of the "New" Policy, 1772–1774

BRITAIN'S decision to pay judges' salaries set off a chain of incidents which ultimately led to the collapse of the new policy. The chronology is familiar—salaries, the Boston Resolves of November 1772, committees of correspondence, the Tea Act of 1773, the Boston Tea Party, and finally the Coercive Acts of 1774. But the way in which democracy affected these events and in turn was affected by them is not so well known.

Boston, as usual, led the way. The selectmen, including John Hancock, could not for long resist popular demand for a town meeting.[1] When a request to the governor elicited the response that independent judges were none of the town's business, the town then asked for a meeting of the General Court. Hutchinson peremptorily refused, as his compliance would weaken the king's prerogative, a response which the town voted "unsatisfactory." Then Samuel Adams moved for a committee to state the rights of the colonists as men, Christians, and subjects, and to communicate this statement to other towns and to publish it to the world as the views of Boston.[2]

[1] Hutchinson, *History*, III, 259–60.

[2] *Boston Town Records*, XVIII, 88–93. Miller, in *Sam Adams*, also treated the salary problem as one which allowed Adams to display his propaganda techniques. According to Miller, the creation of committees of correspondence was essentially

Naturally Samuel Adams, as an effective politician in a democratic society, looked for support from other towns so that Boston would not face the British alone. From his friends Elbridge Gerry of Marblehead and James Warren of Plymouth, neither of whom were proletarians, came assurances that friends of liberty in Marblehead would back Boston and that the pulses of Warren's fellow townsmen in Plymouth were "beating high." [3]

As he often had done, Hutchinson underestimated the gravity of the situation. To show his resentment and to discourage Boston from meddling in affairs beyond its jurisdiction, he not only refused to call a General Court but also postponed the meeting already scheduled. The town meeting was designed to raise a general flame, he said, but he discounted its possible success. [4] The governor mistakenly expressed confidence that the Boston faction had been disappointed in popular reaction to British payment of salaries and would also fail in a system of committees of correspondence, which was "such a foolish scheme that they must necessarily make themselves ridiculous." [5]

The Boston Resolves of November 20, 1772, left no doubt whatever about the sentiments of the people there. The town insisted on *rights*, not *privileges*. These included life, liberty, and property, religious freedom, and laws made by a representative legislature and enforced by independent judges. The colo-

---

a one-man accomplishment against the wishes of practically everyone—Adams' own Whig followers and the citizens of the country towns (pp. 261–73). But, in fact, far from being the work of small cliques of "radicals," the committees of correspondence were the legal organs set up by town meetings, and a perusal of the town records shows how vast was the popular support behind these committees. Miller said that the adoption of committees of correspondence came slowly, but he quoted Hutchinson to show that they came "all of a sudden" (p. 269) and that country towns were just as "radical" as Boston (pp. 269–70). Material in the last chapter shows that committees of correspondence did not mark the rejuvenation of the Whig party or the reappearance of Adams as a menace to the British (p. 269). In spite of occasional efforts to unseat him, Adams and the Whig party had been in complete control throughout.

[3] Gerry to Adams, Oct. 27 and Nov. 10, 1772, and Warren to Adams, Nov. 8, 1772, Adams Papers.

[4] To Dartmouth, Nov. 3, 1772, Mass. Arch., XXVII, 402.

[5] Nov. 13, 1772, *ibid.*, p. 412.

nists were to judge when their rights had been violated and would be justified in restoring to the sword if necessary in defense of them. In sending its views to other towns and requesting their views and correspondence, Boston posed the question of how long the colonies should submit to British treatment of them.[6]

Although at the time Hutchinson underestimated the importance of the Boston Resolves, he was able to look back on them later with a much more accurate view of their importance. When they became public, he considered them as misrepresentations of the facts which were not worth the postage required to transmit them to England, though he did admit that the faction had successfully propagated the doctrine of independence.[7] Later he wrote of the resolves as follows:

Such principles in government were avowed as would be sufficient to justify the colonies in revolting, and forming an independent state, and such instances were given of the infringement of their rights by the exercise of Parliamentary authority, that, upon like reasons, would justify an exception to the authority in all cases whatever. . . . The whole frame of it, however, was calculated to strike the colonists with a sense of their just claim to independence, and to stimulate them to assert it.[8]

[6] *Boston Town Records,* XVIII, 93–105. Schlesinger, in *Colonial Merchants,* contended that merchants had dominated the opposition to British measures up to this point, but that the salary question brought a break between merchants and radicals. Merchants desired to prevent further strengthening of nonmercantile power in provincial politics and were substantially satisfied with concessions made by Parliament (p. 240). Adams labored to keep radical sentiments alive but lacked a compelling issue and an organization divorced from control of merchants. Payment of salaries, said Schlesinger, furnished the issue, and committees of correspondence, set up by Adams, furnished the organization in which merchants were a minority (pp. 254–58). Since he did not consider colonial society as democratic, Schlesinger missed the importance of salaries as a democratic check on Crown appointees. He considered the salary question not as a major grievance, but merely as an excuse for Samuel Adams to show his consummate ability as a master agitator (pp. 257–61). At the same time, Schlesinger failed to account for the fact that the resolve to set up a committee to state colonial rights passed unanimously (p. 257) and that the Boston letters to other towns were an immediate success (p. 259). On page 254, he cited Adams to show that in reality the popular party had used the merchants, not that the merchants had used the popular party.

[7] To Jackson, Dec. 8, 1772, Mass. Arch., XXVII, 428.

[8] Hutchinson, *History,* III, 262–63.

Response to the Boston Resolves was both quick and decisive, a warning to Hutchinson that Boston had wide support for its stand. Often towns accepted the Boston statement as justified, then thanked Boston for its stand in defense of colonial liberties. Sometimes towns made additions to the Boston resolutions, which needed no addition, as they instructed their representatives to defend their rights.[9] Said John Adams: "I said there was no more justice left in Britain than there was in hell; that I wished for war," then chided himself for such rash, boyish statements.[10] Peter Oliver gave Hutchinson this estimate of popular support: "Plymouth folks say there are 90 to 1 to fight Great Britain." [11]

We have Hutchinson's word that backing for Boston was nearly unanimous throughout the province, an indication that the popular party was not simply a Boston faction. He said that there were about 240 towns and districts in the province, that some eighty including the principal towns had voted support for Boston, and that most if not all of the remaining 160 towns would have followed Boston. Alarmed at what he saw, he called a General Court in an effort to stop the flames from spreading to other colonies and to towns which had not yet acted on the resolves.[12]

[9] *Plymouth Town Records*, III, 363–64; *Muddy River and Brookline Records*, pp. 234–36; Malden Town Records, II, 52–54; Sheffield Town Records, Jan. 5 and 12, 1773; Hadley Town Records, Jan. 3, 1773; *Worcester Town Records*, IV, 199–204.

[10] Dec. 31, 1772, Adams, *Works*, II, 308–09.

[11] Dec. 16, 1772, Mass. Arch., XXV, 549. J. T. Adams, in *Revolutionary New England*, discounted the importance of salaries, called the resolves of the Boston town meeting demagogic, and contended that the people were sluggish over the salary issue but that the *Gaspee* affair aroused them (p. 382). The *Gaspee* affair was in June 1772, however, not after the payment of salaries. Channing, *History*, III, did not connect salaries and committees of correspondence. Channing just said that Adams and Joseph Warren devised a system of town committees composed of "leading radicals" to revive and foment interest in a dying cause. Channing also had the *Gaspee* affair coming after the salary controversy (pp. 122–25). On the question of who should get credit for starting committees of correspondence, see Edward D. Collins, "Committees of Correspondence of the American Revolution," American Historical Assn., *Annual Report*, 1901, I, 245–71. The truth is, of course, that committees of correspondence had been used long before 1772.

[12] To Mauduit, Feb. 22, 1773, Mass. Arch., XXVII, 450; to Dartmouth, Feb. 22, 1773, *ibid.*, pp. 451–52; to Mackay, Feb. 23, 1773, *ibid.*, p. 454.

The men who backed Boston were not in any sense radical, lower-class agitators, as Hutchinson on occasion intimated and as some historians have contended. Typical of the committees which acted on the resolves was that of the little western town of Sheffield, where the members were all property owners with varying amounts of property. Included were the following men and their tax ratings: Theodore Sedgwick, £63; Deacon Silas Kellogg, £108; Col. Ashley, £418; Dr. Lem. Barnard, £71; Aaron Root, £215; Philip Callender, £112; Capt. Wm. Day, £116; Deacon Ebenezer Smith, £56; Capt. Nathan Austin, £100; and Capt. Stephen Dewey, £99.[13] The total property of these men would ordinarily be at least ten times their tax rating. This Sheffield committee was similar to the committees of other towns where the records permit a check, and the members are what might be expected to represent a middle-class society.

When Hutchinson met the General Court early in 1773, he found a formidable force arrayed against him. In his opening speech, the governor tried to maintain that Parliament had supreme, absolute, unlimited authority over the colonies, and that there could be no middle ground between this supreme authority and colonial independence. Hutchinson said that this speech was designed to elicit a reply from the faction which would enable him "to make apparent the reasonableness and necessity of coersion [sic] and to justify it to all the world." Naturally, the General Court denied this extreme position, insisting that the very nature of government demanded limitations on the powers of Parliament short of colonial independence.[14] Wrote John Adams: "The governor and general court have been engaged, for two months, upon the greatest question ever yet agitated." [15]

The more the governor attempted to sway public opinion, however, the less became his influence. The Reverend Samuel Cooper said that the Boston Resolves were read in more than one colony "with high approval," and that "the people [were] more confirmed in their sentiments & encouraged to maintain

13 Sheffield Town Records, Jan. 5, 1773; Sheffield Tax List, 1771.
14 Mass. Hist. Soc., *Collections*, 5th ser., IV, 346; Hutchinson, *History*, III, 266–68; Hutchinson to Pownall, Jan., 1773, Mass. Arch., XXVII, 439.
15 Adams, *Works*, II, 315.

them." With all his connections and ability, Hutchinson was not able to alter the views of the people or reconcile them to the measures of government, Cooper continued, and the more openly and strenuously he tried, the less success he had, as the unanimity of both the Council and House as well as of the towns demonstrated.[16] Andrew Oliver wrote that many towns had passed resolves similar to those of Boston, utterly denying the authority of Parliament, and that leading members of the House were behind these denials.[17] Sometimes Hutchinson blamed only the leaders, but again he talked about the absurdity of the strange principles of government which "the greater part of all orders of men seem to have embraced, through an unaccountable infatuation, for if they could be indulged in independency they would become the most distressed & miserable people upon earth." [18]

In particular, Hutchinson accused Samuel Adams of desiring and promoting independence, and if the accusation were not true, Adams was certainly flirting with men who had those ideas. "The restless incendiary laid a new scheme to promote his professed independence," Hutchinson wrote to General Mackay.[19] About the same time, the "restless incendiary" received the following letter from Samuel Parsons in Providence, Rhode Island:

The idea of unalienable allegiance to any prince or state is an idea to me inadmissable, & I cant see but that our ancestors when they first landed in America were as independent on the Crown or King of Great Britain as if they had never been his subjects: & the only rightful authority derived to him over this people was by explicit covenant contained in the first charters. These are but broken hints of sentiments I wish I was at liberty more fully to explain.[20]

In addition to his controversy with the legislature, Hutchinson was taken to task by the Boston town meeting for statements about the Boston Resolves which the governor had made in

16 To Pownall, March 25, 1773, King's MSS., CCIII.

17 To Bernard, Jan. 31, 1773, Oliver Letter Book, II, 108; to Montagu, Jan. 20, 1773, *ibid.*, pp. 111–12.

18 To Dartmouth, Feb. 22, 1773, Mass. Arch., XXVII, 451–52.

19 Feb. 23, 1773, *ibid.*, p. 454.   20 March 3, 1773, Adams Papers.

his speech to the legislature. Hutchinson had called this meeting illegal and claimed that the town had published principles having a tendency to alienate the affections of the people from their sovereign. The town defended the legality of its meeting, but it did not deny the second charge. All it would say was that there was still the great and perpetual law of self-preservation to which every man had a right to concur and that the liberties of the continent had been invaded step by step. That other towns felt as Boston did merely indicated a happy union of sentiment in the colony for a united effort to preserve their liberties, the town declared.[21]

In all this trouble, Hutchinson was virtually alone as a force for upholding British authority—there was certainly no "ruling aristocracy" to aid him. Andrew Oliver wrote that the Council had been garbled, that the ablest men in the House had either been defeated or had refused to run for office, and that some others had not attended the General Court from despair of doing any good.[22] As for popular opinion, Hutchinson wrote to the Earl of Dartmouth, who had replaced Lord Hillsborough as colonial secretary: "I have long had the same hopes with Your Lordship that the absurd principles of so great a part of the people of this country could not continue and that the prejudices against government in England which are the consequences of these principles would cease with them." [23]

"These principles" which the governor condemned so roundly were in reality the product of one element, democracy, according to the governor. He spoke of the constitutions of the towns "being all alike, by one act or law made a corporation as democratic as possible." [24] He urged that this democracy of the towns must be restrained or government would never be orderly, for "by an unfortunate mistake soon after the charter a law passed which made every town in the province a corporation perfectly democratic." [25] The Boston Resolves had been passed

---

21 *Boston Town Records*, XVIII, 110–22.
22 To Montagu, Jan. 20, 1773, Oliver Letter Book, II, 111–12.
23 March 20, 1773, Mass. Arch., XXVII, 468.
24 To Mauduit, Feb. 22, 1773, *ibid.*, p. 450.
25 To Pownall, Feb. 24, 1773, *ibid.*, p. 457; to Gage, March 7, 1773, *ibid.*, p. 461.

by the "lowest orders" in the town, he declared.[26] To Edward Montagu he wrote the same: "Every town in the province is a corporation perfectly democratic. All the absurdities of the present day are therefore easily received by them." [27] It was these "absurd principles" of democracy which caused "the prejudices against government in England," he said, and "the opposition to the salaries of judges springs from the same principles." [28]

If the salary controversy furnished evidence of "absolute democracy," it also furnished evidence that the colonists were resisting, not demanding, changes. This, of course, is what could be expected in a society which was already democratic. Samuel Cooper believed that if an early settlement of the unhappy disputes had been made "only by annihilating innovation, and recurring to the same old course which time and practice had sanctified," there would not be the revolution which Cooper now saw "in the sentiments and hearts of the people." [29] It was to be one of the unique revolutions in history—a revolution to preserve a democratic society rather than to acquire one, a revolution to prevent change rather than to promote it.

The immediate problem of the colonists was to prevent the British from paying judges' salaries and thus gaining control of the judicial as well as the executive branch of the government. Hutchinson tried to forestall whatever measures the colonials might take by demanding assurances from the judges that they would not accept salaries from the General Court after the date of their salary grant from the king.[30] To head off this threat, the General Court raised the salaries of judges, granted salaries for a full year, then did the unheard of by voting them a salary for the following year. This presented Hutchinson with a problem. The king's warrants for salaries dated from July 1772 on, but the governor was afraid that the judges would lose the half-year's salary for early 1772 if they accepted the king's offer, for the General Court would not pay them if they accepted the

26 To Mackay, Feb. 23, 1773, *ibid.*, p. 454.   27 Feb. 22, 1773, *ibid.*
28 To Dartmouth, Feb. 22 and March 20, 1773, *ibid.*, pp. 451–52, 468.
29 To Pownall, March 25, 1773, King's MSS., CCIII.
30 Circular to judges, Feb. 5, 1773, Mass. Arch., XXV, 553.

king's grant. At the same time, he did not want the judges to accept pay from the colony for service after July 1772. So he consented to the salary grant from the House after receiving promises from the judges that they would accept only what was due them before July.[31] The House then attempted to put pressure on the judges to refuse a royal grant, especially by a resolve stating that as judges held office during pleasure only, their acceptance of salaries from the king, independent of grants from the General Court, made them enemies of the constitution and promoters of arbitrary government.[32]

By this time there were indications that the popular party in Massachusetts was going to receive considerable support from other colonies. Boston had sent its resolves to these colonies urging the re-establishment of committees of correspondence. Hutchinson informed Dartmouth that the persons who influenced all public measures triumphed by having these resolves accepted by the Virginia assembly.[33] The governor expected all colonies to appoint committees of correspondence as a result of collaboration between Boston and Virginia. If Parliament took any steps against this union, they must include all the colonies, he said, "as the same spirit prevails everywhere tho not in like degree." [34]

However serious the rift in the popular party in 1772, that rift was well healed by election time in 1773. Hancock had apparently seen the handwriting on the wall and had refused a seat on the Council in 1772 despite Hutchinson's efforts. The vote in 1773 lends even more weight to the suspicion that the governor had made his supreme bid to discredit Adams in 1772 and had finally lost all hope of accomplishing this feat. Out of 419 votes, Cushing had 418, Hancock 417, Adams 413, and Philips 416. The town noted this near unanimity as it instructed its representatives to take a strong stand in defense of colonial rights and to work for a colonial union. The town also withheld permission to use the town house for the usual election dinner if

31 To Dartmouth?, Feb. 22, 1773, *ibid.*, XXVII, 452,
32 Hutchinson, *History*, III, 277–79.
33 April, 1773, Mass. Arch., XXVII, 477.
34 To Pownall, April 19, 1773, *ibid.*, p. 480,

the governor invited persons obnoxious to the town to the dinner.[35] To show his resentment, Hutchinson secured another room and invited the "obnoxious" persons.[36]

Boston was not the only town to send unmistakable instructions, and these were not the work of radical agitators.[37] Andover defeated an attempt to reverse the town's previous approval of the Boston Resolves, then instructed its representative to oppose "not with an indifferent coolness, but with an unremited [sic] resentment" any encroachments on colonial liberties. Among the men responsible for these instructions were the Hon. Samuel Phillips, Esq., the richest man in town and a member of the governor's Council, moderator James Frye, representative Moody Bridges, and committee members John Farnum, Nehemiah Abbot, Asa Foster, Samuel Osgood, and Joshua Holt, all among those who paid the highest taxes in Andover.[38]

Even Hatfield, Tory stronghold and home of Hutchinson's good friend and prerogative man Israel Williams, yielded to the popular sweep. Hatfield had been one of the few towns to support the government, but it could not hold back the rising tide of anti-British feeling, as Israel Williams went down to defeat. In his place came John Dickinson, but this replacement did not represent a class revolution. On the tax lists, Williams was rated at £206, Dickinson at £169, and of the 155 names on the list, only twelve rated higher than Dickinson.[39]

Given the democratic nature of Massachusetts society, it followed naturally that the General Court which met in May 1773 was no more tractable than the constituents who elected and instructed the delegates. Jonathan Judd, Jr., had to stand up in a crowded church in Boston where he heard "a very high liberty sermon." [40] Then the popular party eliminated Harrison Gray and Stephen Hall from the Council before passing, by a vote of 109 to 4, some Samuel Adams resolves to establish a

[35] Boston Town Records, XVIII, 128–37.   [36] Hutchinson, History, III, 282.
[37] Topsfield Town Records, II, 318; Wenham Town Records, p. 271; Worcester Town Records, IV, 199–204.
[38] Andover Town Records, May 17 and 31, 1773; Andover Tax List, 1774.
[39] Hatfield Town Records, IV, 241, 248; Acts and Resolves, XVIII, 798–99; Hatfield Assessors' List, 1772.
[40] Judd Diary, II, May 26 and 27, 1773.

standing committee of correspondence. There was a second vote of 101 to 5 to publish some letters sent from England by Franklin, including the well-known letter by Hutchinson to the effect that there must be an abridgment in the colony of what were called English liberties.[41]

The next show of popular strength came with a vote on resolutions to have the governor and lieutenant governor—Hutchinson and Oliver—recalled. The vote was 83–28, but apparently public sentiment was such that the twenty-eight later desired to change their votes.[42] Hutchinson claimed that most members voted against their judgment or did not know what they were doing.[43] One of the twenty-eight had a different explanation, however. John Pickering of Salem went home to find that he was considered a Tory by his constituents for having voted with the twenty-eight against the governor's removal. Pickering said that he had supported the popular party on every measure except this one and that he had voted in the minority only because he thought the time was not favorable. Pickering was somewhat bitter at being called a Tory for having voted as he did. This hurt the cause, he said, and made it appear that Hutchinson

[41] Hutchinson, *History*, III, 282–94. Robert J. Taylor, in *Western Massachusetts in the Revolution* (Providence, 1954), contended that western Massachusetts was a conservative area under the domination of the "river gods" which supported the prerogative party "right up until 1774." Taylor's whole thesis rests on four men—John Stoddard, who died in 1748, Israel Williams and Oliver Partridge of Hatfield, and John Worthington of Springfield (p. 11). Stoddard must be discounted, of course, and his fortune of some £35,400 (p. 13) was undoubtedly in old tenor and amounted to no more than £3,500 Massachusetts money or about £2,600 sterling. Williams, Worthington, and Partridge certainly supported Bernard and Hutchinson, but these three did not constitute western Massachusetts, which according to Taylor had sixty-two towns by the time of the revolution. The vote on major issues throughout the period, as well as statements by Bernard and Hutchinson on the almost unanimous opposition, simply do not support the Taylor thesis. The vote against rescinding was 92 to 17, that to have Bernard recalled was 109 to 0, and the votes of 109 to 4 and 101 to 5 do not show very solid support from western Massachusetts or anywhere else. The town records also show that some of the western towns were just as "radical" as Boston in their ideas. Taylor was perfectly correct, however, in saying that most men in western Massachusetts could vote and that towns often avoided representation, but this latter point is further evidence that the conflict between east and west was not very significant.

[42] Hutchinson, *History*, III, 292.

[43] To Williams, July 20, 1773, Israel Williams Papers, II, 171.

had more support in the assembly than he really had.[44] How many of the twenty-eight voted for reasons similar to those of Pickering is difficult to say.

The final act of the General Court before Hutchinson prorogued it was to pass a set of resolves dealing with the judges. They were declared enemies of their country if they accepted salaries from the king, and it was their duty to declare whether they intended to accept. If they delayed, the House declared, it would be the indispensable duty of the commons of the province to impeach the judges before the governor and Council.[45] Hutchinson ended this threat by proroguing the assembly, something he would not have dared to do had he been subject to popular election in the colony.

Both in the colony and in England, British officials continued to insist that these actions by the Massachusetts democracy were simply further proof of a desire for independence. "The persons who have been active in promoting the principles of independency" were on the committees, Hutchinson declared. In addition, the Council had ceased to be His Majesty's Council and some were ready "to go all the lengths of the chief incendiary, who is determined he says to get rid of every governor who obstructs them in their course to independency." [46] With reference to the assembly's answer to Hutchinson over the powers of Parliament, Dartmouth told Franklin that Parliament would not "suffer such a declaration of the general assembly, asserting its independency, to pass unnotic'd." [47] And Arthur Lee confided to Samuel Adams that the enemies of America considered any claim to constitutional rights as "a pretense only on our part, for claiming absolute independence." From charging the colonists with this aim, he continued, these enemies had brought them first to consider it, then to claim it, and he hoped, to confirm it.[48]

The near unanimity of opinion in Massachusetts in opposition to British measures did not mean, of course, that there

44 To Samuel Adams, July 5, 1773, Adams Papers.
45 Hutchinson, *History,* III, 295.
46 To Dartmouth, and to?, July 10, 1773, Mass. Arch., XXVII, 511–12.
47 Franklin to Cushing, May 6, 1773, Franklin, *Writings,* VI, 49.
48 June 23, 1773, Adams Papers.

were no differences of opinion. From England, Franklin and Arthur Lee urged the colonies to be ready to take advantage of Britain in case of war, when they could demand rights and withhold aid until these rights were granted.[49] Franklin urged caution, however, as men in England were looking for an excuse to use military force to restrain the Americans. Time was on the side of the Americans, for their growing population and strength would soon force concessions.[50] Thomas Cushing also urged caution, for he, too, believed that colonial increase in wealth and numbers would eventually settle the dispute in favor of America. If the colonies persisted in openly and strenuously denying the right of Parliament to legislate for them in any case whatever, they might bring on a war before they were ready for it.[51]

While some men were willing to let time settle the issues between the two countries, they still did not want the British to get false impressions about the nature of colonial opposition. Thomas Cushing declared that the British should not be misled into believing that the assembly was dominated by a few artful men. The men who passed the resolves in answer to the governor were *"grave and sad men,"* "men of property" who would not stand by while their rights were being taken away.[52] The Reverend Samuel Cooper expressed great pleasure at the unanimous stand of the towns in their sentiments of liberty. This showed the general enlightened state of the people's minds, he said, and demonstrated the falsehood of the opinion, much cultivated in England by partisans of arbitrary power in America, that only a small faction in America were discontented with the late measures.[53]

With the General Court prorogued because of its stand, Hutchinson continued to blame the democratic ideas of Samuel Adams and the democratic Boston town meeting for most of his difficulties. Adams, he said, who headed the faction of the party desiring independence, had long practice in politics which

[49] Franklin to Cushing, July 6, 1773, Franklin, *Writings*, VI, 73–81; Lee to Adams, June 11 and 23, 1773, Adams Papers.
[50] To Cushing, March 9, 1773, Franklin, *Writings*, VI, 22.
[51] To Lee, September, 1773, Mass. Hist. Soc., *Collections*, 4th ser., IV, 360.
[52] *Ibid.*
[53] To Franklin, July 7, 1773, Franklin, *Writings*, VI, 89.

qualified him above others to excite the people. Having complete domination of the Boston town meeting and the House of Representatives, he now controlled the government. The governor branded the political principles of Adams and his followers—"that in political matters the public good is above all other considerations"—as criminal. Adams depended on the town meeting, where he originated measures which were followed by the rest of the towns and adopted or justified by the assembly. Then Hutchinson pointed out the value of parliamentary control of salaries: "Could he have been made dependent I am not sure that he might not have been taken off by an appointment to some public civil office." [54]

Adams and his popular party had been only partially successful as far as judges' salaries were concerned, however. Four of the five justices had agreed to accept salaries for 1772 voted by the General Court, since they would have lost half a year's salary if they refused, but what they would do about their salaries for 1773 was not settled. Only the chief justice, Peter Oliver, had held out. Hutchinson asked the British to apply the money saved on the judges' salaries for the half year to repairing the governor's house. The assembly had declared they would not repair the house unless Hutchinson refused to accept a salary from the king.[55] Obviously the salary question was still a trouble spot.

In the midst of all these troubles, and with the General Court and the towns hurling defiance at Parliament, Parliament passed an act which surpassed all others for arousing popular resentment, and the repercussions showed the influence of colonial democracy. This was the famous Tea Act of 1773. Given the trouble already brewing in the colonies, the question arises as to why the British chose this particular time to pass the Tea Act.

The genesis of the Tea Act went back to the complicated arrangement between Parliament and the East India Company before the Townshend taxes were passed. By this agreement, the East India Company was to have a free hand in exploiting India

[54] To Dartmouth, Oct. 9, 1773, Mass. Arch., XXVII, 550.
[55] Hutchinson to Dartmouth, Sept., 1773, *ibid.*, p. 543.

without British interference; the government was to receive £400,000 a year from the company; the government was to lower taxes on tea to help the company expand its tea market in the colonies; the company had to make up any loss in total revenue from tea; and the £400,000 yearly payment was to cease if East India Company dividends dropped below a certain point.[56]

Because of recalcitrance on the part of the colonies, the agreement between the company and Parliament had not worked as it had been planned. Colonists continued mainly to use smuggled Dutch tea, and surpluses of company tea accumulated in England. The company got behind in its payment to the government; its stock fell 120 per cent, wiping out millions of pounds in stock values and causing bankruptcies, unemployment in manufacturing, and hard times in general. The Bank of England refused to lend the company money, which necessitated lowering dividends, but this in turn threatened the government's promised £400,000 a year. Franklin said that company affairs, plus the threat of war with Russia, probably prevented British action against the Boston resolves.[57]

Eventually Parliament came to the rescue of the East India Company. The company petitioned for permission to export tea to America duty free, for a loan of £1,500,000, and for immunity from prosecution for failure to pay the £400,000 a year to the government.[58] Some of these requests were granted. Parliament passed the Tea Act, which allowed a drawback of the whole duty on tea re-exported to America after May 10, 1773, and also changed the act of 18 Geo. II by which company tea had been auctioned to the highest bidder. Now tea could be sent directly to America without being auctioned in England, but it was not to be sent duty free as the company requested.[59]

[56] The best account of the complicated arrangement between Parliament and the East India Company is to be found in Miller, *Origins of the American Revolution*. Many historians have been unaware of this background. See Gipson, *The Coming of the Revolution*, pp. 217–18; Channing, *History*, III, 129; J. T. Adams, *Revolutionary New England*, p. 388.

[57] Franklin, *Writings*, V, 452–59; VI, 2–3, 12–13, 33.

[58] *Parliamentary History*, XVII, 516, 527, 799–827, 840.

[59] 13 Geo. III, c.44, Pickering, *Statutes*, XXX, 74.

Later the company received a £1,400,000 loan from Parliament and immunity from prosecution for failure to pay the government for its loss of revenue.[60]

According to some accounts, there was more to the Tea Act than met the eye at first glance. Franklin said that the "scheme" was

to take off so much duty here, as will make tea cheaper in America than foreigners can supply us, and confine the duty there to keep up the exercise of the right. They have no idea that any people can act from any other principle but that of interest; and they believe, that 3d in a lb of tea, of which one does not perhaps drink 10 in a year, is sufficient to overcome all patriotism in America.[61]

John Adams later claimed that the government devised this new plan to keep the tea tax but that the company, unwilling to risk its property in a dispute with the colonies, finally agreed by a majority of one vote only after receiving assurances that it would not suffer any losses. Adams also contended that the tea should be called "ministerial tea" instead of company tea, because it "was sent by the ministry, in the name of the East India Company," and the company was compensated for its losses out of the public treasury.[62]

It remained for Arthur Lee in London to place the most extreme interpretation on the Tea Act. He considered the sending of tea as a ministerial trick by Lord North to stir up violence in the colonies so that he could use coercive measures. The directors of the company, said Lee, were "fully appraised of the consequences of sending the tea, & that it would end in a certain loss to the company." [63] In short, colonists and their friends in England considered the Tea Act either as a scheme to induce the colonists to pay the tax or a device to force a showdown between colonies and mother country.

"Great noise about tea and India Company's establishing factors in this country," Jonathan Judd, Jr., of Northampton

[60] 13 Geo. III, c.63, *ibid.*, p. 124.
[61] Franklin to Cushing, June 4, 1773, Franklin, *Writings*, VI, 57.
[62] Adams, *Works*, IV, 79, 85.
[63] To Samuel Adams, Dec. 22, 1773, Adams Papers.

recorded in his diary for September 22, 1773.[64] The noise, according to Hutchinson, was a combination of three factors—fear of monopoly by importers, opposition to parliamentary taxation, and opportunity of the leaders to promote their great purpose, which he had long contended was independence.[65]

Boston, as usual, took the lead in opposition to the Tea Act. The town records for November 5, 1773, give the most graphic account of what happened at that town meeting. First a petition was presented expressing alarm that the East India Company was reportedly sending tea and that this was a political plan of Britain to tax in this way. Next, handbills called "The Tradesmen's Protest against the proceedings of the merchants relative to the new importations of tea" were distributed and read. Someone said he had seen Customs Commissioner Charles Paxton distributing these bills in King Street the day before the meeting. It was then moved that the tradesmen collect in one part of the hall, which some four hundred did. When asked whether they acknowledged the handbill as theirs, they voted unanimously in the negative. They also voted unanimously that they detested as false, scandalous, and base the handbill, its printer Ezekiel Russell, and Paxton. After debating the proj-

[64] Judd Diary, II, Sept. 22, 1773.

[65] Hutchinson, *History,* III, 302–03. Many historians emphasize monopoly rather than taxes as the basis for colonial opposition. See Channing, *History,* III, 129. J. T. Adams said that the Tea Act was a colossal blunder due to sheer political and commercial stupidity, not to a desire to tyrannize. Adams also contended that the real objection to the act was due to its monopolistic rather than its tax features (*Revolutionary New England,* pp. 388–89). He also injected the class struggle into his discussion by saying that merchants, in aiding the radicals, forgot the fear of internal revolution, but that soon the radical voters and the unenfranchised thrust the conservatives and merchants aside in the "body" which replaced the town meeting (*ibid.,* p. 390). Adams said that there "was absolutely no principle at stake" (p. 392).

Schlesinger, *Colonial Merchants,* pp. 262–77, particularly emphasized monopoly rather than taxation as the mainspring of colonial resistance against the Tea Act. Fear of monopoly and the threat to colonial manufacturing were undoubtedly important, but protests against the tax were not made chiefly for rhetorical effects. The monopoly thesis can be maintained only by ignoring the more numerous protests against taxation. If one were to assume class and sectional conflicts, as Schlesinger did, the logical reaction of those in the lower classes and agricultural regions would have been to sit back and let the merchants suffer. Popular reaction cannot be explained on the monopoly thesis.

ect of introducing tea and finding that no one favored the project, the town passed a series of resolves summarized below:

It was the inherent right of freemen to dispose of their own property.

The tea tax was levied without the consent of Americans.

The express purpose of the tax, namely support of government, administration of justice, and defense of His Majesty's dominions rendered assemblies useless and introduced arbitrary government.

A virtuous and steady opposition to the ministerial plan to govern America was necessary to preserve liberty and was a duty every freeman in America owed himself and his country.

Resolutions of the East India Company to send teas subject to duty in America were an open attempt to enforce the ministerial plan and a violent attack on American liberties.

It was the duty of every American to oppose this attempt.

Whoever countenanced this attempt was an enemy to America.

A committee was to call on the consignees appointed by the company to sell the tea and request that they resign their appointments immediately if they had any regard for their own characters and for the peace and good order of the town and province.

Some merchants had imported small quantities of tea in violation of agreements not to import dutied tea. The town determined to prevent the sale of imported East India Company tea and expected that no merchants would import dutied tea.

When consignees Richard Clark and Benjamin Faneuil evaded an answer to the demand that they resign by saying that other consignees Thomas and Elisha Hutchinson were out of town, the town voted unanimously to send Samuel Adams, William Mollineux, and Dr. Warren to inform them that as they were not joint factors, the town supposed they could determine for themselves and expected an immediate answer. Then a committee was sent to get the resignations of the Hutchinsons.

The printer of the handbill, Ezekiel Russell, came to the meeting and asked leave to speak, but as the town had not desired information from Russell, the town would have nothing to do with the printer or author of the handbill. The town also sent word to Clark and Faneuil that it was waiting "impatiently" for their answer. When their answer pleaded commitments in England that would prevent resignation, the town voted the answer "unsatisfactory" and adjourned until the next day to hear the answer of the Hutchinsons.

Next day, November 6, 1773, the committee reported on the Hutchinsons. When they inquired for Elisha Hutchinson, they were told he had gone to Milton, but when they got to Milton, Elisha had returned to Boston. Back in Boston, they were informed that he had gone back to Milton. So they went to Governor Thomas Hutchinson's house and delivered their message. The Hutchinsons later replied that they were not sure of the terms of their appointment as consignees, so that they had to wait for the tea before giving an answer. The town voted this answer "not satisfactory," then voted that all these answers from the consignees were *"Daringly Affrontive* to the Town." The Boston committee of correspondence was to send copies of these transactions to every town in the province.

On November 18, 1773, the town met again with Hancock as moderator to consider a petition expressing concern that the tea was expected momentarily and that the consignees should now know what their position was. A committee was sent requesting "an immediate and direct answer." To this the consignees replied that friends in England had so bound them that they were unable to resign. Again the town voted the answer "not satisfactory," then adjourned, not to meet as an official town meeting again until March 4, 1774.[66]

With the people of Boston in a "great ferment," Hutchinson failed completely in getting the Council to support him. The only answers he received were that the disorders were caused by unconstitutional acts of Parliament, that the plan was a design of the ministers to raise a revenue, and that the only solution was to submit to popular demands.[67]

After November 18, 1773, popular opposition, which increased by the hour, was in the hands of "the body," in effect a town meeting, except for the presence of hundreds from neigh-

[66] *Boston Town Records,* XVIII, 141–47.
[67] To Dartmouth, Nov. 15, 1773, Mass. Arch., XXVII, 570; Hutchinson, *History,* III, 306.

boring towns. Determined that the tea should be sent back to England, "the body" refused to hear the sheriff, whom Hutchinson had sent to dissolve them, until Adams consented; then they "hissed" the message. Hutchinson, equally determined to collect the tax, said that these mass meetings, which included all ranks, were more determined than former assemblies—no mean compliment—but were a model of orderliness.[68] When the first tea ship arrived, no one could buy even a pistol in town as the people prepared to use force. Although the consignees refused to send back "that bainfull weed," as Abigail Adams dubbed it, they prudently sought the sanctuary of Castle William and its British troops.[69] Other towns resolved to back the metropolis with their lives and property or stated that "many would spend their lives in the cause." [70] So high ran popular feeling that field officers in the militia could not prevent their men from acting as guards when "the body" ordered the ship to a wharf and placed a watch over it.[71]

For nineteen days after the tea arrived, the impasse continued between governor and people. Hutchinson took extra precautions to see that the tea ship did not leave until the tax was paid, by ordering Castle William to stop all ships and by stationing two government vessels to guard unused channels.[72] Warnings that the tea might be in danger failed to move either the governor or the consignees. On the nineteenth day, after last-minute efforts had failed, the famous Boston Tea Party took place. Men disguised as Indians dumped the tea into Boston harbor. No property but tea was destroyed, and one man, who filled his pockets, lost both tea and clothing. Reverend Samuel Cooper called this a remarkable instance of order and justice among savages. After the tea party, the town became remarkably quiet.[73]

[68] Mass. Hist. Soc., *Proceedings*, XX, 10–17; Hutchinson, *History*, III, 309–10.

[69] "Letters of John Andrews, Esq., of Boston, 1772–1776," in Mass. Hist. Soc., *Proceedings*, VIII, 324; *Warren-Adams Letters*, I, 18.

[70] *Muddy River and Brookline Records*, p. 242; *Plymouth Town Records*, III, 278–81; Marblehead Town Records, IV, 153–54; Malden Town Records, II, 61.

[71] Hutchinson to Dartmouth, Dec. 14, 1773, Mass. Arch., XXVII, 586.

[72] *Ibid.*

[73] Cooper to Franklin, Dec. 17, 1773, Mass. Hist. Soc., *Collections*, 4th ser., IV, 373–75.

The dumping of the tea nineteen days after its arrival had special significance. By an act of Parliament, customs officers could have seized the tea to collect the duty on the twentieth day, and many believed that this was the plan. Cooper said that the people waited as long as they dared, hoping that Hutchinson would allow the ships to leave, but that they were determined not to be frustrated in preventing the landing of the tea.[74]

Both prerogative and popular parties agreed that the tea episode had produced the strongest union to date of the democratic forces. Hutchinson called the tea party the boldest stroke by the popular leaders to gain independence and to involve the people beyond the point of turning back. When he consulted the Council, he was told that the people were justified and that nothing should be done. He could not depend on grand juries, the House, justices of the peace, sheriffs, or colonels of the militia, he said, for none would act against the popular will.[75] Samuel Cooper was certain that country was united with town and colony united with colony more firmly than ever in the cause. Even military force would not alter the principles of the people not to yield to an insidious ministerial design to establish an American revenue from tea.[76] Boston's representatives declared that the British could not have invented a better method for raising popular spirit or uniting the colonies.[77]

Although the Boston Tea Party has been characterized as the "vandalism" of irresponsible "roughs and toughs," John Adams, at least, did not consider it as such. Adams obviously thought that there were some very fundamental principles at stake, and John Adams was no lower-class radical. It was, he said, "the most magnificent movement of all. There is a dignity, a majesty, a sublimity, in this last effort of the patriots, that I greatly admire." It was "an epocha in history." But was it merely the

[74] *Ibid.*, pp. 375, 377–79, 384; Hutchinson, *History*, III, 312.
[75] Hutchinson, *History*, III, 313–15.
[76] Mass. Hist. Soc., *Collections*, 4th ser., IV, 376.
[77] *Ibid.*, p. 377; *Warren-Adams Letters*, I, 19.

irresponsible action of a mob, or was it a necessary measure? Adams obviously considered it the latter:

I apprehend it was absolutely and indispensably so. There was no other alternative but to destroy it or let it be landed. To let it be landed, would be giving up the principles of taxation by parliamentary authority, against which the continent has struggled for ten years. It was losing all our labor for ten years, and subjecting ourselves and our posterity forever to Egyptian taskmasters; to burthens, indignities; to ignominy, reproach and contempt; to desolation and oppression; to poverty and servitude.[78]

What Hutchinson condemned as the "boldest stroke" yet struck for independence was praised by Adams as "the most magnificent movement of all." The difference depended on their points of view. Yet neither was "radical" in the social sense, and neither saw in the tea party an uprising of lower classes against a ruling aristocracy. To both the trouble was between England and her colonies, not internal class division.

[78] Adams, *Works,* II, 323–24. J. T. Adams, in *Revolutionary New England,* pp. 392–94, called the Tea Party "an irresponsible piece of reckless bravado designed to precipitate a crisis" and stressed the actions of "toughs and roughs" rather than of the people. Adams quoted John Adams as being opposed to tarring, feathering, and other violence, but forgot to point out that Adams completely justified the Tea Party, on the principle of taxation, not monopoly. Miller, in *Sam Adams,* pp. 277–95, interpreted the tea party as an aggressive act by Samuel Adams to create a crisis which would restore Adams' leadership in Boston, Boston's leadership in Massachusetts, and Massachusetts' leadership among the colonies. He credited intercolonial rivalry for leadership in the controversy as a major factor.

Schlesinger, in *Colonial Merchants,* insisted that the merchants were in command at the outset but soon lost control. Merchants dictated the activities of mass meetings for their own economic benefit, he said, even though popular rights were used, presumably for propaganda purposes (p. 279). Samuel Adams, however, had other ideas. By "whispered conferences," infinite craft, and resourcefulness, said Schlesinger, the master maneuverer fostered discontent to drive the populace to extreme measures and thus commit the province irrevocably to the cause of revolution and independence (p. 283). Merchants entered the movement against the East India Company intending to resort only to peaceful opposition, Schlesinger declared, but were swept by popular feeling into measures of which they disapproved (p. 289). Irresponsible mass meetings seized control as sentiment went beyond bounds set by the merchants, he said, and he called the tea party the "Boston vandalism" (pp. 300, 304). Presumably he believed that there were no principles involved.

Although some Tory sentiment remained, resolves of the towns, many of which were passed unanimously, indicated that a large majority of the people agreed with John Adams both as to the purpose of the tax and the need for resistance. Many of these resolves denied Parliament's right to legislate for the colonies as well as to tax them.[79] Braintree in particular expressed the democratic philosophy that government was designed for the good of all, not just the few. Laws must be consented to by the people: no British laws were valid, only those passed by the freemen or their representatives. The Tea Act, said the town, was "craftily calculated" to raise a revenue, not to pay off the British debt, but to pay salaries and prevent future opposition. Branding passive obedience as mischievous in politics and religion, Braintree pointed out that religious as well as political rights were endangered, for if Parliament could deprive the colonists of civil rights and impose taxes, it could also by an act of uniformity impose religious shackles.[80] Among other complaints Sheffield objected to Negro slavery, but postponed action because the General Court was considering this problem.[81] Andover agreed that the "express purpose" of the Tea Act— support of government, administration of justice, and defense of the king's dominions—tended to render assemblies useless and introduce arbitrary government.[82] Worcester spoke of England as a "foreign state," listed all the complaints that other towns listed, and then enunciated the democratic philosophy that as all officials were nothing more than the servants of the people, and should receive their remuneration from the people, the people did not have to submit to officers who were not dependent on the people for their pay.[83] If the people did not elect their officials, they must have an effective check on them by way of salaries.

In the face of this popular opposition, government, as represented by British officials, was virtually helpless. The Council refused to act, then published its minutes to justify resistance

[79] Hadley Town Records, Jan. 3, 1774; *Topsfield Town Records*, II, 322–23.
[80] *Braintree Town Records*, pp. 442–48.
[81] Sheffield Town Records, March 15, 1774.
[82] Andover Town Records, Feb. 3, 1774.
[83] *Worcester Town Records*, IV, 212–14.

by all groups. Representatives, town officials, magistrates, militia officers, leading men of property—all were on the wrong side, said Hutchinson, leaving the governor as the solitary upholder of British authority.[84] The consignees were virtually besieged on Castle William as towns agreed not to give them shelter or protection. One of the consignees, Hutchinson's son, tried to visit his wife's home, but bells tolled, the town met, and the Hutchinsons were forced to depart in a snow storm. The informer Malcolm, previously tarred and feathered for his activities, had the performance repeated so that "the flesh came off his back in steaks." [85] There was little doubt that the popular party was serious in its determination.

Shortly after the tea party the question of judges' salaries again became pressing, and so compelling was popular demand that four of the five judges capitulated. They had agreed not to make separate answers to the assembly, but during the recess of the General Court one judge of "weak nerves and timid spirit," according to Hutchinson, surrendered. The governor did not dare to lengthen the recess, and when the General Court met again, the pressure on the other judges became intense. Faced with an ultimatum of a decision within eight days, three of the four remaining judges chose the popular side. Again only Chief Justice Peter Oliver held out. When the assembly denounced Oliver as an enemy of the constitution and when the House and Council threatened impeachment, Hutchinson prorogued the General Court. This action stopped all proceedings of the Superior Court, for no jury would sit as long as Oliver was under impeachment.[86]

By this time popular feeling had reached fever pitch. Men drilled under their own colonial officers to protect their religious as well as political rights. Word that British regulars had confiscated cannon at Salem brought a convergence of armed men on the town.[87] When Lieutenant Governor Andrew Oli-

[84] Hutchinson to Montagu, Dec. 28, 1773, Mass. Arch., XXVII, 601.
[85] Hulton, *Letters*, p. 69.
[86] Trowbridge to Cushing, Jan. 26, 1774, Adams Papers; Hutchinson, *History*, III, 316–25; Adams, *Works*, II, 331–32.
[87] "Extracts from Textbooks of Deacon Joseph Secombe, 1762–1777," Feb. 26, 1774, in Danvers Historical Society, *Collections*, IX, 114.

ver, the former stamp-tax collector, died March 3, 1774, his brother, impeached Chief Justice Peter Oliver, did not dare visit the death bed or attend the funeral. Peter Oliver also declared that a large crowd at the funeral cheered as the body was entombed.[88] When another tea ship arrived on March 6, John Adams recorded laconically in his diary: "Twenty-eight chests of tea arrived yesterday, which are to make an infusion in water at seven o'clock this evening." On March 8, Adams duly recorded the infusion: "Last night twenty-eight chests and a half of tea were drowned." [89] Since the tea ship had to come by Castle William, there was no excuse for this second tea party unless the governor intended to force a showdown.

If the sending of tea was a ministerial device to force the issue, as some colonists contended, it was eminently successful. Arthur Lee reported that news of the tea party "operated like an electric shock" in England.[90] Colonists were warned to prepare for the worst.[91] Franklin, accused of being "an ambassador from the States of America" rather than a mere colonial agent, was severely castigated before a committee of Parliament and dismissed as postmaster for the colonies. Franklin said that British officials had made up their minds before they heard the evidence and that his dismissal was a warning to other officials not to deviate from ministerial policies.[92]

Despite the actions of a few friends of the colonies, members of Parliament condemned Massachusetts in general and Boston in particular for the democracy there. Lord North blamed Boston, the ringleader which set the example for other towns, where, he said, the colonies and Britain were now considered as two independent states. One member thought that Boston "ought to be knocked about their ears and destroyed," for British laws would never be obeyed until Britain had "destroyed

---

[88] Hutchinson to Thompson, March 17, 1774, Oliver Letter Book, II, 157; Egerton MSS., 2671, pp. 207–08.

[89] Adams, *Works*, II, 334.

[90] To Samuel Adams, Jan. 31 and Feb. 16, 1774, Adams Papers.

[91] Edmund Burke to Charles Lee, Feb. 1, 1774, *Lee Papers*, New York Historical Society, *Collections*, 4 vols. (New York, 1872–1875), I, 119; Franklin, *Writings*, VI, 178–80.

[92] Arthur Lee to Samuel Adams, Feb. 8, 1774, Adams Papers; Franklin, *Writings*, VI, 182–93.

that nest of locusts." Friends of the colonies could not even be heard because of the noise. Edmund Burke made little impression with his warning that American discontent had a wide popular basis. The Boston town meeting consisted of several hundred of the town's leading citizens, he declared, and was not a meeting of a lower-class mob. So universal was support for Boston, he continued, that British officials did not dare ask for military aid. Burke went unheeded, however, as Parliament passed the Boston Port Bill closing the port of Boston until the town paid for the tea.[93]

Then Parliament attacked the real heart of British imperial failures—colonial democracy. North proposed a bill to regulate the government of Massachusetts and to curb this democracy. He said that the democratic part of the constitution was too strong and that he intended to remove the executive from the hands of this democratic element through appointment of all officials by the governor, regulation of town meetings, and elimination of the democratically elected juries. George Germain enthusiastically supported North with proposals to stop town meetings, incorporate towns as the properly subordinate towns of Britain were incorporated, and appoint grand juries for life. Calling the government in Massachusetts a tumultuous rabble, Germain recommended a council similar to the House of Lords and declared that Americans should follow their mercantile interests instead of politics and government, which they did not understand. North thanked Germain for these proposals, which, he said, were worthy of a great mind and ought to be adopted. Only Pownall defended the Americans, but his was a voice in the wilderness.[94]

Another curb on democratic action was a bill for the "impartial" administration of justice in Massachusetts. The purpose, said North, was to punish leaders of the popular party by making possible the sending of an accused man to another colony or to England for trial. British officials could then prevent the least disobedience to British measures. Isaac Barré warned that the British, having stimulated discontent into disaffection,

[93] *Parliamentary History*, XVII, 1159, 1163–79, 1182–89.
[94] *Ibid.*, pp. 1192–97.

were now goading disaffection into rebellion, but Solicitor General Alexander Wedderburne replied that while Britain should carry the olive branch in one hand, she should carry the sword in the other. Lord Carmarthen asked why colonists had been allowed to go to America unless the profits of their labors returned to their masters in England. The debates portended no good for democracy in Massachusetts.[95]

Two closely related ideas, colonial democracy and independence, appeared repeatedly throughout the debates. Sir Richard Sutton claimed that even in quiet times colonists resisted British laws and their actions conveyed a spirit and wish for independence. Ask an American who his master was, Sutton said, and he would answer that he had no master nor any governor but Jesus Christ. British neglect of colonial governments, declared one Mr. Stanley, had allowed the Americans to "throw the government into a wild democracy." Having failed to settle this problem in 1763, the British should settle it now. Lord Carmarthen accused the Americans of wanting independence, and John St. John believed that Parliament had saved Massachusetts from the jaws of tyranny by amending her constitution, because town meetings, with Boston as ringleader, decided questions which were the very foundation of the constitution.[96]

The Port Act, Government Act, Justice Act, Quartering Act, and Quebec Act, called the Coercive or Intolerable Acts in the colonies, passed by such large majorities in Parliament as to leave no doubt of Parliament's intentions. Henry Cavendish approved of the spirit which he saw both there and in the country at large, and Franklin declared that the colonies never had so few friends in England.[97]

How, then, did these Coercive Acts affect colonial democracy? In many ways. A British official was protected, even if he committed murder, by the fact that he could be sent to England for trial. Conversely, a popular leader could also be convicted by the same process. Troops could be quartered where needed, regardless of where the colonists wanted to quarter them. More serious, however, were the changes in the Massachusetts consti-

[95] *Ibid.*, pp. 1197–1210.   [96] *Ibid.*, pp. 1288, 1303, 1305, 1309.
[97] *Ibid.*, pp. 1315, 1351, 1353; Franklin, *Writings,* VI, 223.

tution. Calling the elected Council a disruptive influence which obstructed the execution of laws and weakened the attachment of the subjects to the king, the Government Act provided for a Council appointed and removed at the king's pleasure. The governor could also appoint and remove a long list of officials without the consent of the Council. Democratic town meetings, long the fly in British imperial ointment, could not be held, except for annual elections, without the written consent of the governor expressing the exact business of the meeting. And elected juries, called an obstacle to free and impartial administration of justice, were replaced by juries appointed by a sheriff who held office at the pleasure of the governor. Presumably the selection of jurors by British-appointed officials·would result in "impartial justice." [98]

Another threat to colonial democracy came with the passage of the famous Quebec Act and a tax law for Quebec. The Quebec Act granted freedom of the Catholic religion to the French in Quebec, gave the French the right to use French law in civil suits, and provided for government by a governor and council, both appointed and removable at the pleasure of the king.[99] Parliament also passed an act providing that all taxes, except for local use, were to be raised and controlled by Parliament—the very device, and with the same preamble, that Parliament had attempted so unsuccessfully to impose on the other

[98] 14 Geo. III, c.39, Pickering, *Statutes,* XXX, 367; 14 Geo. III, c.54, *ibid.,* p. 410; 14 Geo. III, c.45, *ibid.,* p. 381. Schlesinger, in *Colonial Merchants,* pp. 306–08, contended that news of the Boston Port Bill completely changed the nature of the contest carried on with Parliament since 1764. Up to this point the merchants inspired and guided the struggle for trade reform, he said, forming alliances with their natural enemies in society, intelligent radicals and the lower classes. The Port Bill divided these allies, already suspicious of each other, and changed the issue from trade reforms to a political dispute. Having lost control of the opposition, in which the issues had changed, the merchants who abhorred mob rule now shifted to the British side.

According to the evidence presented in the preceding chapters, the merchants had never controlled the opposition but had, in fact, been largely under the domination of the democratic town meeting. And the issues did not change in 1774—the political issue had always been present. Furthermore, a listing of merchants in 1774 and after the beginning of the war would show that many of them remained in Massachusetts to become governors, lieutenant governors, councilors, representatives, and town officials.

[99] 14 Geo. III, c.45, Pickering, *Statutes,* XXX, 549–54.

colonies. The law also discriminated against the trade of the troublesome mainland colonies by placing higher taxes on goods coming to Quebec from these colonies in colonial ships.[100]

The Quebec Act requires special explanation. Many historians have considered this act as an enlightened piece of legislation having no relation to the other colonies.[101] The colonists, however, did not think so, and that is the important thing. Whether or not the Quebec Act was intended as one of the Coercive Acts, it was so considered in Massachusetts. When we remember the long opposition in the colony to "popery" and the connection made by John Adams between the Catholic Church and tyranny, it is not difficult to understand how Congregationalists considered the Quebec Act a threat to religious democracy. Asked John Adams: "Have not the ministry shown, by the Quebec Bill, that we have no security against them for our religion, any more than our property, if we submit to the unlimited claims of Parliament?" [102] Customs official Benjamin Hallowell said that the people of Massachusetts had long believed "that not only their charter but their religion was intended to be altered." Passage of the Quebec Act had "an amazing effect, and has increased the clamour and opposition against the Mother Country." [103] Dissenting ministers "kindled the flames of sedition," according to an Anglican minister, and they

[100] *Ibid.*, pp. 570–74.

[101] Victor Coffin, *The Province of Quebec and the Early American Revolution* (Madison, Wis., 1896), Reginald Coupland, *The Quebec Act: A Study in Statesmanship* (Oxford, 1925), Alvord, *Mississippi Valley,* II, and Alfred LeRoy Burt, *The Old Province of Quebec* (Minneapolis, 1933) all agree that the Quebec Act had no relation to the other colonies but was designed merely to settle Canadian questions. At the same time, however, they all recognized that Americans looked on the act as one of the Coercive Acts, which, of course, was the important thing. J. T. Adams, *Revolutionary New England,* p. 397, believed that the innocence of the ministers was open to suspicion as far as the intent of the Quebec Act was concerned. Charles Henry Metzger, *The Quebec Act: A Primary Cause of the American Revolution* (New York, 1936), considered only the religious toleration clauses of the act. Given the religious prejudice against Catholics in the colonies, it was inevitable, he said, that toleration of Catholics would be considered as a major grievance. Metzger did not attempt to weigh the importance of religion as a factor, but he considered it a major one, as it undoubtedly was.

[102] Adams, *Works,* IV, 443.

[103] To Grey Cooper, Sept. 5, 1774, Library of Congress Transcripts, Public Record Office, Colonial Office 5, America and West Indies, CLXXV.

accused Anglicans of conspiring with the administration to establish popery through all the American dominions.[104] Various towns condemned the Quebec Act as an attempt to establish despotism and popery in America.[105]

There is ample evidence that Americans considered the Quebec Act as part of the ministerial plan to deprive them of democratic government, not just a measure for Quebec alone. They were warned from England that the act was "intended to keep the old colonies in awe" and that the British expected to use the Canadian militia and the British fleet "to keep the colonies always in subjection." [106] John Adams lumped the Quebec and Massachusetts Acts together as efforts by the British to establish governments in which the people would have no choice in selecting representatives. "These are such *samples* of what they may, and probably will be that few Americans are in love with them." To Adams, these bills were closely associated with the statements in Hutchinson's letters that "there must be an abridgment of what are called English liberties" and also that Britain must act soon to secure the dependence of the colonies. "The port bill, charter bill, murder bill [i.e. administration of justice act], Quebec bill, making altogether such a frightful system, as would have terrified any people, who did not prefer liberty to life, were all concerted at once," he declared.[107]

The idea seems to have been rather widespread that the Quebec and Massachusetts bills represented the kind of government which the British intended to impose on the colonies. John Adams' statement that these were samples of what might be expected is merely one example. When the Boston committee of correspondence wrote to the inhabitants of Quebec in 1775, the same idea was expressed. Said the committee: "These new governments of Quebec and Massachusetts Bay, of a kind nearly alike, are looked upon by the other colonies from Nova Scotia to Georgia, as models intended for them all." [108] And Franklin believed that British intentions were well expressed by two

104 SPG Archives, XXII, ser. B, pp. 122–25.

105 *Plymouth Town Records*, III, 298; *Tisbury Town Records*, p. 210.

106 Peter Force, ed., *American Archives*, 9 vols. (Washington, 1837–1853), 4th ser., I, 498–99.

107 Adams, *Works*, IV, 92.   108 Adams, *Writings*, III, 185.

court maxims—Grenville's statement that "the King is the legislator of the colonies," and the chancellor of the exchequer's
statement when he was in the House of Commons that "the
Quebec Constitution was the only proper constitution for the
colonies, ought to have been given to them all when first
planted, and what all ought now to be reduced to." [109]

If we accept religious and political democracy in Massachusetts as a fact, colonial reaction to the Intolerable Acts becomes
completely understandable in the light of this statement by
John Adams:

There is so much of a republican spirit among the people, which
has been nourished and cherished by their form of government, that
they never would submit to tyrants or oppressive projects. The same
spirit spreads like a contagion into all the other colonies, into Ireland
and into Great Britain too, from this single Province of Massachusetts Bay, that no pains are too great to be taken, no hazards too great
to run, for the destruction of our charter.[110]

Along with the Intolerable Acts went measures to insure that
British restrictions would be enforced. Thomas Hutchinson
was replaced as governor by General Thomas Gage, who would
combine civil and military authority into an effective working
unit. Gage had orders to persuade the people to return to their
obedience, if possible, but to use force if necessary. Dartmouth
informed Gage that sovereignty of the king in Parliament required a "full and absolute submission," but he also said that
information from Boston left little room to hope that order and
obedience would soon return.[111]

If Dartmouth's demand for a full and absolute submission is
considered in the light of the position taken by Samuel Adams,
there was certainly ample reason for Dartmouth's pessimism.
Adams wrote in April 1774:

[109] Franklin, *Writings*, VIII, 241.

[110] Adams, *Works*, II, 336.

[111] April 9, 1774, *Parliamentary History*, XVIII, 74. See Clarence E. Carter,
"The Significance of the Military Office in America," *American Historical Revue*,
XXVIII (April 1923), 475–88, for the importance of the army as the basis for
control of the colonies and one of the chief instruments of colonial administration.

I wish for a permanent union with the mother country, but only on the principles of liberty and truth. No advantage that can accrue to America from such an union can compensate for the loss of liberty. The time may come sooner than they are aware of it, when the being of the British nation, I mean the being of its importance, however strange it may now appear to some, will depend on her union with America.[112]

Thus did the "new policy" fail. First came the plan to pay salaries out of existing revenues, since the colonies would not submit to taxation. Then came the Tea Act, which the colonists considered as a scheme to impose taxes by devious methods or to force a showdown between colonies and mother country. And finally came the Coercive or Intolerable Acts, a major part of which were aimed at restricting colonial democracy. Having been obstructed in their policies by democratic legislatures and town meetings, the British finally applied the remedy which so many officials had long considered necessary. Democracy and imperialism could not live together: democracy would have to go.

112 Adams, *Writings*, III, 101–02.

[CHAPTER XIV]

Democracy and the American War, 1774–1775

"BUT what do we mean by the American Revolution? Do we mean the American war?" John Adams asked in later years. Then Adams answered his own questions: "The Revolution was effected before the war commenced. The Revolution was in the minds and hearts of the people; a change in their religious sentiments of their duties and obligations." The change involved American attitudes and feelings toward Great Britain, he went on to explain. *"This radical change in the principles, opinions, sentiments, and affections of the people, was the real American Revolution."* [1]

At no time did Adams interpret the conflict as a social revolution involving an uprising of lower classes against a ruling aristocracy. From his point of view, it was strictly a British-American problem—a conflict of principles and interests which stretched back for two hundred years. The attitude of the English and Scotch toward the colonies brought about perpetual discordance between British and American principles and feelings and thus resulted in war.[2] The Revolution was the change in the American attitude toward the British, not a class struggle within the colonies. The war itself was a "War of Independence," not an "American Revolution."

[1] Adams, *Works*, X, 282–83.　　　　[2] *Ibid.*, p. 284.

In the preceding chapters, I have attempted to show that democracy in all its various forms was a major area of conflict. British imperial policies were a threat to this democracy, particularly if the British could enforce the Coercive Acts. How democracy and the change of sentiment led from revolution to war becomes apparent in the following pages.

Perhaps because of his association with men such as Hutchinson, General Gage, who replaced Hutchinson as governor, quickly made the mistake that Hutchinson had made of underestimating the problem facing him. When he arrived, he found all British officials either at Castle William or dispersed in the country, Boston was meeting to solicit aid which came in the form of letters and donations, and grand juries prepared to indict Chief Justice Oliver if he appeared on the bench.[3] Gage was hissed at a function for offering a toast to Hutchinson, who was called the "damn'd arch traitor." [4] Yet in spite of this evidence, Gage said that the Port Bill had staggered the most presumptuous and that the popular party seemed to be breaking.[5]

There was plenty of other evidence—most of it unfavorable —to guide the new governor, if he had had eyes that saw and ears that heard. For example, Hutchinson received addresses of approval from some merchants and other inhabitants in Boston, Salem, and Marblehead, but popular opinion was so antagonistic to the addressers that most of them had to recant.[6] Samuel Adams indicated something of the nature of the controversy by saying that merchants would always be divided on policies depending on their interests, but that far the greatest part of them were and always had been steadfast in the interest of their country.[7] Adams' rule was so absolute, both in the senate and in the street, said one observer, that he could threaten the addressers with tar and feathers without fear of the govern-

---

[3] Judd Diary, II, April 27, 1774; Gage to Dartmouth, May 19 and 31, 1774, *Parliamentary History*, XVIII, 80–81; Mass. Hist. Soc., *Collections*, 4th ser., IV, 1–274. For an account of Gage, see John Richard Alden, *General Gage in America: Being Principally a History of His Role in the American Revolution* (Baton Rouge, 1948).

[4] "Andrews Letters," p. 328.
[6] Hutchinson, *History*, III, 329.

[5] *Parliamentary History*, XVIII, 80–81.
[7] Adams, *Writings*, III, 123.

ment.[8] Marblehead censured the addressers and claimed that they were "but a drop in the bucket" compared with the freeholders of the province.[9] Furthermore, Boston drew up a Solemn League and Covenant to stop the purchase of British goods. Without getting the consent of the Council, which he said he could not have obtained anyway, Gage issued a proclamation against the Covenant in which he threatened to seize anyone who signed it. In spite of the threat, nearly every adult in Boston signed.[10]

The May election of 1774 added little that was hopeful for the new governor. In Boston, where he had thought the people were deserting their popular leaders, these leaders received an almost unanimous vote as representatives.[11] Towns instructed their representatives to uphold charter rights and privileges at any cost and to work for a colonial congress that would unite the opposition. These instructions left no doubt whatever that the colonists in Massachusetts were determined to keep what they had always had, not to get something different. This included justice, the right to control their own lives, liberties, and property, representative and democratic government, and control over judges, justices, sheriffs, and jurors. The representatives were to support Boston, condemn representatives whose actions were inimical to the public good, and oppose British claims to absolute power.[12]

The election of 1774 also enables us to learn a great deal about the men who were responsible for the colonial side of the controversy. An analysis of the House of Representatives from 1760 to 1774 gives some very convincing evidence that the political change in Massachusetts was hardly what one would call revolutionary. Of the representatives in 1774, twenty-five had

---

[8] Robinson to Haldimand, c. May, 1774, Library of Congress Transcripts, British Museum, Additional Manuscript, 21,666.

[9] Marblehead Town Records, IV, 163–67.

[10] "Andrews Letters," p. 329; Mass. Hist. Soc., *Proceedings*, XII, 47; Gage to Dartmouth, July 5, 1774, *Parliamentary History*, XVIII, 87.

[11] Adams, 535; Hancock, 536; Phillips, 534; Cushing, 524 out of 536 votes; *Boston Town Records*, XVIII, 166.

[12] Marblehead Town Records, IV, 169; *Fitchburgh Town Records*, I, 99; *Manchester Town Records*, II, 144–45.

served in the House as early as the period 1760–1764.[13] Seventeen, including some of the most important of the revolutionary leaders, had been elected as early as 1765–1766.[14] Forty-nine had served between 1767 and 1772.[15] Nineteen new members came in

[13] Thomas Cushing, Boston (1761), Benjamin Lincoln, Hingham (on the Council from 1760–1769), Ebenezer Thayer, Braintree (1760), Joseph Gerrish, Newbury (1760), Ebenezer Burrill, Lynn (1764), Aaron Wood, Boxford (1762), John Gould, Topsfield (1760), James Barrett, Concord (1764), Abraham Fuller, Newton (1764), Jonas Dix, Waltham (1764), Joseph Hawley, Northampton (1764), Ebenezer Sprout, Middleborough (1760), John Turner, Pembroke (1763), Woodbridge Brown, Abbington (1760), Jedediah Foster, Brookfield (1761), Henry King, Sutton (1760), Moses Marcy, Sturbridge (1760), Edward Davis, Oxford (1760), John Whitcomb, Bolton (1760), Stephen Nye, Sandwich (1761), David Thacher, Yarmouth (1764), Benjamin Aikin, Dartmouth (1760), Jerathmeel Bowers, Swansey (1760), Thomas Morey, Norton (1760), and Thomas Perkins, Arundell (1760); *Acts and Resolves*, XVI, 563–64; XVII, 3–4, 217–18, 377–78, 507–08.

[14] Samuel Adams and John Hancock, Boston; Hezekiah Gay, Stoughton; Stephen Miller, Milton; Jabez Fisher, Wrentham; Jonathan Adams, Medway; Michael Farley, Ipswich; Isaac Merrill, Almsbury; William Stickney, Billerica; James Prescott, Shirley; Ebenezer Harnden, Malden; Timothy Danielson, Brimfield; James Warren, Plymouth; Gideon Vinall, Scituate; Asa Whitcomb, Lancaster; Israel Taylor, Harvard; Thomas Durfee, Freetown; and Stephen Hussey, Sherburn; *Acts and Resolves*, XVIII, 3–4, 111–12.

[15] William Phillips, Boston (1772); Nathaniel Bayley, Weymouth (1772); Benjamin Lincoln, Hingham, who had served from 1760–1769 in the council; Abner Ellis, Dedham (1771); Moses Bulling, Medfield (1769); William Heath, Roxbury (1770); Benjamin White, Brookline (1768); Richard Derby, Jr., Salem, 1769; John Pickering, Jr., Salem (1769); John Gallison, Marblehead (1769), Samuel Smith, Salisbury (1772); Jonathan Webster, Jr., Haverhill (1771); Daniel Thurston, Bradford (1770); Dr. Samuel Holton, Danvers (1768); Benjamin Greenleaf, Newburyport (1769); Thomas Gardiner, Cambridge (1769); Nathaniel Gorham, Charlestown (1771); Samuel Bancroft, Reading (1769); Peter Bent, Marlborough (1771); Jonathan Browne, Watertown (1772); Josiah Stone, Framingham (1771); Jonas Stone, Lexington (1771); Simeon Spaulding, Chelmsford (1769); Benjamin Hall, Medford (1770); Joseph Reed, Westford (1771); Josiah Pierce, Hadley (1771); John Mosley, Westfield (1768); Isaac Lothrop, Plymouth (1772); Samuel Lucas, Plympton (1772); Joshua Bigelow, Worcester (1767); Thomas Denny, Leicester (1769); Edward Rawson, Mendon (1769); Dr. John Taylor, Lunnenburg (1772); Stephen Maynard, Westborough (1767); Joseph Read, Southborough (1772); John Dickinson, Hatfield (1770); Ephraim Doolittle, Petersham (1772); Edward Bacon (Barnstable, 1772); Barnabas Freeman, Eastham (1772); Benjamin Freeman, Harwich (1770); Joseph Doane, Chatham (1768); Joseph Barney, Reheboth (1770); Elnathan Walker, Dighton (1769); Edward Cutt, Kittery (1771); Nathan Lord, Jr., Berwick (1772); David Ingersoll, Jr., Great Barrington (1770); Isaac Searle, Williamston (1770); Peter Curtis, Lanesborough (1772); Samuel March, Scarborough (1772); Thomas Cooke, Edgartown (1770); *Acts and Resolves*, XVIII, 223–24, 329–30, 371–72, 463–64, 527–28, 615–16.

1773 after the salary controversy of 1772–1773.[16] Twenty-three members were serving in 1774 for the first time, but twelve of these came from towns which had not sent delegates before or had been very lax about sending delegates.[17] This usually implied an increased interest in what was happening rather than a desire for change.

Even a change of representative did not mean that a town was altering its sentiments. Samuel Dexter of Dedham served in the House from 1764 to 1768, was rejected by Bernard as a councilor in 1766 and 1767, then served on the Council until 1774, when he was again negatived by Gage. His place in the House was taken first by Nathaniel Sumner, who served in 1762, 1769, and 1770, then by Abner Ellis, who served on into 1775. Obviously these changes did not mean that Dedham was pro-British. Sometimes a town changed delegates, but kept men with the same surname; so, if there was any internal revolution, it involved a split in families, not in classes. Elisha Adams of Medway served from 1760 to 1765, alternated with Jonathan Adams, 1766–1768, and then Jonathan Adams served the remainder of the time. Samuel Phillips represented Andover most of the time from 1760–1772, then went to the Council, was succeeded in 1773 and 1774 by Moody Bridges, and in 1775 by Samuel Phillips, Jr. Stephen Hall from Medford succeeded Benjamin Hall when the latter went to the Council in 1770, and Jonathan Greenleaf of

[16] Enoch Ellis, Brookline; Azor Orne, Marblehead; Moody Bridges, Andover (replaced Samuel Phillips who was representative 1760–1772 and went to the council 1772); Samuel Wyman, Woburn; Thomas Plympton, Sudbury; John Bliss, Springfield; Samuel Field, Deerfield; Moses Gunn, Sunderland; Phineas Wright, Northfield; Abijah White, Marshfield; Ebenezer White, Rochester; John Gray, Kingston; Joseph Cushing, Hanover; Paul Mandell, Hardwick; Moses Swift, Falmouth; Robert Treat Paine, Tauton; Ebenezer Sawyer, Wells; John Lewis, North Yarmouth; *Acts and Resolves,* XVIII, 705–06.

[17] Lemuel Robinson, Dorchester; Josiah Bachellor, Jr., Beverly; Nathaniel Myghill, Rowley; Peter Coffin, Gloucester; Samuel Bullard, Hopkinton; Josiah Hartwell, Littleton; Ebenezer Brooks, Lincoln; Josiah Hayward, Acton; John Tyng, Holliston; Benjamin Day, West Springfield; George Partridge, Duxbury; John Sherman, Grafton; Israel Nichols, Leominster; Abiel Sadler, Upton; William Baylies, Dighton; Daniel Bragdon, York; Thomas Williams, Stockbridge; Gyles Jackson, Tyringham; James Easton, Pittsfield; John Patterson, Richmont; William Clark, Gageborough; Enoch Freeman, Falmouth; Samuel Thompson, Brunswick; *Acts and Resolves,* XVIII, 797–98; XIX, 3–4.

Newburyport succeeded Benjamin Greenleaf when the latter went to the Council.[18]

The Council for 1774 also reflected a lack of internal class revolution in Massachusetts. As has already been pointed out, councilors had been ousted by the House as fast as they proved to be pro-British. Thomas Hutchinson, Andrew Oliver, Peter Oliver, Israel Williams, and Edmund Trowbridge, all holders of other important offices, had been defeated in 1766. Andrew Belcher, John Worthington, Thomas Flucker, Harrison Gray, Nathaniel Ropes, Timothy Woodbridge, James Russell, Isaac Royal, and John Chandler had been dropped when their views became known. Yet there were several men on the Council who had sat many years or had previously been elected to the Council. Samuel Danforth, John Erving and James Bowdoin had served since 1760; James Otis, Sr., came to the Council in 1762; James Pitts, Jerathmeel Bowers, Jeremiah Powell, and Samuel Dexter came in 1766; Artemas Ward and John Hancock in 1768; Benjamin Greenleaf, William Sever, and Walter Spooner in 1769; George Leonard, Jr., 1770; Caleb Cushing, 1771; Samuel Phillips, 1772; and William Phillips, John Winthrop, John Adams, and Jedediah Prebble in 1773.[19] Some of these councilors were rejected, but the changes paralleled British policies, not internal conflicts, and the men who came to the Council could hardly be said to represent a proletariat.

Many councilors, including newcomers in 1774, had served long terms in the lower house, and so their election to the Council could not be construed as an internal revolution. Caleb Cushing of Salisbury, Samuel Phillips of Andover, Artemas Ward of Shrewsbury, and Jerathmeel Bowers of Swansey had been representatives from 1760 on. Walter Spooner of Dartmouth, Jedediah Foster of Brookfield, and Benjamin Chadbourn came to the House in 1761; George Leonard, Jr., of Norton came in 1764; and Jedediah Prebble of Falmouth, Timothy Danielson of Brimfield, Benjamin Greenleaf of Newburyport, Michael

18 *Ibid.*, XVI, 564–65; XVII, 4–5, 218–19, 378–79, 508–09; XVIII, 4–5, 112–13, 224–25, 330–31, 372–73, 464, 528, 616, 705–06, 797–98; XIX, 4.

19 *Acts and Resolves*, XVI, 563–64; XVII, 3–4, 217–18, 377–78, 507–09; XVIII, 3–4, 111–12, 223–24, 329–30, 371–72, 463–64, 527–28, 615–16, 705–06, 797–98.

334 DEMOCRACY IN MASSACHUSETTS

Farley of Ipswich, and James Prescott of Shirley came in 1766.[20]

Of these elected councilors, none left the country to become a Loyalist, although two or three probably had Loyalist leanings. John Erving had sons who were Loyalists, but of course his son-in-law, James Bowdoin, was one of the leading patriots. Strangely enough, Jerathmeel Bowers seems to have become one of the most pro-British of all the councilors. Bowers had been elected to the Council and negatived by the governor every year from 1766 to 1774. Yet when the showdown came, Bowers' sympathies apparently went with the British.[21] For all practical purposes, however, the significant changes on the Council had occurred before 1774. Gage negatived thirteen members of the 1774 Council, another indication that the popular party was in command.[22]

Again the town records, tax records, and probate records furnish ample evidence that the men who were responsible for the revolutionary movement were not in any sense radical, lower-class proletarians. For the most part, they were substantial, middle-class property owners, men who had long been active in town affairs. Usually the towns' representatives and selectmen were on the important revolutionary committees, such as the committees of correspondence and the committees to draw up covenants.

In Pittsfield, Deacon Josiah Wright was moderator of the town meeting which appointed a standing committee of correspondence and accepted the Covenant. Wright was a town assessor in 1761, and served as assessor or selectman at various times during the ensuing years.[23] Deacon James Easton, who was elected representative in 1774 and delegate to the county convention during the summer, was selectman as early as 1766.[24] Captain David Bush was assessor, moderator, and selectman in 1761, was still selectman in 1771 and 1774, paid the highest price of anybody in town for a pew in the new church in 1765, and was on the committee of correspondence in 1774.[25] Charles Goodrich, who

20 *Ibid.*, XVI, 564–65; XVII, 4–5, 508–09; XVIII, 112–13.

21 Edward Alfred Jones, *The Loyalists of Massachusetts, Their Memorials, Petitions and Claims* (London, 1930), pp. 46–47.

22 *Acts and Resolves*, XVII, 797–98.   23 Pittsfield Town Records, I, 22, 67.

24 *Ibid.*, 68.   25 *Ibid.*, pp. 22, 77–78, 134, 166, 175.

was elected to the revolutionary provincial congress in 1775, served as representative in 1763, 1769, 1770, and 1773, paid a good price for a pew in the church, and served in various town offices from moderator down.[26]

The town and tax records are especially complete for Andover, records which show exactly who the leading men in the revolutionary movement were and how they rated with their fellow townsmen on the tax lists. The committee to prepare a covenant included: [27]

Name	*Town Tax, 1774* [28]
Moody Bridges	£1.0.2.0
Samuel Phillips	5.17.4.2
Samuel Osgood, Jr.	0.17.10.2
Capt. John Farnum	1.2.7.2
Joshua Holt	0.15.8.0
Capt. Asa Foster	0.13.4.1
Asa Abbot	0.12.2.2
Nehemiah Abbot	1.10.9.1
Lt. Henry Abbot, Jr.	0.12.9.2

The committee of safety included the above and these additional names:

Deacon Joseph Abbot	£1.5.2.1
Capt. Samuel Johnson	0.14.0.0
Josiah Blanchard	0.14.0.0
John Barker	1.0.9.2
Col. George Abbot	1.13.11.2
Col. James Frye	1.4.8.0
Nathan Chandler	0.9.0.3
Benjamin Poor	0.11.10.0
Isaac Osgood	1.2.8.2

[26] *Ibid.,* pp. 22, 65, 67, 117, 125, 159, 203. For a similar account confined to western Massachusetts, see Lee Nathaniel Newcomer, "Yankee Rebels in Inland Massachusetts," *William and Mary Quarterly,* 3d ser., IX (April, 1952), 156–65 and *The Embattled Farmers: A Massachusetts Countryside in the American Revolution* (New York, 1953). Newcomer shows that the leaders in the towns were the substantial property owners, not lower-class radicals, and that these substantial citizens were in power before, during, and after the war. Taylor, *Western Massachusetts,* has a somewhat contrasting account.

[27] Andover Town Records, July 18, 1774.   [28] Andover Tax List, 1774.

Name	*Town Tax, 1774*
Dr. Joseph Osgood	£0.16.2.3
Darius Abbot	0.18.4.3
John Ingalls	0.17.7.3
Baracius Abbot	0.14.5.0
Stephen Holt	0.14.5.0
John Abbot 4th	0.11.0.2
Sarg. John Abbot	0.14.5.3
William Foster	0.10.9.0
Ebenezer Poor	0.11.11.2
Deacon John Dean	0.16.11.1
Benjamin Farnum	0.10.5.0
Samuel Frye	0.19.7.2

An analysis of the Andover tax lists yields some interesting results. Only eighteen people on a list containing 473 names
(including widows, guardians, and estates) paid £1 or more in
taxes. Nine, or half, of these £1 taxpayers were on the two committees. Asa Abbot, with £0.12.2.2, was low on the first committee, but on the list, 114 people paid that much or more.
And 181 paid as much tax as Nathan Chandler, who was low
taxpayer on both lists with £0.9.0.3. In other words, these two
committees were drawn from the top half of the town's taxpayers; yet many men paid as much in taxes as did some of the
committee members.

The probate records furnish the material needed to show
how widespread property ownership was in Andover and how
many men in the town could meet the £54 voting qualification.
When he died, committeeman Nathan Chandler, "Gentleman,"
had an estate of £615,[29] yet, as cited above, 181 men paid as much
or more in taxes. A "blacksmith," Josiah Osgood, paid £0.8.8.1
in taxes and was worth £668,[30] a "yeoman," Joseph Faulkner,
paid £0.7.11.3 and had an estate of £781,[31] and Deacon Isaac
Abbot paid £0.7.10.0 and was worth £642.[32] This was a town
tax, not a province tax, so it was based on taxable property, not
polls. Therefore, anyone who paid 1s. should have had ample

[29] Essex County Probate Records, CCCLVII, 207–08.
[30] *Ibid.*, CCCLIV, 254–55. [31] *Ibid.*, pp. 304–05.
[32] *Ibid.*, CCCLVIII, 60–61.

property to vote. Only three men—Philip Fowler, David Jones, and Joseph Jackson—paid less than 1s., and 143 paid between 4s. and 9s., indicating property worth several hundred pounds.[33]

There is also other information to show that these "revolutionaries" were not "radicals" but were the town's most substantial citizens. Moody Bridges replaced Samuel Phillips in the House of Representatives when Phillips, who had served in the House most of the time since 1760, went to the Council. Phillips paid three times as much taxes as anyone else in the town, yet he was on the Council, which had long given the governor so much trouble. Many of these men had been influential in town affairs for years. In 1766, Samuel Phillips was town clerk, treasurer, and warden; George Abbot, John Farnum, Nehemiah Abbot, and Asa Abbot were selectmen, and James Frye was warden.[34] At that time, Phillips paid the most taxes, John Farnum and James Frye were tied at fourth place, George Abbot was twenty-sixth on the list, Asa Abbot, forty-first, and Nehemiah Abbot fifty-first.[35] In 1769, James Frye was moderator, Samuel Phillips was clerk and treasurer, and John Farnum, George Abbot, James Frye, and Joshua Holt were selectmen.[36] Samuel Phillips continued to be moderator from 1775 on except for 1777, when Moody Bridges took his place, and 1778 when Samuel Osgood was moderator. The same names appear over and over as the important men in town affairs.[37]

In Hatfield, another typical agricultural town, but one in which Tory sentiment was strong, the committee of correspondence was composed of men whose property was above average, but not the wealthiest men. Real estate ratings in 1772 for the members were as follows: John Dickinson, £156; Elijah Morton, £147; Perez Graves, £88; John Hastings, £86; and Elihu White, £50. Six men rated higher than Dickinson: Oliver Partridge, £230; Reuben Belding, £215; Salmon Dickinson, £194; Elisha Allis, £323; Joseph Billing, £215; and Col. Israel Williams, £158. At the same time, some fifty-two had less taxable real

[33] Andover Tax List, 1774.   [34] Andover Town Records, March 3, 1776.
[35] Andover Tax List, 1776.   [36] Andover Town Records, March 6, 1769.
[37] Ibid., March 5, 1775, March 4, 1776, March 3, 1777, May 14, 1777, March 2, 1778, March 6, 1780, March 5, 1781.

estate than did Elihu White, who was rated lowest on the committee of correspondence. Forty-five men had ratings between White's £50 and Dickinson's £156.[38] Reuben Belding died in 1775, leaving an estate of £2,468.[39] Since Belding was rated at £215, Elihu White, the lowest man on the committee with a rating of £50 should have been worth over £500, as would half the men in Hatfield.

These figures should be kept in mind when we see Gage and others use the term "better sort" to indicate the friends of government and "lower class" to designate members of the popular party. The figures indicate that the opposition Gage would be forced to deal with was a society of middle-class property owners.

Gage had no more success in stemming the popular torrent in its rush toward revolution than Hutchinson had. To avoid popular influence in Boston, he met the General Court at Salem; but instead of adopting conciliatory measures, the legislature sent out a call for a continental congress, as many towns had suggested.[40] An effort to condemn Samuel Adams and the Boston committee for circulating the Covenant failed completely when the town supported Adams and the committee by a "vast majority." [41] Gage said that some of the "better sort" had attended a town meeting to try to pay for the tea and also to annihilate the committee of correspondence, but they were

[38] Hatfield Town Records, IV, 254; Hatfield Assessors' List, 1772.

[39] Hampshire County Probate Records, XIII, 167–68.

[40] To Dartmouth, June 26, 1774, *Parliamentary History*, XVIII, 85.

[41] *Boston Town Records*, XVIII, 176–78. From the town records, it does not appear that Samuel Adams and the Boston committee of correspondence were in "serious danger" of being thrown overboard by irate citizens and that they "finally weathered" the storm (Miller, *Sam Adams*, p. 304). This was another futile attempt by the pro-British group to "get" Samuel Adams, but it failed completely. Instead of being in danger, Adams apparently used the occasion to demonstrate his power in the town by a sort of cat and mouse technique. So confident of success was Adams that he stepped down as moderator, allowed his opponents to be "patiently heard" until dark, even though the meeting was so large that it had to be moved from Faneuil Hall to Old South Meeting House and it was obvious that Adams could have annihilated the opposition at any time. After arguments against the committee were continued next day the motion failed by a "great majority" and another motion to approve was passed by a *"Vast Majority."* Adams was never in the slightest danger of suffering defeat.

outvoted "by a great majority of the lower class." [42] The town
of Fitchburgh voted to raise money to send the colony's delegates to a continental congress—then to use any money left over
to purchase powder.[43] By July 9, 1774, the "continued noise
about liberty" had "almost unhinged the firmness of government" out in agricultural Southampton.[44] And John Adams
began to talk of the need for legions rather than nonimportation
agreements as the only effective way to get justice from the British.[45]

In the early summer of 1774, Governor Gage seemed to be
torn between two conflicting forces—the desire to believe that
events were developing satisfactorily and the realization that
they were not. In June, he believed that the Coercive Acts would
enforce themselves as soon as Boston felt the pinch and found
out that she could expect little except fair words by way of support.[46] By early July, Gage was contradicting himself. The "better sort" had been overwhelmingly outvoted in Boston, and the
Council had not consented to his proclamation against the Covenant, yet he said that now there was an open opposition to the
popular party by friends of government which had not previously been possible. On the other hand, he said, town meetings,
issuing edicts enforced by mobs, had taken over all forms of
government and would not easily be dislodged.[47] By July 20,
Gage was sure that New York and Philadelphia would not back
Boston, and he also believed that the Covenant had not achieved
its expected results. Yet, he said, a fast day designated by the
popular party had been kept everywhere as punctually as if it
had been authorized by authority.[48]

Ann Hulton, the customs commissioners' sister, saw events
much more clearly than did Gage. She, too, sometimes identified
the "better sort" with those people who favored government, for
she said the people of property, sense, and character would have
submitted to the penalties of the Coercive Acts. But even these

[42] To Dartmouth, July 5, 1774, *Parliamentary History,* XVIII, 87.
[43] *Fitchburgh Town Records,* I, 104.   [44] Judd Diary, II, July 9, 1774.
[45] *Warren-Adams Letters,* I, 29.
[46] To Dartmouth, June 26, 1774, *Parliamentary History,* XVIII, 85.
[47] To Dartmouth, July 5, 1774, *ibid.,* p. 87.
[48] To Dartmouth, July 20, 1774, *ibid.,* p. 88.

"better sort" were pro-British "more from interest than principle it's to be feared," she said, for "Tories" were also unwilling to acknowledge the authority of Parliament. But Ann Hulton did not see that the popular party was losing any of its power as Gage said it was. There was no discernible disposition to obey the Coercive Acts, she declared, and the leaders of the faction were more active than ever. Instead of the lower classes being responsible for agitation, she believed that the leaders were doing all they could to draw the people into resistance. When the Tories tried to wrest power from the patriots, they were overwhelmed by numbers. The "Leader," Samuel Adams, governed absolutely, she said; the Covenant was a "deep and diabolical scheme," and Boston would receive aid which would result in complete independence for the colonies.[49]

By this time, Samuel Adams was ready to agree with the British accusation that the colonies wanted independence, but he thought the British, not the popular party, were responsible. Wrote Adams: "If Britain by her multiplied oppressions is now accelerating that independency of the colonies which she so much dreads, and which in process of time must take place, who will she have to blame but herself?" [50] Nowhere in Adams' writings is there the idea that the lower orders were trying to get more internal democracy.

That "the Leader" was extremely popular in Boston is attested by another observer. John Andrews, Boston Merchant, said the ultimate aim of the high government party was to get Samuel Adams out of the way; then they could accomplish their plans. But however much one might despise Adams, Andrews continued, he certainly had *"very"* many friends. These friends had built him a new barn, repaired his house, bought him clothing, and given him money. Andrews said he mentioned this to show how much Adams was esteemed by the people. They valued him for his good sense, great abilities, amazing fortitude, noble resolution, and undaunted courage—for being firm and unmoved in face of reports that he was to be seized and sent to England.[51]

---

[49] Hulton, *Letters*, pp. 72–76.   [50] Adams, *Writings*, III, 128.
[51] "Andrews Letters," p. 340. This evidence was intended to show how popular Adams was, not to demonstrate that he was too poor to buy his own clothing.

How well the parliamentary act to restrict town-meeting democracy was to be enforced was soon made evident to the governor. Gage called in the Boston selectmen, gave them the act, then told them that he was going out of town and that if they wanted a meeting they should apply to him. If he considered it expedient, he would give his consent. The selectmen blandly informed him that they would not need to call a new town meeting as they still had two meetings alive by adjournment. Concerned at this news, Gage realized that by this method the selectmen "might keep the meetings alive for ten years" without ever asking the governor's permission, as the act of Parliament stipulated. With "some degree of temper," he informed the selectmen that he was determined to enforce the acts of Parliament and that the selectmen would be responsible for any bad consequences.[52] Except for a representatives' election on September 21, 1774, the town met constantly by adjournment from this time on, thus making the act of Parliament for checking town-meeting democracy a dead letter.[53]

The political leanings of the mandamus councilors who were appointed by the British furnish another indication of the nature of the "revolution." [54] Of the thirty-six councilors, only three, Samuel Danforth, John Erving, Sr., and Jeremiah Powell were on the elected Council of 1774, and of the three, only Danforth accepted the appointment. Danforth's views were apparently not known until the showdown came in 1774. He was referred to as the "amphibious Danforth" and was accused of accepting the appointment for fear of losing the positions he held.[55] Fourteen of the thirty-six mandamus councilors had sat

52 Boston Selectmen's Minutes, 1769–75 in Reports of the Record Commissioners, XXIII, 224.

53 Boston Town Records, XVIII, 188ff.

54 Thomas Oliver*, Thomas Flucker*, Peter Oliver*, Foster Hutchinson*, Thomas Hutchinson*, Harrison Gray*, Samuel Danforth*, John Erving, Sr., James Russell, Timothy Ruggles*, Joseph Lee*, Isaac Winslow*, Israel Williams, George Watson*, Nathaniel Ray Thomas*, Timothy Woodbridge, William Vassel, William Brown(e)*, Joseph Green, James Boutineau*, Andrew Oliver, Josiah Edson*, Richard Lechmere*, Joshua Loring*, John Worthington, Timothy Paine*, William Pepperrell*, Jeremiah Powell, Jonathan Simpson*, John Murry*, Daniel Leonard*, Thomas Palmer, Isaac Royal, Robert Hooper, Abijah Willard*, John Erving, Jr*. Those marked * took the oath required of councilors, Force, American Archives, 4th ser., I, 781.

55 Thomas Young to Samuel Adams, Aug. 19, 1774, Adams Papers.

on the Council at one time but had been defeated as their views became known.[56] Five had at one time or another been representatives, some of whom had been defeated along the way. Josiah Edson alternated with Edward Mitchell as Bridgwater representative from 1766 to 1773, then went with the British. Daniel Leonard and Robert Treat Paine represented Taunton. Leonard became a Loyalist; Paine became a well-known patriot.[57] Many of these councilors, however, had never been able to win a popular election in their towns, but obviously their appointment showed where their sympathies were expected to be. So it is clear that the "revolution" had taken place in the Council long before 1774.

John Adams explanation of the appointment of the mandamus Council shows that the colonists were opposing the British in an effort to keep the social order they had, not fighting an internal revolution to acquire more democracy. Said Adams:

Every man, of every character, who, by voting, writing, speaking, or otherwise, had favored the Stamp Act, the Tea Act, or every other

[56] Thomas Flucker, Peter Oliver, Thomas Hutchinson, Harrison Gray, Samuel Danforth, John Erving, Sr., James Russell, Timothy Ruggles, Israel Williams, Timothy Woodbridge, Andrew Oliver, John Worthington, Timothy Paine, and Jeremiah Powell.

[57] Joseph Lee (Cambridge), William Brown (Salem), Josiah Edson (Bridgwater), John Murry (Rutland), and Daniel Leonard (Taunton), *Acts and Resolves*, XVII and XVIII, *passim*. For favorable accounts of the Loyalists, stressing their numbers and upper-class social status, see Moses Coit Tyler, "The Party of the Loyalists in the American Revolution," *American Historical Review*, I (Oct. 1895), 24–46; Claude H. Van Tyne, *The Loyalists in the American Revolution* (New York, 1902); Adams, *Revolutionary New England*, pp. 448–49.

Schlesinger, *Colonial Merchants,* p. 604, gave an erroneous impression of the importance of Loyalist merchants in Boston. Merchants, actuated by class interests, had been converted to loyalism earlier than in other provinces, Schlesinger said, and "more than two hundred members of the trade accompanied the British troops upon the evacuation of Boston in March, 1775" (i.e., 1776). Schlesinger cited Lorenzo Sabine, *Biographical Sketches of Loyalists of the American Revolution,* 2 vols. (Boston, 1864), I, 25, but Sabine does not say this. What Sabine did say was that "of merchants and other persons who resided in Boston, two hundred and thirteen" left with the British troops. This number included the women and children, which might reduce the figure to less than fifty adult men, and Sabine did not say how many of these were merchants and how many were other persons. In short, the merchants did not support the Loyalist cause in anything near the number that Schlesinger implied. Sabine also said that only some 2,000 people left Massachusetts (p. 26). If there were 300,000 people in the colony, this would be 0.00666 or two-thirds of one per cent.

measure of a minister or governor, who they knew was aiming at the destruction of their form of government, and introducing parliamentary taxation, was uniformly, in some department or other, promoted to some place of honor or profit for ten years together; and, on the other hand, every man who favored the people in their opposition to these innovations, was depressed, degraded, and persecuted, so far as it was in the power of the government to do it.[58]

The Mandamus Council of 1774 definitely consisted of those men who had always favored the British rather than the colonial cause or who finally decided to go with the British when they had to decide.

Popular pressure, however, forced many councilors to resign or to seek the protection of British troops in Boston. Abijah Willard of Lancaster soon resigned after signing a confession to uphold all charter rights and expressing regret at taking the councilor's oath. Timothy Paine, Lieutenant Governor Thomas Oliver, superior court justices Peter Oliver, Foster Hutchinson, and Joseph Lee, and councilors Isaac Winslow, Samuel Danforth, and George Watson quickly followed Willard's example, leaving only fifteen of the original thirty-six appointees. Gage at one time planned to send troops into the country to protect councilors and judges, "but finding from undoubted authority, that the flames of sedition had spread universally throughout the country beyond conception," he was at a loss to know where troops would be effective.[59] Some five hundred

[58] Adams, *Works*, IV, 53. Taylor, *Western Massachusetts*, contended that from 1740 right down to 1774 the western towns either remained indifferent to larger political questions that agitated the province or openly showed their hostility to Boston's leadership. As evidence he cited the fact that six of the seventeen rescinders in 1768 were from western Massachusetts and that three were re-elected compared with two from the remainder of the province, and also that the west did not support Boston at the Convention of 1768 (pp. 52–58). The first evidence appears legitimate but the second is open to question, since many towns did not have sufficient time to elect delegates.

The selection of a Mandamus Council, however, does not substantiate Taylor's interpretation of conservatism in the western counties. Since the Council was appointed before the Port Bill reached the colony, the selection obviously had no relation to colonists' views or change of views as a result of the Coercive Acts. Yet of thirty-six mandamus councilors, only two from the west, Israel Williams of Hatfield and John Worthington, were appointed, and neither one accepted. This was certainly not the west's proportion, especially if the west had long been considered a stronghold of Toryism.

[59] To Dartmouth, Sept. 12, 1774, *Parliamentary History*, XVIII, 94.

of Daniel Leonard's neighbors in Taunton attempted to dissuade him from accepting the appointment, "but the sudden disappearance of that gentleman" prevented further action. Timothy Ruggles was ordered out of Dartmouth, but before he could depart, his horse was painted and had its mane and tail cut off. "Such is the spirit in this county," wrote one observer. "It is more dangerous being a tory here than at Boston, even if no troops were there." [60]

That the "revolution" sometimes cut across family lines rather than class lines is well demonstrated by a letter from Solomon Williams to his brother Israel, one of the mandamus councilors. Solomon said his brother's political ideas were very different from his own, but that even so he hoped his brother would not accept the appointment as mandamus councilor. The names of those who did would "be execrated by your countrymen to all posterity." Then Solomon Williams condemned Parliament for acts which took the property and estates of the people of Boston, since "that power which has right to take away their estates has as good a right to take your lands or mine, our houses, or inheritances, or any other man's in America." The Massachusetts Government Act placed the colony under the arbitrary will of British ministers—ministers who had no love for the colonies except for what the colonies could be made to yield. Solomon Williams reminded his brother that their ancestors had left England to obtain political, religious, and economic freedom.[61]

Another indication that the people were trying to preserve a social order rather than change it was their refusal to submit to the act of Parliament making judges appointive at pleasure rather than during good behavior. To have allowed the courts to conduct business would have meant sanctioning the change of the constitution, so the courts did not sit. The Pittsfield town meeting expressed the general feeling when it declared that the people should "utterly refuse the least submission" to the acts of Parliament and must "resist them to the last extremity." The town therefore resolved that no courts should sit until

[60] Force, *American Archives,* 4th ser., I, 732, 745, 766, 799.
[61] Solomon Williams to Israel Williams, Aug. 20, 1774, Library of Congress, Massachusetts Miscellaneous, 1769–1778.

the act of Parliament was repealed.[62] As a result, the courts were stopped universally throughout the province, sometimes by persuasion, often by force.[63] In Boston, Chief Justice and Mandamus Councilor Peter Oliver attempted with the aid of the sheriffs to hold a superior court, but they could not find a grand or petit juror who would be sworn. The reasons given were that Oliver had been impeached, that the constitution had been changed, and that three judges, Oliver, Foster Hutchinson, and William Brown had taken the oath as councilors.[64]

With Gage and the British army in Boston, the center of opposition shifted from Boston to county conventions during the summer of 1774. These conventions passed resolves which leave little doubt that the issues were British-American rather than upper-lower class. One after another the counties took positions which boded no good for anyone who would try to enforce changes in the Massachusetts constitution. Although the Suffolk County resolves have become the best known, all were about the same in content. All protested against arbitrary changes of government which would allow British control of colonial politics. All insisted that a free people must have constitutional checks on government and that appointment of officials at pleasure, destruction of trial by jury, and payment of officials by a power over which the people had no control destroyed these constitutional checks. All insisted directly or indirectly that the colonists would be justified in appealing to the sword to prevent enforcement of the act of Parliament. And all called for a provincial congress to mobilize the opposition. The adoption of the Middlesex County resolves by a vote of 146 to 4 gave some indication of the unanimity of sentiment in the towns.[65] Far from insisting on change, these people were saying that they would fight to prevent it.

Actions and resolutions of the town meetings merely emphasized the proceedings of the county conventions. Gage tried to prevent by use of troops the Salem town meeting which was

[62] Pittsfield Town Records, I, 182. [63] Judd Diary, II, Aug. 19–31.
[64] Force, *American Archives*, 4th ser., I, 747–48.
[65] *Ibid.*, pp. 750–53, 776–79, 795–97, 798–802; *Journals of Each Provincial Congress of Massachusetts in 1774 and 1775* . . . (Boston, 1838), pp. 601–60.

called without his consent to elect county delegates, but this move failed.[66] Watertown sent its selectmen to the convention, then adopted the convention's resolves and voted to exercise the militia two hours a week.[67] Some called special meetings to elect delegates "for this special reason, to show our contempt of the act of Parliament touching town meetings." One delegate said that all men must now "appear undisguised upon one side or the other." [68] Braintree wanted to obtain county indemnification for anyone fined for noncompliance with the government act.[69] Malden unanimously accepted the resolves of the county convention,[70] and Brookline voted to protect and indemnify any town official who incurred any penalty for violating the act of Parliament.[71]

The best available picture of the nature and extent of the revolution in 1774 is to be found in the letters from Gage to Dartmouth which were laid before Parliament in January 1775. Gage had started his term in office with the idea that the trouble was due to a few leaders in Boston, but that the people were deserting these leaders. The signing of the Covenant by most Bostonians probably influenced him in believing that the malady had infected all Boston, but he did not expect other towns or colonies to aid Boston. In August, however, he confessed that the frenzy had spread to all the counties in Massachusetts, not just Boston, that popular rage appeared throughout the province, and that everyone agreed that popular fury was never greater in the colony. By this time he began to suspect that he might have to discipline both Massachusetts and Connecticut, for Connecticut was now alarmed at the attack on the Massachusetts charter, but he was sure that the other colonies would not assist these two.[72]

Before September was over, Gage realized that he had been seriously mistaken in his judgment of the revolutionary move-

[66] Force, *American Archives,* 4th ser., I, 1730.
[67] *Watertown Records, 1769–92,* pp. 109–10.
[68] Benjamin Kent to Samuel Adams, Aug. 20, 1774, Adams Papers.
[69] *Braintree Town Records,* p. 450.
[70] Malden Town Records, II, 67.
[71] *Muddy River and Brookline Records,* p. 247.
[72] *Parliamentary History,* XVIII, 80–90.

ment. On September 2, 1774, he wrote "that the flames of sedition had spread universally throughout the country, beyond conception." Now Connecticut and Rhode Island were "as furious as they are in this province." Gage said he got his information "from gentlemen thoroughly acquainted with the country, and who knew the pitch of enthusiasm to which the people are now raised." By September 12, he believed it would be necessary to conquer all New England, and by September 20, revolt seemed universal to him. He expressed surprise "that so many other provinces interest themselves so much in the behalf of this." Support came unexpectedly from New York and Philadelphia, and he had learned from an officer who left South Carolina in August "that the people of Charlestown are as mad as they are here." [73] Perhaps the other colonies, too, thought they had something worth while to lose if the British were successful in Massachusetts.

When these letters were laid before Parliament, one Governor Johnstone declared that Gage had regularly deceived the administration. Nothing turned out as Gage had predicted, he said, and each letter contradicted the previous letter as an evaluation of the situation in the colonies. Johnstone said the only letter to believe was the last one in which Gage told of total disaffection in America.[74]

By the end of September, then, Gage's estimate of popular feeling in the colonies conformed almost exactly with the estimates of the popular party. Joseph Warren of the Boston committee wrote that the spirit displayed by different parts of the continent dampened the spirits of the pro-British faction who hoped to be the colonists' masters. Some believed or pretended to believe that if the faction in Boston were quelled, the other provinces would submit, he declared, but now they saw a firm union of all America which the most powerful monarch on earth could not break.[75] Gage's seizure of the province powder in Boston "set the whole country aflame." About 20,000 men in

[73] *Ibid.*, pp. 90–94; Thomas Gage, *The Correspondence of General Thomas Gage,* ed. by Clarence E. Carter, 2 vols. (New Haven, 1931, 1933), I, 375; Force, *American Archives,* 4th ser., I, 795.

[74] *Parliamentary History,* XVIII, 261.

[75] Mass. Hist. Soc., *Collections,* 4th ser., IV, 59.

the western towns started to march on Boston and were persuaded to turn back only with difficulty.[76] If there had been much animosity between backcountry and seacoast, the backcountry could easily have stood by and watched Boston suffer in solitude. Jonathan Judd of Southampton suspected that the reported seizure was put out with a design to discover the spirit of the people. If so, it succeeded very well, he said, for the spirits were alive through that part of the country as far as New York.[77] Even James Bowdoin, who had been at the center of events for a long time, expressed surprise at the spontaneous spirit that had burst forth in all the colonies.[78]

The spirit of unanimity obviously pleased "the Leader," Samuel Adams. One correspondent wrote as follows: "By the inclosed papers you will perceive the temper of your countrymen in the condition your every wish, your every sigh for years past, panted to find it." This man particularly stressed the enthusiasm in the western towns—those agricultural towns which were already overrepresented in the legislature. "By all our advices from the westward the body of the people are for resuming the old charter [the charter of 1629 under which all officials were elected] and organizing a government immediately," he said. Even Joseph Hawley, who opposed the Covenant and was called "the cautious Major Hawley," was "so strongly convinced of the necessity of resuming the old charter that he declared that if the four New England governments alone adopt the measure he will venture his life to defend it against the whole force of Great Britain, in case she resents it." [79] Adams and Hawley had worked together closely in the assembly from the time Adams was elected to that body.

Customs official Benjamin Hallowell concluded that popular sentiment had already carried the issue beyond resistance to obedience to an act of Parliament to a desire for independence itself. He believed that "the brains of most of the people in this country" had been turned, and though arguments sufficient

---

[76] Benjamin Church to S. Adams, Sept. 4, 1774, Adams Papers.
[77] Judd Diary, II, Sept. 5, 1774.
[78] Mass. Hist. Soc., *Proceedings*, XVIII, 153.
[79] Young to S. Adams, Sept. 4, 1774, Adams Papers.

to convince rational men had been used, the frenzy was now so great that reason was entirely out of the question. "What evinces most the strength of the party against government is that not one person has dared to ask protection of the General," he declared. Even Lieutenant Governor and Councilor Thomas Oliver had been forced to resign in Cambridge, just across the river from Boston, yet had not dared to call for troops. Hallowell stressed the Quebec Act as a major grievance, as did also all the county conventions. "In a word sir," he wrote, "the people here are not now contending for this or that matter about acts of Parliament, but dominion is the principle upon which they now act." [80] Obviously Hallowell and these other contemporary observers had never heard of the interpretation, accepted by later historians, that one-third of the people were patriots, one-third were Loyalists, and one-third were indifferent.

Such was the spirit displayed throughout the country that Gage, who had been sent to enforce acts of Parliament, soon found it expedient to take measures to protect his own troops. Instead of talking about sending troops to various parts of the province to protect the courts, the general decided to fortify the narrow neck of the peninsula on which Boston was built at that time.[81] And well he might have taken these precautions, for the towns as well as the county conventions were calling for the resignations of commissioned officers and demanding that militia officers increase military training. Marblehead wanted its men trained two hours a day, four days a week.[82] Artificers in Boston refused to work for the British in spite of the economic distress brought on by the closing of the port, and Gage had to admit that he did not find the spirit abating anywhere.[83]

In late September, Gage finally gave an account of the situation which seemed to agree with those of other observers. He had called for an assembly to meet at Salem. The old councilors were there, and he did not dare take the mandamus councilors out of Boston, but under the act of Parliament he could not

[80] To Grey Cooper, Sept. 5, 1774, Library of Congress Transcripts, Public Record Office, Colonial Office 5, America and West Indies, CLXXV.

[81] Force, *American Archives*, 4th ser., I, 775.

[82] Judd Diary, II, Sept. 7, 1774; Marblehead Town Records, IV, 183.

[83] Gage to Dartmouth, Oct. 3, 1774, Force, *American Archives*, 4th ser., I, 814–15.

meet with the old Council. So he decided not to hold a General Court. There were reports of military preparations from Boston to New York and the whole seemed united. Rumors that British soldiers had killed six people and that ships and troops were firing on Boston had put the whole country in arms and in motion. Numerous bodies from Connecticut had begun to march before the report was contradicted. This, said Gage, would indicate how Massachusetts was supported and abetted by others beyond the conception of most people and foreseen by none. The disease was believed to have been confined to Boston at one time but now the malady was so universal there was no knowing where to apply the remedy.[84]

The problem, in fact, was not how to arouse popular enthusiasm against the British but how to restrain that enthusiasm to prevent an open break between the two countries, particularly before an effective union of the colonies had been formed. James Warren wrote of clashes between civilians and soldiers, making it difficult to keep the people from taking action.[85] From Philadelphia, Samuel Adams urged the "vast importance of union." He did not want the people of Massachusetts to precipitate events by taking up the old charter as Joseph Hawley had suggested. Better that the colony should follow the present charter to the letter to unite the people in a constitutional opposition to tyranny.[86] Even Benjamin Franklin, who still talked of reconciliation between the two countries, feared that some little incident might occur to prevent it.[87] Because of his compromise position, Franklin said he was considered too much an American by the British and too much an Englishman by the Americans.[88]

There can be little doubt that all this popular enthusiasm had its roots in democracy, but not in the way we have generally believed. If there had been popular discontent with the franchise, with internal economic conditions, with inequitable representation, or with a ruling aristocracy, some of this discontent would

---

[84] To Dartmouth, Sept. 25, 1774, *Parliamentary History,* XVIII, 99.
[85] To S. Adams, Sept. 29, 1774, Adams Papers.
[86] Adams, *Writings,* III, 156–57.   [87] Franklin, *Writings,* VI, 249–51.
[88] *Ibid.,* pp. 269–76.

have appeared in the mass of evidence available. People who talked of sacrificing their lives and property would certainly have mentioned these internal grievances had they been important. On the other hand, if we accept the fact that a democratic society existed, popular opposition to British measures seems entirely logical. People accustomed to democratic government would naturally oppose changes which gave the British control of governors, councilors, judges, sheriffs, justices of the peace, taxes, juries, and town meetings. The problem was not one of attaining a democratic society but of keeping the democracy they had, a democracy threatened by British imperialism.

Actions of the First Continental Congress, which met in Philadelphia in the late summer of 1774, are of interest here only as they throw light on the revolution in Massachusetts. Statements were made that the Virginia and Carolina delegates were "much among the Bostonians" and that the Bostonians were "moderate men when compared with Virginia, South Carolina, and Rhode Island." [89] This would indicate that Massachusetts was going to be supported by the others and that the issue was not back-country against coast, as the Massachusetts delegation was referred to as Bostonians. Furthermore, we need not take seriously Joseph Galloway's later statement that the popular party at the Congress were "congregational or presbyterian republicans, or men of bankrupt fortunes." [90] The Massachusetts delegation, John Hancock, John Adams, Thomas Cushing, and Robert Treat Paine (Bowdoin was chosen but could not attend) were perhaps "congregational and presbyterian republicans," but they were not exactly men of bankrupt fortunes.

Members from some other colonies were not as far advanced in their thinking about colonial independence as were the men from Massachusetts, and there was undoubtedly much political maneuvering, but on the whole the Congress backed Massachusetts. It sanctioned the strongly worded Suffolk County Re-

[89] Burnett, Letters, I, 9–10, 27. For accounts of the Continental Congress, see Edmund Cody Burnett, The Continental Congress (New York, 1941), which depicts the Continental Congress as the center of the revolutionary scene, and Lynn Montross, The Reluctant Rebels: The Story of the Continental Congress, 1774–1789 (New York, 1950).

[90] Burnett, Letters, I, 54–56.

solves, agreed to shut off trade with England, and approved opposition by Massachusetts to enforcement of the Coercive Acts, especially the Massachusetts Government Act.[91] John Dickinson, who was not a social "radical," said that the first act of violence on the part of Britain would "put the whole continent in arms, from Nova Scotia to Georgia." [92] And Gage believed that the Congress had "violently espoused" the cause of Massachusetts, thus emphasizing his belief that the revolt was widespread.[93]

More important than the Continental Congress in this study, of course, was the Provincial Congress, which met in October 1774. This came about when Gage, alarmed by the growing realization of the serious problem confronting him, decided not to hold the General Court which he had called to meet at Salem on October 5, 1774.

In electing their representatives for this General Court which was later canceled, the towns again placed the accent on the status quo. Many assumed that the governor's purpose was to see whether the assembly would acquiesce in the Government Act. Almost as one they instructed their delegates not to submit to charter changes. Many towns also assumed that Gage would dissolve the assembly for its refusal, so at the same time they elected delegates to a provincial congress, which many towns and the county conventions had called for. Pittsfield did not bother to elect a representative to the General Court but simply sent its delegate to the Provincial Congress.[94]

Most of the towns couched their instructions in terms strong enough to discourage the most intrepid governor, but Worcester exceeded even this limit. The town's instructions stated that the charter of 1629 had been wrongfully wrested from the colony and the second charter had been nullified by acts of Parliament,

[91] *Journals of the Continental Congress, 1774–1789*, 35 vols. (Washington, 1904–1937), I, 43, 51–52, 58, 60; Adams, *Writings*, III, 158–59; Mass. Hist. Soc., *Collections*, 2d ser., VIII, 311.

[92] Burnett, *Letters*, I, 83.

[93] To Dartmouth, Oct. 3, 1774, *Parliamentary History*, XVIII, 100.

[94] For example, see *Boston Town Records*, XVIII, 191; Andover Town Records, Sept. 15, 1774; Marblehead Town Records, IV, 187–88; *Plymouth Town Records*, III, 292–93; Malden Town Records, II, 71; Pittsfield Town Records, I, 189.

troops, and a governor rendered independent of the people. The representatives, therefore, should open the port to restore free trade, get the troops removed, demand that the troops restore confiscated ammunition, impeach the mandamus councilors as traitors and secure them for trial, send a delegation to get aid from Canada, and follow the advice of the Continental Congress to preserve unity. Then, declared Worcester, if all wrongs had not been redressed and all charter rights restored by the day the Provincial Congress met, the representatives were to consider the people of Massachusetts in a state of nature, absolved from all charter obligations to Britain, and were to raise a new form of government in which all officials would be elected by the people.[95] Little wonder that Gage decided to cancel the meeting of this General Court.

Again these elections to the General Court and the Provincial Congress were remarkable only because they demonstrated an absence of internal revolution. The Boston delegation was elected unanimously by the 362 voters—except for Samuel Adams, who received only 361 votes.[96] Generally towns sent their regular representatives; some of them added more men to meet in the Provincial Congress. Andover sent Moody Bridges as usual.[97] Marblehead elected representatives Azor Orne and Elbridge Gerry to go to Salem, then added Jeremiah Lee, the town moderator, to join the other two at the Congress.[98] Malden elected Ebenezer Harnden, its representative since 1765, and added John Dexter, who had represented the town in 1763 and 1764.[99] Plymouth sent James Warren, representative since 1766, and Isaac Lathrop, who had come to the House in 1772.[100] Wenham had sent only two representatives since 1760—Nathaniel Brown in 1762 and Benjamin Fairfield in 1767—but now it sent Fairfield again.[101] Benjamin White, the Brookline delegate, had

[95] *Worcester Town Records*, IV, 240–43.

[96] *Boston Town Records*, XVIII, 191.

[97] Andover Town Records, Sept. 15, 1774.

[98] Marblehead Town Records, IV, 187–88.

[99] Malden Town Records, II, 68; *Acts and Resolves*, XVII, 378–79, 508–09; XVIII, *passim*.

[100] *Plymouth Town Records*, III, 292–93; *Acts and Resolves*, XVIII, 112–13, 617.

[101] *Wenham Town Records*, p. 274; *Acts and Resolves*, XVII, 218–19, XVIII, 224–25.

represented the town since 1768.[102] John Remington and Jonathan Brown of Watertown had served in the House from 1768 and 1772 respectively, Josiah Pierce of Hadley from 1771, Joshua Bigelow of Worcester from 1767.[103] Northampton sent Seth Pomeroy, described as "very high in liberty." [104] Pomeroy, listed as a "blacksmith" on the tax rolls, was rated more than twice as much as any other man in Northampton.[105]

Even where a town changed delegates, the change did not signify a social revolution. In Weston the call for a Provincial Congress resulted in a political "revolution" which again shows that these "revolutionaries" were not lower-class proletarians. Weston was one of the few towns where the progovernment party had maintained control. In 1765, the town had voted to compensate Hutchinson and the other sufferers in the Stamp Act riots. When the assembly voided the election of Colonel Elisha Jones in 1773, the town re-elected him. Then, in January 1774, Captain Braddyl Smith and others petitioned the town to set up a committee of correspondence, but the town, with Colonel Jones as moderator, rejected the petition. Jones was again elected representative in May 1774, but events of the summer finally resulted in the election of Captain Braddyl Smith, Samuel Savage, and Josiah Smith.[106]

Fortunately, the Weston records are sufficiently complete to give us a great deal of information on these "revolutionaries." The tax lists yield the following ratings: [107]

Braddyl Smith	£139
Josiah Smith	201
Elisha Jones	162
Abraham Bigelow	201

[102] *Muddy River and Brookline Records*, pp. 247–49; *Acts and Resolves*, XVIII, *passim*.

[103] Hadley Town Records, Oct. 3, 1774; *Worcester Town Records*, IV, 240; *Acts and Resolves*, XVII and XVIII, *passim*.

[104] Judd Diary, II, Sept. 29, 1774.

[105] Northampton Town Records, I, 296–99; II, 123–24; Judd MSS., Northampton, II, 69.

[106] *Weston Town Records*, pp. 125–27, 194, 198, 204.

[107] *Weston Tax Lists*, p. 83.

Bigelow was the town's representative from 1764 to 1773, when Elisha Jones was elected.[108] From these figures we might assume that Bigelow and Josiah Smith had roughly about the same amount of property and that Braddyl Smith had about two-thirds as much as the other two. Bigelow died in 1775, leaving an estate, which was settled in 1784, of about £3,325.[109] Braddyl Smith died in 1780 and his estate by 1784 added up to some £1,725.[110] With both Bigelow and Smith, real estate was worth about fifteen times the tax rating. In personal estate, Smith was rated at £39.18.0, yet his inventory showed only £53.14.0, while Bigelow had a tax rating of £26 for personal estate but an inventory of £460. This would indicate that Smith had a great deal more in personal estate in 1774 and that probably his total property was about two-thirds as much as Bigelow's. At any rate, these figures show that the "revolution" in Weston did not result in the election of "debtor" farmers or men of the lower classes. They were not rich men—Bigelow's house was worth £200 compared with Andrew Oliver's £2,000 home in Boston—but they were substantial, middle-class, property owners.

In its three sessions during 1774 and 1775, the Provincial Congress did nothing which could be called a social revolution. The men were the same who had been in the legislature or had long been important in their town affairs. There was an increase in representation to 302 in the first Congress, but there is no discernibly significant pattern in the increase. Seaport towns such as Boston, Salem, and Marblehead sent more members, but so did many of the agricultural towns.[111] As often happened, important events brought increased representation, and this seems to have been the explanation for the increase. By the second Congress, the number had dropped to 229, but again the decrease does not show any significant pattern.[112] The Congress did decide not to pay taxes to Harrison Gray, the regular treasurer, but to have them collected by Henry Gardner of Stow.

108 *Acts and Resolves,* XVII and XVIII, *passim.*
109 Middlesex County Probate Records, LVII, 415–16; LXVIII, 40–45.
110 *Ibid.,* LXIV, 71; LXVI, 68, 404.
111 *Journals of Each Provincial Congress,* p. 78.
112 *Ibid.,* pp. 77–78.

Gardner had represented Stow in the assembly since 1761.[113] The delegates had come with orders to prevent change, not to promote it.

If there is little evidence of internal revolution during the fall of 1774, there is ample proof that the issue was opposition to British measures. This involved the carrying out of proposals by the Continental and Provincial Congresses—raising troops, getting arms and ammunition, establishing committees to enforce regulation and to prevent any unlawful activities, and putting pressure on those who favored the British cause.[114] In Marblehead, twelve who had signed the Hutchinson address recanted, leaving only six men to be censured by the town as enemies of their country.[115] A traveler reported that the people all the way from Boston to Salem and Marblehead were "furious in the cause of liberty" and that political writings were bought up "with amazing avidity." [116]

Gage was now fully aware of the seriousness of his situation. He expected the colony to assume all functions of government. Edicts of the Provincial Congress were implicitly obeyed throughout the country, the people were in ferment, many were armed, and other colonies supported Massachusetts. Britain, he declared, never had occasion for more wisdom, firmness, and unanimity. He was afraid the people would try to provoke his troops so that they would have reason to retaliate. At one time he thought the people would listen to reason if they were allowed to cool off a little, but by December 1774 he had changed his mind. They had had time to cool and listen to reason, he said, but they had not altered their views about Parliament and its powers over the colony.[117]

In late 1774 and early 1775, John Adams wrote a series of newspaper articles signed Novanglus in answer to articles signed Massachusettensis. Massachusettensis was the Tory attorney gen-

[113] *Acts and Resolves,* XVII and XVIII, *passim.*

[114] Malden Town Records, II, 68; *Worcester Town Records,* IV, 248; Sheffield Town Records, Nov. 3 and 5, 1774; Marblehead Town Records, IV, 185.

[115] Marblehead Town Records, IV, 194–98.

[116] Honyman, *Colonial Panorama,* pp. 41, 49, 58.

[117] To Dartmouth, Nov. 2 and Dec. 15, 1774, *Parliamentary History,* XVIII, 104, 106.

eral and mandamus councilor, Daniel Leonard, who attempted to convince the people that British policy was just and right and that colonial leaders were misleading the people either from ignorance or personal gain. As Novanglus, John Adams attempted to offset the influence of Massachusettensis by writing his version of the controversy. Naturally, Adams justified the actions of the colonists and attempted to prove that Tories were acting from selfish motives. This paper controversy tells us much about the pre-Revolutionary social order in the colony.[118]

Both Leonard and Adams agreed that democracy was in operation—that the people made the final decisions—though they differed as to the ultimate significance of this fact. Leonard inferred that the popular leaders were working for their own gain at the expense of the people and the colonies. Adams disagreed:

I appeal to all experience, and to universal history, if it has ever been in the power of popular leaders, uninvested with other authority than what is conferred by the popular suffrage, to persuade a large people, for any length of time together, to think themselves wronged, injured, and oppressed, unless they really were, and saw and felt it to be so.

Popular leaders held their position because the people were behind them and believed that the leaders were working for the interests of the people. Otherwise, the leaders could not have held the confidence of the people for long.[119]

Throughout the Novanglus writings, Adams argued that the revolutionary movement had wide popular support. The people, he said, were much more apt to overlook mistakes of government and to suffer multiplied oppression than they were to resist government. The wide extent of opposition proved that the grievance must be extremely serious.[120] Another argument he used was that the press was almost universally pro-patriot, not because the Tories could not present the government side, but because the people favored the Whig side. The most influential of Tory writers had not been able to change the minds of the people.[121] All America, Adams contended, was united in op-

[118] John Adams, "Novanglus," in *Works,* IV, *passim.*
[119] Adams, *Works,* IV, 14–15.   [120] *Ibid.,* p. 17.
[121] *Ibid.,* pp. 29–32.

position to the claims of the ministers and Parliament. Every colony, county, city, town, and hamlet had taken up Samuel Adams' suggestion of committees of correspondence.[122] The public record of votes in the assembly, with the consequent ousting of Tory delegates, was another indication to Adams that the Whigs were the party of the people.[123] If the militia refused to carry out orders to enforce a British act, did "not this prove the universal sense and resolution of the people not to submit to it?" he asked.[124] Nine-tenths of the people were "high whigs," so it would be difficult to get a Tory jury in the colony by democratic processes. The only way was to have the sheriff choose a jury.[125] In another place, Adams placed the majority in favor of the popular party at nineteen to one,[126] all of which is a far cry from his later statement that a third of the people were patriots, a third Loyalists, and a third indifferent.

There was a junto in the colony, Adams declared, but it was made up of appointed officials, the Bernards, Hutchinsons, Olivers, and others. He mistakenly accused the junto of originating the changes in policy which occurred after 1760, but he was correct in saying that they proposed a colonial nobility.[127] This junto held office by royal favor, however, and was not an elected aristocracy which held office because of a limited franchise or unequal representation.

Adams cited Thomas Hutchinson as a prime example of a man who had held important offices under a democratic system but who had forfeited his position because of his principles. At one time, Hutchinson had been popular. He acted with ability and integrity in several important capacities when his actions did not affect his political philosophy. "Had he continued steadfast to those principles in religion and government, which, in his former life, he professed, and which alone had procured him the confidence of the people and all his importance," Adams declared, "he would have lived and died, respected and beloved, and have done honor to his native country." By renouncing these principles, he had lost the respect of the people and the popular support which had raised him to positions of

122 *Ibid.*, pp. 33–34.   123 *Ibid.*, p. 58.   124 *Ibid.*, p. 65.

125 *Ibid.*, p. 73.   126 *Ibid.*, p. 98.   127 *Ibid.*, pp. 18–27, 63.

influence. It was a matter of principles, not class, which had gained and lost Thomas Hutchinson his position. Adams, in fact, claimed that Hutchinson never really understood the true character of his native country or the temper, principles, and opinions of its people.[128]

According to Adams, the men who were behind the "revolution" were substantial, respected gentlemen, not lower-class proletarians. Under the new militia organized by the Provincial Congress, officers commissioned by the governor had been forced to resign, to be replaced by officers with colonial commissions. The two were often the same. Now they held their commissions, not as a favor from a governor, but because they were "gentlemen, whose estates, abilities, and benevolence have rendered them the delight of the soldiers." [129] Furthermore, the councilors after 1766, when Hutchinson, Oliver, and others were defeated, were little if any inferior to the councilors before 1766 "in point of fortune, family, note, or abilities." [130] Even Leonard had to admit that "first rate whigs" were elected to juries, although he attributed this to maneuvering against government. Adams simply claimed that most of the freeholders were Whigs, so naturally a jury chosen by lot would be Whig.[131] And if you took "the whigs and tories on an average, the balance of principle, as well as genius, learning, wit, and wealth, is infinitely in favor of the former." [132]

Throughout their discussion there is no hint by Adams that the conflict involved internal social issues. Both Leonard and Adams referred to the republican spirit in the colony, one with disapproval, the other with praise.[133] Leonard also called the colony, once it was under popular control, "a democracy or republic," indicating that aristocratic influence was nonexistent once the people took affairs in their own hands.[134] The issues were imperial—the right of Britain to regulate trade, control colonial officials, levy taxes, pay salaries, and change the Massachusetts charter.

During the winter of 1774–1775, General Haldiman of the

128 *Ibid.*, pp. 67–68.   129 *Ibid.*, p. 41.   130 *Ibid.*, p. 64.
131 *Ibid.*, p. 73.   132 *Ibid.*, p. 97.   133 *Ibid.*, p. 68.
134 *Ibid.*, p. 79.

British army told a story which captures the popular spirit of the times about as well as any. Some boys in Boston had used a certain hill for sledding, but one of Haldiman's servants, unhappy about the treacherous footing thus created, had sprinkled ashes over the ice and snow and had spoiled the boys' fun. With the true spirit of sons of Boston, according to the general, the boys chose a committee to complain. Demanding to see the general, the committee explained that the servant had thrown ashes on a spot of ground which they and their fathers before them had always used for coasting. Haldiman then ordered his servant to throw water on the spot to rectify the damage, after which he treated the committee to a glass of wine. Later the general afforded Gage's dinner party much amusement by repeating this incident. Gage observed that the boys had only caught the spirit of the times and that what was bred in the bone would creep out in the flesh.[135]

In England, the great majority in Parliament still seemed to misunderstand the situation in the colonies, perhaps because they neither appreciated nor sympathized with the type of social order which had developed there. William Pitt warned that the ministry had deluded the people into thinking that the affair concerned Boston only and could be easily put down, but, said he, the cause of Boston would be the cause of America. Others, however, refused to listen. The Earl of Suffolk wanted to use force first, then make concessions. Lord Lyttelton believed that the Navigation Acts would be attacked next and that then the colonies would demand independence. Lord Townshend believed that the colonies intended to throw off the Navigation Acts, not just procure a redress of grievances. And Earl Gower said he was well informed that the language now held by the Americans was the language of the rabble and a few factious leaders. It did not express the true sense of the respectable part of the people.[136] In the House, one Colonel Grant said the Americans would never fight, then ridiculed them for their religious enthusiasm, manners, and ways of living.[137]

Edmund Burke, on the other hand, seems to have had a fairly accurate understanding of colonial society and the issues at stake

---

[135] *Belknap Papers,* in Mass. Hist. Soc., *Collections,* 6th ser., IV, 77.
[136] *Parliamentary History,* XVIII, 150–67.　　　　　[137] *Ibid.,* p. 226.

in the dispute. Colonial governments were popular governments, he declared, with the popular representative branch the most important element. The people, inspired with lofty sentiments by having a share in their own government, were averse to anything that would deprive them of this share. Colonial political ideas were strengthened by religious beliefs, he said, for religion to the colonists was important. Their extreme Protestant views were one of the main causes for their free spirit, since their religion was not only favorable to liberty but was built upon liberty. Whereas Catholic and Anglican churches were closely connected with government, Burke continued, dissenting churches, having grown by opposition to state churches, could justify their existence only on a strong claim to natural liberty. And New England religion was one of the most Protestant of the Protestant. In the South, slavery placed such a premium on freedom that a free Southerner was more jealous of freedom than was the New Englander. Burke also said that education promoted freedom in America, where most people could read. He maintained that Britain should have won over the lawyers, presumably part of the "upper classes," who took the lead in opposition.[138]

Burke was particularly explicit in pointing out that there was no internal class revolution in the colonies and that the colonies were trying to maintain the old order. Britain had resolved that none but an obedient assembly should sit, he said, but the people there had willed otherwise. They had formed a government sufficient for its purposes without the bustle of a revolution or the troublesome formality of an election. This new government was obeyed better than the old ones ever were. Britain had tried coercion in Massachusetts, expecting immediate submission, but a vast province had existed a year without governor, judges, or magistrates. Burke listed six reasons for colonial dissension—form of government, religion in the northern colonies, manners in the southern colonies, education, English descent, and remoteness. But above all, he emphasized that the trouble involved differences between British and American interests and principles.[139]

Psychological factors, though difficult to evaluate, were cer-

[138] *Parliamentary History*, XVIII, 478–96.   [139] *Ibid.*, pp. 496–536.

tainly important, as the following from Franklin indicates. Franklin warned the British of their mistaken belief that Americans were a pack of cowardly runaways and that five hundred men with whips would make them all dance to the tune of "Yankee Doodle." It would take at least seven years to conquer the Americans, if they could be conquered, he contended, and then only at a tremendous cost in men, money, and trade.[140] Franklin said the ministers were proceeding under advice from America that Americans were divided, that a very great part disapproved the resolutions of the Continental Congress, and that these loyal subjects would break the resolutions if supported by an army. He said the ministers had no conception that such a thing as public spirit or public virtue existed.[141] A little later, Franklin had this reaction to a visit which he made to the House of Lords:

I was much disgusted, from the ministerial side, by many base reflections on American courage, religion, understanding, &c, in which we were treated with the utmost contempt, as the lowest of mankind, and almost of a different species from the English of Britain; but particularly the American honesty was abused by some of the Lords, who asserted that we were all knaves, and wanted only by this dispute to avoid paying our debts. . . . I went home somewhat irritated and heated.[142]

Members of Parliament who made so much noise that Edmund Burke could not speak, however, were not apt to listen to a Franklin.[143]

Franklin also proposed a plan for reconciliation in which he pointed out that the issues involved were some pretty fundamental differences of interests and principles between Britain and the colonies, not internal class divisions. In general, Franklin demanded equal treatment for colonists within the Empire. All acts such as the Tea Act, Massachusetts Government Act, Quebec Act, and treason act of Henry VIII were to be repealed. The Navigation Acts and acts restricting colonial manufacturing were to be reconsidered and re-enacted in the colonies. There were to be no British troops in the colonies without the con-

140 Franklin, *Writings,* VI, 299–300.   141 *Ibid.,* pp. 303–07.
142 *Ibid.,* p 396.   143 *Parliamentary History,* XVIII, 193.

sent of the colonists and a fixed system of colonial contributions to imperial defense was to be set up. Castle William must be restored to Massachusetts, the Crown could not build fortifications without the consent of the legislature, governors were to be supported by assemblies, judges were to be appointed on good behavior and given a fixed salary or appointed at pleasure with a salary voted by the legislature, admiralty courts were to be reduced to the same powers as admiralty courts in England, and acts establishing them were to be re-enacted in America, and Parliament was to disclaim all powers of internal legislation in the colonies.[144]

These, of course, were the very issues that had long been in contention. But given the sentiment in Parliament that the colonies were aiming at independence and must be controlled by the British, and also the belief that subjection of the colonies would not be difficult, Franklin's plan had no chance whatever of acceptance.[145] Even former Governor Thomas Pownall, who said that he saw the trouble as early as the Albany Congress in 1754, now supported the government, though he had previously defended the colonists.[146]

Franklin later warned that the New England colonies in particular had good reason to consider the Quebec Act as one of the Intolerable Acts. No notice had been taken of the petition sent by the Continental Congress, he said, and a petition by the colonial agents had been "rejected with scorn in the Commons." All colonies except those in New England could still make peace by acknowledging the supreme authority of Parliament, Franklin continued, but New England was "absolutely to be conquered. After which possibly they may obtain a Quebec Constitution." [147]

Given the attitude in England that the colonies were aiming at independence and must be placed under governments embodying British principles of colonial government, it was not to be expected that Britain would retreat again. But given the kind of social order that existed in Massachusetts, plus the

---

144 Franklin, *Writings*, VI, 328–40.
145 *Parliamentary History*, XVIII, 240–98.   146 *Ibid.*, pp. 322–27.
147 Franklin, *Writings*, VI, 315–17.

knowledge that British measures would bring fundamental changes in democracy, it was not to be expected that the colonists would back down either. During the winter, stores of arms and ammunition, which Gage desired to capture or destroy, were collected at strategic points near Boston.[148] This situation, combined with orders from England calling for the seizure of colonial leaders, led to the opening shots of the war—the Battle of Lexington and Concord. By this time, as John Adams had said, the "revolution" was well over in Massachusetts and the "American War" had begun.

As Adams said, the revolution was not the war: it was the change in sentiment of the colonists toward Great Britain. By 1775, the change was sufficiently complete so that the people of Massachusetts were willing to defend their institutions and property by force of arms. That democracy was a fundamental institution there can be little doubt, and that its preservation was equally fundamental seems beyond question. Enforcement of the Coercive Acts would have greatly curtailed, if not annihilated, democratic government in the colony. The people, therefore, were simply determined that the Coercive Acts should not be enforced.

The people who constituted the popular party were not what we could call the lower class or propertyless proletariat. Neither were they attempting to overthrow a local aristocracy which had entrenched itself through voting qualifications and restricted representation. The Hutchinsons and Olivers could hold office in Massachusetts only through appointment from Great Britain, and when the showdown came, even an army was not effective in preserving whatever authority they retained. But for the British, these so-called "aristocrats" would have been eliminated from politics in the colony long before 1775.

[148] *Warren-Adams Letters,* I, 94. For details of events leading up to and following the Battle of Lexington and Concord, see Harold Murdock, *The Nineteenth of April, 1775* . . . (Boston, 1923); Allen French, *General Gage's Informers* . . . (Ann Arbor, 1932), *The Day of Concord and Lexington* . . . (Boston, 1925), *The First Year of the American Revolution* (Boston, 1934), *The Siege of Boston* (New York, 1911); Richard Frothingham, *History of The Siege of Boston* . . . (Boston, 1851).

[C H A P T E R   X V]

Democracy and the
"Revolution"

IF THE "revolution" in Massachusetts was an internal social movement for a more democratic society, the evidence for such an interpretation would have to appear after the Battle of Lexington and Concord. Up to this point, there is certainly little to support such a view. Events after April 1775 should tell us a great deal about the issues involved—whether the conflict was a War of Independence against British imperialism or an American Revolution involving internal class conflict.

Instead of achieving colonial submission, the Battle of Lexington and Concord merely deepened the gulf between the colonies and Britain. Franklin said the battle had united the colonies and widened the breach between the two countries to the point of being irreparable.[1] Jefferson believed that hostili-

[1] Franklin, *Writings*, VI, 400. In addition to texts and other works already cited, the following are some of the writers who have stressed the "internal revolution": James Truslow Adams, *New England in the Republic, 1776–1850* (Boston, 1926); John Richard Alden, *The American Revolution, 1775–1783* (New York, 1954); Carl Becker, review of Hugh Edward Egerton, *The Causes and Character of the American Revolution* (Oxford, 1923), in *American Historical Review*, XXIX (Jan. 1924), 344–45; John Franklin Jameson, *The American Revolution Considered as a Social Movement* (Princeton, 1926); Merrill M. Jensen, *The Articles of Confederation: An Interpretation of the Social-Constitutional History of the American Revolution* (Madison, 1940); Leonard Woods Labaree, *Conservatism in Early American History* (New York, 1948), and "The Nature of American Loyalism," in American

ties in Massachusetts had cut off the last hope of reconciliation and that a "phrenzy of revenge" had seized "all ranks of people." Gage should have known that the people were more apt to be provoked than frightened by "haughty" actions, he declared, and that the people would not permit the punishment of men "whose sole crime has been the developing and asserting their [the people's] rights." [2] There is little of internal revolution here.

From the Second Continental Congress, which met in the spring of 1775, came indications as to the social structure of the coming revolution. John Adams reported that the military spirit throughout the continent was "truly amazing," that the martial spirit in Pennsylvania after Lexington and Concord was astonishing, and that "men of property and family, some of them of independent fortunes," were among the Pennsylvania riflemen sent to aid Massachusetts.[3] In the appointment of Washington as commander of the army, Adams declared that Washington's "independent fortune" was one of the many factors which helped him to "command the approbation of all America." [4] A man who is universally admired because of his independent fortune is not good evidence for a class struggle.

Historians have been accustomed to using the terms radical and conservative to characterize those for and against the Revolution, but these are misleading terms when applied to men of the time. Now we designate men as radical, liberal, conservative, or reactionary to indicate their social philosophies, and the point between liberal and conservative we generally call middle-of-the-road. In our present connotation of the words

---

Antiquarian Society, *Proceedings*, LIV, 15–58; Ronald S. Longley, "Mob Activities in Revolutionary Massachusetts," *New England Quarterly*, VI (March 1933), 98–130; Herbert Monfort Morais, *The Struggle for American Freedom: The First Two Hundred Years* (New York, 1944); John C. Miller, *Triumph of Freedom, 1775–83* (Boston, 1948); Arthur M. Schlesinger, "The American Revolution Reconsidered," *Political Science Quarterly*, XXXIV (March 1919), 61–78, and *New Viewpoints in American History* (New York, 1922).

[2] Jefferson, *Writings*, I, 453–54. For a factual account of political changes in Massachusetts from 1775 to 1780, see Cushing, *History of the Transition from Province to Commonwealth Government in Massachusetts, passim.*

[3] Adams, *Familiar Letters*, p. 58; *Warren-Adams Letters*, I, 57, 76.

[4] Adams, *Works*, II, 417.

then, the leaders of the Revolution were extreme left-wingers; those who opposed them were mild right-wingers. Since they believed in democracy, the revolutionary leaders could certainly be considered on the liberal side. Conversely, those who believed in aristocratic government, such as the British proposed, would undoubtedly be conservative. But the term radical does not apply to most of the people of the time, if by that term we mean a leveler, socialist, or communist. The wildest stretch of the imagination cannot make radicals out of Washington, Adams, Hancock, and the others.

John Adams was one of the early advocates for independence, yet he could scarcely be considered a champion of the lower classes against the upper classes. Adams would have been willing to see a reconciliation of Britain and the colonies if this could be obtained on a constitutional basis that would guarantee colonial rights. Given the attitude in England, however, he did not expect such a constitutional union to take place.[5] Consequently, he thought the Congress ought to set up governments in all the colonies like the government of Connecticut, which was completely elective, and federate together for mutual defense. This, he said, was the system which he had promoted from first to last.[6] Adams chafed at the delays concocted by such men as John Dickinson, who could not be considered very "radical" either.[7] But in desiring independence, Adams showed no evidence of fearing that a lower class would take over once the British were eliminated.

The reason for Adams' lack of fear of any social revolution is not difficult to find. Adams was perfectly satisfied with the democratic structure of New England society. He considered the religious and moral institutions of New England to be superior to those of any other area. Of education, he had this to say: "The public institutions in New England for the education of youth, supporting colleges at public expense, and obliging towns to maintain grammar schools, are not equaled, and never were, in any part of the world." The multifarious activi-

5 To Moses Gill, June 10, 1775, *ibid.*, IX, 356.
6 Adams to James Warren, July 6, 1775, *Warren-Adams Letters*, I, 152.
7 Burnett, *Letters*, I, 176.

ties of the town meeting gave "every man an opportunity of showing and improving that education which he received at college or at school, and makes knowledge and dexterity at public business common." And finally, the laws governing inheritance brought frequent divisions of landed property and prevented monopolies of land. These were the institutions, he said, which had preserved colonial liberties.[8] These, of course, were the institutions that Adams was trying to preserve. They were not institutions which would foster class conflict.

Under the circumstances, it is not surprising that there was not a violent overthrow of government in Massachusetts. Some of the towns and some individuals had urged that a government be established in which British influence would be eliminated and all offices would be elected by the people. But other than the elimination of the British, there was no demand for change in the structure of government itself. There was no suggestion of inequities in the franchise or in representation.[9] What the Continental Congress did was to advise that Massachusetts refuse to acknowledge any changes in her constitution and to assume the powers of government by eliminating British officials. Qualified voters were to elect representatives who in turn would elect a Council, then the House and Council would govern until a British-appointed governor agreed to abide by the charter.[10] This did not satisfy all the people in Massachusetts, some of whom were ready to eliminate Britain from colonial government completely, but the colony did not dare do anything that would disturb colonial union.[11]

The result was anything but revolutionary. Gone were the men who had upheld British policy, naturally. In their place came men who had long been active in the American cause. The Council, for example, contained few men who had not been around the General Court for many years, some as councilors, others as representatives. The Boston leaders—Bowdoin, Hancock, Samuel Adams, John Adams, Thomas Cushing—

8 Adams, *Familiar Letters*, pp. 120–21.
9 *Worcester Town Records*, IV, 240–43, 251.
10 *Journals of the Continental Congress*, II, 83–84.
11 *Warren-Adams Letters*, I, 59, 64, 66.

were all there, indicating that there was neither a sectional nor a class conflict in operation. Several men had had years of experience on the Council—James Bowdoin, James Otis, Benjamin Lincoln, James Pitts, Joseph Gerrish, Caleb Cushing, Benjamin Greenleaf, William Sever, and Walter Spooner. Others had come in 1773 or 1774—John Winthrop, Michael Farley, James Prescott, Enoch Freeman, Benjamin Chadbourn, and Jedediah Foster—but some of these had served many years in the House. Men like Artemas Ward were not on the Council as usual because they were serving as officers in the army.[12]

Of the new men on the Council, Jabez Fisher had represented Wrentham since 1766, Dr. Samuel Holton had represented Danvers since 1768, Eldad Taylor had come from Westfield in 1762, Dr. John Taylor came from Lunnenburg in 1772, and Robert Treat Paine came from Taunton in 1773. Joseph Palmer, Charles Chauncy, and Moses Gill were the only men completely new to the General Court. Palmer had replaced Ebenezer Thayer of Braintree, who had served steadily from 1760 on, but when Palmer was elected to the Council, Thayer was sent to the House again; so the election of Palmer indicated no significant change.[13] Charles Chauncy was the well-known Boston minister who had long been active in the popular cause. Moses Gill represented Princeton, which was sending a representative to the General Court for the first time. Gill married the sister of Thomas and Nicholas Boylston, the latter, according to John Adams, having one of the most magnificent homes in America. Gill, who was chairman of the committee on supplies for the army around Boston, was also noted as a money-lender and later became lieutenant governor of the state.[14]

The same absence of political revolution that characterized the Council also characterized the House of Representatives. Many of the delegates were the same men who had been coming to the General Court for years. Many representatives carried military titles of colonel, major, and captain, and just how many left the legislature to serve in the army would be difficult to say, but there were undoubtedly many. The number of rep-

---

[12] *Acts and Resolves*, XVII and XVIII, *passim.*; XIX, 3–4. [13] *Ibid.*
[14] Adams, *Works*, II, 178–79, 322, 336; IX, 356.

resentatives dropped to some 207, which was not surprising. James Warren of Plymouth replaced Thomas Cushing as speaker, when Cushing went to the Council, but again this did not represent much of a change.[15] As Warren said, the new House of Representatives had pretty nearly the same complexion that the old one had.[16]

And why would one expect a social revolution? The House of Representatives had undoubtedly reflected popular sentiments for years. Everyone at the time said this, so there is no reason to question it. We also know that councilors publicly had to hold views similar to those of the popular party, whatever they believed in private, or they were soon ousted. Given a society in which most men were middle-class property owners and therefore voters, and in which there was adequate representation, we would not expect internal revolution. The elections of House and Council in 1775 confirm this analysis.

Other incidents make it possible to judge the nature of the revolutionary movement and the men who favored and opposed it. In Hatfield, for example, Tory sentiment was perhaps as strong as it was in any other town, largely because of the influence of Israel Williams. To curb Tory activities, the town voted that anyone suspected of being inimical to the interests of the country should take an oath to defend colonial rights and oppose the late acts of Parliament. Six men were named —Israel Williams, William Williams, Elisha Allis, Samuel Partridge, David Billing, Elijah Dickinson, and Reuben Belding.[17] On the tax lists for 1772, these seven men all rated from £100 up; on the same list were twenty other men who had ratings of £100 or more.[18] Reuben Belding, who was worth £2,468 when he died in 1775,[19] was rated at £273, which would mean that anyone rated at £100 would have some £800 or £900 in property. The town's two representatives in 1775, John Hastings and Elihu White, were rated at £93 and £66 respectively.[20] So Tories were represented by some substantial citizens, pa-

[15] *Acts and Resolves*, XIX, 3–5.
[16] To S. Adams, July 20, 1775, Adams Papers.
[17] Hatfield Town Records, IV, 261.   [18] Hatfield Assessors' List, 1772.
[19] Hampshire County Probate Records, XIII, 167–68.
[20] *Acts and Resolves*, XIX, 5; Hatfield Assessors' List, 1772.

triots were represented by nearly three times as many substantial citizens, and the town's representatives were in the middle economic group.

That sectional conflict was not involved is attested by the actions of Worcester. Worcester from time to time had passed some of the strongest resolves and instructions to representatives passed by any of the towns. In May 1775, the town had repeated these strong instructions, including a statement that the representative should do everything possible to subject Gage and his army. Yet the town voted not to send more than one representative, then voted down two motions to reconsider its decision to send only one delegate. Worcester sent a new man, David Bancroft, in 1775 but in July the town sent a second representative, Joshua Bigelow, who had been the town's delegate since 1767.[21] If representation or other internal conflicts had been the issue, towns like Worcester would certainly have sent as many delegates as possible.

This new General Court, which was organized in July 1775, on instructions from the Continental Congress, did pass one act which at first glance might be misconstrued as evidence of internal unrest. This was an act for equalizing representation in the colony. In October 1774, the First Provincial Congress had appointed a committee of Hawley, Cushing, and Gerry to bring in a resolve on equal representation, but nothing seems to have been done. In May 1775, however, the Third Provincial Congress voted to recommend that towns and districts send as many representatives as they considered "necessary and expedient." This vote was reconsidered the following day and a committee was appointed to bring in a resolve on equal representation, but again nothing was done.[22] Finally, Hawley introduced a bill in August 1775, which passed within a short time.[23]

One might expect that any change of representation would be done to benefit the underrepresented larger towns, especially those along the seacoast. But did this happen? No. The bill con-

---

[21] Representatives' lists, *Acts and Resolves*, XVIII, *passim.*; XIX, 4–5; *Worcester Town Records*, IV, 263–67.

[22] *Journals of Each Provincial Congress*, pp. 40, 196, 198, 208.

[23] *Acts and Resolves*, V, 411.

demned the old British policy of restricting representation through the formation of districts without the right of representation. This practice was branded as "against common right, and in derogation of the rights granted to the inhabitants of this colony by the charter." The new law provided that these unrepresented districts could have a representative. Any town with thirty voters, qualified according to the charter, could henceforth send a delegate.[24] Since these towns had always voted with neighboring agricultural towns, and since they seldom sent as many delegates as they were entitled to send anyway, the act simply gave more representation to the agricultural towns which had not used what they already had. Why the General Court did this is not clear from the records, unless it was anxious to get the support of as many towns as possible, for the towns themselves do not appear to have demanded representation.

Not until the General Court had granted additional delegates to the overrepresented agricultural towns did the seaport towns become concerned about the problem of representation. A convention of Essex County towns was called in April 1776 to protest against the new representation law. The broadside calling for the convention stated that independence was near and undoubtedly the people would establish a republic or a commonwealth. It was important, therefore, that each man should have equal liberty and equal right of representation. The mode of representation had long been somewhat inequitable, the broadside stated, and was made more so by the late act which allowed a town of thirty voters to send a representative but did not increase representation for towns with 300 to 3,000 freeholders.[25]

Although representation had not been an internal issue until the law of 1775 was passed, there is no doubt whatever that representation under the charter was inequitable. The Essex Convention pointed out that one town in Essex County paid more taxes than thirty other towns in the province, yet these thirty towns had fifteen times the representation.[26] As a matter

24 *Ibid.*, p. 419.
25 "Broadside," in Essex Institute, *Historical Collections*, XXXVI, 104.
26 *Acts and Resolves*, V, 542–43.

of fact, the combined taxes of more than forty other towns were less than the taxes paid by Salem. One town, which paid £9 in taxes, had half the representation of Salem, which paid £1,372.[27]

Within a few days after the Essex Convention, the General Court passed another representation law to remove the injustice by increasing representation for large towns. The new law said that towns with 120 voters could send two delegates, just as the old colonial law had done, but each additional 100 voters in a town entitled it to an additional representative.[28] This law still favored towns with less than a hundred voters, but certainly it was more equitable than the old law had been. The change of representation might have been important if representation had been an internal issue during colonial days, but it never was.

Aside from the controversy over representation, there was little evidence during the summer of 1775 that the conflict was an American Revolution, but there was a great deal that it was a War of Independence.

Popular enthusiasm for the American cause and against Britain and her adherents still continued to run high. An Anglican minister reported that the "predominant infatuation" of the time had reached his parish in Falmouth and spread "with increasing and frightful rapidity." Resolutions of both congresses were "carried into execution with relentless and inhuman severity." As soon as a man was marked as a friend of government, this minister continued, his property and life were in danger. In spite of the fact that the inhabitants were being reduced almost to starvation, however, they showed no disposition to submit. This man did think that friends of government were more numerous than was commonly imagined. But dissenting ministers fanned the flames of sedition, accusing the Anglican clergy of being inimical to their country and "conspiring with administration to establish popery thro' all the American dominions." [29] This, of course, was a reference to the Quebec Act.

[27] Ibid., pp. 423-33.   [28] Ibid., pp. 502-03.
[29] SPG Archives, XXII, ser. B, pp. 122-25.

Two other observers believed that pro-American sentiment was much stronger and certainly more universal than the Anglican minister had thought. One wrote that anyone who did not encourage the people to resist was apt to be considered a Tory. Encouragement did not seem necessary, however, he continued, "as they are much higher & determined than either of us imagined. The uninimity [*sic*] of ye colonies is amazing; & their determination to suffer ye last extremity before they submit is beyond the conception of any person in G. Britain." [30]

Another writer tried to correct the misconception in England that the trouble in the colonies was due to the efforts of a few men only. "You no doubt have been told that the quarrel on this side, has been fomented by a few factious men but I assure you this is not the case, the people throughout the colonies are as generally for the measures pursued, as we can suppose . . . such a body of people to be." Some people whose property was affected by measures enacted for the public good naturally complained, he continued, and this was especially true in New York. There some people had long benefited by the fact that the British army and navy had been stationed in the city for many years. Consequently, there were more Tories in New York City than in half the country. [31]

If there was any fear at the time that a break with England might result in an uprising of lower classes, it is not apparent in the actions of John Adams. Instead of fearing independence, Adams, by the summer of 1775, was afraid that something would happen to make a reconciliation possible. He said Congress was greatly divided over what to do. Some men believed that the British would back down when they heard of the Battle of Lexington and Concord, the spirit in New York and Philadelphia, and the strength of colonial union. These men would be deceived, he thought, yet they must be humored for the sake of union. So Congress presented a strange sight—preparations for war and negotiations for peace, petitions to the king and proposals for negotiation. Adams dreaded this negotiation, yet

[30] Library of Congress Transcripts, Public Record Office, Colonial Office 5, XL, 167.
[31] *Ibid.*, pp. 156–57.

it must be proposed, he said, to avoid colonial discord and disunion. He hoped that the ministers would fear negotiation and refuse it, for otherwise the colonies might be deceived, wheedled, threatened, or bribed out of their freedom.[32]

By October 1775, John Adams thought the colonies should prepare for the worst, that is, a War of Independence. Adams said he had been engaged in the public cause of America from his earliest entrance into public life, and from first to last, he had had a strong impression that things would eventually reach their present crisis. He had seen from the beginning that the controversy was of such a nature that it would never be settled, and every day confirmed this conviction. He had long held, and greatly dreaded, the thought that the colonies would be driven to independence. Even now, he would willingly have given up public life, public honor, and his own property for peace and liberty; but these had to be sacrificed before he would surrender the right of his country to a free constitution.[33] As this passage shows, Adams believed that his efforts were designed to preserve the free constitution which Massachusetts had, not to achieve a more democratic constitution.

The following examples reflect little of an internal class conflict. William Palfrey wanted the colonies to become independent so that they could unite in the most glorious of all causes, "the defense of our liberties and property." [34] The General Court recommended that Harvard examine the political principles of its instructors to see whether their past or present conduct appeared unfriendly to the privileges and liberties of the colonies.[35] When the Continental Congress sanctioned a new government in New Hampshire, the New Hampshire delegates recommended the constitution of Massachusetts as the best model—one with "a free representation." The delegates expressed joy with their new government and hoped "never to return to our former despotick state." [36] And in a proclamation, the General Court declared that the only foundation of government was the consent of the people. The British had ignored

32 *Warren-Adams Letters*, I, 73.   33 Adams, *Works*, I, 190.
34 Palfrey to S. Adams, Oct. 3, 1775, Adams Papers.
35 *Acts and Resolves*, XIX, 103.   36 Burnett, *Letters*, I, 246–47.

this principle in attempting for many years to establish a sovereignty over the American people without their consent. Government had consequently been suspended, the General Court continued, "And mankind has seen a phenomenon without example in the political world, a large and populous colony subsisting in great decency and order for more than a year under such a suspension of government." [37]

When the question of independence was under consideration during the winter of 1775–1776, it is not surprising that there was little fear of an internal change which might accompany independence. John Pitts was ready to make a complete break with England as early as October 1775, and Pitts believed that this was the general sentiment in Massachusetts. [38] In November, James Warren proposed that the colonies stop petitioning and declare independence. [39] When Warren wrote to John Adams that there was universal sentiment for independence in the colony, Adams replied that the colonies had been independent since the Battle of Lexington and Concord. [40] Councilor John Winthrop said that the people of Massachusetts were impatiently waiting for Congress to declare independence, and if Congress did not act soon, he would not guarantee that Massachusetts would not go ahead with its own declaration. [41]

To these men, the "revolution" was the break with England, not an internal class conflict. "For God's sake let there be a full revolution, or all has been done in vain," exclaimed Joseph Hawley, as he pointed out all the advantages of independence. "Independency, and a well planned continental government, will save us." [42] John Adams wrote in June 1775 that committees were appointed to draw up a continental constitution and a declaration of independence. When these committees reported, he said, "the last finishing strokes will be given to the politics of this revolution. Nothing after that will remain but war." [43]

Carter Braxton of Virginia also explained why the conflict was a War of Independence and not an internal social revolu-

[37] Adams, *Works*, I, 193.　　　[38] To Adams, Oct. 25, 1775, Adams Papers.
[39] To S. Adams, Nov. 12, 1775, *ibid.*　　　[40] *Warren-Adams Letters*, I, 225.
[41] Mass. Hist. Soc., *Collections*, 5th ser., IV, 296.
[42] Force, *American Archives*, 4th ser., V, 1168–69.
[43] Adams, *Works*, IX, 409.

tion. The colony already had a democratic social order and was determined to keep what it had. Said Braxton:

Two of the New England colonies enjoy a government purely democratical the nature and principle of which both civil and religious are so totally incompatible with monarchy that they have ever lived in a restless state under it. The other two tho' not so popular in their frame bordered so near upon it that monarchical influence hung very heavy on them. The best opportunity in the world being now offered them to throw off all subjection and embrace their darling democracy they are determined to accept it.

Braxton did believe that there were serious conflicts, potential or actual, between some of the colonies, especially over land claims, but he did not seem to question the idea that Massachusetts had a democratic society.[44]

When it finally came, independence was something of an anticlimax in Massachusetts. John Adams suggested that, instead of declaring its own independence, the colony should wait for the others but that it could instruct its delegates to vote for independence.[45] Even this move was carried out in a democratic fashion. The General Court passed a resolution which was sent out and voted on by the towns. In the town meetings there was very little controversy over the issue; and, in fact, one might say there was very little interest. Some towns recorded the vote as unanimous; others merely said they would support independence with their lives and property, but they did not indicate that there was any opposition.[46] In Pittsfield, only two men voted against independence.[47] One significant measure of the general indifference was the total Boston vote of only 272.[48] Apparently these people all believed that the revolution was over and, as Adams said, all that remained was the war.

In voting for independence, many of the towns adopted instructions to their representatives which further emphasize the

[44] Burnett, *Letters*, I, 420–21.
[45] Mass. Hist. Soc., *Collections*, 5th ser., IV, 300–01.
[46] Andover Town Records, June 12, 1776; Malden Town Records, II, 85; *Worcester Town Records*, IV, 277; Hadley Town Records, May 30, 1776; Hatfield Town Records, IV, 268.
[47] Pittsfield Town Records, June 15, 1776.
[48] *Boston Town Records*, XVIII, 234.

absence of social revolution in Massachusetts. Topsfield wanted the state to continue to use the rules of government as found in the charter, which, said the town, was what the province had been contending for.[49] Plymouth demanded a government which would insure permanent harmony among the colonies, particularly one in which the legislative and executive offices were completely separated.[50] Boston declared that preservation of internal peace and harmony required that the constituent body be satisfied that it was fully and fairly represented. It was particularly essential to liberty that the legislative, executive, and judicial powers be separated from each other. When they were united in the same persons, there was a lack of check which was the principal security against arbitrary laws. Judges were to hold office during good behavior, not at the pleasure of someone else.[51] Boston's instructions represented years of experience with arbitrary British measures and methods by which arbitrary power could be checked in the future. But none of these towns gave instructions which signified violent or even mild social change. In fact, such items as separation of powers, checks and balances, and the appointment of judges for life, when they were incorporated into the federal Constitution, have been considered quite conservative.

An examination of the town records reveals that the men who were responsible for these resolutions and instructions for independence were hardly lower-class proletarians. Malden resolved itself into a committee of the whole with the Reverend Mr. Willis as chairman.[52] The Sheffield committee to instruct its representative was headed by Colonel John Ashley, the largest property owner in town.[53] In Andover, Samuel Phillips, the town's wealthiest citizen, headed the committee of correspondence, inspection, and safety, Asa Foster was moderator of the town meeting which voted for independence, and other leading men were on the committee with Phillips.[54] Northampton's

[49] *Topsfield Town Records,* II, 359.
[50] *Plymouth Town Records,* III, 315.
[51] *Boston Town Records,* XVIII, 236–38.
[52] Malden Town Records, II, 85.
[53] Sheffield Town Records, June 18, 1776; Sheffield Tax Lists, *passim.*
[54] Andover Town Records, March 4 and June 17, 1776.

committee of correspondence, inspection, and safety was headed by Joseph Hawley and contained such names as Deacon Josiah Clark, Seth Pomeroy, Joseph Lyman, and Caleb Strong.[55] Indicative that these "revolutionary" leaders were neither up-starts nor propertyless is the fact that nine of the committee of sixteen had substantial ratings on the tax list for 1765, and one, Seth Pomeroy, was rated more than twice as much as any other man in town.[56]

A few isolated incidents might be taken as evidence for in-ternal revolution except for the fact that they do not appear to have been representative of any important segment of the population. The Reverend Thomas Allen of Pittsfield de-nounced the charter as a bad constitution and advocated that the people oppose it. He warned the people that while they were fighting against oppression by king and Parliament, usurp-ers might rise up among them. Allen was very suspicious of the General Court and the Continental Congress. He did not seem to understand that the delay in declaring independence and the expedient of using the old charter were both done to insure support from other colonies. He branded as wrong any gov-ernment in which officials were not elected directly by the people instead of being appointed. Just what Allen wanted is not too clear and apparently was not too clear to the General Court, for it appointed a commission to investigate and report any grievances.[57]

Then there is the account by John Winthrop of efforts to prevent the courts from sitting in Hampshire and Berkshire Counties and in Taunton, Bristol County. Winthrop said there were three grounds for complaint: (1) fees and court charges were extravagantly high, (2) commissions of judges and justices ran in the name of the king, and (3) some men who were ob-noxious to the people had been commissioned. The General Court had answered the first complaint with an act which con-siderably reduced fees and the second with an act to eliminate the king's name in commissions. The third grievance remained as no officers had yet been displaced. Then Winthrop went

55 Northampton Town Records, III, 24. 56 *Ibid.*, II, 123–24.
57 Mass. Arch., CXXXVII, 76–78; Judd Diary, II, March 12, 1776.

on as follows: "Some suspect these are only feasible reasons, and that the true ground . . . is the unwillingness to submit to law and pay their debts." [58]

If we accepted what "some suspect" to be the real cause, we would certainly have some basis for internal social conflict. But since the government eliminated two of the grievances, it is just possible that these were actually the real grievances. Some rather bitter feeling had been generated between men who had upheld the king's authority and those who favored the American cause. If men who had been suspected of Toryism or had been only lukewarm in the patriot cause still held commissions, opposition to the courts on the part of the people would be perfectly understandable. After all, they had prevented the sitting of the courts when the judges were British-appointed and held their commissions under one of the Intolerable Acts.

This same letter from John Winthrop to John Adams contains other suggestions of social revolution. Winthrop spoke of the "spirit of innovation" which prevailed and which might alter everything. The newspapers were continually teeming with new projects. And what were they? Some people wanted such "revolutionary" innovations as county assemblies, a registry of deeds in each town, and the probating of wills to be made in each town by an elected committee.[59] The first was probably the result of the county conventions in 1774 and the Essex County convention on representation in 1776. It might be considered as revolutionary, but it is difficult to see what county assemblies could accomplish that town instructions to representatives would not do equally well. The other two proposals were merely devices which would lessen the expense for property owners in registering deeds and probating estates. John Adams spoke of these proposals as "that rage for innovation which appears in so many wild shapes in our province." [60] But even if these proposals were widely supported, which apparently they were not, they would hardly constitute evidence of an internal social revolution.

[58] Mass. Hist. Soc., *Collections*, 5th ser., IV, 306–07.
[59] *Ibid.*, pp. 307–08.   [60] *Ibid.*, p. 310.

A petition from Salem to the General Court might also be mistaken as evidence of discontent of a "city proletariat" and a downtrodden lower class. The town asked for an abatement of taxes because of its distressing circumstances. Salem was a maritime town, said the petition, with few people engaged in agriculture. Now all their trade, fishing, and handicraft work had been stopped because of the impending war, making it difficult for Salem citizens to earn a living. Many owned their homes—seamen, fishermen, housewrights, masons, coopers, and others—but these houses yielded nothing but a shelter for their owners. Men without work and traders without goods could not pay taxes.[61] But it should be noted that the conditions were unusual, that the men referred to were skilled workers, not "laborers," and that they owned their homes, which would make them voters.

If the purpose of the revolution in Massachusetts was to preserve a social order rather than to change it, we would expect to find little alteration in the social structure after the revolution started. The prediction would be correct, for perhaps the most significant feature of the revolution was the absence of internal change. As Samuel Adams put it: "We have however gone from step to step, till at length we are arrived at perfection, as you have heard, in a Declaration of Independence. Was there ever a revolution brought about, especially so important as this without great internal tumults & violent convulsions!" [62] Had there been sharp class conflicts or important sectional disputes in the colony, Adams could never have made this statement.

For one thing, the election of the council in 1776 makes the election of the Council of 1775 look even less revolutionary than it previously had. In 1775, Timothy Danielson, Benjamin Austin, William Phillips, Artemas Ward, Richard Derby, and Jeremiah Powell were all omitted from the Council, though all had served in 1774. But these men were back on the Council in 1776, indicating that their absence in 1775 was probably due to causes other than their political views. Names such as Samuel

[61] Mass. Arch., CLXXX, 275–77.   [62] Adams, *Writings*, III, 304.

Adams, John Adams, John Hancock, and Robert Treat Paine were naturally missing in 1776 for these men had other work to do.[63]

Absence of change is also evident in the one area in which change might have been expected—representation. The law of 1776 permitting larger towns to send more than two representatives did bring a short flurry of increased representation, but the flurry did not last long. Boston increased its delegation from four to twelve and nine other towns in Suffolk County sent more than the one member they customarily sent. But in 1777, Boston decreased its number to seven and all the other towns went back to one. From 1777 to 1787, only four towns in the county ever sent two delegates—Roxbury in 1785, Hingham in 1778, Dedham in 1781 and 1785, and Stoughton in 1780. Towns in Essex County did a little better, but not much. In 1776, Salem sent seven representatives; Ipswich, Newbury, Newburyport, Marblehead, and Gloucester sent five each; and Andover sent four. But after 1776, only three towns ever sent more than two delegates and sometimes they sent only two. In total numbers, the county representation went from twenty-three in 1775 to forty-eight in 1776, then dropped back to thirty-two, twenty-six, twenty-nine, twenty-six, twenty-eight, twenty-seven, eighteen, twenty-four, twenty-four, twenty-eight, and twenty-seven during the next few years. Worcester County apparently did not realize what had happened for not a single town sent more than one delegate in 1776. The next year, however, fifteen towns sent from two to four representatives each. Then in 1778, only one town sent more than one delegate, and from that time until 1787, not a single town in the county ever sent more than one representative.[64]

The increased representation for a short time can probably be explained as apprehension that some significant changes *might* be made. When nothing happened, most of the towns simply reverted to their old practice of sending only one delegate.

[63] *Acts and Resolves,* XIX, 417.

[64] Data from representatives lists in *ibid.,* XIX, XX, and XXI; *Acts and Laws of the Commonwealth of Massachusetts* (Boston, 1780– b), I–IV.

Certainly the new law did not materially change the dominance of the agricultural over the seaport towns. Most of the inland towns could have sent from two to six delegates at any time, which was enough to insure control of the legislature whenever the agricultural towns desired.

If the views of the Reverend Allen of Pittsfield had been widely held—that the charter was an unacceptable constitution—one of the first evidences of internal revolution should have been the adoption of a new frame of government. That this did not take place for four years is in itself testimony that there was not much dissatisfaction with the form of government. In fact, Topsfield, one of the small agricultural towns, specifically stated that the rules of government in the charter were to be retained after independence as these were the very things for which the province had been contending.[65]

If there had been unrest because property qualifications for voting prevented democratic representation, one of the first internal changes should have been an attack on the voting franchise. But again nothing of this sort took place. There seemed to be no question that the new state would continue to use the old qualifications both for province and town voting. After the long period of agitation in which the common people talked of dying for their rights and liberties, it is inconceivable that property restrictions on voting could have been considered a grievance and still have remained undisturbed. Among the innovations mentioned by John Winthrop, nothing was said about changing the voting franchise. On the other hand, if most men could vote, it would be natural that voting qualifications would not be an issue and would not be altered.

Similarly, there were no indications of internal revolution in other institutions and practices where internal discontent should have manifested itself. The Congregational Church remained as it had been, a semiestablished church, and there seemed to be little if any dissatisfaction over this arrangement in a society composed mainly of Congregationalists. Education, which John Adams had called the best in the world for the ordinary citizen,

[65] *Topsfield Town Records*, II, 359.

continued as it had been. There was no change in the laws governing property holding or inheritance, since Massachusetts did not employ the practices of entail and primogeniture.

Writing in 1778, John Adams explained why there was so little internal change after the Declaration of Independence. First, there already was economic democracy. "The agrarian in America is divided among the common people in every state, in such a manner, that nineteen twentieths of the property would be in the hands of the commons, let them appoint whom they could for chief magistrate and senators," he wrote.[66] In the second place, Adams believed that there had always been political democracy. "The truth is," he continued, "that the people have ever governed in America; all the force of royal governors and councils, even backed by fleets and armies, has never been able to get the advantage of them, who have stood by their houses of representatives in every instance, and have always carried their points." [67]

The process by which Massachusetts adopted a state constitution and the kind of constitution which the state adopted are perhaps the best evidence available that there was little internal revolution involved. If ever a constitution was adopted democratically, it was the Massachusetts constitution. If ever men had the opportunity to express their direct views on the kind of government they wanted and to influence the kind of government they got, it was in the adoption of the Massachusetts constitution.

The method by which the constitution was to be written and accepted seems to have been proposed by Pittsfield. The town vetoed suggestions that the General Court adopt a constitution, calling such suggestions "the rankest kind of Toryism, the self same monster we are now fighting against." Pittsfield contended that the General Court could write the constitution, but it could not become effective until the people had sanctioned it.[68] But the General Court did not proceed with a constitution until it had consulted the towns. *All adult men,* not just the qualified voters, were to vote on whether the General Court

[66] Adams, *Works,* IV, 359.   [67] *Ibid.,* p. 360.
[68] Pittsfield memorial, May 29, 1776, Mass. Arch., CLXXXI, 42–45.

should write a frame of government; and though some towns objected to this method of forming a constitution, a substantial majority seem to have agreed. There was no discernible sectional pattern in the returns.[69] With this popular mandate, the General Court decided that the next election would be held with the understanding that the General Court so elected would write a constitution.[70]

Some of the instructions drawn up by the towns to their representatives show us what the people wanted and how the democratic process worked. Hatfield, for example, sent John Hastings, who was *first* to concern himself with "the public honor of God, the secure establishment of the Christian religion & the preservation of the rights of conscience." In other words, religion was the most important item to these people. Next came civil rights and privileges. The town wanted a bill of rights specifying the inalienable rights of the people so that freedom and property would be protected. There should also be a *reduction* in the number of representatives in the assembly, to be chosen by persons who had sufficient interest and property in the state to make them attentive to its welfare. Governor and Council, as well as representatives, were to be elected directly by the people in such a way that they would represent the whole commonwealth, not just sections of it. Hastings was to work for these items in his instructions, but if the majority of the people decided differently, Hatfield would acquiesce in the will of the majority, provided there was "no capital infringement of the essential privileges of the people." [71]

These Hatfield instructions are not at all surprising, given the background that has been presented here. That they would want religion safeguarded would be natural in a society which emphasized religion, especially the Congregational religion. Since the state was so completely represented, the demand for a reduction of representatives was also logical. We would expect

[69] *Plymouth Town Records*, III, 317; Marblehead Town Records, IV, 248; Springfield Town Records, IV, 438; Sheffield Town Records, Sept. 26, 1776; Pittsfield Town Records, I, 230.

[70] *Journal of the Convention for Framing a Constitution of Government for the State of Massachusetts Bay* . . . (Boston, 1832), pp. 255–56.

[71] Hatfield Town Records, IV, 273–74.

a middle-class society, accustomed to property qualifications for voting, to demand that voters have property, especially since the revolution was not designed to change the social order. And finally, in a society long accustomed to the democratic process, we would expect the town to be willing to acquiesce in the will of the majority.

Space does not permit an analysis of the Constitution of 1778 and the reasons for its rejection. Suffice to say that it was submitted to a vote of *all* adult males and was rejected by a vote of nearly five to one as best we can tell from records that are not too clear. Some of the reasons were these: The constitution should have been drawn up by a special convention, in order to make the constitution superior to the legislature. In general, qualifications for voting and office holding were not considered sufficiently high, though a few towns did favor abolition of property qualifications. There was not a sufficient check and balance or separation of powers provided. Towns objected that qualified Negroes and Indians were to be excluded from the franchise. Some of the towns, and particularly a convention in Essex County, objected that property rights were not sufficiently safeguarded. Several towns suggested that the drawing up of a government be postponed until the soldiers came home and could participate. What some towns approved, others disapproved, so it is almost impossible to get a clear picture of the objections, but there was no doubt that the constitution was unsatisfactory.[72]

After the Constitution of 1778 was rejected, there was a threat of a mild uprising in Berkshire County which might be taken as evidence of class conflict. Delegates from several towns met to petition the General Court. These delegates said that they had contributed their share of men and supplies in the war, but despite their efforts, designing men had called them a "mobbish ungovernable refractory, licentious and dissolate [sic] people." The reason seems to have been that they had stopped the courts because of a fear that they were to be deprived of a constitution.

[72] *Result of the Convention of Delegates Holden at Ipswich in the County of Essex* . . . (Newbury-Port, 1778), *passim.* Town returns are in Mass. Arch., CLVI, 304–432, CLX, 1–31.

But they said that it was better to stop the courts than have justice dealt out piecemeal without any foundation to support it. What they demanded was a bill of rights and a constitution. They said that four-fifths of the people were against the sitting of courts until a constitution had been established and accepted by the people. In closing, the delegates threatened that if their demands were refused, there were other states with constitutions which would gladly accept them—presumably New York and New Hampshire.[73]

The General Court soon acted to put out this potential fire. It sent a committee to investigate all grievances or anything the people supposed to be a grievance.[74] The committee investigated and discovered that the people were opposed to "executive" courts instead of regularly constituted civil courts. Apparently the committee satisfied most of the towns that there was no sinister design against their freedom, for the delegates praised the justness of the investigating committee, and fourteen of the sixteen towns represented voted that the present constitution was valid until a new one could be adopted. The committee reported that if proper civil officers were appointed for Berkshire County, the clamors about executive courts would quickly subside.[75]

If the Berkshire attitude had been general, an interpretation of the situation at the time would be relatively easy. We might well believe that a class conflict existed and that an upper class

[73] Mass. Arch., CLXXXIV, 196–98; CCXX, 456–61.   [74] *Ibid.*, CCXX, 134.

[75] *Ibid.*, pp. 452–60. Taylor, in *Western Massachusetts,* emphasized the importance of the "Berkshire Constitutionalists," but his evidence does not always substantiate his thesis. The evidence shows that Hampshire did not back Berkshire consistently and that even Berkshire was badly divided (pp. 81–82, 92–94). On the Constitution of 1780, the author emphasized the six towns which objected to property qualifications for voting, not the eighty or more which did not object. Placing the emphasis on the small minority rather than the large majority results in the tail wagging the dog (pp. 89–91). Since Pittsfield led the fight for a constitution, why is it necessary to assume that the town voted unanimously for the constitution "more in despair than in hope probably" (p. 91)? Since the town had never been backward in expressing its views, why not assume that the unanimous vote signified satisfaction with the constitution? Taylor claimed that action by Stockbridge "clearly illustrates the class conflict underlying the Constitutional struggle," but two petitions cited as evidence do not show class conflict. Neither does the fact that the *average* assessment of the nine signers of one petition was

was attempting to maintain control by preventing the adoption of a more democratic government. But the facts do not bear out such an interpretation. About the same time as the Berkshire complaint, the General Court, still functioning under the Charter of 1691, sent out a request for the towns to vote whether they wanted a new constitution and, if so, whether they wished for a special convention.[76] This was a logical step, for anyone in Boston who had access to all the returns and petitions from the towns would not have known what the people as a whole wanted. Some demanded a new constitution, others demanded that the old charter be used, and some wanted to wait until the soldiers had returned so that they could participate.

The vote on whether to have a new constitution shows definitely that the attitude in Berkshire County was the exception rather than the rule. The total vote was 5,654 to 2,049 in favor of a new constitution, but the significant point is that this represented less than 15 per cent of the qualified voters.[77] Furthermore, the fact that some little towns, such as Beckley, Gorham, Boxford, Acton, Pembroke, and Medway voted unanimously against the proposition while other small agricultural towns voted unanimously for it simply defies interpretation. We cannot even tell the significance of the vote in the seacoast towns. Boston and Marblehead voted unanimously for a constitutional convention, but only thirty people voted in Marblehead, a town which could send at least five representatives to the General Court. Plymouth, Salem, and Newburyport voted

---

£1,900 while the average of signers of the other petition was only £671. We would need to know how much the assessments of individuals overlapped before we could determine the class connotations (p. 97). Petitions of both factions, which were similar, were voted on by the town and the result was 54 to 54. The vote of 66 to 0 by which the town agreed to abide by the Pittsfield convention resolutions accepting the government as legal does not prove either class conflict or abstention by the constitutionalists. Perhaps they were just satisfied. And the fact that several towns where constitutionalists had controlled failed even to suggest changes in the Constitution of 1780 does not prove that the people so longed for the re-establishment of law and order that they were willing to sacrifice their principles (p. 100). It would be much simpler to say that they approved of the constitution and voted accordingly. And we should not forget that the Reverend Allen of Pittsfield, leader of the Berkshire Constitutionalists, was, like Samuel Adams, an opponent of Shays' Rebellion.

[76] Mass. Arch., CLX, 32.   [77] *Ibid.*, CCXXIII, 192.

unanimously against it; Ipswich split its vote 41 for and 68 against; and Gloucester apparently did not vote.[78] The vote simply did not indicate a great popular upsurge for a new constitution; in fact, one might say it represented a great deal of indifference.

There is much humor to be found in the returns from the towns to the General Court, of which this report from Oakham is but a sample: "Voted unanimously in the affirmative except one person who is an old insignificant Torry and never ought to vote in any case." [79]

Before the returns were in there was still some agitation in the western part of the state because of the lack of a constitution and the refusal by some men to recognize the legality of the General Court. On March 22, 1779, Stockbridge voted on whether the present government was valid and split its vote 54 to 54. A week later, March 29, however, the town voted unanimously to support the General Court.[80] A convention of twenty-three towns in Hampshire County requested a special convention for a constitution in spite of the fact that the towns were then voting on just this question.[81] Hadley decided to allow the courts to sit as usual in the county,[82] but Pittsfield refused to permit the holding of courts until a constitution was adopted.[83] Sheffield voted on whether to petition the General Court that Berkshire County be allowed to join a neighboring state that had a constitution if the people of Massachusetts failed to adopt one themselves.[84]

In deciding to have a constitutional convention, many of the towns confirmed the view stated in an earlier chapter that there was no dissatisfaction with the apportionment of representation before 1775. Some of the towns specifically stated that they wanted the constitutional convention called on the apportionment in effect before 1775. Petersham elaborated. The town declared that the new system was unsafe as it gave the mercan-

[78] *Ibid.,* CLX, 33–52; CCXXIII, 198–201; Marblehead Town Records, IV, 309.
[79] Mass. Arch., CLX, 98.
[80] Stockbridge Town Records, March 22 and 29, 1779.
[81] Mass. Arch., CLXXXV, 147.
[82] Hadley Town Records, March 10, 1779.
[83] Pittsfield Town Records, II, 51.   [84] Sheffield Town Records, II, 7.

tile interest too much power in the legislature in comparison with agriculture and manufacturing. The mercantile interest would discourage manufacturing and both were equally important to the farmer. Furthermore, the sharp practices of the merchant tended to corrupt the morals of the people.[85] The division here was obviously that of rival economic or property groups, not upper against lower class, but again it shows that the small agricultural towns were satisfied with representation before the Revolution.

Both the election of delegates to the constitutional convention and the ratification of the constitution which this convention would devise were to be as democratic as manhood suffrage could make them. The General Court decided that towns could send as many delegates as they were allowed to send representatives. *Every free adult man* could vote for these delegates and *every free adult man* could vote on ratification. There were no property restrictions in either instance. If two-thirds of those voting approved, the constitution was to be adopted.[86] In brief,

[85] Mass. Arch., CLX, 107; CLXXXV, 167–68.

[86] *Ibid.*, CLX, 125; CCXXIII, 190; *Journal of the Convention, 1779–1780*, p. 6. The most widely accepted interpretation of the constitution, that by Samuel Eliot Morison ("The Struggle over the Adoption of the Constitution of Massachusetts, 1780," Mass. Hist. Soc., *Proceedings*, L[1917], 353–412), is the conspiracy thesis that the convention rigged ratification to insure acceptance regardless of the people's wishes.

The Morison interpretation is open to many criticisms. Morison stressed the severe winter of 1780 as a factor in creating a thin final session of the convention, but this did not account for the declining attendance in the fall session of 1779 or the decline from 82 on February 16 to 36 on February 28. The material on pages 360–64 is completely unsupported except for John Adams' fear of innovations in 1776 and Pittsfield's claim that the constitution would have been defeated if it had been submitted in toto. If the people were as tenacious of power and jealous of their rights or if they did not understand the constitution, as Morison said, they could have defeated the constitution. If fourteen weeks of discussion were not enough, how many were needed? There is no evidence for the inference that the "gloomy spring" of 1780 had any influence. And if the people showed remarkable insight into problems of government and anticipated future amendments (p. 365), they must have been fully aware of what they were doing.

Article III on religion was not liberal, but it did not "virtually" establish Congregationalism as the state religion (p. 368). If it was "reactionary" (p. 371), it was also customary and was accepted by the people. It is not necessary to assume that the people could not vote or that they were misled in order to explain the adoption of "conservative" measures. Universal suffrage in this country has not guaranteed the election of "liberals." As a matter of fact, Morison shows (pp. 365–68) that it is impossible to tell how many people favored or opposed Article III.

no instrument of government could be adopted unless it met the approval of a large portion of the adult men, including any "disfranchised masses" if such existed.

Again the election of delegates to the constitutional convention signifies a great deal of indifference in the state rather than sharp class or sectional conflict. We would expect Berkshire and Hampshire Counties to flood the convention with as many delegates as they could if there had been really serious disaffection there. But nothing of the sort happened. Pittsfield, the ringleader, sent only one delegate, though the town had once sent three representatives, and that delegate was William Williams, Esquire, who had first represented the town in the General Court in 1765.[87] Returns in the *Boston Gazette* show that twenty-three out of fifty-six towns in Hampshire County and nine out of thirty-one in Berkshire County did not even send delegates.[88] Marblehead elected only two, Thomas Gerry and Joshua Orne, instead of the five or more to which the town was entitled, and when both men refused to serve, the town voted not to send any delegates. Later Marblehead reconsidered and sent four men, but there did not seem to be much enthusiasm in the town over a constitution.[89] Northampton voted to send delegates to the convention, but as the meeting was "thin," the town suspended the choice of men "untill the people should be more generally collected." Then Northampton elected Ephriam Wright and Caleb Strong.[90]

If the analysis of Massachusetts society thus far is correct, we would not expect to find a very "radical" convention even

---

Morison also misinterpreted the franchise requirements in the Constitution of 1780 (pp. 389-90). There was little objection to property qualifications, these qualifications were not 50 per cent higher than the province qualification, and an "important segment of the population" did not formally consent "to its own disfranchisement." It is not logical to assume that the people fought to democratize American society, then voted to disfranchise themselves.

As others have done, Morison emphasized the few who objected rather than the vast majority who approved, but the 90 per cent who approved most articles are at least as important as the 10 per cent who opposed. And finally, as Morison said, no one at the time accused the convention of dishonesty—not even its bitterest opponents.

[87] Mass. Arch., CLX, 124–292 for returns.
[88] *Boston Gazette*, Sept. 6, 1779.
[89] Marblehead Town Records, IV, 309.
[90] Northampton Town Records, III, 53–54.

though it was elected by manhood suffrage. The expectation would prove correct. The list of delegates was replete with the names of such substantial citizens and old-time "revolutionary" leaders as John Hancock, Samuel Adams, James Bowdoin, John Adams, Robert Treat Paine, Walter Spooner, Jabez Fisher, Benjamin Greenleaf, Jonathan Greenleaf, Samuel Holden, Timothy Danielson, William Williams, Samuel Osgood, Samuel Phillips, Benjamin Chadbourne, Jedediah Foster, Azor Orne, and many others. A vast majority of the delegates carried some kind of honorary or professional title—reverend, doctor, deacon, esquire, honorable, brigadier, colonel, captain, or lieutenant. In short, the convention did not give the appearance of having been elected by a propertyless, unenfranchised mass of men.[91]

Under these circumstances, we would also expect that the constitution produced by such a convention would not be very radical, either. This expectation would likewise prove correct. In fact, the instructions which the towns sent with their delegates give a fairly good picture of what the people wanted. For the most part they demanded the things to which they had been accustomed or rights which they had demanded from the British. Occasionally towns desired to depart from customary practices; for example, Gorham requested a single-house legislature with neither governor nor council and the elimination of all property qualifications for voting and office holding.[92] But most towns desired such items as a bill of rights to protect life, liberty, property, religion, jury trial, and other rights. They also wanted equitable representation, separation of powers, and adequate property qualifications for both voters and office holders to insure that they would have a stake in society.[93]

For all practical purposes, the Constitution of 1780 continued practices that had been customary before the Revolution. There was a bill of rights setting forth all the claims which the colonists had made while they were under the British. First among these was a statement that all men were born free and equal and that they had the right of enjoying and defending their lives

[91] Mass. Arch., CLX, 124–292. [92] *Ibid.,* p. 288.
[93] *Ibid., passim.*

and liberties as well as the right of acquiring, possessing, and protecting property. The church was to be semiestablished as it had been in colonial times. Other provisions were for a free press, freedom of speech, trial by jury, free elections, freedom from unlawful search, and frequent elections. These all reflected ideas which had long been current.[94]

There was also little that was new in the structure of government itself. A two-house legislature, each branch able to veto acts of the other, an executive with power of veto, and a judiciary with tenure of good behavior were all familiar landmarks in government to the people of the state. Naturally there was the tremendous difference that the British had no check on government, but otherwise the structure was what the people were accustomed to. A senate replaced the old colonial Council, with the slight alteration that it was to be apportioned by counties instead of being elected at large. Representation in the lower house was determined by polls rather than qualified voters, but this still favored the small towns. All incorporated towns of any size could send a delegate, but in the future a new town must have 150 ratable polls to elect a representative. Towns could send additional representatives for each 225 additional polls in the town. This was the most accurate way to determine representation, as the tax rolls always contained the number of polls, and towns did not always know how many voters they had.[95]

In theory, the Constitution of 1780 was more conservative than the Charter of 1691, although in practice there was probably not much change. There was the stipulation that the governor, lieutenant governor, councilors, senators, and representatives were to swear that they believed in the Christian religion and possessed a certain amount of property. The governor and lieutenant governor had to possess a freehold of £1,000 in the state. Senators were required to possess a freehold of £300 or a total estate of £600. Representatives had to own a freehold of £100 or any ratable estate worth £200.[96] As we have already seen, many farmers in every town could qualify for gov-

---

94 Thorpe, *Charters and Constitutions*, III, 1888–1911.   95 *Ibid.*
96 *Ibid.*, pp. 1897, 1898, 1900, 1903.

ernor, and there were not many who could not qualify for representative. It is very doubtful that many with less than these qualifications had been elected in the past or would be elected in the future. It should also be noted that the qualifications greatly favored the agricultural interests, since the governor and lieutenant governor had to own substantial freeholds, and the freehold qualifications for representatives and senators were only half as much as the personal property qualifications.

Voting qualifications under the constitution of 1780 were also slightly more conservative than they had previously been, though they were not nearly as conservative as they have been pictured. All adult men who had a freehold of £3 (60s.) annual income or any estate worth £60 could qualify as voters. On the surface this appears to be a 50-per-cent increase over the charter qualifications, but actually it was not. In the charter, the 40s. freehold of £40 qualifications were in sterling. These new qualifications, on the other hand, were in Massachusetts lawful silver money at 6s.8d. an ounce.[97] At that time, £40 sterling was equal to £53.6.8 lawful money, so that the increase to £60 amounted to 12.5 per cent.

If there had been much internal discontent, particularly over

---

[97] *Ibid.,* pp. 1898, 1910. For interpretations of the Massachusetts Constitution of 1780 as a conservative document, see Allan Nevins, *The American States during and after the Revolution, 1775–1789* (New York, 1924), pp. 175–82, 211; J. T. Adams, *New England in the Republic,* pp. 85–93; Miller, *Sam Adams,* pp. 355–74. Adams had the property qualifications "doubled" over those under the provincial charter. Miller pictured Samuel Adams as having become a rank conservative by 1780. After depicting Adams as a leader of the lower classes throughout his book, Miller declared that Adams was no Jacksonian democrat for he never made extension of the suffrage a part of his revolutionary propaganda. Since practically every adult man in Massachusetts could vote, Adams' failure to push extension of the suffrage was only natural. Adams might appear as a conservative after the war started, but if so, it was only because he was never as "radical" as Miller contended. Adams was perfectly consistent in opposing county conventions and Shays' Rebellion. He had opposed the British because he believed that constitutional government meant a government based on the consent of the governed. Once Massachusetts had a constitutional government adopted by the people and under which they elected their officials yearly, there was no longer any need for extra-constitutional bodies. This did not make Adams conservative or undemocratic. How can a democratic government operate, if any minority can defy the will of the majority at any time? Samuel Adams and Abraham Lincoln would have seen eye to eye on democracy.

qualifications for voting and office holding, this constitution would certainly have been defeated. An examination of the actions by the towns, however, shows a remarkable amount of agreement on the kind of government the people wanted. In fact, the very parts of the constitution which theoretically should have received the most criticism were often the parts which were accepted the most readily.

Article III of the bill of rights encountered more opposition than any other item in the constitution. This article stipulated that towns were to provide churches and support Protestant ministers where they were not supported voluntarily, though the citizen could say which church would receive his tax money. The legislature could pass a law forcing all people to attend church, but all denominations of Christians were to enjoy equal protection and equal rights under the law. This was the same provision that had prevailed in colonial times except that now all Christians were to be equally protected by the law.

There were three general objections to Article III. Some towns, such as Acton and Ashby, believed that it gave the legislature too much power over religion. Ashby claimed that religious bodies were more important than political bodies and should not be subordinated to political groups. The town was worried more about the state having power over the church than about the church having power over the state.[98] Some towns did not object to the religious provisions but simply wanted the language of the article stated more clearly.[99] Then there were towns which approved the article except for the fact that it granted religious toleration to Catholics. They wanted the word Christian changed to Protestant Christian on the ground that the state should not encourage idolatry.[100] It is impossible to tell from the returns how many people opposed the connection of church and state, how many merely wanted the article written more clearly, or how many desired to exclude Catholics. It would also be interesting to know how many

98 Mass. Arch., CCLXXVII, 1–3.
99 Andover Town Records, May 22, 1780.
100 Mass. Arch., CCLXXVII, 10; Hatfield Town Records, IV, 292–93.

of the towns which opposed the article actually enforced its provisions in practice.

Other objections to the Constitution of 1780 merely emphasize the fact that the war was not being fought to democratize American society. There was provision for checks and balances or separation of powers, which is often considered conservative and undemocratic, but the only criticism of that provision was that the constitution did not go far enough. Groton and Lincoln demanded a more complete separation of executive, legislative, and judicial branches. Newburyport believed the governor should have an absolute veto, since he was elected by all the people annually and could therefore be trusted.[101] Some towns desired to retain the old limit of twenty-eight senators instead of the forty provided in the constitution.[102] In the choice of representatives, a few towns contended that the House would be too large, while a few others wanted a sliding scale of apportionment which would favor the small towns as they had been favored under the charter.[103] Less than half a dozen towns objected to property qualifications for those who voted for representatives and none opposed property qualifications for representatives. These towns thought that any adult man who paid taxes should vote for representatives, though they had no objection to property qualifications for those electing the governor and senators. One such town, Framingham, rejected the voting qualification 79-0, but this was the rare exception, not the rule.[104] Given the fact that all free adult men voted on these provisions, there was surprisingly little objection to property qualifications for both voting and office holding. This can be explained logically only on the assumption that the constitution would allow most men to vote.

There were other objections to the constitution, but again they do not indicate internal social revolution. There was no objection to the high qualifications for governor, as one might expect if there had been a social revolution, or to the stipula-

[101] Mass. Arch., CCLXXVII, 14, 17; attested copy of Newburyport Town Records collected by Professor Samuel Eliot Morison, Massachusetts Historical Society.

[102] Mass. Arch., CCLXXVII, 10; Malden Town Records, II, 126–27.

[103] Mass. Arch., CCLXXVII, 12–13, 17; Andover Town Records, May 22, 1780.

[104] Mass. Arch., CCLXXVII, 12–13.

tion that the governor must be a Christian. The only objection to the religious qualification was that many towns insisted he should be Protestant.[105] There was practically no protest against appointment of judges during good behavior, a fact to be expected since the colonists had long demanded that kind of appointment. Instead of objecting to property qualifications for office holding, many towns believed that the state's delegates to the Continental Congress should have the same high qualifications as the governor.[106] There was a fairly general demand that the oaths for governor, lieutenant governor, senators, and representatives in Chapter VI of the Constitution should contain the word Protestant as well as Christian and that revision of the Constitution take place before 1795.[107]

Instead of creating dissension and political conflict, as a constitution with checks and balances and property and religious qualifications might have done, the Constitution of 1780 met with general agreement, sometimes amounting to indifference. With the exception of Article III, most of the towns voted overwhelmingly for the constitution if they bothered to vote at all. Many towns did not bother to vote. Even Pittsfield, with the recalcitrant Reverend Allen playing an active role, accepted the document without much argument.[108] In other towns, the people were aroused from their lethargy only with great difficulty. Marblehead, for example, met and adjourned several times, then had the selectmen urge the people to attend and had the ministers read notices in their services. All this was sufficient to bring out but eighty-five men in a town that had 831 adult men in 1780. Even this number soon dwindled to the point where the last parts of the constitution were being accepted by a vote of 36 to 0.[109] Framingham started with 141 present, but after the controversial Article III of the bill of rights was passed, the number dropped to eighty and finally to thirty-eight.[110]

105 *Ibid.*, pp. 1, 8, 15, 20; Hatfield Town Records, IV, 292–93.
106 Mass. Arch., CCLXXVII, 20, 23, 25; Malden Town Records, II, 126–27.
107 Mass. Arch., CCLXXVII, 10, 15, 16, 22.
108 *Ibid., passim.;* Pittsfield Town Records, II, 73–75.
109 Marblehead Town Records, IV, 338–42, 364.
110 Mass. Arch., CCLXXVII, 12.

One of the most striking features about the ratification of the constitution was the often-expressed willingness of the people to compromise their differences, which is certainly the mark of a democratic society. Most of the towns agreed to accept the constitution as it was if the people voted for it or if the convention amended it to meet general demands. Cambridge objected to several parts but said these objections were not so strong that the town would reject the whole if the amendments failed. Cambridge would submit to majority rule for the sake of an established government.[111] Newburyport ordered its delegates to work for amendments, but the town said that differences of education, interests, and various other factors precluded the possibility that a government could be devised that would please everyone. "Mutual concessions must be made," the town declared, for there was need of a government and this constitution was "in general a wise and good one." [112] These views seem to have been fairly representative of the towns in general.

The widespread approval of the constitution was summed up by two contemporary observers who had participated in the ratification. Jonathan Judd, Jr., of Southampton said there was "a much greater vote in favor of it than was expected." [113] And Samuel Adams wrote as follows: "The people of Massachusetts have at length agreed to form a civil constitution. . . . This great business was carried through with much good humour among the people, and even in Berkshire, where some persons led us to expect it would meet with many obstructions." [114]

One might argue, as the town of Middleborough did and as some might still do today, that the Constitution of 1780 was not democratically adopted because three-fourths of the voters did not vote, even though two-thirds of those who did vote approved the constitution.[115] This, however, was confusing the issue of those who could vote and those who did vote. Unless we fix a quorum or define democracy as a system in which all voters *must* vote, democracy generally means a majority of those

111 *Ibid.,* p. 5.
112 Attested copy of Cambridge Records, Massachusetts Historical Society.
113 Judd Diary, II, May 22, 1780.   114 Adams, *Writings,* IV, 199–200.
115 Selectmen of the town of Middleborough to the selectmen of the town of Plymouth, Library of Congress, Massachusetts Miscellaneous, 1779–1864.

who are interested enough to vote. In this latter sense, the Massachusetts Constitution of 1780 was certainly ratified democratically.

The Massachusetts Constitution of 1780 is convincing evidence that the people of that state considered the conflict in progress as a War of Independence rather than as an internal revolution. John Adams summed it up as follows: "I say again that resistance to innovation and the unlimited claims of Parliament, and not any new form of government, was the object of the Revolution." [116] It would have been inconceivable that a convention, elected under manhood suffrage, could have written such a frame of government had there been much internal dissatisfaction with the kind of political system in effect before the Revolution. It would have been even more inconceivable that this constitution could have been ratified under manhood suffrage by such a large majority if there had been much demand for change. The contradictions are resolved if we accept the fact that the people of Massachusetts were trying to keep the type of middle-class democracy that they had.

Thus did events after Lexington and Concord demonstrate the absence of an "internal" revolution to democratize society. There was much continuity in the House and Council (now Senate) as members of long standing took over control of the government. With the exception of a few men who went with the British, the leading men in the towns continued to run town affairs and to organize the "revolutionary" movement. Not until the General Court gave representation to the districts that had been denied representation by the British did the larger towns demand increased membership in the House, and then they failed to take advantage of their increased representation. There were no changes in the franchise or in the position of the churches and schools until the Constitution of 1780, and then the changes were of little significance. The property requirement for the franchise was actually increased about 12 per cent, qualifications for office holding were put into effect, but Catholics were given a greater amount of toleration than prevailed under the charter.

[116] Mass. Hist. Soc., *Collections*, 5th ser., IV, 532.

Historians who have stressed the internal revolution as an interpretation have long noted the contradictory fact that the results of the American Revolution were not very revolutionary. The logical explanation for this otherwise seemingly illogical phenomenon is that society in Massachusetts was already democratic and that there was no need for an internal revolution.

Conclusion

IN MASSACHUSETTS, therefore, we find one of the unique "revolutions" in world history—a revolution to preserve a social order rather than to change it. It was not, as we have often assumed, a dual revolution in which Americans won their independence from the British on one hand, and in which unenfranchised and underprivileged lower classes wrested democratic rights from a privileged local aristocracy on the other.

To understand what happened, we must first have a clear picture of Massachusetts society. Economically speaking, it was a middle-class society in which property was easily acquired and in which a large portion of the people were property-owning farmers. There was undoubtedly more economic democracy for the common man then than there is now. A large permanent labor class was practically nonexistent; men could either acquire land and become farmers or work for themselves as skilled artisans. If we insist that Americans who came to this country brought their accustomed class or caste lines with them, we must do so in the face of all the evidence to the contrary. If there was anything that observers at the time agreed on, it was that American society was almost the exact opposite of European society. There was nothing approaching the spread between the rich and the poor that Europe had at that time or that we have at present; a much larger proportion of society owned property then than now. Yet today, many people, even including many laborers, look on American society as predominantly middle class, though the opportunity for almost universal ownership of property is far less now than it was before the Revolution.

Economic opportunity, or economic democracy, in turn contributed to political democracy. While it is true that property ownership was a prerequisite for province and town voting, it is also true that the amount of property required for the franchise was very small and that the great majority of men could easily meet the requirements. There were probably a few men who could not qualify for voting, but the number could not have been very large. We cannot condone the practice of excluding even those few, but we should try to place the unenfranchised in their proper perspective. It makes a tremendous difference in our understanding of colonial society whether 95 per cent of the men were disfranchised or only 5 per cent. Furthermore, representation was apportioned in such a way that the farmers, not a merchant aristocracy, had complete control of the legislature.

It is not enough to say that the people of Massachusetts perhaps had more democracy than the people of Europe, but that they still did not have what we call democracy today. Neither is it sufficient to say that the germs of democracy were present, or that democracy, as a growing process if not as a reality, could be found in colonial times. When Hutchinson said that anything that looked like a man was a voter and that policy in general was dictated by the lower classes, he was certainly using the term "democracy" as we mean it now. A Hutchinson might deplore the view that government existed for the benefit of the people and that the people were to decide when government had served its proper functions, but this is the democratic idea. He might also deplore the fact that the people not only elected their representatives but also told them how to vote, yet this, too, is democracy.

In many respects, the people of Massachusetts had a government more responsive to the popular will than we have at the present time. There were far more representatives in proportion to population than we now have, and the representatives were more responsible to their constituents for their actions than are legislators at present. If a man votes against his belief to please his constituents so that he can hold his elected position, we cannot demand much more of democracy.

The number of men who could vote in the colony must not be confused with the number who did vote. These are entirely different problems, for the fact that there was much indifference on election day did not mean that many men could not participate. If we are attempting to explain events in terms of class conflict or internal revolution, it is especially important that we do not confuse the unfranchised and the disinterested. It is one thing if a man wants the vote but cannot meet the property requirements; it is another if he has the vote but fails to use it. Neither should we confuse the issue by giving percentages of voters in terms of the entire population, for probably less than 20 per cent of the people in colonial times were adult men.

In addition to economics and politics, there were also other manifestations of democracy in colonial Massachusetts. The system of education was, for its day, undoubtedly the best provided for the common people anywhere, and the correct comparison is with other educational systems at the time, not with our own. Many democratic practices were used in the operation of the Congregational church, and again we should remember that some 98 per cent of the people were Congregationalists. Furthermore, the Congregational church was not established as it was in England. Men who belonged to other churches did not pay taxes to the Congregational church; education and political office were open to those who were not Congregationalists. Perhaps there was not the complete religious freedom—or religious indifference—that we now associate with a liberal society, but there was also little dissatisfaction with religion to contribute to internal conflict. Even the colonial militia was democratic in its organization and in the influence which it exerted on politics.

In brief, Massachusetts did not have a social order before the American Revolution which would breed sharp internal class conflicts. The evidence does not justify an interpretation of the Revolution in Massachusetts as an internal class conflict designed to achieve additional political, economic, and social democracy. Although democracy was important as a factor in the conflict, it was a democracy which had already arrived in the colony long before 1776.

If we turn to British-American relations, however, we do not need to search long to find areas of conflict. The British for many years had developed a mercantilist-imperialist colonial system that had not functioned as expected. The aim of the system, as men at the time frankly admitted, was the ultimate benefit of the mother country. They believed that colonies should be regulated, both economically and politically, to further the well-being of the parent state. British officials were fully aware of the shortcomings in colonial administration, but, until 1760, Britain was not in a favorable position to remedy these defects. British officials were also fully aware of the fact that colonial democracy was one of the chief obstacles to effective enforcement of British colonial policy.

These two ingredients—an effective middle-class democracy and British imperial policies which had been thwarted by this democracy—explain what happened in Massachusetts from 1760 to 1776. In order to make their colonial system effective, the British believed that they had to recover authority over colonial officials. This, in turn, called for a colonial revenue which would be administered by Parliament, especially to pay the salaries of colonial officials and thus remove them from under the dominating influence of colonial assemblies. But of course the assembly of Massachusetts was fully aware of the power which control of the purse conferred and was equally determined to retain this power over British officials.

Throughout the story runs another thread—the threat, or at least what the British considered the threat, of colonial independence. This gave an air of urgency to British measures. There was the frequently expressed fear that time was on the side of the colonists. A rapidly growing population, bolstered by a phenomenal birthrate due to economic opportunity and by immigrants attracted by economic and political democracy, posed the problem to the British of recovering authority before the colonies became too large. When the showdown came with

the Tea Act and the Coercive Acts, there was no doubt whatever that the British intended to curtail colonial democracy as
a necessary step toward recovery of British authority and the
prevention of colonial independence. The result was the very
thing the Brtish had tried to prevent—American independence.

Obviously democracy played an important part in the events
before 1776, not as a condition to be achieved but as a reality
which interfered with British policies. If the British had been
successful, there would undoubtedly have been much less
democracy in Massachusetts—hence the interpretation that
the Revolution was designed to *preserve* a social order rather
than to change it. We search in vain for evidence of class conflict that was serious enough to justify revolution; we do not
have to look far for copious quantities of proof that colonial
society was democratic and that the colonists were attempting to
prevent British innovations.

Furthermore, the results of the Revolution more than confirm the interpretation presented here. There is a logic to
what happened after the Revolution—or perhaps it would be
more accurate to say what did not happen—if we accept the
fact that the people of Massachusetts were not conducting an
internal revolution. We are not confronted with the contradiction, which most writers fail to resolve, of a social revolution
which was presumably successful but which failed to achieve
social change. Why would a people, who were supposedly demanding a more democratic government, adopt a constitution
which restricted democracy even more than it had been restricted in colonial days? On the other hand, the Massachusetts
Constitution of 1780 was a logical consequence of a middle-
class society which believed in the protection of property because most men were property owners. The almost complete
absence of social revolution in Massachusetts should stand as
convincing evidence that internal social revolution was not one
of the chief aims of the American Revolution as far as the people of Massachusetts were concerned.

It is not necessary to explain whatever conservatism existed
in colonial times in terms of a limited electorate. There is
implied in this approach an assumption that universal suffrage

will result in increased liberalism, but this is not necessarily so. The elections of 1920, 1924, 1928, and even 1952, when women as well as men had the vote, should convince us that "the people" can and do vote for conservatism. If the people of Massachusetts believed that a man should own property to be a voter or that an official should be a Protestant to be elected to office, they might well vote for both propositions and not be out of character. And since most men in Massachusetts were Protestants and property owners, the fact that both property and religious qualifications found their way into the Constitution of 1780 should not be surprising.

We do not need a "conservative counterrevolution" or a thermidorean reaction to explain either the Massachusetts Constitution of 1780 or the adoption of the federal Constitution in 1788. If there was no "social revolution," there could hardly be a "conservative counterrevolution." Both constitutions must be explained in terms of a middle-class society in which most men could vote.

In recent years it has been frequently said that the British did not intend to tyrannize the colonies by the policies which they adopted. Colonists thought otherwise, however, and judging by the material presented in these chapters, one might suspect that many British policies looked like tyranny to them. Perhaps we of today would also consider as tyranny trials without juries, instructions by the king which were supposed to be law, taxation by a people who were considered foreigners, a declaration by the Parliament of these same "foreign people" that it had the power to legislate in all cases whatsoever, appointed governors who could dissolve assemblies or determine town meetings, and navigation acts regulating colonial trade in British interests. It would be interesting to speculate on the reaction of a modern oleomargarine manufacturer whose suit against the butter interests was to be tried in Wisconsin by a jury of Wisconsin dairy farmers presided over by a judge appointed by the governor of Wisconsin. This hypothetical case might seem exaggerated, but it is not too far removed from the attitude expressed by colonists toward their relations with the British. The fact is that colonists looked on British measures as tyrannical, and if we are going to explain colonial actions, we must consider the colonial point of view.

How should we rate in importance the various factors that entered into this British-American war? That, of course, is difficult to answer, but it is not so difficult to say that many items contributed and that some were probably more important to some individuals than to others.

There is no doubt that economic motives were fundamental. That Americans would oppose a mercantilist system which they considered inimical to their interests should not be surprising. After all, they looked on many British regulations as simply devices by which some segments of the Empire were favored at the expense of other segments. The tax program also had its economic side, for as many men said, a mother country which could collect a stamp tax could also tax a man's land, his cattle, or his home. Undoubtedly, too, the threat of monopoly contained in the Tea Act had its economic influence. In fact, a middle-class society would almost inevitably place great emphasis on property and its economic interests, a fact which is only too apparent in the sources. The importance of economic factors, however, did not lie in their contribution to class conflict as a cause of the American Revolution.

But economic elements were not the only forces making for revolution. Equally significant was the fact that Massachusetts had long been accustomed to democratic government and intended to maintain its accustomed system. Politics inevitably include economics, since economic subjects are some of the most important items in politics, but not all politics is economic. The very fact that people govern their own destinies is important in itself. As one old soldier of the Revolution put it, the British intended to govern the Americans and the Americans did not intend that they should. To a people accustomed to the democracy both of province and town affairs, the danger inherent in British imperial controls was far more than a mere threat. When the common people talked of dying for their liberties or pledging their lives and property for the defense of their liberties, they were not dealing in abstractions; and they would not have talked in this way if their society had been dominated by a merchant aristocracy.

Neither can religious democracy be ignored as a factor in the Revolution. We must remember that the people of Massachusetts were accustomed to a church organization which lived by democratic procedures and opposition to the Church of England. We must not forget, either, that many people at the time considered religion more important than politics. The threat that the British might impose the Church of England on them and enforce conformity was not a threat to be taken lightly. As many of them often said, religious and political freedom were inextricably connected and would rise or fall together. Little wonder, then, that the Congregational clergy supported the Revolution almost to a man.

This study of Massachusetts raises some rather serious questions about our interpretation of colonial society and the Revolution in other colonies. Were the other colonies as undemocratic as we have supposed them to be? Was their economic and social life dominated by a coastal aristocracy of planters in the South and merchants in the North? How was property distributed? Exactly how many men could meet the voting qualifications? Was representation restricted in such a way that conservative areas could dominate the legislature? These are questions for which we need well-documented answers before we interpret the colonial and revolutionary periods with any assurance of accuracy.

Evidence which has turned up in the course of this study suggests that Massachusetts was not fundamentally different from the other colonies and states. If so—and the idea is certainly worth extensive investigation—we might be forced to make some drastic revisions in our interpretation of American history before 1830. Perhaps we will find in America as a whole, as in Massachusetts, that American democracy as we know it goes far deeper than the election of 1828 and that the "common man" in this country had come into his own long before the era of Jacksonian Democracy.

Bibliography

I. SOURCES

Printed Sources

Adams, Abigail. *New Letters of Abigail Adams, 1788–1801*. Ed. by Stewart Mitchell. Boston: Houghton Mifflin Co., 1947.

Adams, John. "Correspondence between John Adams and John Winthrop," in Mass. Hist. Soc., *Collections*, 5th ser., IV, 287–313.

———. *Correspondence of John Adams and Thomas Jefferson, [1812–1826]*. Selected by Paul Wilstach. Indianapolis: Bobbs-Merrill Co., 1925.

———. "Correspondence between John Adams and Mercy Warren Relating to Her 'History of the American Revolution,' July–August, 1807," in Mass. Hist. Soc., *Collections*, 5th ser., IV, pt. III, 315–511.

———. *A Defence of the Constitutions of Government of the United States of America. . . .* In *The Works of John Adams*, IV, 271–588; V; VI, 3–217.

———. *Familiar Letters of John Adams and His Wife Abigail Adams, during the Revolution.* Ed. by Charles Francis Adams. New York: Hurd and Houghton, 1876.

———. *James Otis, Samuel Adams, and John Hancock. John Adams' Tributes to These as the Three Principal Movers and Agents of the American Revolution.* [Boston: Directors of Old South Work, 1907.]

———. *The Works of John Adams.* Ed. by Charles Francis Adams. 10 vols. Boston: Little, Brown and Co., 1850–1856.

Adams, Samuel. *The Writings of Samuel Adams.* Ed. by Harry Alonzo Cushing. 4 vols. New York: G. P. Putnam's Sons, 1904–08.

American Antiquarian Society. *Proceedings.* May 31, 1843–April 28, 1880. New ser., 1880–1919.

American Archives. . . . Ed. by Peter Force. 9 vols. Washington: Prepared and published under authority of an Act of Congress, 1837–1853.

American Statistical Association. *Collections.* Boston: For the Association by T. R. Marvin, 1847.

Amory, Katharine (Greene). *The Journal of Mrs. John Amory (Katharine Greene) 1775–1777, with Letters from Her father, Rufus Greene, 1759–1777.* Boston: Private printing, 1923.

Andrews, John. "Letters of John Andrews, Esq. of Boston, 1772–1776," in Mass. Hist. Soc., *Proceedings,* VIII, 316–412.

The Annual Register, a Review of Public Events at Home and Abroad . . . 1758—. London: Printed for J. Dodsley, 1761–19–.

The Aspinwall Papers. Comp. by Thomas Aspinwall. In Mass. Hist. Soc., *Collections,* 4th ser., vols. IX and X.

Austin, James T. *The Life of Elbridge Gerry. With Contemporary Letters. To the Close of the American Revolution.* 2 vols. Boston: Wells and Lilly, 1828–1829.

Barker, John. *The British in Boston, being the Diary of Lieutenant John Barker of the King's Own Regiment from November 15, 1774, to May 31, 1776.* Ed. by Elizabeth Ellery Dana. Cambridge, Harvard University Press, 1924.

Barnard, John. "Autobiography of the Reverend John Barnard of Marblehead," in Mass. Hist. Soc., *Collections,* 3d ser., V, 177–242.

Barrington, William Wildman, and Bernard, Sir Francis. *The Barrington-Bernard Correspondence and Illustrative Matter, 1760–1770, Drawn from the "Papers of Sir Francis Bernard" Sometime Governor of Massachusetts-bay.* Ed. by Edward Channing and Archibald Cary Coolidge. Cambridge: Harvard University Press, 1912.

Belcher, Jonathan. *Belcher Papers.* In Mass. Hist. Soc., *Collections,* 6th ser., vols. VI and VII (1893–1894).

Belknap, Jeremy. *Belknap Papers.* In Mass. Hist. Soc., *Collections,* 5th ser., vols. II and III; 6th ser., vol. IV.

Bernard, Sir Francis. *Select Letters on the Trade and Government of America; and the Principles of Law and Polity, Applied to the American Colonies.* London: Printed for T. Payne, 1774.

——. *Letters to the Ministry, from Governor Bernard, General Gage, and Commodore Hood.* Boston: Printed by Edes and Gill, 1769.

——. *Letters to the Right Honourable the Earl of Hillsborough from Governor Bernard, General Gage and the Honourable His Majesty's Council of the Province of Massachusetts-Bay.* Boston: Printed by Edes and Gill, 1769.

Boardman, Benjamin. "Diary of Rev. Benjamin Boardman," July 31–Nov. 12, 1775, in Mass. Hist. Soc., *Proceedings,* 2d ser., VII, 400–413.

[Bollan, William]. *A Succinct View of the Origin of Our Colonies, with Their Civil State. . . .* London: 1766.

Boston Committee. "Correspondence of the Boston Committee to Receive Donations for the Poor," in Mass. Hist. Soc., *Collections,* 4th ser., IV, 1–275.

Bowdoin, James. *The Bowdoin and Temple Papers.* In Mass. Hist. Soc., *Collections,* 6th ser., vol. IX; 7th ser., vol. VI.

"Broadside," in Essex Institute, *Historical Collections,* XXXVI, 104.

Canada. *Statutes, Treaties and Documents of the Canadian Constitution, 1713–1929.* Ed. by W. P. M. Kennedy. 2d ed. Toronto and London: Oxford University Press, 1930.

Chastellux, François Jean. *Travels in North-America, in the Years 1780, 1781, and 1782.* (London, 1787). Tr. by George Grieve. New York: White, Gallaher, and White, 1827.

Clough, Gibson. "Extracts from Gibson Clough's Journal," in Essex Institute, *Historical Collections,* III, 99–106, 195–201.

Colonial Currency Reprints, 1682–1751. Ed. by Andrew McFarland Davis. 4 vols. Boston: Prince Society, 1910–1911.

Colonial Society of Massachusetts. *Publications.* 33 vols. Boston, 1895–1940.

Continental Congress. *Journals of the Continental Congress, 1774–1789.* Library of Congress ed. 34 vols. Washington, D.C., 1904–1937.

Cooper, Samuel. "Diary of Samuel Cooper, 1775–76," *American Historical Review,* VI (Jan., 1901), 301–41.

Cooper, Samuel. "Letters of Samuel Cooper to Thomas Pownall, 1769–1777," *American Historical Review,* VIII (Jan., 1903), 301–30.

Crèvecoeur, Hector St. John de. *Letters from an American Farmer.* Ed. by Ernest Rhys. Everyman's Library. New York and London: E. P. Dutton and Co., Inc., 1940.

Danvers Historical Society. *Historical Collections.* 32 vols. Danvers, Mass.: The Society, 1913—.

Documents Relative to the Colonial History of the State of New York. Ed. by E. B. O'Callaghan and E. Fernow. 15 vols. Albany: Weed, Parsons, and Co., 1853–1887.

Douglass, William. *A Summary, Historical and Political, of the First Planting, Progressive Improvements, and Present State of the British Settlements in North America.* . . . 2 vols. [Boston: Rogers and Fowle, 1749–1752]. London: Reprinted for R. Baldwin, 1755.

Dummer, Jeremiah. *A Defense of the New-England Charters.* Boston: Reprinted and sold by Thomas and John Fleet, 1765.

Eliot, Andrew, and Hollis, Thomas. "Correspondence of Andrew Eliot with Thomas Hollis," in Mass. Hist. Soc., *Collections,* 4th ser., IV, 398–461.

Essex Institute. *Historical Collections.* 82 vols. Salem: Printed for the Essex Institute, 1859–1946.

The Federal and State Constitutions, Colonial Charters, and Other Organic Laws. . . . Ed. by Francis Newton Thorpe. 7 vols. Washington: Government Printing Office, 1909.

The Federal and State Constitutions, Colonial Charters, and Other Organic Laws of the United States. . . . Comp. by Ben: Perley Poore. 2d ed. 2 vols. Washington: Government Printing Office, 1878.

Franklin, Benjamin. *The Writings of Benjamin Franklin.* Ed. by Albert H. Smyth. 10 vols. New York: Macmillan, 1907.

Gage, Thomas. *The Correspondence of General Thomas Gage.* . . . Ed. by Clarence E. Carter. 2 vols. New Haven: Yale University Press, 1931, 1933.

The General Magazine and Historical Chronicle for All the British Plantations in America. Pub. by Benjamin Franklin. Reproduced from the original edition, Philadelphia, 1741. New York: Columbia University Press, 1938.

George III. *The Correspondence of King George the Third from 1760 to December 1783.* . . . Ed. by Hon. Sir John Fortescue. 6 vols. London: Macmillan, 1927–1928.

Goelet, Francis. "Extracts from Capt. Francis Goelet's Journal. . . ." *New-England Historical and Genealogical Register,* XXIV (1870), 50–63.

Great Britain. *Acts of the Privy Council of England.* Colonial ser.

Ed. by W. L. Grant and James Munro. 6 vols. Hereford and London, 1908–1912.

——. *Calendar of State Papers, Colonial Series, American and West Indies.* . . . Numerous editors and publishers. 40 vols. London, 1860–1939.

——. *Journal of the Commissioners for Trade and Plantations.* . . . Preserved in the Public Record Office. 14 vols. London: His Majesty's Stationery Office, 1920–1938.

——. *The Parliamentary History of England From the Earliest Period to the Year 1803.* Ed. by W. Cobbett. 36 vols. London: T. C. Hansard, 1813.

——. *Proceedings and Debates of the British Parliaments Respecting North America.* Ed. by Leo Francis Stock. 5 vols. Washington: Carnegie Institute, 1924–1941.

——. *Royal Instructions to British Colonial Governors, 1670–1776.* Ed. by Leonard Woods Labaree. 2 vols. New York and London: D. Appleton–Century Co., 1935.

——. *Statutes at Large from Magna Charta.* . . . Ed. by D. Pickering. 46 vols. Cambridge and London, 1762–1814.

Grenville, Richard Temple Grenville-Temple. *The Grenville Papers.* . . . Ed. by William J. Smith. 4 vols. London: J. Murray, 1852–1853.

Harvard College. "Subjects for Master's Degrees, 1655–1791," in Mass. Hist. Soc., *Proceedings,* XVIII, 123–51.

Haskell, Caleb. *Caleb Haskell's Diary, May 5, 1775–May 30, 1776.* . . . Ed. by Lothrop Withington. Newburyport, Mass.: W. H. Huse and Co., 1881.

Heath, William. *The Heath Papers.* In Mass. Hist. Soc., *Collections,* 5th ser., IV, 1–285; 7th ser., vols. IV and V.

Historical Collections Relating to the American Colonial Church. Ed. by William Stevens Perry. 5 vols. Hartford: Church Press, 1870–1878.

Honyman, Robert. *Colonial Panorama, 1775: Dr. Robert Honyman's Journal for March and April.* Ed. by Philip Padelford. San Marino, Calif.: Huntington Library, 1939.

Hulton, Ann. *Letters of a Loyalist Lady, Being the Letters of Ann Hulton, Sister of Henry Hulton, Commissioner of the Customs at Boston, 1767–1776.* Cambridge: Harvard University Press, 1927.

Hutchinson, Thomas. *Additions to Thomas Hutchinson's History of Massachusetts Bay.* Ed. by Catherine B. Mayo. Worcester: American Antiquarian Society, 1949.

—— and others. *Copy of Letters sent to Great Britain, by His Excellency Thomas Hutchinson, the Hon. Andrew Oliver, and Several Other Persons, Born and Educated among Us. . . .* Boston: Printed by Edes and Gill, 1773.

——. *The Diary and Letters of His Excellency Thomas Hutchinson. . . .* Ed. by Peter Orlando Hutchinson. 2 vols. London: S. Low, Marston, Searle & Rivington, 1883–1886.

——. *The History of the Colony and Province of Massachusetts-Bay.* Ed. by Lawrence S. Mayo. 3 vols. Cambridge: Harvard University Press, 1936.

——. *Hutchinson Papers.* In Mass. Hist. Soc., *Collections,* 2d Ser., X, 181–88; 3d Ser., I, 1–152.

Jefferson, Thomas. *The Writings of Thomas Jefferson.* Ed. by Paul Leicester Ford. 10 vols. New York: G. P. Putnam's Sons, 1892–1899.

Kalm, Peter. *The America of 1750: Peter Kalm's Travels in North America.* 2 vols. New York: Wilson-Erickson Co., 1937.

Lee, Charles. *The Lee Papers . . . 1754—.* In New York Historical Society, *Collections,* vols. IV–VII (1872–1875).

Letter to the Freeholders, and Qualified Voters, Relating to the Ensuing Election. Boston, 1749.

Letters of Members of the Continental Congress. Ed. by Edmund C. Burnett. 8 vols. Washington: Carnegie Institute of Washington, 1921–1936.

Lynde, Benjamin and Benjamin Lynde, Jr. *The Diaries of Benjamin Lynde and of Benjamin Lynde, Jr.* Ed. by Fitch Edward Oliver. Boston: Private printing [Cambridge: Riverside Press], 1880.

Massachusetts. *Acts and Laws of Her Majesties Province of the Massachusetts-Bay in New England.* Boston: B. Green, 1714.

——. *Acts and Laws of His Majesty's Province of the Massachusetts-Bay in New England.* Boston: B. Green, 1726.

——. *Acts and Laws of His Majesty's Province of the Massachusetts-Bay in New England.* Boston: Samuel Kneeland and Timothy Green, 1742.

——. *Acts and Laws of His Majesty's Province of the Massachusetts-Bay in New England.* Boston: S. Kneeland, 1759.

——. *Acts and Laws of the Commonwealth of Massachusetts.* Boston: Benj. Edes and Sons, 1780. Reprint, Wright and Potter, 1890.

——. *The Acts and Resolves, Public and Private, of the Province of Massachusetts Bay. . . .* 21 vols. Boston: Wright and Potter, 1869–1922.

——. *Journal of the Convention for Framing a Constitution of Government for the State of Massachusetts Bay . . . Sept. 1, 1779 to the Close of Their Last Session, June 16, 1780. . . .* Boston: Dutton and Wentworth, 1832.

——. *Journal of the House of Representatives. . . .* 25 vols. Boston and Watertown, 1715–1777.

——. *The Journals of Each Provincial Congress of Massachusetts in 1774 and 1775, and of the Committee of Safety. . . .* Boston: Dutton and Wentworth, 1838.

——. *Speeches of the Governors of Massachusetts, from 1765 to 1775; and the Answers of the House of Representatives to the Same; with Their Resolutions and Addresses for That Period.* Ed. by Alden Bradford. Boston: Russell and Gardner, 1818.

Massachusetts Historical Society. *Collections.* Vols. I–. 1792–19–. Special collections as cited; other documents as noted in footnotes.

——. *Proceedings.* Vols. I–. 1859—.

Mauduit, Israel. *A Short View of the History of the Colony of Massachusetts Bay, with Respect to Their Charters and Constitution.* 3d ed. London: J. Wilkie, 1774.

——. *Jasper Mauduit, Agent in London for the Province of the Massachusetts-Bay, 1762–1765.* In Mass. Hist. Soc., *Collections,* vol. LXXIV.

Military Affairs in North America, 1748–1765: Selected Documents from the Cumberland Papers in Windsor Castle. Ed. by Stanley M. Pargellis. New York: D. Appleton–Century Co., 1936.

Moore, Frank. *Diary of the American Revolution. From Newspapers and Original Documents.* 2 vols. New York: Charles Scribner, 1860.

The New England Historical and Genealogical Register. 94 vols. Boston: Samuel G. Drake and others, 1847–1941.

Otis, James. *Some Political Writings of James Otis.* Coll. by Charles F. Mullett. 2 vols. (University of Missouri *Studies.*) Columbia, Mo.: University of Missouri, 1929.

Paine, Thomas. *The Complete Writings of Thomas Paine.* Ed. by Philip S. Foner. 2 vols. New York: Citadel Press, 1945.

Pennsylvania Archives. Various editors. 120 vols. Philadelphia and Harrisburg: J. Severns and Co., and others, 1852–1856, 1874–1935.

Pepperrell, Sir William. *The Journal of Sir William Pepperrell.* . . . Ed. by Charles Henry Lincoln. In American Antiquarian Society, *Proceedings,* n.s., XX (1910), 133–83.

——. *The Pepperell Papers.* In Mass. Hist. Soc., *Collections,* 6th ser., vol. X (1899).

Pitt, William. *Correspondence of William Pitt.* . . . Ed. by Gertrude S. Kimball. 2 vols. New York: Macmillan, 1906.

Pownall, Thomas. *The Administration of the Colonies.* London: J. Wilkie, 1764.

Pynchon, William. *The Diary of William Pynchon of Salem. A Picture of Salem Life, Social and Political, a Century Ago.* Ed. by Fitch Edward Oliver. Boston and New York: Houghton, Mifflin and Co., 1890.

Quarry, Colonel. *Colonel Quarry's Memorial to the Lords Commissioners of Trade and Plantations.* . . . In Mass. Hist. Soc., *Collections,* 3d ser., VII, 222–242.

Result of the Convention of Delegates Holden at Ipswich in the County of Essex. . . . Newbury-Port: John Mycall, printer, 1778.

Rowe, John. *Letters and Diary of John Rowe, Boston Merchant, 1759–62, 1764–1779.* Ed. by Anne R. Cunningham. Boston: W. B. Clarke Co., 1903.

Secombe, Joseph. "Extracts from Textbooks of Deacon Joseph Secombe, 1762–1777," in Danvers Historical Society, *Historical Collections,* vol. IX.

Shirley, William. *Correspondence of William Shirley, Governor of Massachusetts and Military Commander in America 1731–1760.* Ed. by Charles Henry Lincoln. 2 vols. New York: Macmillan, 1912.

Stiles, Ezra. *Extracts from the Itineraries and Other Miscellanies of Ezra Stiles, D.D., L.L.D., 1775–1794, with a Selection from His Correspondence.* Ed. by Franklin Bowditch Dexter. New Haven: Yale University Press, 1916.

Trumbull, Jonathan. *Trumbull Papers.* In Mass. Hist. Soc., *Collections,* 5th ser., vols. IX and X (1885, 1888).

Warren, James and Adamses. *Warren-Adams Letters.* . . . In Mass. Hist. Soc., *Collections,* vols. LXXII and LXXIII.

Weare, Comptroller. "Observations on the British Colonies on the Continent of America . . . ," in Mass. Hist. Soc., *Collections,* 1st ser., I, 66–84.

Whitmore, William Henry. *The Massachusetts Civil List for the Colonial and Provincial Periods, 1630–1774.* Albany: J. Munsell, 1870.

The Winthrop Papers. In Mass. Hist. Soc., *Collections,* 3d ser., X, 1–127.

Woolman, John. *The Journal and Essays of John Woolman.* Ed. by Amelia Mott Gummere. New York: Macmillan, 1922.

Newspapers

The Boston Evening Post.
The Boston Gazette.
The Boston News-Letter.
The Boston Post-Boy. Later became *The Boston Post-Boy and Advertiser.*
The Independent Advertiser [Boston].
The Massachusetts Gazette.
The Massachusetts Spy.
The New-England Weekly Journal.
The New York Gazette.
The Pennsylvania Gazette.

Printed town records

Barnstable, Mass. *Barnstable Town Records.* Yarmouthport, Mass.: C. W. Swift, 1910.

Boston, Mass. *Boston Selectmen's Minutes.* In *Report of the Record Commissioners of the City of Boston.* 39 vols. Boston: Rockwell and Churchill, 1876–1909. Vols. I–XXVIII were issued under above title; vols. XXIX–XXXIX have the following title: *Records Relating to the Early History of Boston.* . . .

———. *Boston Town Records.* In *Reports of the Record Commissioners of the City of Boston.*

Braintree, Mass. *Records of the Town of Braintree, 1640–1793.* Ed. by Samuel Austin Bates. Randolph, Mass.: D. H. Huxford, 1886.

Cambridge, Mass. *The Records of the Town of Cambridge (Formerly Newtowne) Massachusetts, 1630–1703.* Cambridge: Printed by order of the City Council, 1901.

Charlestown, Mass. *Charlestown Land Records, 1638–1802.* In Boston, *Reports of the Record Commissioners,* vol. III.

Danvers, Mass. "Records of Overseers of the Poor of the Old Town of Danvers, for the Years 1767 and 1768," in Essex Institute, *Historical Collections,* II, 85–92.

——. *Danvers Town Records.* In Danvers Historical Society, *Collections,* vol. III.

——. "Danvers Tax List, 1775," in Essex Institute, *Historical Collections,* XXIX, 181–83.

——. *Vital Records of Danvers, Massachusetts. . . .* 2 vols. Salem, Mass.: Essex Institute, 1909–1910.

Dorchester, Mass. *Dorchester Town Records.* In Boston, *Report of the Record Commissioners,* vol. IV.

Dudley, Mass. *Town Records of Dudley, Massachusetts. . . .* 2 vols. in 1. Pawtucket, R.I.: Adam Sutcliffe Co., 1893–1894.

Fitchburgh, Mass. *The Old Records of the Town of Fitchburgh, Massachusetts. . . .* Comp. by Walter A. Davis. 8 vols. Fitchburg: Sentinel Printing Co., 1898–1913.

Manchester, Mass. *Town Records of Manchester.* 2 vols. Salem, Mass.: 1889.

——. *Vital Records of Manchester, Massachusetts, to the End of the Year, 1849.* Salem: Essex Institute, 1903.

Mendon, Mass. *The Proprietors' Records of the Town of Mendon, Massachusetts.* Boston: Rockwell and Churchill press, 1899.

Milton, Mass. *Milton Church Records, 1681–1754.* Milton, Mass.: Milton Historical Society, 1916.

[Muddy River] Brookline, Mass. *Muddy River and Brookline Records. 1634–1838.* [Boston]: J. E. Farwell and Co., 1875.

Oxford, Mass. *Records of Oxford, Mass.* Albany, N.Y.: J. Munsell's Sons, 1894.

——. *Vital Records of Oxford, Massachusetts to . . . 1849.* Worcester, Mass.: F. P. Rice, 1905.

Plymouth, Mass. *Records of the Town of Plymouth [1636–1783].* 3 vols. Plymouth, Mass.: Avery and Doten, 1889–1903.

Roxbury, Mass. *Roxbury Land Records.* In Boston, *Report of the Record Commissioners,* vol. VI.

Tisbury, Mass. *Records of the Town of Tisbury, Mass., Beginning June 29, 1669, and Ending May 16, 1864.* Boston: Wright and Potter, 1903.

Topsfield, Mass. *Town Records of Topsfield, Massachusetts. . . .* 2 vols. Topsfield, Mass.: Topsfield Historical Society, 1917–1920.

Watertown, Mass. *Watertown Records. . . .* 6 vols. Watertown, Mass.: Prepared for publication by the [Watertown?] Historical Society, 1894–1906.

Wenham, Mass. *Wenham Town Records, 1730–1775.* Salem, Mass.: 1940.

Weston, Mass. *Town of Weston, The Tax Lists, 1757–1827.* Ed. by Mary Frances Peirce. Boston: A. Mudge and Son, 1897.

——. *Town of Weston, Records of the First Precinct, 1746–1754 and of the Town, 1754–1803.* Boston: A. Mudge and Son, 1893.

Worcester, Mass. "Worcester Tax List, 1789," in Worcester Historical Society, *Collections,* XVI (1899).

——. *Worcester Town Records . . . [1722–1848].* Ed. by Franklin P. Rice. 7 vols. in 6. (Worcester Historical Society, *Collections,* II, IV, VIII, X, XI, XV.) Worcester, Mass.: Worcester Society of Antiquity, 1879–1895.

Manuscripts

GENERAL

Adams, Samuel. Adams Papers. New York Public Library.

Alden Papers. Papers of the Alden Family. 4 bound volumes. Library of Congress, Division of Manuscripts.

Attested copies of town records, collected by Professor Samuel Eliot Morison. Massachusetts Historical Society, Boston, Mass.

Barnes, Mrs. Henry. Letters of Mrs. Henry Barnes of Marlborough, Mass., c.1768–74. Library of Congress, Division of Manuscripts.

Berkshire County Register of Deeds.

Bernard, Francis. Letters, 1768–1769. Force transcripts. Library of Congress, Division of Manuscripts.

Emmet Collection. New York Public Library.

Essex County Probate Records.

Hampshire County Probate Records.

Hancock, John. Chamberlain Collection. Boston Public Library.

Hawley, Joseph. Joseph Hawley Papers. New York Public Library.

Hutchinson and Oliver Papers. Massachusetts Historical Society, Boston, Mass.

Judd, Jonathan. Diary of Jonathan Judd, Jr. 4 vols. Forbes Library, Northampton, Mass.

Judd Manuscripts. Forbes Library, Northampton, Mass.

Madison, James. Madison Papers. New York Public Library.

Massachusetts Archives. State House, Boston, Mass.

Massachusetts Miscellaneous Manuscripts, 1620–1864. 6 portfolios. Library of Congress, Division of Manuscripts.

Middlesex County Probate Records.

Miscellaneous Manuscripts, XIII, 1761–70. Massachusetts Historical Society, Boston, Mass.

Morris, Robert. Robert Morris Papers. New York Public Library.

Oliver, Andrew. Andrew Oliver Letter Book. 2 vols. Massachusetts Historical Society, Boston, Mass.

Pownall, Thomas. "The State of the Government of Massachusetts-Bay as It Stood in the Year 1757." Miscellaneous Manuscripts, 1757. Library of Congress, Division of Manuscripts.

Stockbridge, Mass. "Indian Proprietors, 1749–1790." Stockbridge Library, Stockbridge, Mass.

Suffolk County Probate Records.

Williams, Israel. Israel Williams Papers. Massachusetts Historical Society, Boston, Mass.

MANUSCRIPT TOWN RECORDS IN THE TOWNS

Andover Tax Lists. Andover, Mass.

Andover Town Records. Andover, Mass.

Hadley Town Records. Hadley, Mass.

Hatfield Assessors' List. Hatfield, Mass.

Hatfield Town Records. Hatfield, Mass.

Malden Town Records. Malden, Mass.

Marblehead Town Records. Marblehead, Mass.

Milton Town Records. Milton, Mass.

Northampton Town Records. Northampton, Mass.

Pittsfield Town Records. Pittsfield, Mass.

Sheffield Tax Lists. Sheffield, Mass.

Sheffield Town Records. Sheffield, Mass.

Springfield Town Records. Springfield, Mass.

Stockbridge Town Records. Stockbridge, Mass.

Sudbury Town Records. Sudbury, Mass.

LIBRARY OF CONGRESS TRANSCRIPTS

British Museum. Additional Manuscripts.

     15,486. Papers relating to Massachusetts, 1720–1724.

     21,666. Correspondence of General Haldimand.

     35,427. Hardwicke Papers. Vol. 79.

     35,621. Hardwicke Papers. Vol. 621.

     35,907. Hardwicke Papers. Vol. 559.

     35,908. Hardwicke Papers. Vol. 560.

———. Egerton Manuscripts.

     Vol. 2669. Diary of Elisha Hutchinson.

Vol. 2671. The Origins and Progress of the Rebellion [Peter Oliver].

——. King's Manuscripts.

202. Original letters from Governor Pownall to the Reverend Dr. Cooper, 1769–1774, on American Politics.

203. Letters from the Reverend Dr. Cooper to Dr. Franklin and Governor Pownall, 1769–1775, on American politics.

205. Reports of the State of the American colonies, 1721–1766.

206. State of manufactures, mode of granting land, fees of office, etc., in America. 1766–1768.

212. Journal of General Braddock's expedition in 1755.

213. Journal of an Officer [Lord Adam Gordon] who travelled over a part of the West Indies, and of North America, 1764–1765.

Manuscripts of Dr. Bray's Associates.

Public Record Office. Admiralty Office, Admiralty 1. Admirals Dispatches

Vol. 480. 1745–1763. Admirals Warren, etc.

——. Colonial Office 5: America and West Indies

Vol. 38.—Pelham and Copley letters and other papers, 1739–1775.

Vol. 40.—Intercepted letters from various sources, 1775–1782.

Vol. 175.—New Hampshire, Massachusetts, etc.

Vol. 232.—Précis of documents relating to the American Revolution.

——. Colonial Office 323. Plantations General.

Vol. 19. A collection of papers on financial matters, etc.

——. War Office 34. Amherst Papers.

Vol. 25. Letters from the governor of Massachusetts to the commander-in-chief. Sept. 1757–Dec. 1759.

Vol. 26. Letters from the governor of Massachusetts to the commander-in-chief. Jan. 1760–Oct. 1763.

Vol. 27. Letters from the commander-in-chief to the governor of Massachusetts.

Vols. 71–72. Letters from secretaries of state and government departments in England to the commander-in-chief, North America, 1753–1763.

Vols. 73–74. Letters from the commander-in-chief, North America, to secretaries of state and government departments in England. May 1754–Feb. 1764.

Shelburne (Lansdowne) Papers.

Vols. 66, 67. "American Affairs." Vols. I, II. Papers from 1765 to 1783 relating chiefly to American politics.

Vol. 85. "American Affairs," 1766–1769.

Society for the Propagation of the Gospel in Foreign Parts. Archives.

Series A. Vols. I–XXVI. Contemporary copies of letters received, 1702–1736, chiefly from the American colonies.

Series B. Vols. I–XXV. Original letters received from the American colonies, etc.

II. SECONDARY WORKS

Adams, Brooks. *The Emancipation of Massachusetts.* Boston and New York: Houghton, Mifflin, and Co., 1887.

Adams, Charles Francis. *Massachusetts, Its Historians and Its History; an Object Lesson.* 2d ed. Boston: Houghton, Mifflin, and Co., 1894.

Adams, Charles Francis, and others. *The Genesis of the Massachusetts Town and the Development of Town-meeting Government.* Cambridge, Mass.: J. Wilson and Son, 1892.

Adams, Herbert B. *The Germanic Origin of New England Towns.* (Johns Hopkins University, *Studies in Historical and Political Science,* I, no. 2.) Baltimore: Johns Hopkins University, 1882.

Adams, James Truslow. *The American: The Making of a New Man.* New York: Charles Scribner's Sons, 1944.

——. *Building the British Empire: To the End of the First Empire.* New York: Charles Scribner's Sons, 1938.

——, ed. *Dictionary of American History.* 5 vols. New York: Charles Scribner's Sons, 1940.

——. *New England in the Republic, 1776–1850.* Boston: Little, Brown and Co., 1926.

——. *Provincial Society, 1690–1763.* New York: Macmillan, 1927.

——. *Revolutionary New England, 1691–1776.* Boston: Atlantic Monthly Press, 1923.

——. "The Unexplored Region in New England History," *American Historical Review,* XXVIII (July 1923), 673–81.

Adams, Randolph G. "New Light on the Boston Massacre," in American Antiquarian Society, *Proceedings,* n.s., vol. XLVII (1938).

——. *Political Ideas of the American Revolution . . .* Durham, N.C.: Trinity College Press, 1922.

Akagi, Roy Hidemichi. *The Town Proprietors of the New England Colonies.* . . . Philadelphia: University of Pennsylvania Press, 1924.

Alden, John Richard. *The American Revolution, 1775–1783.* New York: Harper and Brothers, 1954.

——. *General Gage in America: Being Principally a History of His Role in the American Revolution.* Baton Rouge, La.: Louisiana State University Press, 1948.

Allan, Herbert S. *John Hancock, Patriot in Purple.* New York: Macmillan, 1948.

Alvord, Clarence Walworth. "The Genesis of the Proclamation of 1763," in Michigan Pioneer and Historical Society, *Historical Collections,* XXXVI (1908), 20–52.

——. *The Mississippi Valley in British Politics.* . . . 2 vols. Cleveland: Arthur H. Clark Co., 1917.

Ames, Ellis. Paper on the qualifications for voting in the province charter, in Mass. Hist. Soc., *Proceedings,* X (1867–1869), 370–75.

Anderson, William. *American Government.* 3d ed. New York: Henry Holt and Co., 1946.

Andrews, Charles McLean. "The American Revolution: An Interpretation," *American Historical Review,* XXXI (Jan. 1926), 219–32.

——. "Anglo-French Commercial Rivalry, 1700–1750: The Western Phase," *American Historical Review,* XX (April, July, 1915), 539–56, 761–80.

——. "The Boston Merchants and the Non-Importation Movement," in Colonial Society of Massachusetts, *Publications,* XIX (1918), 159–259.

——. *Colonial Background of the American Revolution.* New Haven: Yale University Press, 1924.

——. "Colonial Commerce," *American Historical Review,* XX (Oct. 1914), 43–63.

——. *Colonial Folkways: A Chronicle of American Life in the Reign of the Georges.* New Haven: Yale University Press, 1918.

——. *The Colonial Period of American History.* 4 vols. New Haven: Yale University Press, 1934–38.

——. "Current Lawful Money of New England," *American Historical Review,* XXIV (Oct. 1918), 73–77.

[——.] *Essays in Colonial History.* Presented to Charles M. Andrews by his students. New Haven: Yale University Press, 1931.

——. "On the Writing of Colonial History," *William and Mary Quarterly,* 3d ser., I (Jan. 1944), 27–48.

——, and others. *George Louis Beer: A Tribute to His Life and Work.* . . . New York: Macmillan, 1924.

Armitage, Thomas. *A History of the Baptists.* New York: Bryan, Taylor and Co., 1899.

Atkins, Gauis G., and Fagley, Frederick L. *History of American Congregationalism.* Boston and Chicago: Pilgrim Press, 1942.

Backus, Isaac. *Church History of New England, from 1620 to 1804.* Philadelphia: American Baptist Publication Society, 1853.

Baldwin, Alice M. *The New England Clergy and the American Revolution.* Durham, N.C.: Duke University Press, 1928.

Baldwin, Leland D. *The Stream of American History.* 2 vols. New York: American Book Co., 1952.

Bancroft, George. *History of the United States.* . . . 10 vols. Boston: Little, Brown, and Co., 1834–1875.

Barck, Oscar Theodore, Jr., and others. *The United States: A Survey of National Development.* New York: Ronald Press, 1950.

Baxter, W. T. *The House of Hancock: Business in Boston, 1734–1775.* Cambridge, Mass.: Harvard Press, 1945.

Becker, Carl Lotus. *The Beginnings of the American People.* Boston and New York: Houghton, Mifflin and Co., 1915.

——. *The History of Political Parties in the Province of New York, 1760–1776.* (University of Wisconsin *Bulletin,* no. 286, history series.) Madison, Wis.: 1909.

——. Review of Hugh Edward Egerton, *The Causes and Character of the American Revolution* (Oxford, 1923), *American Historical Review,* XXIX (Jan. 1924).

Beer, George Louis. *British Colonial Policy, 1754–1765.* New York: Macmillan, 1907.

——. *The Commercial Policy of England toward the American Colonies.* New York: Columbia College, 1893.

——. *The English-Speaking Peoples, Their Future Relations and Joint International Obligations.* New York: Macmillan, 1917.

Bell, Herbert C. "The West India Trade before the American Revolution," *American Historical Review,* XXII (Jan. 1917), 272–87.

Bidwell, Percy W., and Falconer, John I. *History of Agriculture in the Northern United States, 1620–1860.* Washington: Carnegie Institute of Washington, 1925.

Bining, Arthur Cecil. *A History of the United States.* 2 vols. New York: Charles Scribner's Sons, 1950.

——. *British Regulation of the Colonial Iron Industry.* Philadelphia: University of Pennsylvania Press, 1933.

Bishop, Cortlandt F. *History of Elections in the American Colonies.* (Columbia University *Studies*, III, no. 1.) New York: Columbia College, 1893.

Bond, Beverley W. "The Colonial Agent as a Popular Representative," *Political Science Quarterly*, XXXV (Sept. 1920), 372–92.

Bowen, Catherine Drinker. *John Adams and the American Revolution.* Boston: Little, Brown and Co., 1950.

Brennan, Ellen Elizabeth. "James Otis: Recreant and Patriot," *New England Quarterly*, XII (Dec. 1939), 691–725.

Bridenbaugh, Carl. *Cities in the Wilderness: The First Century of Urban Life in America, 1625–1742.* New York: Ronald Press Co., 1938.

——. *The Colonial Craftsman.* New York: New York University Press, 1950.

——. "The New England Town: A Way of Life," in American Antiquarian Society, *Proceedings*, LVI (1947), 19–48.

Brown, Ernest Francis. *Joseph Hawley, Colonial Radical.* New York: Columbia University Press, 1931.

Brown, Robert E. "Road to Revolution in Massachusetts." Unpublished thesis, University of Wisconsin, 1946.

——. "Democracy in Colonial Massachusetts," *New England Quarterly*, XXV (Sept. 1952).

——. "Restriction of Representation in Colonial Massachusetts," *Mississippi Valley Historical Review*, XL (Dec. 1953).

Brubacher, John S. *A History of the Problems of Education.* New York and London: McGraw-Hill Book Co., 1947.

Bullock, Charles J. *Essays on the Monetary History of the United States.* New York: Macmillan, 1900.

Burnett, Edmund Cody. *The Continental Congress.* New York: Macmillan, 1941.

Burns, James J. *Colonial Agents of New England.* Washington: Catholic University of America, 1935.

Burt, Alfred LeRoy. *The Old Province of Quebec.* Minneapolis: University of Minnesota Press, 1933.

Butler, James D. "British Convicts Shipped to the American Colonies," *American Historical Review*, II (Oct. 1896), 12–33.

Carter, Clarence E. "The Significance of the Military Office in America, 1763–1775," *American Historical Review*, XXVIII (April 1923), 475–488.

Chamberlain, Mellen. *John Adams, the Statesman of the American Revolution.* . . . Boston and New York: Houghton, Mifflin and Co., 1898.

Channing, Edward. *A History of the United States.* 6 vols. New York: Macmillan, 1905–1925.

———. *Town and County Government in the English Colonies of North America.* (Johns Hopkins University, *Studies in Historical and Political Science,* II.) Baltimore, 1884.

Chitwood, Oliver Percy. *A History of Colonial America.* New York: Harper and Brothers, 1931.

Clark, Dora Mae. "The American Board of Customs, 1767–1783," *American Historical Review,* XLV (July 1940), 777–806.

Clark, Joseph S. *A Historical Sketch of the Congregational Churches in Massachusetts, from 1620 to 1858.* Boston: Congregational Board of Publication, 1858.

Clark, Victor Selden. *History of Manufactures in the United States, 1607–1860.* Washington: Carnegie Institute of Washington, 1916.

Clarke, Mary Patterson. *Parliamentary Privilege in the American Colonies.* (Yale, *Historical Studies,* Miscellany, XLIV.) New Haven: Yale University Press, 1943.

Coffin, Victor. *The Province of Quebec and the Early American Revolution.* Madison, Wis.: University of Wisconsin, 1896.

Cole, Arthur H. *The American Wool Manufacture.* 2 vols. Cambridge, Mass.: Harvard University Press, 1926.

Coleman, Roy V. *Liberty and Property.* New York: Charles Scribner's Sons, 1951.

Collins, Edward D. "Committees of Correspondence of the American Revolution," in American Historical Association, *Annual Report,* 1901, I, 245–71.

Commons, John R., and others. *History of Labor in the United States.* 2 vols. New York: Macmillan, 1918.

Coupland, Reginald. *The Quebec Act: A Study in Statesmanship.* Oxford: Clarendon Press, 1925.

Cremin, Lawrence A. *The American Common School: An Historic Conception.* New York: Columbia University, 1951.

Cremin, Lawrence A., and Butts, R. Freeman. *A History of Education in American Culture.* New York: Henry Holt, 1954.

Cross, Arthur Lyon. *The Anglican Episcopate and the American Colonies.* New York: Longmans, Green, 1902.

Curti, Merle. *The Growth of American Thought.* New York and London: Harper and Brothers, 1943.

——. *The Social Ideas of American Educators*. New York: Charles Scribner's Sons, 1935.

——, and others. *An American History*. 2 vols. New York: Harper and Brothers, 1950.

——. *American Issues*. 2 vols. Chicago and Philadelphia: J. B. Lippincott and Co., 1941.

Cushing, Harry Alonzo. *History of the Transition from Province to Commonwealth Government in Massachusetts*. (Columbia University, *Studies in History, Economics and Public Law*, VII.) New York: Columbia University Press, 1896.

Davidson, Philip. *Propaganda and the American Revolution, 1763–1783*. Chapel Hill: University of North Carolina Press, 1941.

Davis, Andrew McFarland. "Boston Banks, 1681–1740; Those Who Were Interested in Them," *New England Historical and Genealogical Register* (July, 1903).

——. "Certain Considerations Concerning the Coinage of the Colony and the Public Bills of Credit of the Province of Massachusetts Bay," in American Academy of Arts and Sciences, *Proceedings* XXXIII, no. 12 (Feb. 1898).

——. *Currency and Banking in the Province of Massachusetts Bay*. 2 vols. New York: Published for the American Economic Association by the Macmillan Company, 1900, 1901.

——. "Currency Discussion in Massachusetts in the Eighteenth Century," *Quarterly Journal of Economics*, XI (Oct. 1896, Jan. 1897).

——. "The General Court and Quarrels between Individuals Arising from the Land Bank," in American Antiquarian Society, *Proceedings*, n.s., XI (1898), 351–68.

——. "Land Bank Mortgages in Worcester County," in American Antiquarian Society, *Proceedings*, n.s., XVI (1904), 85–90.

——. "Legislation and Litigation Connected with the Land Bank of 1740," in American Antiquarian Society, *Proceedings*, n.s., XI 1898), 86–123.

——. "Papers Relating to the Land Bank of 1740," in Colonial Society of Massachusetts, *Publications*, vol. IV (1910).

DeGrazia, Alfred. *Public and Republic; Political Representation in America*. New York: Alfred A. Knopf, 1951.

Dickerson, Oliver M. *American Colonial Government, 1696–1765*. . . . Cleveland, Ohio: Arthur H. Clark Co., 1912.

——. "British Control of American Newspapers on the Eve of the Revolution," *New England Quarterly*, XXIV (Dec. 1951), 453–68.

——. "The Commissioners of Customs and the 'Boston Massacre,' " *New England Quarterly,* XXVII (Sept. 1954), 307–25.

——. "England's Most Fateful Decision" [1767], *New England Quarterly,* XXII (Sept. 1949), 388–94.

——. "John Hancock: Notorious Smuggler or Near Victim of British Revenue Racketeers?" *Mississippi Valley Historical Review,* XXXII (March 1946), 517–40.

——. *The Navigation Acts and the American Revolution.* Philadelphia: University of Pennsylvania Press, 1951.

——. "Writs of Assistance as a Cause of the Revolution," Richard B. Morris, ed., *Era of American Revolution.* New York: Columbia University Press, 1939. Pp. 40–75.

Dorfman, Joseph. *The Economic Mind in American Civilization.* 3 vols. New York: Viking Press, 1946–1949.

Douglass, Elisha P. *Rebels and Democrats: The Struggle for Equal Political Rights and Majority Rule during the American Revolution.* Chapel Hill, N.C.: University of North Carolina, 1955.

Edmonds, John Henry. "How Massachusetts Received the Declaration of Independence," in American Antiquarian Society, *Proceedings,* n.s., XXXV (1926).

Farrand, Max. "The Indian Boundary Line," *American Historical Review,* X (July 1905), 782–91.

——. "The Taxation of Tea, 1767–1773," *American Historical Review,* III (Jan. 1898), 266–69.

Felt, Joseph Barlow. *An Historical Account of Massachusetts Currency.* Boston: Perkins and Marvin, 1839.

——. "Statistics of Population in Massachusetts," in American Statistical Association, *Collections.* Boston: T. R. Marvin, 1847.

Ferguson, E. James. "Currency Finance: An Interpretation of Colonial Monetary Practices," *William and Mary Quarterly,* ser. 3, X (April 1953).

Ferguson, John H., and McHenry, Dean E. *Elements of American Government.* New York: McGraw-Hill Book Co., Inc., 1950.

Foner, Philip S. *History of the Labor Movement in the United States from Colonial Times to the Founding of the American Federation of Labor.* New York: International Publishers, 1947.

Fortescue, Sir John William. *A History of the British Army.* 13 vols. in 14. New York and London: Macmillan, 1899–1930.

Franklin, W. Neil. "Some Aspects of Representation in the American Colonies," *North Carolina Historical Review,* VI (Jan. 1929), 38–66.

French, Allen. *The Day of Concord and Lexington.* . . . Boston: Little, Brown and Co., 1925.

——. *The First Year of the American Revolution.* Boston: Houghton Mifflin Co., 1934.

——. *General Gage's Informers.* . . . Ann Arbor, Mich.: University of Michigan Press, 1932.

——. *The Siege of Boston.* New York: Macmillan, 1911.

Frothingham, Richard. *History of the Siege of Boston.* . . . Boston: Chas. C. Little and James Brown, 1851.

Gifford, Frank Dean. "The Influence of the Clergy on American Politics from 1773 to 1776," *Historical Magazine of the Protestant Episcopal Church,* X (June 1941), 104–23.

Gipson, Lawrence Henry. *The American Revolution as an Aftermath of the Great War for the Empire, 1754–1763, and Other Essays in American Colonial History.* Bethlehem, Pa.: Institute of Research, Lehigh University, 1950.

——. *The British Empire before the American Revolution.* 8 vols. Vols. I–III, Caldwell, Idaho: Caxton Printers, 1936; vols. IV–VIII, New York: Alfred A. Knopf, 1939–1954.

——. *Charles McLean Andrews and the Re-orientation of the Study of American Colonial History.* Bethlehem, Pa.: Lehigh University, 1935.

——. *The Coming of the Revolution, 1763–1775.* New York: Harper and Brothers, 1954.

Good, Harry G. *A History of Western Education.* New York: Macmillan, 1949.

Gordon, William. *The History of the Rise, Progress, and Establishment of the Independence of the United States of America.* . . . 3 vols. 3d American ed. New York: John Woods, 1801.

Grant, William Lawson. "Canada versus Guadeloupe," *American Historical Review,* XVII (July 1912), 735–43.

Green, Samuel A. "The Boston Massacre, March 5, 1770," in the American Antiquarian Society, *Proceedings,* n.s., XIV (1901), 40–53.

Greene, Evarts B., and Harrington, Virginia D. *American Population before the Federal Census of 1790.* New York: Columbia University Press, 1932.

Greene, Evarts Boutell. *Provincial America, 1690–1740.* New York and London: Harper and Brothers, 1905.

——. *Religion and the State; the Making and Testing of an American Tradition.* New York: New York University Press, 1941.

——. *The Revolutionary Generation, 1763–1790.* New York: Macmillan, 1943.

Greene, Lorenzo Johnston. *The Negro in Colonial New England, 1620–1776.* New York: Columbia University Press, 1942.

Griffith, Ernest S. *History of American City Government: The Colonial Period.* New York: Oxford University Press, 1938.

Grinnell, Frank W. "A Forgotten Patriot, Jedediah Foster of Brookfield," in Mass. Hist. Soc., *Proceedings,* LXVII (1945), 128–34.

Haley, R. H. "Louisbourg—Prelude to Revolution," *National Historical Magazine,* LXXIV (Jan. 1940).

Handlin, Oscar and Mary F. "Radicals and Conservatives in Massachusetts after Independence," *New England Quarterly,* XVII (Sept., 1944), 343–55.

Harlow, Ralph V. *Samuel Adams, Promoter of the American Revolution.* . . . New York: Henry Holt and Co., 1923.

Harper, Lawrence A. "The Effect of the Navigation Acts on the Thirteen Colonies," in Richard B. Morris, ed., *The Era of the American Revolution.* . . . Pp. 3–39.

Haynes, George H. *Representation and Suffrage in Massachusetts, 1620–1691.* (Johns Hopkins University, *Studies in Historical and Political Science,* 12th ser.) Baltimore: Johns Hopkins Press, 1894.

——. "Representation in New England Legislatures," in American Academy of Political and Social Science, *Annals,* VI, no. 2, pp. 254–67. Philadelphia, 1895.

Hicks, John D. *A Short History of American Democracy.* Boston: Houghton, Mifflin Co., 1949.

Hickman, Emily. "Colonial Writs of Assistance," *New England Quarterly,* V (Jan. 1932), 83–104.

Humphreys, R. A. "Lord Shelburne and a Projected Recall of Colonial Governors in 1767," *American Historical Review,* XXXVII (April 1935), 269–72.

Jameson, J. Franklin. *The American Revolution Considered as a Social Movement.* Princeton, N.J.: Princeton University Press, 1926.

——. "Did the Fathers Vote?" *New England Magazine,* n.s., I (Jan. 1890), 484–90.

Jensen, Merrill. *The Articles of Confederation.* . . . Madison, Wis.: University of Wisconsin Press, 1940.

Jernegan, Marcus Wilson. *The American Colonies, 1492–1750.* . . . New York: Longmans, Green and Co., 1941.

——. *Laboring and Dependent Classes in Colonial America, 1607–1783*. . . . Chicago: University of Chicago Press, 1931.

Johnson, Claudius O. *Government in the United States*. 3d ed. New York: Thomas Y. Crowell Co., 1944.

Jones, Edward Alfred. *The Loyalists of Massachusetts, Their Memorials, Petitions and Claims*. London: Saint Catherine Press, 1930.

Jones, Rufus Matthew. *The Quakers in the American Colonies*. London: Macmillan, 1911.

Kaplan, Sidney. "Rank and Status among Massachusetts Continental Officers," *American Historical Review*, LVI (Jan. 1951), 318–26.

Kelso, Robert W. *The History of Poor Relief in Massachusetts, 1620–1920*. Boston and New York: Houghton Mifflin Co., 1922.

Labaree, Leonard W. "The Conservative Attitude toward the Great Awakening," *William and Mary Quarterly*, 3d ser. I (Oct. 1944), 331–52.

——. *Conservatism in Early American History*. New York: New York University Press, 1948.

——. "The Nature of American Loyalism," in American Antiquarian Society, *Proceedings*, LIV (1945), 15–58.

——. *Royal Government in America*. . . . New Haven: Yale University Press, 1930.

Lamb, George Woodward. "Clergymen Licensed to the American Colonies by the Bishops of London: 1745–1781," *Historical Magazine of the Protestant Episcopal Church*, XIII (June 1944).

Laprade, William T. "The Stamp Act in British Politics," *American Historical Review*, XXXV (July 1930), 735–57.

Long, John Cuthbert. *Lord Jeffery Amherst, a Soldier of the King*. New York: Macmillan, 1933.

Longley, Ronald S. "Mob Activities in Revolutionary Massachusetts," *New England Quarterly*, VI (March 1933), 98–130.

Lord, Eleanor. *Industrial Experiments in the British Colonies of North America*. Baltimore: Johns Hopkins University Press, 1896.

Martin, George H. *Evolution of the Massachusetts School System*. New York: D. Appleton Co., 1894.

Mayo, Lawrence Shaw. *Jeffery Amherst: A Biography*. New York and London: Longmans, Green and Co., 1916.

McClellan, William Smith. *Smuggling in the American Colonies at the Outbreak of the Revolution*. . . . New York: Moffat, Yard and Co., 1912.

McCormac, Eugene Irving. *Colonial Opposition to Imperial Authority during the French and Indian War.* Berkeley, Calif.: University of California Press, 1911.

McIlwain, Charles Howard. *The American Revolution: A Constitutional Interpretation.* New York: Macmillan, 1923.

McKinley, Albert Edward. *The Suffrage Franchise in the Thirteen English Colonies in America.* (University of Pennsylvania, *Publications,* series in history, no. 2.) Philadelphia: University of Pennsylvania, 1905.

McLennan, J. S. *Louisbourg from Its Foundation to Its Fall, 1713–1758.* London: Macmillan, 1918.

Merriam, Charles Edward. *A History of American Political Theories.* New York: Macmillan, 1920.

Metzger, Charles Henry. *The Quebec Act: A Primary Cause of the American Revolution.* New York: United States Catholic Historical Society, 1936.

Meyer, Jacob Conrad. *Church and State in Massachusetts from 1740 to 1833.* . . . Cleveland, Ohio: Western Reserve University Press, 1930.

Miller, John C. "The Massachusetts Convention: 1768," *New England Quarterly,* VII (Sept. 1934), 445–74.

——. *Origins of the American Revolution.* Boston: Little, Brown and Co., 1943.

——. "Religion, Finance and Democracy in Massachusetts," *New England Quarterly,* VI (March 1933).

——. *Sam Adams, Pioneer in Propaganda.* Boston: Little, Brown and Co., 1936.

——. *Triumph of Freedom, 1775–83.* Boston: Little, Brown and Co., Atlantic Monthly Press, 1948.

Miller, Perry. "Declension of a Bible Commonwealth," in American Antiquarian Society *Proceedings,* LI (1942), 37–94.

——. *Jonathan Edwards.* New York: W. Sloane Associates, 1949.

——. "Jonathan Edwards' Sociology of the Great Awakening," *New England Quarterly,* XXI (March 1948), 50–77.

——. *The New England Mind: From Colony to Province.* Cambridge: Harvard University Press, 1953.

Montross, Lynn. *The Reluctant Rebels: The Story of the Continental Congress, 1774–1789.* New York: Harper and Brothers, 1950.

Morais, Herbert M. *Deism in Eighteenth Century America.* New York: Columbia University Press, 1934.

——. *The Struggle for American Freedom.* . . . New York: International Publishers, 1944.

Morgan, Edmund S. "Colonial Ideas of Parliamentary Power, 1764–1766," *William and Mary Quarterly,* 3d ser., V (July 1948), 311–41.

——. "The Postponement of the Stamp Act," *William and Mary Quarterly,* 3d ser., VII (July 1950), 353–92.

——. "Thomas Hutchinson and the Stamp Act," *New England Quarterly,* XXI (Dec. 1948), 459–92.

——, and Morgan, Helen M. *The Stamp Act Crisis.* . . . Chapel Hill: University of North Carolina Press, 1953.

Morison, Samuel Eliot. "The Struggle over the Adoption of the Constitution of Massachusetts, 1780," in Mass. Hist. Soc., *Proceedings,* L (1916–1917), 353–412.

——. "Vote of Massachusetts on Summoning a Constitutional Convention, 1776–1916," in Mass. Hist. Soc., *Proceedings,* L (1916–1917), 241–49.

——, and Commager, Henry Steele. *The Growth of the American Republic.* 2 vols. New York: Oxford University Press, 1950.

Morris, Richard B., ed. *The Era of the American Revolution: Studies Inscribed to Evarts Boutell Greene.* New York: Columbia University Press, 1939.

——. *Government and Labor in Early America.* New York: Columbia University Press, 1946.

——. "Primogeniture and Entailed Estates in America," *Columbia Law Review,* XXVII (1927), 24–51.

——. *Studies in the History of American Law, with Special Reference to the Seventeenth and Eighteenth Centuries.* New York: Columbia University Press, 1930.

Mullett, Charles Frederic. *Fundamental Law and the American Revolution, 1760–76.* New York: Columbia University Press, 1933.

Murdock, Harold. *The Nineteenth of April, 1775: Exhibiting a Fair and Impartial Account of the Engagement Fought on that Day.* . . . Boston: Houghton Mifflin Co., 1923.

Nettels, Curtis P. "The Menace of Colonial Manufacturing," *New England Quarterly,* IV (April 1931), 230–269.

——. *The Money Supply of the Thirteen American Colonies Before 1720.* Madison, Wis.: University of Wisconsin Press, 1934.

——. "The Place of Colonial Markets in the Old Colonial System," *New England Quarterly,* VI (Sept. 1933), 491–512.

——. *The Roots of American Civilization.* New York: F. S. Crofts and Co., 1939.

Nevins, Allan. *The American States During and After the Revolution, 1775–1789.* New York: Macmillan, 1924.

Newcomer, Lee Nathaniel. *The Embattled Farmers: A Massachusetts Countryside in the American Revolution.* New York: King's Crown Press, 1953.

———. "Yankee Rebels of Inland Massachusetts," *William and Mary Quarterly,* 3d ser., IX (April 1952), 156–65.

Newman, Albert H. *History of the Baptist Churches in the United States.* New York: Christian Literature Co., 1894.

Norton, William B. "Paper Currency in Massachusetts during the Revolution," *New England Quarterly,* VII (March 1934), 43–69.

Nye, Russell Blaine. *George Bancroft, Brahmin Rebel.* New York: Alfred A. Knopf, 1944.

Ogg, Frederic A., and Ray, P. Orman. *Introduction to American Government.* 9th ed. New York: Appleton-Century-Crofts, Inc., 1948.

Osgood, Herbert L. *The American Colonies in the Eighteenth Century.* 4 vols. New York: Columbia University Press, 1924–1925.

———. "The American Revolution," *Political Science Quarterly,* XIII (March 1898).

———. "England and the Colonies," *Political Science Quarterly,* II (Sept. 1887), 440–69.

Paine, Robert Treat, Jr. "Massachusetts' Historic Attitude in Regard to Representative Government," *Arena,* XXXVIII (1907), 14–18.

Pargellis, Stanley M. "Braddock's Defeat," *American Historical Review,* XLI (Jan. 1936), 253–69.

———. *Lord Loudoun in America.* New Haven: Yale University Press, 1933.

Parkman, Francis. *A Half-Century of Conflict.* 5th ed. 2 vols. Boston: Little, Brown and Co., 1892.

———. *Montcalm and Wolfe. France and England in North America.* 2 vols. Boston: Little, Brown and Co., 1910.

Parrington, Vernon Louis. *Main Currents in American Thought.* 3 vols. in 1. New York: Harcourt, Brace and Co., 1930.

Porter, Kirk Harold. *County and Township Government in the United States.* New York: Macmillan, 1922.

———. *A History of Suffrage in the United States.* Chicago: University of Chicago Press, 1918.

Reed, Susan M. *Church and State in Massachusetts, 1691–1740.* Urbana, Ill.: University of Illinois, 1914.

Riker, Thad W. "The Politics Behind Braddock's Expedition," *American Historical Review,* XIII (July 1908), 742–52.

Rossiter, Clinton L. *Seedtime of the Republic.* . . . New York: Harcourt, Brace and Co., 1953.

Sabine, Lorenzo. *Biographical Sketches of Loyalists of the American Revolution, with an Historical Essay.* 2 vols. Boston: Little, Brown and Co., 1864.

Sachs, William S. "Agricultural Conditions in the Northern Colonies before the Revolution," *Journal of Economic History,* XIII (Summer 1953), 274–90.

Savelle, Max. *Seeds of Liberty: The Genesis of the American Mind.* New York: Alfred A. Knopf, 1948.

——. *The Diplomatic History of the Canadian Boundary, 1749–1763.* New Haven, Yale University Press, 1940.

Sawtelle, William Otis. "Thomas Pownall, Colonial Governor," in Mass. Hist. Soc., *Proceedings,* LXIII, 233–87.

Schlesinger, Arthur M. "The American Revolution Reconsidered," *Political Science Quarterly,* XXXIV (March 1919), 61–78.

——. *The Colonial Merchants and the American Revolution, 1763–76.* New York: Columbia University Press, 1918.

——. "Colonial Newspapers and the Stamp Act," *New England Quarterly,* VIII (March 1935), 63–83.

——. *New Viewpoints in American History.* New York: Macmillan, 1922.

——. "The Uprising against the East India Company," *Political Science Quarterly,* XXXII (March 1917), 60–69.

Schutz, John A. *Thomas Pownall, British Defender of American Liberty: A Study of Anglo-American Relations in the Eighteenth Century.* Glendale, Calif.: A. H. Clark Co., 1951.

Sears, Lorenzo. *John Hancock, The Picturesque Patriot.* Boston: Little, Brown and Co., 1912.

Seybolt, Robert Francis. *Apprenticeship and Apprenticeship Education in Colonial New England and New York.* New York: Teachers College, 1917.

——. *The Evening School in Colonial America.* Urbana, Ill.: University of Illinois, 1925.

——. *The Private Schools of Colonial Boston.* Cambridge: Harvard University Press, 1935.

——. *The Public Schools of Colonial Boston, 1635–1775.* Cambridge: Harvard University Press, 1935.

——. *The Town Officials of Colonial Boston, 1634–1775.* Cambridge: Harvard University Press, 1939.

Shipton, Clifford K. "Secondary Education in the Puritan Colonies," *New England Quarterly,* VII (Dec. 1934), 646–61.

——. "The Shaping of Revolutionary New England, 1680–1740," *Political Science Quarterly,* L (Dec. 1935), 584–97.

Sly, John Fairfield. *Town Government in Massachusetts, 1620–1930.* Cambridge: Harvard University Press, 1930.

Smith, Abbot Emerson. *Colonists in Bondage: White Servitude and Convict Labor in America, 1607–1776.* Chapel Hill: University of North Carolina Press, 1947.

Smith, Joseph. *Appeals to the Privy Council from the American Plantations.* New York: Columbia University Press, 1950.

Spector, Margaret. *The American Department of the British Government, 1768–1782.* New York: Columbia University, 1940.

Spencer, Henry Russell. *Constitutional Conflict in Provincial Massachusetts.* . . . Columbus, Ohio: Fred J. Heer, 1905.

Stark, James Henry. *The Loyalists of Massachusetts.* . . . Boston: W. B. Clarke Co., 1910.

Stokes, Anson Phelps. *Church and State in the United States.* 3 vols. New York: Harper and Brothers, 1950.

Sumner, William Graham. "The Spanish Dollar and the Colonial Shilling," *American Historical Review,* III (July 1898), 607–19.

Sweet, William Warren. *Religion in Colonial America.* New York: Charles Scribner's Sons, 1942.

——. *Religion in the Development of American Culture, 1765–1840.* New York: Charles Scribner's Sons, 1952.

——. *Revivalism in America, Its Origin, Growth, and Decline.* New York: Charles Scribner's Sons, 1944.

——. *The Story of Religions in America.* New York: Harper and Brothers, 1931.

Sydnor, Charles A., and Cunningham, Noble E., Jr., "Voting in Early America," *American Heritage,* IV (Fall 1952), 6–8.

Tanner, Edwin P. "Colonial Agencies in England during the Eighteenth Century," *Political Science Quarterly,* XVI (March 1901), 24–49.

Taylor, Robert J. *Western Massachusetts in the Revolution.* Providence: Brown University Press, 1954.

Thayer, Theodore. "The Land-Bank System in the American Colonies," *Journal of Economic History*, XIII (Spring 1953), 145–159.

Torbet, Robert George. *A History of the Baptists*. Philadelphia: Judson Press, 1950.

Tryon, Rollo Milton. *Household Manufactures in the United States, 1640–1860: A Study in Industrial History*. Chicago: University of Chicago Press, 1917.

Tudor, William. *The Life of James Otis of Massachusetts*. Boston: Wells and Lilly, 1823.

Turner, Frederick Jackson. *The Frontier in American History*. New York: Henry Holt and Co., 1920.

Tyler, Moses Coit. *The Literary History of the American Revolution, 1763–1783*. 2 vols. New York and London: G. P. Putnam's Sons, 1897.

——. "The Party of the Loyalists in the American Revolution," *American Historical Review*, I (Oct. 1895), 24–46.

Van Tyne, Claude H. *The American Revolution*. (American Nation Series.) New York and London: Harper and Brothers, 1905.

——. *The Causes of the War of Independence: Being the First Volume of a History of the Founding of the American Republic*. Boston and New York: Houghton Mifflin Co., 1922.

——. *England and America, Rivals in the American Revolution*. New York: Macmillan, 1927.

——. "The Influence of the Clergy, and of Religious and Sectarian Forces, on the American Revolution," *American Historical Review*, XIX (Oct. 1913), 44–64.

——. *The Loyalists in the American Revolution*. New York: Macmillan, 1902.

——. *The War of Independence*. Boston and New York: Houghton Mifflin Co., 1929.

Vedder, Henry C. *Short History of the Baptists*. Philadelphia: American Baptist Publication Society, 1897.

Wainger, Bertrand M. *Liberal Currents in Provincial Massachusetts, 1692–1766*. Ithaca, N.Y.: Cornell University, 1934.

Walker, Williston. *A History of the Congregational Churches in the United States*. 6th ed. New York: Charles Scribner's Sons, 1903.

Walett, Francis G. "James Bowdoin, Patriot Propagandist," *New England Quarterly*, XXIII (Sept. 1950), 320–38.

——. "The Massachusetts Council, 1766–1774: The Transformation of a Conservative Institution," *William and Mary Quarterly*, 3d ser. VI (Oct. 1949), 605–27.

Washburne, George A. *Imperial Control of the Administration of*

Justice in the Thirteen American Colonies, 1684–1776. New York: Columbia University Press, 1923.

Wells, William V. *The Life and Public Services of Samuel Adams.* . . . 3 vols. Boston: Little, Brown and Co., 1865.

White, Eugene E. "Decline of the Great Awakening in New England: 1741–1746," *New England Quarterly*, XXIV (March 1951), 35–52.

Whitmore, William H. *Massachusetts Civil List for the Colonial and Provincial Periods, 1630–1774.* . . . Albany, N.Y.: 1870.

Winslow, Ola Elizabeth. *Jonathan Edwards, 1703–1758: A Biography*. New York: Macmillan, 1940.

——. *Meetinghouse Hill, 1630–1783*. New York: Macmillan, 1952.

Wolkins, George G. "Malcom and Writs of Assistance," in Mass. Hist. Soc., *Proceedings*, LVIII (1925), 5–84.

——. "The Seizure of John Hancock's Sloop *Liberty*," in Mass. Hist. Soc., *Proceedings*, LV (1923), 239–84.

Wood, George A. *William Shirley, Governor of Massachusetts, 1741–1756: A History*. New York: Columbia University Press, 1920.

Wood, William Charles Henry. *The Great Fortress: A Chronicle of Louisbourg, 1720–1760*. Toronto: Glasgow, Brook and Co., 1915.

Wrong, George M. *The Conquest of New France.* . . . New Haven: Yale University Press, 1918.

——. *The Rise and Fall of New France*. 2 vols. New York: Macmillan, 1928.

Index

Abercrombie, General, 154-155

Acts of Trade and Navigation, 123, 161, 224; enforcement of 1763, 126, 198; and writs of assistance, 177-179; colonial view of, 180-181; and Townshend Acts, 240n.; repeal advocated, 362; *see also* British colonial policy, Mercantilism, *and* Imperialism

Adams, Brooks, interpretation by, 101n.

Adams, Charles Francis, interpretation by, 79n., 101n.

Adams, Herbert Baxter, interpretation by, 79n.

Adams, James Truslow, interpretation by, 6n., 11n., 14n., 17n., 38n., 39n., 61n., 80n., 103n., 110n., 114n., 121n., 151n., 153n., 176n., 199n., 214n., 268n., 299n., 310n., 312n., 317n., 324n., 342n., 365n., 394n.

Adams, John, 10, 102n., 121n., 146, 228; value of homestead, 18; views on democracy, 56, 96, 185-186, 367-368, 384; views on religion, 112, 185-186; views on education, 118, 186, 217-219; interpretation of American Revolution, 120; on Land Bank, 130; opinion of Samuel Adams, 131-132; views of Louisbourg episode, 137; on British fears of colonial union, 151; on conduct of French and Indian War, 162; on independence, 162, 367, 374-377; on Massachusetts government, 175; on appointment of Hutchinson as chief justice, 178; on trade acts, 180-181; on writs of assistance, 179-180, 182; on

retention of Canada, 192; on Stamp Act, 216-220; on election of 1766, 229; and Boston Resolves 1772, 299; on British authority in colonies, 300; on Tea Act and Tea Party, 311, 316-317, 320; on Quebec Act, 324-325; on Coercive Acts, 326; on meaning of "revolution," 328; attitude toward Britain 1774, 339; on Mandamus Council, 342-343; on colonial rights, 356-359; as Novanglus, 356-359; view of Hutchinson, 358-359; on social and economic position of revolutionary leaders, 359; on social structure of revolution, 366; on War of Independence, 375; on innovations, 380; delegate to Constitutional Convention 1779, 392; denies internal revolution, 399

Adams, Randolph G., interpretation by, 264n.

Adams, Samuel: controls Boston town meeting, 51, 57; early leader of the Revolution, 131-132; and Land Bank, 132, 132n.; career at Harvard, 132, 132n.; interpretation of, 211n., 212n., 222n., 223n., 237n., 268, 268n., 298, 317n., 338n., 394n.; and Stamp Act, 214, 222; as popular leader, 223, 338n.; and election 1766, 228-229; attempt to discredit 1768, 247; on salary question, 248, 282; delegate to Convention of 1768, 252; and Convention of 1768, 254; and election 1769, 258; and Sons of Liberty, 261; on independence, 262, 307, 340; and election

439